RETROSPECTIVE

Other books by Juan Gabriel Vásquez

The Informers
The Secret History of Costaguana
The Sound of Things Falling
The All Saints' Day Lovers
Reputations
The Shape of the Ruins
Songs for the Flames

Juan Gabriel Vásquez

RETROSPECTIVE

Translated from the Spanish by
Anne McLean

MACLEHOSE PRESS
A Bill Swainson Book
QUERCUS · LONDON

First published in the Spanish language as *Volver la vista atrás*
by Penguin Random House Grupo Editorial, S.A.U., in 2020

First published in Great Britain in 2022 as A Bill Swainson Book by

MacLehose Press
An imprint of Quercus Publishing Ltd
Carmelite House
50 Victoria Embankment
London EC4Y 0DZ

An Hachette UK company

All translations of excerpts from poetry or prose by writers other than
Juan Gabriel Vásquez are by Anne McLean unless noted here:
"Martians", from *Mythologies* by Roland Barthes, translated by
Richard Howard and Annette Lavers, New York: Hill and Wang, 2012.
"Huichang", "Mount Liupan" and "Militia Women" from *Poems: Selected Works of Mao Tse-Tung* on
Marxists Internet Archive: http://www.marxists.org/reference/archive/mao/selected-works/poems
"A man walks by with a stick of bread" by César Vallejo, from *The Complete Poetry: A Bilingual Edition*,
edited and translated by Clayton Eshleman, © 2009, The Regents of the University of California Press
The Autobiography of Maxim Gorky, translated by Isidor Schneider, New York: Citadel Press, 1949

The seventeen images in this book are reproduced courtesy of Sergio Cabrera

A CIP catalogue record for this book is available from the British Library.

(HB) 978 1 52941 862 0
(TPB) 978 1 52941 863 7
(Ebook) 978 1 52941 864 4

10 9 8 7 6 5 4 3 2 1

Designed and typeset in Albertina by Libanus Press, Marlborough
Printed and bound in Great Britain by Clays Ltd, St Ives plc

MIX
Paper from
responsible sources
FSC® C104740

Papers used by Quercus Books are from well-managed forests and
other responsible sources.

For Sergio Cabrera and Silvia Jardim Soares
For Marianella Cabrera

For, according to our view of the thing, a novel should be the biography of a man or of an affair, and a biography whether of a man or of an affair should be a novel.

Ford Madox Ford
Joseph Conrad: A Personal Remembrance

CONTENTS

PART ONE

Encounter in Barcelona

I

According to what he told me himself, Sergio Cabrera had been in Lisbon for three days when he got the phone call telling him of his father's accident. The call reached him in the Praça do Império Gardens, a park with wide paved paths where his daughter Amalia, who was then five years old, was trying to tame the rebellious bicycle she'd just been given. Sergio was sitting beside Silvia on a stone bench, but at that moment he had to walk over to the park gates, as if the proximity of another person would prevent him from concentrating on the details of what had happened. Apparently, Fausto Cabrera had been in his apartment in Bogotá, reading the newspaper on the sofa in the living room, when it occurred to him that the door might not be locked properly, and he stood up suddenly and fainted. Nayibe, his second wife, who had followed him to ask him to sit back down and not to worry, the door was locked and bolted, caught Fausto in her arms before he hit the floor. She immediately called their daughter Lina, who was spending a few days in Madrid, and it was Lina who was now giving Sergio the news.

"She says the ambulance is on its way," she told him. "What should we do?"

"Wait," Sergio said. "Everything's going to be alright."

But he didn't really believe it. Although Fausto had always enjoyed enviable good health and the strength of someone twenty years younger, it was also true that he'd recently turned ninety-two, and at that age everything is more serious: illnesses are more threatening and accidents more harmful. He was still getting up at five in the morning for his sessions of t'ai chi ch'uan, but with ever dwindling energy, making increasingly noticeable concessions to the erosion of his own body. Since he hadn't lost a sliver of his lucidity, that irritated him enormously. Living with him, from the little Sergio knew, had become tense and difficult, so nobody had objected when he announced that he was going on a trip to Beijing and Shanghai. It was a three-month visit to places where he'd always been happy, and on which his old students from the Foreign Languages Institute would pay him a series of homages: what could go wrong? Yes, taking such a long trip at such an advanced age might not seem like the most prudent idea, but nobody had ever convinced Fausto Cabrera not to do something he'd already set his mind on. So he went to China, received the homages and came back to Colombia in time to celebrate his birthday. And now, a few weeks after returning from the other side of the world, he'd had a fall in the space between the sofa and the front door of his own home, and was clinging to life.

It was not just any life, it has to be said. Fausto Cabrera was a renowned figure of whom theatre people (but also television and cinema people) spoke with the respect due to pioneers, in spite of being always surrounded by controversy and as many enemies as friends. He'd been the first to use the Stanislavsky method to interpret poems, not just to perform dramatic characters; he had founded experimental theatre schools in

Medellín and Bogotá, and once dared to turn the Santamaría bullring into a stage for a Molière play. At the end of the 1940s he made radio programmes that changed the way people understood poetry, and then, when television arrived in Colombia, he was one of the first directors of television drama and one of its most acclaimed actors. Later, in more agitated times, he used his reputation in the dramatic arts as a cover for his engagement in Colombian communism, and that earned him the hatred of many until those years began to be forgotten. Younger generations remembered him mostly for a role he'd played in a film: *The Strategy of the Snail*, Sergio's best-known film, and perhaps the one that had brought him the most satisfaction, in which Fausto played Jacinto, a Spanish anarchist who leads a small popular revolution in the heart of Bogotá. He embodied him with such naturalness, and seemed so comfortable in the skin of his character, that Sergio, when talking about his father's role in the film, usually summed it up this way:

"He was just playing himself."

Now, coming out of the park with Silvia at his side, walking between the Jerónimos Monastery and the waters of the Tagus, watching Amalia who, up ahead, was struggling with the handlebars of her bicycle, Sergio wondered if he shouldn't have made more of an effort to visit him more frequently. It wouldn't have been easy, in any case, since in his own life two things were happening that consumed his time and attention, and barely left him space for other preoccupations. On the one hand, there was a television series; on the other, the attempt to save his marriage. The series told the story of the journalist Jaime Garzón, his friend and accomplice, whose brilliant political satire programmes ended in 1999, the morning he was shot dead by right-wing hit men while waiting for a traffic light to change to green. The marriage, for its part, was going off the rails, and the reasons were not clear to either Sergio or his wife. Silvia was Portuguese and twenty-six years younger than him; they'd met in 2007, in Madrid, and they'd managed to live happily together for several years in Bogotá, until something stopped working the way it should. But what was it? Although they hadn't figured it out with certainty, separation seemed the best possible option, or the least damaging, and Silvia travelled to Lisbon not as one returning to her country and her language, but as if she were coming home to shelter from a storm.

Sergio endured life without his wife and daughter as well as he could, but was always aware that the separation was doing him more harm than he admitted. Then the opportunity he'd unknowingly been waiting for arrived: the Filmoteca de Catalunya was organizing a retrospective of his films, and the programmers asked Sergio to travel to Barcelona to spend a long weekend with them, from Thursday, October 13 until the following Sunday. There would be the opening, one of those ceremonies with cava and live music, full of handshakes and generous praise, which had always embarrassed his natural shyness but which he'd never refused, because deep down he felt that not even a shyness like his justified ingratitude. And then, for three days, Sergio would attend the showings of his films and speak about them with an interested and educated audience. The occasion was perfect. Sergio decided immediately that he'd take advantage of the invitation to Barcelona to stop over in Lisbon, spend some days with his wife and daughter and mend the family that had come apart, or at least come to understand the reasons for the rupture. The film institute booked his flights in accordance with those requests.

So on October 6, when Sergio arrived in a yellow taxi at Bogotá airport, he already had his connecting flight to Lisbon booked for the next day. He called his father from the departure lounge: never in his life had he left the country without saying goodbye to him over the telephone. "When will you be back?" Fausto asked. "In a couple of weeks, Papá," Sergio said. "OK, OK," Fausto said. "We'll see you when you get home." "Yes, see you then," Sergio said, thinking they were both repeating the same phrases they'd said a thousand times on a thousand identical phone calls, and that those simple words weren't what they used to be: they'd lost value, like coins no longer in circulation. In El Prat Airport one of the assistants in charge of the retrospective was waiting for him, because Sergio had offered to bring in his hand luggage all the material they needed: the hard discs with the films, of course, but also stills from the shoots and even one or two original screenplays that the film institute would show in their display cases. The assistant was a thin and bearded young man, with thick black-framed glasses and a cartoon convict T-shirt, who received the bag with an expression of unshakeable seriousness and then asked Sergio if anyone else was coming with him. "To reserve a double room," the young man clarified. "If that's the case."

"My son is coming," Sergio said. "His name is Raúl. But they already know at the Filmoteca."

Sergio had decided some time ago. Silvia would not have been able to accompany him even if the relationship had been good, and not just because of her own work, which she couldn't be away from, but because Amalia was about to start at a new school. The most natural thing in the world was to invite Raúl, the only child from his previous marriage, who'd just started his last year of secondary school and in every email asked when they would see each other again. That hadn't happened for two years, since Raúl lived with his mother in Marbella, far from the routes Sergio normally travelled. So he would take a flight on Thursday afternoon, after class, and land in Barcelona just in time to attend the opening and spend almost three whole days with his father, seeing films he'd never seen and watching some that he'd seen before, but this time with the sound and image on a cinema screen. As if these weren't reasons enough, Raúl had never been to Barcelona, and the idea of showing him the city at the same time as showing him his films struck his father as extremely tempting. That's what Sergio was thinking when he landed in Lisbon, just before nine that night, and was greeted by Silvia's face with her luminous smile, which made him feel he was arriving home rather than coming for a visit. Then he realized that Amalia had come to welcome him too; and even though it was too late for her, the little girl had the energy to stretch out her arms and wrap them around his neck, and Sergio understood why this whole detour was worth the effort.

The reunion was so lovely that he didn't even care that the airline had lost his luggage. Of the three bags Sergio had checked in at Bogotá airport, only one had arrived safe and sound at its destination, and the woman at the yellow counter offered no solution other than returning to the airport on Monday morning. But there was no misunderstanding or incident that could take away Sergio's happiness at seeing his family. On Saturday, much earlier than his jet lag might have recommended, he let Amalia take him by the hand and show him around the Benfica neighbourhood, which for her consisted of Manuel Ferreira de Andrade Street and its most important shop: the Pastelaria Califa. He bought her favourite *croquetes*, took her to a friend's birthday party, listened to her Portuguese songs and tried to sing along with her, and on Sunday, with Silvia as well, they repeated the routine. That night he told Silvia: "I'm glad I came." And it was true.

The call from his half-sister Lina was like smashing his face against impertinent reality. That morning, he and Silvia had collected the missing suitcases at the airport, and on the way back they bought Amalia a bicycle with a very pink frame, battery-operated lights on the handlebars, a doll-carrier on the back, and a helmet that matched the frame's dazzling colour; and that was the reason they had gone to the Praça do Império Gardens, across from the Jerónimos Monastery, where they were when he got the call. It was a day of clear skies and the waters of the Tagus sparkled; the stones of the walkways shone so much that Sergio's eyes hurt, and he had to put his sunglasses on just to walk to the place they'd parked Silvia's car. But his strides were not the light steps of before; the frivolous happiness of the new bicycle, and the satisfaction he got from the concentrated face of the little girl trying to go in a straight line, had all suddenly gone to shit.

It was seven in the evening when they arrived back at Manuel Ferreira de Andrade Street. In front of number 19, Sergio unloaded the heavy suitcases and dragged them as far as the covered walkway in front of the building, while Silvia drove around the block to find a free parking space. And that was when the phone in his pocket vibrated again and the same number appeared on the screen. The moment he answered, Sergio already knew what Lina's voice would say to him, he already knew all the words, because there are not so many to say what Lina was going to say. When his wife and daughter arrived he was still there, in the marble-floored walkway, between the green-tiled columns, paralysed even though gusts of air blew in his face, with his phone still in his hand and his forlorn luggage beside him like two lapdogs, feeling in spite of everything that a conjunction of fates had been favourable to him, as he wouldn't have wanted to receive that news in any other place in the world, or in any other company. He took Silvia's hand, while letting Amalia ride a little way away on her bicycle, and said:

"He's dead."

The first thing he did when they got up to the apartment was shut himself in Silvia's bedroom to call his sister Marianella. They wept together for long telephonic seconds, with no need to say anything, just sharing the terrifying feeling that a whole life – not only that of Fausto Cabrera – had just ended. Marianella was two years younger than Sergio, but, for reasons they'd never tried to explain, that distance had something unreal or arbitrary about it, maybe because features of their personalities compensated for it: the younger sister had always been bolder, more rebellious, more insubordinate, and the older brother seemed to have been born with the vices of over-thinking and hesitancy. But they had lived through so many things together, and such different things from what they should have experienced, that since they were very young they had shared a special loyalty: that of those who know that their life is incomprehensible to others, and that the only way to be happy is to accept it without getting incensed. Sergio tried to alleviate his sister's sadness from afar, and could think of no better way than to tell her everything he knew about their father's death. He told her about the sofa where he had been reading the newspaper, about his insistence on checking that the already locked door was bolted, about his fainting into the arms of his wife. He told her that Fausto didn't even make it into the ambulance, since he had no vital signs when the paramedics arrived. The death certificate had just been signed there in his own living room, and right now they were waiting for the people from the funeral home. That's what Lina had told him, and she'd finished with a strange sentence, at once cryptic and bombastic:

"He died on his feet, Sergio. Just as he lived."

It was Monday, October 10, 2016. The opening ceremony at the film institute was planned for Thursday 13, at seven-thirty in the evening. After his call with Marianella, Sergio suddenly found himself doing mental arithmetic, calculating flight times, sitting at the computer, comparing available itineraries between Spain and Colombia. Although the time difference was not in his favour, he realized that it wasn't impossible, if he hurried, to fly to Bogotá and see his father's face one last time, speak to Nayibe, embrace Marianella and be back in Barcelona barely a day late, to participate in the rest of the retrospective, watch his films and answer audience questions. But that night, after having dinner with Silvia and Amalia, Sergio lay down on the grey sofa in front of the television without turning it on, and at some point began to feel an emotion he'd never known before. There, in that foreign apartment with wooden floors, was his family, the family that had escaped him once already; as if that weren't enough, Raúl was expecting him in Barcelona, and

21

suddenly the whole trip had started to feel like the possibility of a second chance. Maybe Sergio was thinking of this when he made the decision that didn't strike him as strange as it would later seem to him.

"I'm not going to go," he told Silvia.

He would not travel to Bogotá: he would not attend his father's funeral. The commitment he'd made to the film institute, he would explain to those needing explanations, did not give him enough time to go and come back again, and he could not disparage the work and money the organizers had put into the tribute. Yes, that was the solution. *I'm so sorry*, he would say to his father's wife, and he would not be lying. He had a cordial relationship with her, but never, in so many years of coexistence, had they ever shared anything remotely resembling intimacy. She wouldn't miss Sergio's presence; he, for reasons he could find no clear words for, didn't feel entirely welcome in Bogotá.

"Are you sure?" Silvia said.

"I'm sure," Sergio said. "I've already thought it through. And my place is here with the living, not with the dead."

All the Colombian media covered the death of Fausto Cabrera. By the time Sergio arrived in Barcelona, late on that grey Wednesday morning, the Colombian press was inundated with accounts of his father's life. Reading the news from those days, it seemed there was no actor in the whole country who had not shared the famous Seki Sano's acting classes with Fausto, nor had a single fan not been present in the bullring to see *The Imaginary Invalid*, nor had any colleague not called to congratulate him when he won the Ministry for Culture's Lifetime Achievement

Award. The radio stations discovered old recordings in which Fausto recited poems by José Asunción Silva or León de Greiff, and in some corner of the internet an article resurfaced that Sergio had published several years earlier in the Madrid paper *ABC*. "A good citizen," he wrote there, "is not one who spends his life trying to prove his country is the best; it's the one who tries to make the country that received him great, because this is the best way to honour the one where he was born." Social media also did what it does: from its sewers emerged anonymous silhouettes and high-sounding pseudonyms – Patriot, Standard Bearer, Great Colombian – reminding people of Fausto Cabrera's militant history and his relationship with the Maoist guerrillas, and declaring that the only good communist was a dead communist. Sergio's phone received non-stop calls from unknown or concealed numbers, and his WhatsApp filled with requests or pleas, which he ignored as politely as he could. He knew he couldn't hide for ever, but for a few hours, the more the better, he wanted to hold onto his own recollection of his father, the memories – good ones and otherwise – that were already beginning to assault him.

The Filmoteca de Catalunya put him up in a luxurious hotel on the Rambla del Raval, one of those places where all the walls are windows and all the lights are coloured, but he had no time to enjoy the room: the organizers took him out immediately for a welcome lunch in a nearby restaurant. Even though they hadn't said so, Sergio realized that everyone knew what had happened: they had the strained expression of people feeling out the terrain to see how much sympathy to allow, where the legal limit of the smiles was. Before dessert arrived, the director of programming, a friendly man with big eyes and frameless glasses, whose thick eyebrows rose almost affectionately when he talked about cinema, interrupted the conversation to thank Sergio for his presence and tell him how delighted they were to have him in Barcelona, but that he was free to fly back to Colombia if he chose to: the retrospective was already organized, the films were already at the institute, the exhibition had been set up, and if Sergio decided to cancel his participation to be with his family and bury his father, they would understand perfectly. Sergio had by then had time to size him up: Octavi Martí had directed several things for television and cinema, and spoke about the great directors with that intimacy that only those who have truly understood them can pull off. Sometimes it seemed he'd seen all the films in the world, and, sometimes, that he'd written about all of them as a critic. Sergio liked him immediately, but that wasn't the only reason he answered as he did.

"No, I'm staying," he said.

"You could go and come back for the closing, if you want. We could have a final cocktail party, you could talk to people then."

"Thank you," Sergio said. "But commitments are commitments."

At the end of the lunch, in the chair to his right, which had been left mysteriously empty when the coffee was served, a young woman appeared with a folder the contents of which – several pages of well-ordered information – she began to explain with the overly patient voice of a teacher. One by one she listed the interviews that the guest of honour would have to give over the following days, a long list of press and radio and television that there, on the white page, was a torrential river that Sergio would have to swim across, as if he were once again undergoing the military training of days gone by. The programme for the retrospective also came out of the folder.

Oct. 13. *Everybody Leaves* (2015). On-stage discussion and audience questions.

Oct. 14. *Time Out* (1998). Discussion and Q & A.

Oct. 15. *The Strategy of the Snail* (1993). Discussion and Q & A.

Oct. 16–19 *The Art of Losing* (2004), *Ilona Arrives With the Rain* (1996), *A Matter of Honour* (1989) and *Eagles Don't Hunt Flies* (1994). Films shown without the participation of Sergio Cabrera.

Sergio thought he could have added a few words: Films shown in a world in which my father no longer exists. The idea shook him, because the trace of Fausto Cabrera was present in each of his films, and in many of them he was not a trace, but a flesh and blood presence: the Spanish anarchist, the porter at the sailors' hotel, the priest presiding over a funeral. Never, since the first short he ever made – an episode of Alexander von Humboldt's travels in Colombia – had he finished a film without wondering what his father would think of it; never had he wondered what it would be like to see his films in this new orphaned world, or if his films might change when the outside world, the unfilmed world, had changed in such an uncomfortable way: if the stills or the lines of dialogue would be transformed by the disappearance of the person who, in more than one sense, had made them possible. Now, while he was talking through the programme with the young woman, Octavi Martí came over to say something. He had noticed that the first three films, which they'd be showing in Sergio's presence, formed a sort of reverse chronology: from the latest to the earliest. Had that been on purpose?

"No, but it's good that way," Sergio said with a smile. "Looking back, you know? This is going to be a real retrospective, after all."

After leaving the restaurant he went straight to his room. That Barcelona afternoon was the Colombian morning: the morning of the day of the funeral. He wanted to speak to Marianella, who was feeling very sad. In recent times, after a series of unresolvable arguments, her contact with their father had become marred to the point of ceasing completely. That's why there was fury in her cry when she answered the phone: because now, after that painful distancing, she would have liked to be part of her father's death. But no-one had told her of the accident in time, even if just to give her the chance to worry, nor had they invited her to her father's house, to accompany him in the rituals of death. "They didn't tell me," Marianella complained. "They're saying I abandoned Papá in his last years, that I left him alone in his old age . . . They don't understand, Sergio, they don't know anything and they don't understand anything." The hidden or never expressed bickering that goes on in all families, the misunderstandings and words not said or said at the wrong time, the false idea we create in our head or heart of the other: that complex network of silences conspired now against serenity, and Marianella, in the midst of her sadness, was telling Sergio that she wasn't going to attend the funeral either.

"No, that can't be," Sergio said. "You're there, you have to go."

"And you?" she said. "Why aren't you here?"

Sergio didn't know what to tell her. He insisted with vague reasons, and finally got his sister to accept that, their mother having died nine years earlier and with Sergio out of the country, she was the family, she had to represent the family.

That afternoon he had his first interview in the lobby of the hotel. The journalist explained that it would be a special page – the back page of *La Vanguardia* – and that the format always started with a brief inventory of biographical information, so Sergio found himself filling in a police dossier: he was sixty-six years old, three marriages and four children; he'd been born in Medellín, lived in China and worked in Spain; he was an atheist. He was not surprised that the first question, after that interrogation, was not a question, but condolences: "Sorry to hear about your father." His own reply, however, took him by surprise, not because not even he expected it, but because as he said it he had the impression of giving away more than he meant to, as if denouncing someone.

"Thanks," he said. "He died today and I won't be able to get to his funeral."

It was a lie, of course, a deliberate forty-eight hour lag, which didn't matter there, in the strident hotel lobby armchair: it was unlikely the journalist would notice, and if she did, she'd put it down to confusion brought on by grief, that disorientation a person feels when they've just lost a loved one. But why? Why had he lied? He wondered if he was belatedly ashamed of his decision not to go to the funeral, as if shame could be a travelling companion that catches up on us after a late start. The journalist wanted to know more about his father, the Republican exile in Colombia, son of a military family that had not supported Franco's coup, and Sergio kept answering her questions judiciously, but that betrayal of his own emotions continued to trouble him.

"Oh, so he lived here?" the journalist asked. "Here, in Barcelona?"

"Not for long, but yes," Sergio said.

"And where did he live?"

"That, I don't know," Sergio said. "He never told me. I don't think he remembered."

He gave two more interviews and then he made his apologies to the film institute: he was tired, he would have dinner on his own and get some sleep. "Good, good," they said, "tomorrow the serious work begins." He went up to his room, where the thick glass repelled the din of the groups drinking under the palm trees, and he tried to lie down, close his eyes and rest a little. But he could not. He was thinking about the questions he'd been asked and the replies he'd willingly given, always thinking that talking about cinema was one of the hardest things to do in the world, for words tangled everything up and did nothing but provoke misunderstandings; nevertheless, now he was grateful for that obligation, which distracted him from his grief and kept his sadness at bay. He'd praised Wendy Guerra's novel, on which he'd based the plot of his latest film, and he'd talked about *Time Out*, a comedy in which the guerrillas and the police declare a truce so they can watch a football match, and he'd also talked about *The Art of Losing* and his friendship with the novelist Santiago Gamboa; and a thousand times, as he answered questions about *The Strategy of the Snail*, he'd had to refer briefly to his father, who went through the Civil War right there in Barcelona, before beginning the years of exile or wandering that would eventually take him to Colombia. But where, in what part of the city had he lived? His father had never told him, or perhaps Sergio had forgotten.

He could not get to sleep: the tiredness, if it had really existed, had evaporated from his eyes. Maybe it was the remains of jet lag, as it hadn't been five days since he left Colombia, or maybe a current of insomnia was running through his body, but Sergio could not stay in bed. He put on a jacket, because the temperature had suddenly dropped, he looked at the pamphlets in the room and found a few photos he liked, and in a few minutes he was on his way up to the hotel's rooftop terrace, looking for a seat and settling down to watch the young night, the night falling over the old city that extended from there down to the sea. The sky had cleared and a breeze ruffled the paper napkins. His was a high seat that, placed there in front of a glass table, seemed about to fall down into the street. He didn't know which arrived first, the waitress with the glass of red wine or the uncomfortable question, but there it was again: if he had to explain why he'd decided not to travel to Bogotá to see his father's face for the last time, what would he say? To be with Silvia and Amalia, of course; to meet up with his son Raúl here in Barcelona. All well and good, but was that it? Was there not something more?

The city lights shone below, as they began to come on, and to his left, the line of light of the Ramblas summoned his gaze and guided it towards the port, towards the invisible statue of Columbus. In the sky he could see the lights of planes approaching El Prat. He took out his phone – the white light broke the comfortable semi-darkness of the bar and caught the attention of his neighbours – and checked his WhatsApp messages. He counted twenty-seven condolence messages before reaching a line from Silvia: *How are you?* He answered: *Fine. I won't pretend I'm not thinking about you. I want this to work.* And she: *It's important now to think of your father. Are you thinking about him?* And he: *I'm remembering things, yes.* But they were badly formed memories he couldn't see clearly or that resisted letting themselves be seen, disagreeable memories that burst halfway into the calm night, into this solitude that tomorrow, when Raúl arrived, would be irretrievable. *So many conflicts, Sergio wrote. In spite of doing so many things together, in China, with the guerrilla forces, in the cinema, on television, the compendium of memories, no matter how hard I try to sweeten them, is not positive.* He looked up: another plane was flying over, but this time it must have been closer, because its noise could be heard in the distance. *But I know, and I say it every chance I get, that I am my father's disciple. I would never have been able to do the things I've done had I not grown up in his world.* He lowered the phone and looked up at the sky, because the plane was still flying towards the south, towards the airport, or towards the place where Sergio imagined the airport must be. At that moment his phone vibrated (Silvia had answered), but Sergio didn't look at the screen, because his gaze, which had fixed on the plane or on its tiny lights, had begun taking in the whole city of low structures, and now ran into something else: the silhouette of a mountain, lying on the horizon like a sleeping animal, and above the silhouette, the glowing radiance of the castle. He felt something come undone in his chest, because, although he was sure he'd never been on that rooftop or on any similar one in Barcelona, there had to be some reason for the unpredictable emotion that was coming over him now, as he realized that from there, from the hotel terrace, he could see Montjuic.

II

From the rooftop he could see Montjuic. Fausto, who was then thirteen years old, liked to go up with his brother Mauro to see the sky and the distant sea, and, in the sky, Franco's planes that flew over the defiant city. The Civil War was many things: it was a priest who, from the belfry of a neighbourhood church, shot at an unarmed crowd, and it was also the hissing of a cat in heat a bomb produces as it falls, and it was also the tremor of the explosion, which you felt in the pit of your stomach like a belly ache. The war, for the two brothers, was hiding under the dining room table while the silhouettes of the enemy Junkers were crossing the blue sky. Later they learned to seek shelter when the sirens sounded, but very soon, when the sirens became routine, they lost the habit: from a certain moment, only Pilón, the family wolfhound, kept hiding in the shelter. Fausto listened to bombs falling elsewhere – near or far, but elsewhere – and then, by asking the adults, found out that the planes were coming from the Balearic Islands, that they were Franco's, but he received the reassuring news that Barcelona would never fall into the hands of the fascists. Why not? Because his father said so.

His name was Domingo Cabrera. When the war began, he

still had an athletic build, but he was also an amateur poet and a guitarist with a good voice and a film star's face. He was an adventurer: at the age of sixteen he'd packed up his few belongings, tired of the provincial life in the Canary Islands, and had boarded the first ship heading to the Americas. He barely managed to scrape together enough money to be allowed on board, so he had to pay the rest of his passage with the sweat of his brow: and this was more true in his case than in any other, for what he did, to the shock and fascination of the passengers, was reach an agreement with another lad and stage wrestling exhibitions on deck. On that adventurous trip he went to Cuba, worked in the countryside in Argentina and administered an estate in Guatemala, a few kilometres from the city of Antigua. There he met a Spanish colonel, Antonio Díaz Benzo, who had been sent by the king himself to open a military school. And that changed his life.

The colonel was a hero of the Cuban war whose medals would not fit on his dress uniform. Nobody could have predicted what happened: Domingo, the young adventurer, fell in love with Julia, the colonel's daughter; and what was worse, the colonel's daughter fell in love with the young adventurer. Julia Díaz Sandino was a Madrid aristocrat, monarchist to the marrow; it was the most improbable relationship in the world until one realized that the monarchist was also a good reader of Spanish poetry, and recited Lope as long as the poem wasn't obscene, and told the Guatemalans about Rubén Darío as if he were from Madrid. The newlyweds returned to Las Palmas. There, in a house on calle Triana with a view of the sea, in a room with window frames constantly stripped of their paint by the force of the salty sea air, their children were born – Olga, Mauro and Fausto – and there they would have stayed for their whole lives had their lives not taken an unexpected turn.

One night, after putting little Fausto to bed, Julia complained for the first time of a sore throat. They attributed it to the arrival of autumn – she must have caught something, they said – but the pain got stronger as the days went by, and then became almost intolerable. In a matter of weeks, a doctor had diagnosed a very aggressive cancer and given her an honest recommendation: she should travel to the capital because they had discovered a new treatment there.

"And what kind of treatment is it?" Domingo asked.

The doctor replied in his way:

"It is a trigeminal touch," he said. "Even has a pretty name."

Times were difficult when they arrived in Madrid. Alfonso XIII's monarchy had been suffering the siege of the ghosts of the Republic for months, and, although he was managing to keep them at bay, it was obvious to everyone that something in Spain was going to change. Doña Julia was suffering like her king, for in her family the figure of the heroic colonel, defender of the Crown's territories in the Cuban war, weighed heavily, and she suffered doubly because of what happened to her brother. Felipe Díaz Sandino was one of the great pilots of Spanish aviation. Flight Commander Díaz Sandino, of the Catalan Air Force, was one of those characters who seem to live with their family crest tattooed across their chests, and this family's contained ominous words: *Vive la vida de suerte que viva quede en la muerte.* Live life in such a way as to stay alive in death. Julia would have felt proud of him, and would have transmitted this pride to her family if Uncle Felipe, who visited the Cabrera household every other day, didn't have three flaws: one, he was a committed Republican; two, he was conspiring to overthrow the king; and three, he had convinced Domingo to join the plotters.

One night in 1930, Domingo, who usually came home early to look after his ailing wife, did not show up. Nobody knew where he was, nobody had seen him all day, nobody had heard of anything strange going on. In Madrid there was already an atmosphere of subversion, and in a city like that serious things can happen without anyone finding out about them. So they went to bed – and Fausto would remember later his perfect awareness that his mother was lying when they said that no, nothing was going on, these were adult matters – and he had managed to get a couple of hours' sleep before he was awakened by rifle butts banging on the door. Three agents of the security forces burst in without removing their hats or holstering their pistols, the way they would burst into a criminal's house, asking for Felipe Díaz Sandino, kicking open doors and looking under beds. When they were convinced that Uncle Felipe was not there, they asked for the head of the household. Julia looked at each one in turn.

"He's not here either," said Doña Julia. "And I don't know where he might be. And if I did know, I wouldn't tell you either."

"Well, tell him as soon as you see him, Señora," one of the agents said, "that we're expecting him at the Station."

"And what if I don't see him?"

"Of course you'll see him," the man said. "Of course you'll see him."

She saw him just before dawn. Domingo arrived so quietly that young Fausto was only alerted to his presence by the sound of his mother weeping. The news was not good: the police had followed them, Domingo and Uncle Felipe, and after they'd been hiding for hours, changing houses and slipping into cafés to confuse their pursuers, they'd caught them up. Domingo had managed to elude them, but Felipe was arrested, and now they were accusing him of conspiring against Alfonso XIII and were holding him in a military prison.

"Well, let's go see him," Doña Julia said.

"What are you saying?" Domingo reproached her. "You're ill."

"Not for this I'm not," she said. "We're going right now. And what's more we're all going."

Fausto was six when he visited a prison for the first time. For Olga and Mauro it was a dark and ugly place; for Fausto, however, the prison was sordid and dangerous, and Uncle Felipe was suffering there for being fair and fighting injustice. In reality, it was not like that: it was not a sordid place, and there were no claustrophobic walkways, and Uncle Felipe had not been tortured or mistreated. Prisons for military officers, more so if they were officers with lineage and medals on their chests, were rather comfortable places. But none of that mattered to Fausto: those days in prison turned Uncle Felipe into his hero. The family visited him every week of his captivity, and Fausto embraced Uncle Felipe as if he had just returned from the battlefield. Julia begged her brother: "Tell him that everything's going to be alright, please, the poor boy can't sleep. Tell him they're not torturing you, that they treat you well and you'll soon be released." Uncle Felipe went further: "I'll be out soon, Fausto," he said, "and when I get out, Spain will be a republic."

Fausto remembered that conversation later, when he saw people rushing out onto the streets to celebrate. Uncle Felipe carried him on his shoulders around Madrid, holding on to a leg with one hand while waving a tricolour flag with the other, and singing the "Himno de Riego", the Republican anthem, at the top of his voice while Doña Julia cried in her bedroom and said the world was going to end. For months the conversations round the dinner table were unbearable, since Julia was convinced the family was condemned to hell, and the priest she invited every chance she got backed her up. At the same time, Domingo and Uncle Felipe had formed an alliance that closely resembled a mafia. Thanks to Felipe, Domingo had found part-time work in the Ministry for the Interior, but at night he was another person: secret agent for the Department of Security. Fausto and his brother and sister had received precise instructions not to speak of this job, because – it was explained – the walls had ears.

The afternoon when his father brought him the news, Fausto had spent the morning alone in the house, wandering through the rooms, and at some point found himself in front of the wardrobe where Domingo kept his things. It was a miracle that it was not locked. Fausto was not going to let that opportunity slip by: he found the detective's badge, he found the gun without its cartridge and took it out of its holster, and was caressing it, imagining dangerous and violent scenes, when his father suddenly opened the door. His face was tangled with emotions and, in a voice Fausto had never heard before, gave him an order that was more like a plea: "Come and say goodbye." He took him to another bedroom. Fausto found himself with a body in a bed and a face covered with a white bandage that left only a pair of closed eyes uncovered. He kissed the bandage, and would later think that not having touched his mother's cold face with his lips, far from being a consolation, was a lost opportunity he'd always regret.

His mother's death foreshadowed other disasters. Years later, when the war broke out, Fausto didn't know if it was better that his mother hadn't seen it, but he always had the uncomfortable certainty that the war would have been different for him, less terrifying and less lonely, if he could have relied on her. By that stage he had already begun to seek consolation in the books that she had left behind, some of which were falling apart from having been read so often; the pages of others, however, remained uncut. Thus he discovered Becquer (coming apart) and Pedro Salinas (uncut), García Lorca (uncut) and Manuel Reina (coming apart). Domingo did not raise any objections, and began to give him new books every once in a while, for any remedy was good if it could spare his son the pain he was feeling. So Fausto got to know the poems of *Las islas invitadas*, the book in which Manuel Altolaguirre dedicated a poem to his dead mother. In those verses, which might have been alarming, there was something resembling tranquillity.

> *I would have preferred*
> *To be an orphan in death,*
> *Than to be missing you*
> *There, in the mystery,*
> *Not here, in what's known.*

Meanwhile, the Cabrera family had become *personae non gratae*. Uncle Felipe, who had known Franco, who had fought with him in Africa and been decorated, who had become famous in Africa for climbing out of the trenches, so they said, to defy enemy bullets, now was remaining faithful to the Republic, for which he'd fought. In those days, when the major part of the army had taken the side of those who were staging the coup, that fidelity was suicidal. "Your uncle is very brave," his father told Fausto. "It takes courage to not do what everyone would have forgiven him for doing in the end." But the family's life in Madrid was getting more and more difficult. After the death of Julia, whose mere presence served to deactivate the hostility of monarchists, the Cabrera household was nothing but a nest of sedition, and the military officers loyal to the king, who supported Franco's rebellion, began to harass them shamelessly. The situation rapidly became untenable. One night, while Domingo and his children were having dinner at home, Uncle Felipe made a surprise visit and said:

"We're leaving. For everyone's safety."

"Where to?" Domingo said.

"Barcelona, where I have friends," Felipe said. "After that, we'll see."

A week later, Fausto was climbing into an airplane for the first time in his life. It was a Junkers G24 of the Republican air fleet, piloted by Colonel Felipe Díaz Sandino – his beloved uncle, his audacious uncle, saviour of the family – the nine seats of which easily accommodated the entire family. Uncle Felipe knew he was doomed, because officers who turned their backs on Franco went onto a black list and were pursued more viciously than if they were communists, so he thought he would get his loved ones to safety in order to continue fighting his war. Domingo became his chief bodyguard: the safety of Uncle Felipe, who had become a nuisance to the officers trying to topple their government, could not have been in better hands. Olga once asked her uncle what her father's job was, and he explained: "He's the one who doesn't let them kill me."

"And what if they kill him?" asked Olga.

Her uncle was lost for words.

The Cabreras settled into an apartment with a view of the sea and windows that went from the floor to the ceiling, and from the terraced roof they could see Montjuic. The family carried on their lives in bombarded Barcelona: Fausto went to school and discovered that he liked it, and he discovered it was frustrating not to be able to boast about being the nephew of Felipe Díaz Sandino, the Republican hero who ordered the bombing of Franco's barracks in Zaragoza. A long time later Fausto would find out what had been going on during that time: Uncle Felipe had confronted his political superiors about the way they were waging the war (especially a war as dysfunctional as that one, where sometimes the Republicans' worst enemies were other Republicans); the confrontations heated up to such an extent that the only way to cool them off was a political move, and Uncle Felipe accepted a diplomatic post in Paris, thinking that way he could raise support from other European countries for the Republican cause. On the occasion of his appointment, the labour unions of Barcelona gave him a gift nobody was expecting: a Hispano-Suiza T56, made in La Sagrera, with room for five passengers and a 46-horsepower engine. When he came to show the Cabreras, he said it was a waste to have so many horses: to get to Paris he only needed three.

That's how Fausto found out that Uncle Felipe was taking him and his brother Mauro along on his trip, while the rest of them were to stay in Barcelona. He never knew who decided that, whether the trip had been planned with his father's complicity or simply with his consent, but later, as they crossed the Pyrenees in the Hispano-Suiza, Fausto saw the expression of respect with which the gendarme received the papers of that Republican diplomat and for the rest of the trip he realized he'd never known that sense of security. Uncle Felipe seemed to have the keys to the world. During their first days in Paris he took them to the best restaurants, so Fausto and his brother could eat everything the war had kept them from eating, and then he got them accepted into the Lycée Pothier, a boarding school for well-off people in Orléans. For Fausto, an adolescent by then, these were days of fist fights with French kids who looked down on him for no reason he could fathom, days of discovering sex, or rather fantasies of sex, with fifteen-year-old girls who visited him at night to learn Spanish. Fausto let them recite lines of Paul Géraldy and in exchange gave them whole Bécquer poems that he'd memorized without trying by reading his mother's books, those verses of contagious music in which all pupils were improbably blue and all lovers wondered what they would give for a kiss. Meanwhile, in interviews with the French newspapers, Felipe Díaz Sandino accepted that yes, his side had also committed excesses, but it was a grave moral error to equate them with the excesses of the other side: with Nazi aircraft that razed defenceless villages, for example, while the so-called democratic nations looked the other way, unaware that the defeat of the Republic would, in the long run, be their own defeat.

The diplomatic mission did not last long. The news arriving from Spain was disheartening, and the French government, overwhelmed by the attempt to manage a serious economic crisis, dodging the nationalists of La Cagoule, who were assassinating union leaders or planning coups d'état, did not seem to have the time or patience to listen to his complaints. It was better to keep fighting the war in Spain. But when they returned to Barcelona, Uncle Felipe discovered that the pro-Franco newspapers had published news of his escape and capture. He had an experience very few get to have: he saw a photograph of his dead body in the press and read the news of his execution by firing squad. Seeing himself there, shot dead in the plaza Cataluña and repudiated as a traitor and a red, Uncle Felipe for the first time felt certain that the war was being lost.

Fausto and Mauro also found life changed: Domingo had met a woman. One night he gathered his three children and announced that he was going to be married. Josefina Bosch was Catalan and much younger than Domingo, and she leaned too close to her husband's children when she spoke to them, as if she thought they couldn't understand her closed accent with its stubborn Ls, and seemed much more at ease with dogs. Her temperament was so difficult that Fausto wondered why he couldn't have stayed in France, and for the first time felt something like resentment towards Uncle Felipe, thinking it was not good to do something like that to a boy who's just awakening to life: it wasn't right to bring him back to a country at war, a city being bombed by planes that weren't even Spanish, to a family that had been mended like a broken piece of porcelain.

After Domingo and Josefina were married, the Cabrera family moved to a large house not far from plaza Cataluña. By day the sirens went off continually, but in the new house there was no way to get up on a roof and see the planes. The city was living in fear: Fausto could see it in Josefina's face and talked about it with his siblings, and he could feel it in the air each time his father took them to their Aunt Teresa's house. Less than a week after they'd moved house the sirens went off as they were always going off, but this time the family, sitting at the table having lunch, didn't have time to hide. An explosion shook the building and broke one of the windows, and it was so strong that the soup leaped out of the bowls and Fausto fell off his chair. "Under the table!" shouted Domingo. It would have been a useless precaution, but they all obeyed. Olga clung to her father's arm, and Josefina, still chewing a piece of bread, hugged Fausto and Mauro, who were crying at the tops of their lungs. "Check to see if they're injured," Domingo said to Josefina, and she lifted their shirts and felt their backs and bellies and chests, and Domingo did the same with Olga. "It's nothing, it's nothing," Domingo said then. "Stay here, I'll be right back." And a few minutes later he brought the news: Italian airplanes had been fiercely attacking Barcelona, and one of the bombs had fallen onto a truck loaded with dynamite that was parked around the corner. Josefina listened patiently and then came out from under the table, brushing off her dress.

"Well, now we know," she said. "Let's finish eating, then, there's still some soup left."

A few days later, the family gathered to make some decisions. They were losing the war, and Barcelona was the fascists' favourite target. The Italians, on board the Savoia bombers, were not going to stop destroying the city. Uncle Felipe made the decision for everyone: "It's time you left Spain. I can't protect you here." So they packed their things into the Hispano-Suiza, and one morning they set off for the French border. Fausto, squashed in with his brother and sister in a car designed for fewer people, thought about various things during the trip: his dead mother, poems by Bécquer and Géraldy, fifteen-year-old French girls; and also his father, who had stayed behind to protect Uncle Felipe. But most of all he was thinking of his uncle: Colonel Felipe Díaz Sandino, Republican, conspirator and war hero. From that moment on, Fausto would see Uncle Felipe and would think: That's how I'm going to be. He'd think: That's what I want to be like when I'm grown up. He'd think: Live life in such a way as to stay alive in death.

The scene resembled the set and props of a bad play: a road, some trees, a bleaching sun. There, in that lacklustre setting, were Josefina and the Cabrera children, squeezed into the Hispano-Suiza five kilometres from the French border, in the middle of nowhere. But they weren't alone: like them, many other occupants of many vehicles, and other men and women who had arrived on foot with their bundles on their shoulders, were waiting for the same thing. They were fleeing the war: they were leaving behind their houses; they were leaving behind, more than anything else, their dead, with that audacity or that desperation that lets anyone, even the most cowardly, set off into the uncertainties of exile. The border was closed and there was nothing to do but wait; but while they were waiting, while the morose hours of the first day went by and then the second, the food started to run out and women began to get more nervous, perhaps aware of something the children didn't know. Some waits are horrible because they have no visible conclusion, because the powers with the ability to end the wait or to make something happen that will set the world in motion again are not in view: for example, that the authorities – but who are they? Where are they? – give the order to open a border. And that's what Fausto and his brother Mauro were wondering: who could give the order and why had they refused to give it so far, when a murmur was heard in the air, and then the murmur turned into a roar, and before the family realized, a fighter plane was bearing down on them, firing its machine guns.

"Take cover!" someone shouted.

But there was nowhere to hide. Fausto took shelter behind the Hispano-Suiza, but soon, when the plane had flown away, he suspected the attack had not finished, and realized that behind the car when a plane's coming from one direction would be in front of it if the plane came from the other direction. And that's what happened: the plane banked and came back from the opposite direction. Fausto crawled under the Hispano-Suiza, and from there, with his face pressed against the ground, feeling the stones on his skin, he heard the roar again and the machine guns and recognized Josefina's shout, which was a shout of fear and rage: "Sons of bitches!" And then there was silence again. The attack had passed without loss of life: fearful faces everywhere, women crying, children leaning against car tyres, bullet holes – dark holes looking out – in the bodywork. But no dead. No wounded either. It was unreal.

"But we haven't done anything!" Fausto said. "Why are they shooting us?"

Josefina answered: "Because they're fascists."

They slept fearing another attack. Fausto, in any case, was afraid, and it was a different sort of fear because they were outside. The next day they decided that the worst decision was not making any decision, so they moved: they went along the border, from control post to control post, until they found movements in the crowd, those recognizable movements because they are the opposite of despair or defeat: because they could see in them something we identify with the urge to go on living. Someone in the family asked what was happening, and the reply was the one they were hoping for:

"They've just opened the border."

"They've opened it," Fausto said.

"Yes, they've opened it," Josefina said.

Then they saw the problem they were about to confront. The gendarmes had opened the pass, but they were separating the men from the women and children.

"What's going on?" Fausto asked. "Where are they taking them?"

"To concentration camps," Josefina said. "Fucking frogs."

Then she asked Fausto to come over. She spoke looking up in the air with her eyebrows raised, and Fausto understood that he shouldn't be looking at her eyes, but at her hands: her hands that were now handing him a wallet as if revealing a secret.

"Try to speak to them," she said.

"To whom?"

"To the gendarmes. You speak French, don't you? Well then."

Fausto and Mauro made their way through the crowd and found the door to some offices. They tried to go in, thinking, rightly, that on the other side of the door they could get the authorizations they needed, but the gendarmes kicked them out rudely. "They treat us like scum," Mauro said. "Sons of bitches." Then Fausto noticed a man in an elegant suit walking with his hat in his hand, and there was something in the way he held his hat that transmitted authority. Fausto grabbed his brother by the arm and they began to walk behind the man with the hat, stepping right behind his shoes, so close that they could have tripped him. A couple of gendarmes tried to stop them. "Where are you going?" one of them spat out. Fausto answered in his impeccable French:

"What do you mean, where? Where my uncle is going."

The gendarme, confused, looked at his comrade.

"Well if they're coming with *Monsieur*..." the other said.

Fausto quickened his pace in the direction of the man with the hat, and wasn't worried about losing sight of him: they had got round the obstacle. "Now what?" Mauro said. "Now we look for an office," Fausto said. It was not difficult: an abundance of people, a movement of bodies thronging together at the back of the building. One of the bodies was wearing a uniform: he was a burly man, with white hair and a moustache less white than his hair, and Fausto walked up to him. "They told us," he assured the man with all the aplomb he could summon up in his adolescent voice, "that we should speak with you." And he explained their case.

He told him of his uncle, hero of the resistance to Franco. He told him of his Republican family desperate to leave the country where the fascists were bombing women and children. He told him he had studied in Paris and that the values of the République were his values. "We can't make exceptions," the officer said. And after those words, the only result of which was entrance into an office and the briefest of audiences with a clerk, Fausto took Josefina's wallet out of his pocket, and from the wallet, the bundle of notes. He left it there, on his outstretched hand, floating in mid-air. The officer looked at the clerk.

"We'll make an exception," he said.

Fausto handed over the money and in exchange received a permit to go to the railway station. In minutes they were all reunited in front of the ticket office, asking with a smile which train was leaving next. Josefina paid for the tickets.

"Where are we going?" Fausto asked Josefina. "Where is this train going?"

"We're getting on it even if it's going to Siberia," she said.

But it wasn't Siberia: it was Perpignan. Fausto didn't remember anything about that city, for the Cabreras spent the days hiding in a fleabag hotel, distressed at not knowing anything of Domingo or Uncle Felipe. But they could do nothing but send notice of their whereabouts and news. They had agreed they would use an Orléans address, the house of a family Fausto had known when he was studying at the Lycée Pothier, for their correspondence. Several days later they received news: the men had been confined to the Argelès-sur-Mer concentration camp, but Uncle Felipe, using his contacts from his time as military attaché in Paris, had got them released. In the letter, Uncle Felipe instructed the family to reunite in Bordeaux. There, the two families would decide what to do.

And what they did was the same thing all those who could afford it did: flee Europe. For once it was not Uncle Felipe's decision. He had a profound conviction that Hitler would lose the war and that Franco would fall sooner rather than later. The rest of them did not agree: perhaps they were more pessimistic, perhaps they were more realistic or just more afraid. Whatever the reason, they eventually prevailed. And that's how Fausto came to be with his father again, after months that seemed like centuries, and the family of stinking reds began to roam the streets to find anyone who would accept them. They visited all the Latin American consulates and endured rejection after rejection until a country they knew little about opened its doors, and in a matter of days they were arriving at the port on the estuary and posing together with a small crowd of strangers for an onboard photographer, a small man with a moustache who would sell them the photo before the journey was over. In the front row, closest to the camera, are the women and children, but also a smiling priest and a man in uniform. Behind, in almost the back row, his woollen jacket buttoned up and one hand resting on the ship, is Fausto Cabrera, happy to be among the men, many of them Spanish like him, saying farewell to Spain confident that he will soon return, commenting on the news of a Europe in flames, cheering their good fortune at having escaped death and asking day and night, in the cabins and on deck, what life will be like, the new life, in the Dominican Republic.

III

Everything was strange in Ciudad Trujillo, the new name of old Santo Domingo. Fausto was a very white little Spaniard dressed in woollen trousers, and the dock workers, watching him disembark, began to shout: "Jew! Jew!" It was strange that reds like them, hounded by Franco, escapees from the concentration camps of collaborationist France, had been accepted by a military dictatorship. They didn't know it at the time, but President Franklin Delano Roosevelt had asked a favour of General Rafael Leónidas Trujillo: to take in some of the many refugees the war in Europe was producing. Trujillo did as he was told: for his regime, at least at that moment, the wishes of the United States were commands. Domingo was content, for he suspected it was better to arrive in a country where everything had yet to be done. He was right. Uncle Felipe, after carefully studying the city, found a Galician fisherman, proposed a partnership, and, in a matter of weeks, was setting up a business.

It was called Caribbean Fisheries. One sailing boat, a few nets that were a luminous white at first and grew weathered as the days went on, a pickup truck on the back of which the fish sparkled and a spot in the old city: with those tools

Uncle Felipe planned to support the family. Fausto got up every morning before dawn, and a shirtless young man drove him to the fishing village. There, on the docks, the family's boat would be waiting for him, and Fausto used a stout wheelbarrow to load the truck and then they would make the return journey, stopping in every village to shout out the catch of the day. He arrived at Ciudad Trujillo with weary arms and silver scales stuck to his skin, but after swimming in the ocean, looking back at the breakwater from the waves and imagining, beyond it, Ramfís Park and the family's large house, he did so with the satisfaction of doing his share to provide for everyone. And for a time it seemed they were going to manage it: the exiles had found a place in the world.

One morning a man arrived at the fishery wearing a light suit and tie with a silk handkerchief in his breast pocket, and asked if he could speak to Felipe Díaz Sandino. He brought a proposal from General Arismendy Trujillo, the dictator's brother, who was interested in becoming a partner of the Spanish businessmen: with the support of his surname, he said, the success of Caribbean Fisheries was assured. Uncle Felipe sent him away politely, saying that the business didn't need any more partners. As he did so, however, he knew the matter was not going to end there, and that's what he told the rest of the family. And after a few days had passed, the elegant man returned, bearing renewed reasons and seductive offers, paying lip service to the benefits the partnership would bring to the fishery and the nation, and listing the advantages a foreigner could have if he partnered with the first family of the Dominican Republic. Uncle Felipe refused again. The third meeting was in General Trujillo's offices.

"I understand that you were a colonel," Trujillo said.

"That's right," Uncle Felipe said. "A career officer."

General Trujillo smiled: "Of that career, Colonel, only weariness remains."

Then he said he wanted to help: that he liked military officers, that he liked dealing with them, that fishing was an essential part of the Republic's future and that Caribbean Fisheries was the most promising business in the field. From this moment on, General Trujillo announced, they would be partners. He announced it with a smile and a slight bow behind his solid desk, and Uncle Felipe understood it would be not only futile but dangerous to continue to refuse. At this meeting, they did not discuss the terms of the partnership, but that wasn't necessary. They were very simple: the fishery would give General Trujillo a generous monthly sum; General Trujillo, for his part, would give nothing. In a matter of months, the dictator's family had taken over Caribbean Fisheries. Uncle Felipe summed up the situation in words that Fausto would remember for his whole life: "Every man for himself."

A few days later, Uncle Felipe announced that he was going to Venezuela. Olga, who hadn't found a job in Ciudad Trujillo, decided to travel with him, but Fausto stayed with Mauro and their father: Uncle Felipe had turned into a defeated man. Yes, he had been a hero, but now it seemed as though life had passed him over. He left the island taking nothing with him: not enough money, or projects, or hopes. Felipe Díaz Sandino was a man broken by exile, or by the fate of the exiled. For all practical purposes, Fausto, who had so admired him as a boy, felt he was losing him for ever. But he didn't even have time to miss Uncle Felipe, because the Cabreras had already embarked on yet another attempt to survive in exile. And his uncle had left when Domingo announced the project.

"We're going to plant peanuts," he said.

It was a piece of land near the Haitian border: a dense, damp forest where the heat never seemed to abate and where a thick cloud of mosquitos hovered above every puddle. Twenty families of Spanish refugees cultivated the lands where the Dominican government wanted to produce its own oil, and each family received a generous endowment from the Ministry for Agriculture: a plough, a team of oxen, a mule and a two-room house, if those boxes separated by sheets of plywood that threatened to topple over in the first gust of wind could be called rooms. The Cabreras had to dig their own latrines. Fausto would later speak of the satisfaction of seeing one's own shit well-channelled. The company of other Spaniards was a consolation. One of them was Pablo, an Asturian who had left Spain in the same beret Fausto saw him in every day, and he would not take it off, he claimed, until that bastard Franco fell. They met with him on Sunday mornings for the call to matins, and often to sing "The Army of the Ebro" at the tops of their lungs. It was the only moment when Pablo would take off his beret. He would throw it up in the air and shout:

"Death to Franco!"

And everyone, especially Fausto, would shout back: "Let him die!"

It was with him, or at his request, that Fausto began to recite poetry. He'd liked it since childhood, reading his mother's books and listening to poems read by his father, but a stroke of luck had turned his pastime into a vocation. On the ship that had brought them from Spain, in one of the first-class cabins, was Alberto Paz y Mateos, one of the most recognized actors of his day, who had introduced Stanislavsky's theories to Spain and was turning on their heads all the ideas people in his country had about dramatic interpretation. Fausto had barely left his side during the whole voyage. He looked for him to talk about Lorca, whose verses he knew by heart, and about Chekhov, whose name he was hearing for the first time; and then, in Ciudad Trujillo, they had continued to meet occasionally. Thanks to Paz y Mateos's advice, Fausto had begun to experiment with his voice and gestures to use Stanislavsky's method in the service of poetry. A colony of exiles stuck in the jungle, where two out of three people fell ill with malaria, did not seem like the ideal place to put what he'd learned into practice, but Fausto was not daunted. In the evenings, when the black neighbours in the surrounding villages gathered to sing their songs, he liked to take advantage of the sporadic silences, and there, beside the smoky, mosquito-repelling bonfire, confronting the locals' terminal boredom, he would bring out a Machado poem or one by Miguel Hernández. The "Song of the Husband Soldier" for example:

> *The peace I am forging will be for our child,*
> *And in the end, your heart and mine*
> *Will be shipwrecked in an ocean of inevitable bones*
> *Leaving only a woman and a man worn out by kisses.*

Pablo, the Asturian, liked "Mother Spain":

> *To say mother is to say earth that gave birth to me;*
> *to say to the dead: brothers, rise up.*

These were the verses that Fausto was rehearsing on the morning of the accident. He had grown accustomed to reciting while harvesting the peanuts, to create the illusion that he was making good use of his time, and that afternoon, as he moved along the rows in the field under the sun that pressed on the nape of his neck, he was saying in his head: *Earth: earth in the mouth, and in the soul, and everywhere.* Later, telling the tale to the adults, he found that his bad luck caused only laughter, because the words could not have been more appropriate. Only a cruel and mocking god could have made Fausto, at the moment of saying these words – and those that followed: *Earth that I am eating, that in the end I must swallow* – step unwittingly into a live anthill. They were, as he later learned, fire ants, and everyone agreed that Fausto had been lucky: the viciousness of the bite and the intensity of the venom made him lose consciousness, but they remembered cases of people who had not survived. Late that night, when he awoke from a fever dream and found himself with his father and his brother Mauro, the first thing he did was say he wanted to get out of there.

"We have to wait," his father said.

"Until when?" Fausto said. "Wait until when? I'm wasting my life in this jungle. Do you think I want to spend my whole life here?"

"And what do you want, then?"

With a thread of a voice, still trembling with fever, Fausto said: "To be an actor. And I don't see much of a future here."

It was the first time he said it. Instead of mocking or humouring him, his father handed him a towel soaked in cold water and said:

"Two harvests, no more. And then we'll go."

They didn't even last for two. Winter – what Dominicans call winter – arrived without warning, with its downpours and changeable temperatures, and one night Mauro woke up in bed bathed in sweat and with his face burning. The quinine they'd started taking weeks earlier was not a sufficient preventive, and the fever was so high that Mauro stopped recognizing his family. When that happened, when Domingo arrived home one day to find that his son had confused him with the wizard Mandrake, he knew they had to return to Ciudad Trujillo. They sold the last crop at a loss and all squeezed into the first truck that could get them out of the jungle, a rickety beast with wooden rails around the flatbed. Fausto travelled there, lying among their belongings, seeing as they advanced how the clouds of malaria-carrying mosquitos became visible against the white clouds.

During the months that followed in Ciudad Trujillo, Fausto went from job to job – print worker and then lift operator and finally an assistant in a pharmacy – barely scraping by. Meanwhile, in stolen moments, he visited the Spanish Republican Centre. Similar places had been founded all over Latin America, from Mexico City to Buenos Aires, which led many to believe that the real winners of the Spanish Civil War were Latin Americans: hundreds of exiles – artists and journalists, actors, editors and novelists – brought their work and their talent with them, and the continent was never the same. Paz y Mateos was at the Ciudad Trujillo Republican Centre, and there, amid lectures and recitals, between a discussion on the possible return of the Republic and a reading of *Human Poems* by someone called César Vallejo, Fausto began his training as an actor, or continued what he had started on his own almost without knowing it. Under the guidance of exiles he discovered new poets and learned how to deliver their verses in such a way that his audience, strangely, would seem to be discovering them as well. Nobody recited Lorca better than Fausto, although recite was a weak verb for what really went on in those sessions. Paz y Mateos realized that Fausto, with his baritone voice and sinewy body, with a couple of tricks learned in Saturday workshops, was able to turn the most peaceful of verses into a call to subversion. The name of Fausto Cabrera began to appear frequently on the Centre's posters, and after one of those recitals, Fausto's father was walking over to say hello to Paz y Mateos when he heard him say:

"That boy is going to make a big splash one day."

The fantasy of being an actor took up more and more space in his head. His job at the pharmacy, with its long hours, was becoming a nuisance. Fausto kept the shop clean, which he didn't mind, but he also had to take care of the shop window, and he didn't like that so much: finding himself there, in his work clothes, with a bucket of soapy water in one hand and a rag in the other, when the girls from the nearby school walked by, was like being subjected to public ridicule. He had also noticed that he wasn't on the good side of the manager, an embittered, prematurely bald Dominican with a prominent belly, for whom the young Spaniard was the most fearful of threats. But Fausto noticed that very late, when he'd already given the manager the pretext he needed to fire him.

The error happened bit by bit. In the back of the pharmacy was a glass container full to the brim with translucent capsules: it was cod-liver oil, and Fausto began to take a capsule each time he walked past. The effect was immediate: he felt more awake and better able to concentrate. In those capsules, he thought, was the remedy for his family. For it was true that the Cabreras, subjected to months of privations and strenuous work harvesting peanuts, had arrived in Ciudad Trujillo several kilos underweight and convinced they were malnourished. After taking one capsule a few days in a row with impunity, he grabbed a generous handful and put them in his pocket. "They gave them to me at the pharmacy," he told his father.

"Oh, that's great," he said, holding the amber capsule between his fingers. "Just what we need. Bring more when you can."

"Sure," Fausto said. "Whenever I can."

But he couldn't. He was putting some capsules in his pocket, without even worrying about the one that had fallen under the table, when he realized the manager had seen the whole operation: from the other side of the counter, where a customer was waiting for a box of Gillette blades, the manager made a sign of slicing his throat with his finger, but waited till the customer had left before telling him he was fired. Fausto, ashamed, didn't even show his face to the owner. That evening, at home during dinner, he announced: "I don't work at the pharmacy anymore."

"You don't?" his father said. "So what will you do?"

"I don't know," Fausto said. "I just can't stand it anymore, Papá. What I want is something else." His face lit up. "What I want is to go to Venezuela," Fausto said. "Like Mateos did. He seems to be going great guns."

Paz y Mateos had travelled to Caracas around then. He had left the Republican Centre in the hands of another actor, and without him it was no longer the same.

"And what would you do?" Domingo asked.

"Devote myself to what I enjoy doing," Fausto said. "Devote myself to acting, devote myself to truth. Stop wasting my time. If other Spaniards have gone, why can't I go too?"

"Because you can't afford it," his father told him. "But, go ahead. I don't know how you'll do it without a job, but that's your problem now."

Fausto got a job, as a receptionist in a Dominican doctor's office, but he would have accepted anything. Now that he had the idea of acting nobody was going to get it out of his head. Once a week he walked to the Ciudad Trujillo radio station and recorded a programme about poetry; he did so for free, as hearing his own voice over the airwaves, so transformed that it sounded like someone else's voice, and receiving compliments from the few people who identified him as the radio reader, was a satisfaction he didn't try to explain to anyone, because no-one would have understood. His brother Mauro, errand boy at a Spanish grocery store, helped him out with bottles of milk and handfuls of lentils he got from work, and Fausto, relying on his tiny bit of celebrity, began to seek appointments with rich compatriots to ask for financial help. Sometimes they recognized him, but more frequently they would never have heard his name or voice. Anyway, after a few months he managed to acquire the sum that he needed. But when he tried to buy a flight he found that the routes had changed: the direct flight from Ciudad Trujillo to Caracas no longer existed, and a stopover in Curaçao was required. That, of course, increased the price. He no longer had enough money.

That night, talking to his father, he cried as he had not cried since he was a child. "I'm never going to get away from here," he said. "We're all going to rot on this island." That was when his father unbuckled his belt. A sash appeared in his hands; under the sash, some dark and damp banknotes.

"The savings from the peanut harvest," his father said. "How much are you short for the airfare?"

"That money's for emergencies," Fausto said.

"This money is for what I say it is," his father said. "And right now you're the one who needs it."

It turned out something similar had happened to him. When he wanted to leave the Canary Islands, when he was sixteen, a good friend lent him the pesetas to make up his fare.

"And now," his father said to Fausto, "I want to be that friend for you."

A long time later, with the perspective time provides, Fausto would understand that Venezuela had never been a destination but simply a stopover. During the months that followed, while he divided his time between an absurd job – winding bolts of material at the Gallo de Oro department store – and the always frustrating search for the cultural life of Caracas, his father and brother were arriving in Colombia, where Uncle Felipe had settled. When Olga decided to join the others, Fausto was left alone in Caracas, making contact with theosophy groups and reading Khalil Gibran, and receiving news that made him feel a mixture of nostalgia and envy. "We're all working," his father told him in his letters. "Olga is the secretary in a Spanish refugee's office. Mauro is the sales agent – an elegant title – for a perfume factory. And I can give you another piece of news you'll like: your Uncle Felipe is here too. Not in Bogotá with us, but in Medellín. It's the country's second city. A man from

Ecuador founded a chain of pharmaceutical laboratories and Felipe is the manager. I am running a hotel in the centre of Bogotá. This country is treating us well. All that's missing is you."

All that's missing is me, Fausto thought. But he also thought of those lives that the letter summarized. They were the lives of those who had lost their country, for whom happiness was precarious: a pitiful salary for jobs they wouldn't have done in their own country. Fausto told himself it wouldn't be like that for him: he would do what he wanted to do or die trying. In the following months, he recited poetry, a lot of poetry, and he built up a reputation with his voice and his talent, but also with other weapons. In the Pegasus Art Salon he single-handedly organized a Lorca recital, and he was well aware that his success owed in part to the tiny mythology he had constructed: he had told everyone that he was a disciple of the poet. The truth was that when Fausto was very small, his cousin Ángel had brought Lorca to visit the family home. "Federico, this is my cousin Fausto," Ángel said. "He loves to recite poetry." And Federico congratulated him, placed a firm hand on his head and gave him a kiss. That was it, but now, years after Lorca had been murdered, he didn't think it impermissible to make his way with that exaggerated anecdote. No, he was not a disciple of Lorca, but something better or more profound. And he was going to use that however he could.

Fausto was twenty when he arrived in Bogotá, after crossing the border from Venezuela and a fifteen-hour road trip, but he felt his soul had already been through several lives. It was June 1945: Hitler had committed suicide in his bunker a few weeks earlier, two days after Mussolini was hanged by the Italians, but Franco was alive, very much alive, and nothing seemed to indicate that Spain could become a republic again. The family lived in a house on calle 17, a few steps away from Parque Santander. It was not a small house, but the rest of them had occupied all the available rooms, and to make room for Fausto they had to open up non-existent spaces in the storeroom – take out boxes of food, move wooden stools – and fit in a camp bed on which anyone taller or fatter than Fausto would not have been able to sleep a single night. The storeroom was a place with a schizophrenic climate: during the day, when the kitchen was in use, it was warmer than the rest of the house, but at night the fires went out and gusts of wind blew in from the courtyard and the cold clung to the tiled walls, and Fausto climbed into bed convinced that someone had sprinkled his sheets with icy water. After Caracas and Ciudad Trujillo he thought it absurd that compatriots of his had once decided to found a city under these grey skies, in this permanent winter where it rained every day, without exception, where men walked down the street carrying umbrellas and wearing gloves and frowns, and where the women rarely came out of their houses, and, when they did, only to buy food and seek out a ray of sunshine like lost cats.

He began to walk the city streets with his scrapbook in hand, showing it to anyone he could. It contained newspaper cuttings that recounted his story as a budding actor, marginal notes, a few poor-quality photographs that had appeared in publications in Venezuela or the Dominican Republic, in which Fausto could be seen in histrionic poses in front of a microphone or extravagantly dressed against a black background. The captions were often ridiculous, and the texts patronising;

but the important thing was that the news had been published, and now Fausto, in Bogotá, wasn't a son of exiles who had grown peanuts in the jungle, or even an employee at a department store who wound bolts of cloth for sale and recited poetry in his spare time, but a young Spanish actor, survivor of the European debacle, come to enrich the cultural life of the city with his talent. Maybe, he thought, here he would at last have the chance to be someone else, to leave behind who he'd been before: he was arriving here with very little baggage, without the troubling weight of his recent past. He had escaped from the other's life and here he was, inventing himself anew, and when he had a stroke of luck, he thought it was not so strange: fortune favours the bold.

One day, walking in the city centre with no firm intentions, he came across a stone plaque that read: MINISTRY OF EDUCATION. He was most surprised when a certain Darío Achury Valenzuela, director of something called the Department for Cultural Extension, received him straight away. Fausto suspected he'd confused him with someone else, but the suspicion soon evaporated: Achury was a man of voracious curiosity, and yes, it's true that he was unusually free that day, but talking about poetry was one of the things he most enjoyed doing. He was forty years old and had the diction and manners of an older man; he was wearing a three-piece suit, and his hat and umbrella hung on a coat stand behind his desk. Fausto had never met anyone like him: it was like talking to Ortega y Gasset one autumn morning. Achury quoted Schiller in German and could reel off pages of *Don Quixote* from memory, and spent a quarter of an hour soliloquizing against the critics who had called Cervantes an uncultured wit. He did not hesitate to lay into Unamuno or Azorín, or to declare Ganivet an incompetent, and Varela undocumented.

"More fool them," he said.

The conversation lasted more than two hours. They talked about Spanish and Latin American poets; Achury mentioned Hernando de Bengoechea, a Colombian poet who had died fighting for France in the war of 1914, and from there they went on to the Civil War and spoke of the death of Machado. When they arrived – as they evidently would – at García Lorca, Fausto didn't miss his chance.

"Oh, yes, Federico," he said. "I knew him, you know? I still remember the kiss he planted on my head."

He left the ministry with the promise of a recital at the Teatro Colón. He was an unknown twenty-year-old, but he'd been given a space in the most important theatre in the country. Things could not have gone better. The theatre was not full the day of the recital, but the audience crowded into the front rows, so the empty seats remained in the shadows. Fausto had never performed somewhere that had seats fixed to the floor, and those seats were upholstered in red velvet, and under the light from the chandelier were the colour of blood on sand. He began the recital with something simple: a seductive music and an inoffensive meditation to warm the audience up.

I never chased glory
Nor sought to leave
In memory my song.

They were Antonio Machado's *Proverbs and Songs*, and there, on stage, Fausto became Machado and was at the same time the

63

man who loved subtle, weightless, genteel worlds, and the pursued man who had died at the French border, not far from where he, Fausto, might have died under the fascist bombing raids.

> As we walk we make our way
> And turning our gaze to look back
> We see the path that we shall
> Never tread again.

The audience approved in the stalls, and in the boxes the rare faces, all at the lowest level, leaned out over the railing a bit further, circles of skin emerging from the shadows. Nobody seemed to be occupying the presidential box, and that, absurdly, disappointed Fausto. It was too much to ask that a dignitary attend, of course, but at least he could have lent his box to some relatives or friends. The attentive faces had not been distracted; after the applause, scattered like a threat of rain, Fausto continued with another dead poet:

> The onion is frost-stung
> tight and small:
> frost of your days
> and of my nights.
> Hunger and onion
> black ice and frost
> big and round.

But it was not a poem about an onion, the audience in their red velvet seats understood, but about a child: a hungry child, son of a dark-skinned woman, suckling onion blood.

The child flies in the double
moon of the breast.
He, onion saddened.
You satisfied.
Do not give up.
May you not know what is happening
or what has come to pass.

And now Fausto was the poet Miguel, writing in prison the verses for his son: the poet Miguel, countryman imprisoned by the fascists as Uncle Felipe had been. Fausto was Uncle Felipe and also the six-year-old boy who had visited him in prison, with fear and sadness, and he was the hungry adolescent who had stolen cod-liver oil capsules from a pharmacy in Ciudad Trujillo. A muffled sound reached him from the front row, and as he finished the poem (with his hands straight by his sides and a potent vibrato in his voice) Fausto realized someone was crying. It was not just one woman, but several: two, four, ten: the velvet seats were sobbing. Then the applause began.

IV

The Colón triumph was at the same time modest and extraordinary, and put Fausto on the theatre map of Bogotá. People started talking about the Spanish actor – the disciple of García Lorca, yes, the relative of Republican heroes – and newly founded companies took an interest in him. When he returned from a brief tour full of Seville courtyards and children and onions, he found an invitation to recite poetry at the Municipal Theatre. This was not a theatre like the others. At that time, the Liberal leader Jorge Eliécer Gaitán, a politician of humble origins who had become a feared leader of the masses and was seen by the elites as a palpable threat, gave his speeches there at the end of the week – the Cultural Fridays, he called them – masterpieces of oratory that convened more people than Fausto had ever seen in one place, and were broadcast over the radio to a country seduced by the left-wing ideas and Mussolini-inspired rhetoric of that man with indigenous features and firmly brilliantined hair. Fausto began to rehearse his usual repertoire there – Machado, Lorca, Hernández – and one Friday, realizing that Gaitán had stayed after his broadcast to hear his poems, he approached him and they began to talk. Gaitán spoke knowledgeably of Colombian poetry, he quoted Silva and Julio

Flórez and suggested to Fausto that he should include Neruda. When they said goodbye, Fausto heard someone say:

"Why wouldn't they see eye to eye? They're both communists. With people like that, this country is going to the dogs."

It was not true: Gaitán was no communist, and Fausto even less. Until that moment, he had never even had the time to ask himself such questions, for he was still struggling with the bigger ones: God, for example. In his brief stay in Caracas he had mixed with some occultist groups to try to figure things out, and he had approached the theosophist Madame Blavatsky, and then he was a Rosicrucian and then a freemason. He got as far as graduating *into the temple*, an important first step for masons, but little by little he became disenchanted with all of them: the masons, the Rosicrucians and the theosophists. But not of the quest: the quest remained alive, because nobody had been able to give him the answers he needed. And something in Gaitán's tone suggested that this popular leader knew things he still didn't. Gaitán asked Fausto if he had never thought of wearing a sash around his waist, as he did, so the pressure over his diaphragm made his voice stronger. Fausto knew that this man, who was not imposing, was able to speak without a microphone in a packed plaza de Bolívar, and he did not rule out any of his advice. He was especially impressed by what Gaitán praised about his recitation. It wasn't only the quality of the poems, of course, or the emotions, but the conviction.

"You hate tyrants," he said to Fausto. "That's where you and I agree. An hour or two away from here *campesinos* are being killed, and we're reciting poems. And I say to you, young man: if those poems are not good for fighting, they're probably not good for anything."

Gaitán was talking to him about a distant reality. From the countryside and the mountains news reached Bogotá of horrible scenes where men were dying of machete blows and women were raped in front of their children; Fausto Cabrera, reciter of dead poets from the other side of the Atlantic, had lived until now with other preoccupations, but the conversations with Gaitán suggested a wider reality. Maybe it was not a coincidence that around then he began to frequent the Spanish Republican Cultural Centre, a meeting place where artists and writers wished for Franco's death and gave a hand to the hungriest of the exiles, but where they also spoke quietly of the Communist Party and the guerrillas in the Eastern Plains. At the Cultural Centre there was no room for theosophists or occultism: there, Fausto discovered, real reality was realer than ever. The discussions revolved around the Soviet Union and bringing about revolution, although the same ones who punched the table went on, without a solution, to recite poetry. One of the regulars, a Colombian with a singsong accent called Pedro León Arboleda, talked to Fausto about names nobody had ever mentioned to him, from Porfirio Barba Jacob to León de Greiff, and then explained that they were all great poets and, most of all, Antioqueño poets.

"You're wasting your time here, Cabrera," Arboleda said. "The poets, in Colombia, are in Medellín."

It's possible that a short time later, when Fausto decided to spend a few days in that city, Arboleda's words may have carried as much weight as his desire to see his family. Fausto arrived with the idea of being in the city for some days, giving a few readings and spending time with Uncle Felipe, manager of the Ecuadorean Pharmaceutical Labs. Medellín was wedged between beautiful mountains and its climate felt like a caress on the skin: it was easy to understand why Felipe had stayed there. When he arrived to see him, Fausto found a man who was stubbornly the same. His uncle hadn't lost a letter of his peninsular accent, was still creating illusions with his Spanish pride and was quite capable of refusing the subsidies that the Republican government in exile, in Mexico, offered him far too late. The memory of Spain, or his past in Spain, hurt as if he'd just been expelled. Everything referred to his lost land. One of those nights, after dinner, he showed Fausto a recent issue of the magazine *Semana*, open to a three-column article with the headline "The Nation". "Read it," he said. And Fausto read.

Is there, as we seem to glean from the newspapers, a wave of violence? Has anyone proved what connection the bloody and criminal acts of this time have with normal times? No. But without doubt, a foreigner who seeks to inform himself about Colombia's current situation, glancing through the country's press, would believe it to be on the brink of catastrophe or the edge of revolution. Colombians, however, are not alarmed. Why? Are we indifferent when every 24 hours a new violent crime is attributed to political struggles? No. We cannot have reached such a level of insensitivity. Something must happen, however, so that we, old Christians, realize the importance of such a situation. And it is that we do not accept those versions as they are presented to us. Neither the conservatives murdered by the liberals, nor the liberals murdered by the conservatives, provoke our alarm or our indignation, because all those reports are received with considerable initial disbelief. We hope, people say, to see how things go. And that – how things go – is never known.

"You're not old enough to remember," Uncle Felipe said. "But that's how it was. That's exactly how it was."

"What was?"

"Spain," said his uncle. "Spain in those years."

"Before the war?"

"Everything is too similar, you see. There's something in the air. Something serious is going to happen here."

Fausto did five readings in Medellín, but the most important was one he attended not as an actor, but as an audience member. It was at the Language Institute: a poet was reading his own work, a series of sonnets that seemed like they'd never end; and later, when he finally reached the implausible finale, a blonde woman with big eyes, whose swanlike neck emerged elegantly from her flowered dress, approached Fausto, flanked by her mother and sister, and held out a slender notebook she was clutching with both hands. "I was listening to you a few days ago, Señor Cabrera. May I have your autograph?" Fausto had the presence of mind to know he'd never see her again if he acceded immediately to her request; he said he would need to think it over as he didn't want to write just any old thing, that he would call her to arrange a visit at a less hectic moment. And so he did: he visited the house on avenida La Playa two or three times, always in the presence of one of her sisters and sometimes along with other poets, but she never brought out her autograph book; and he must have done something better than the other visitors, because after a few months he was receiving exclusive invitations from the girl.

Her name was Luz Elena. She was one of the four daughters of Don Emilio Cárdenas, a *paisa* from a well-off Medellín family who had made a fortune of his own setting up with nobody's help a pharmaceutical laboratory that competed with Uncle Felipe's: ECAR. In spite of being only sixteen years old, Luz Elena was much less predictable than her flowery dresses, ubiquitous chaperones and bourgeois family might suggest. Fausto never figured out when she had read so much, but that young girl talked to him with insolent self-possession of Sor Juana Inés de la Cruz and Rubén Darío, and the family said her high school diploma had been offered ahead of time so she'd stop showing her teachers up. Inés Amelia, the youngest of the sisters, told the story of one time, when the Spanish teacher had fallen ill at the last minute, Luz Elena had taught a whole class on the old ballads without looking at a single note. Don Emilio was so proud of her that he didn't mind being scolded by her for making it so obvious. Fausto witnessed this for the first time one Sunday, after a long postprandial conversation during which he was sitting in a chair that could easily have been labelled *Suitor*. In a moment of silence, apropos of nothing, Don Emilio said:

"You know about these things, young man, haven't you heard my daughter recite? Come on, child, let your guest hear the poem of the little soldier."

"Not now, Papá."

"That's the one I like best," Don Emilio said to Fausto. And then: "Don't make us beg, Luz Elena, it's not polite."

She played along, not to please her father, but to feel the gaze of this Spanish man who understood poetry and recited

71

it so well. She stood up, smoothed her dress and, enunciating well, said:

> —Soldadito, dear soldier — whence have you come?
> —From the war, señorita — how can I serve thee?
> —Have you seen my husband — ever, in the war?
> —No, señora, I haven't seen him — nor do I know what he's like.
> —My husband is tall, fair — tall and fair, from Aragón
> And by the tip of his sword — he carries an embroidered cloth
> I embroidered it when I was a girl — as a girl I embroidered,
> Another one I am embroidering now — and another I shall.
> —From the description you give — your husband is dead,
> They took him to Zaragoza — to the house of a colonel.
> —Seven years I've waited for him, — another seven I'll wait,
> If after fourteen he has not come — I'll become a nun.
> —Hush, hush, Isabelita, — hush, hush, Isabel,
> I am your dear husband — you are my beloved.

The table applauded and Luz Elena, under Fausto's attentive eye, sat back down again.

"I love that one," Don Emilio said. "The husband pretending not to be himself to test his wife's love. So pretty, isn't it?"

"A pretty poem," Luz Elena said quietly. "But I don't think anyone should do that to their wife."

In a matter of months they were engaged, and in a few months they had planned the wedding as if they had some unholy urgency. They agreed that the day of the wedding they did not want ceremonies full of strangers and photographers from the social pages, so Luz Elena chose the Sagrado Corazón church, which had an advantage over the others: in Medellín there were two churches with that name. One was in a residential neighbourhood with clean streets and elegant families, and busybodies would assume the ceremony would be there; meanwhile, the couple were married almost clandestinely in the other, darker and more modest, in one of the city's poorer neighbourhoods. When Fausto signed the marriage register, Luz Elena looked at him ironically.

"At last," she said. "I've never had to do so much to get an autograph."

It was December 1947. For the next two years, while Colombia descended into the bloodshed of partisan violence, the newlyweds travelled around Latin America on a reading tour that was like a honeymoon they would never have been able to afford. News of the country arrived late and badly, but Fausto never forgot where he was when he heard of the murder of Gaitán. It was April 9, 1948, and he had just recited a Lorca poem in Quito. According to the news, Juan Roa Sierra, a young, unemployed and paranoid Rosicrucian, had waited for Jorge Eliécer Gaitán outside his office, on carrera Séptima at the corner of avenida Jiménez, and had fired three shots that not only ended the life of the next president of Colombia, but were also the starting pistol for a war that in a short time devoured the country. Fausto said to Luz Elena:

"Just as my uncle predicted."

Fausto did not see the city of Bogotá burning in the midst of mass protests, or the snipers stationed on the roofs of carrera Séptima, or the priests who were also firing from the roof of San Bartolomé College, or the looters who smashed shop windows to make off with lamps or refrigerators or cash registers, or the overturned tramcars in flames in front of the cathedral, or the thousands of dead who were piled up in the arcades over the three following days before any relative could even come out of their homes to identify them. The centre of Bogotá was left in ruins and only a downpour was able to put out the flames when they had already consumed whole buildings, and those flames lit the fuse of violence in the rest of the stirred-up country. While Fausto and Luz Elena travelled around Peru and Bolivia, the conservative police entered the hamlet of Ceilán, in the Cauca Valley, and left fifty people dead, many of them incinerated. While they travelled from Chile to Argentina, in the Casa Liberal in Cali twenty-two people attending a political conference were murdered by plain-clothes conservatives, and the first resistance committees, which were nothing more than armed *campesinos* assembling to defend themselves as best they could, began forming in remote places. The repression was ferocious: in Antioquia as well, as they learned from the letters that reached them as they continued on their tour. That's why Fausto thought it so strange that one day, in Buenos Aires, Luz Elena told him it was time to go back to Colombia. But the reason was incontrovertible: she was pregnant.

Sergio Fausto was born on April 20, 1950, the midpoint of the century, at the San Vicente de Paul Hospital; two years later Marianella was born. Fausto was enjoying something resembling economic security for the first time in his life: he had a job with *La Voz de Antioquia*, on a radio programme everyone listened to (*Dream and Harmony* it was called), and time to found experimental theatre companies in a city where few people had heard of such a thing. He didn't have friends, but true accomplices. They were a doctor, Héctor Abad Gómez, a journalist, Alberto Aguirre, a painter, Fernando Botero, and a poet, Gonzalo Arango. They were all in their twenties; they all wanted to do important things. They would get together to drink aguardiente, talk politics and recite poems while making their livings however they could. With his wife's help and talent, Emilio Cárdenas, his father-in-law, had set up a small pasta production company in the kitchen of their home, a sort of side business that was almost a pastime, and Fausto earned a few pesos driving a dilapidated van all over Medellín, delivering noodles and collecting bills. That's how he got enough money together to buy one of the first portable tape recorders that arrived in Colombia. Gonzalo baptized it with three drops of aguardiente. "You shall be called 'The voice of the gods', recorder," he said solemnly. The group of friends was fascinated by the machine. "My voice, that's my voice," said Alberto after being recorded. "This thing's going to change the world." They broke it in by recording Miguel Hernández poems, for Franco had imposed an implacable censorship on his work: his verses were not recited anywhere in the world, and that was enough to turn him into a sort of totem for the group.

When he wasn't driving the pasta van, Fausto recited poems in front of small, captivated audiences where Luz Elena was always in the front row, moving her lips as Fausto said that as we walk we make our way and turning our gaze to look back we see the path that we shall never tread again. He also founded theatre groups to perform classical plays that few had ever heard of, but that were beginning to win over loyal and curious audiences. Meanwhile, the massacres had become so numerous that they were covered by the newspapers. Fausto remembered the magazine article Uncle Felipe had shown him, and wondered if he wasn't the foreigner who saw the Colombian reality, and then he wondered why nobody seemed to care about what was going on. Or maybe only the people in the countryside cared: for those in the cities, all those dead people were very far removed. The situation was so grave for so long that what everyone expected happened. In June 1953, a military officer, Lieutenant-Colonel Gustavo Rojas Pinilla, staged a coup d'état with the ostensible purpose of stopping the country from bleeding to death.

"Something like this had to happen," Uncle Felipe said. "I'm going to die from one dictatorship to another."

A few weeks later he announced he was going to Chile. Nobody understood: Felipe had married a woman from Medellín, still had the same job, liked the city. Why leave? Luz Elena's parents, who'd grown fond of him, asked: why on earth did he want to go to Chile? Only Fausto understood, though he didn't know how to explain it very well, for Uncle Felipe had contracted the virus of exile, the compulsion to move all over the place since life had forbidden him from staying in his own land. Just as he'd left Ciudad Trujillo for Bogotá and from Bogotá he'd moved to Medellín, now, well settled and with a wife who loved him and looked after him, he was going to Chile. "If it goes well, I'll stay there," he said, "if it goes badly, I'll come back. As my wife says: the worst return is the one that doesn't happen." By the following year, when the government's propaganda began to appear, he had left.

The propaganda was for large celebrations to commemorate the one-year anniversary of the dictatorship. Nobody knew what they would consist of, but Fausto had not the slightest confidence in them. "All dictatorships are the same the world over," he said. "When they start having birthday parties for themselves, they're not planning on going anywhere." But he could not have imagined the nature of the celebrations: Rojas Pinilla announced the arrival of television in Colombia. In long addresses on the radio, he explained that he had discovered it in Berlin, at the end of the 1930s, and he'd never been able to get the idea out of his head that this invention had to come to his country. He explained that it had not been easy, because in this mountainous country the signal ran into too many obstacles, but he had given the order to get the project off the ground without concern for the cost. A highly skilled committee had travelled to the United States to do studies, buy the equipment and import the technologies. Rojas ordered a thirty-metre antenna to be erected on top of the Military Hospital, one of the highest spots in Bogotá, another on the Nevado del Ruiz mountain and a third up on the high La Rusia plateau in Boyaca. Thus the whole country would be covered, for the good of the nation. What he didn't say, but what became known as the days went by, was that then, after the antennae were installed in their positions and the apparatuses ready in their stations, they realized there was nobody in Colombia who knew how to make them work. Nobody even knew what images were going to be transmitted, or who might receive them: Colombians didn't have television sets in their houses, after all, each one cost three years' salary on minimum wage. In a matter of weeks the government brought twenty-five technicians from Cuba, who had worked for a station that had just gone bankrupt, and invented generous credit plans so Colombians would buy 1,500 Siemens television sets, and filled the department store windows with televisions so that nobody, not even those who couldn't buy their own, would be unable to enjoy the invention.

On June 13, 1954, one year after taking power, the dictator peered out of that luminous box that looked at the people and told them he was speaking to them from San Carlos Palace, in the centre of Bogotá, and delivered a stirring speech that declared television inaugurated in Colombia. When the national anthem played, Colombians knew that this time was not like the others, because now they could hear the Colombian Symphony Orchestra at the very instant they played the music: see them without being in the same place as the orchestra. The first broadcast lasted three hours and forty-five minutes, and Fausto, who followed it with fascination from Medellín, knew that the world, this time for sure, had changed for ever, and thought that maybe there was room for him in that world. Then, when he heard a man called Fernando Gómez Agudelo, the one who had brought the teams from the United States and the technicians from Cuba, was now recruiting the most talented theatre people in the country so they could choose which stories television viewers were going to receive in their boxes, he did not hesitate. He said that his Uncle Felipe had gone to Chile and that his painter friend Fernando Botero had gone to Bogotá. Domingo, Fausto's father, was also in the capital, still running a downtown hotel – the Roca, it was called – and living his life as if he'd been born Colombian.

"Why don't we go too?" Fausto asked his wife.

"Well yes," she said. "Let's not be the last ones left in Medellín."

*

The Cabrera Cárdenas family moved into a two-storey apartment on calle 45, a place with small but comfortable rooms where the luminous screen occupied the centre of the living room, and in it moved men in black and white who disappeared into a hole of light and static when you pressed a button. In those days, a short man who dragged one leg often visited the Cabrera home. Fausto explained to his children that his name was Seki Sano, that he was Japanese and had just arrived from Mexico, hired by the Colombian government to teach actors and directors how to do things on television. He had a wide forehead and wore thick, heavy-framed glasses that kept his eyes from being seen, and always carried a pipe that he put between his lips whether it was lit or not. He had lost the use of his leg as a result of the tubercular arthritis that he suffered as a child, but someone had told a war story to account for it, and he had never bothered to clarify things. After fleeing from Japan, he had sought refuge in the Soviet Union, and from there the Stalinists had expelled him, just as they had Trotsky. Now he was coming to Colombia to apply the Stanislavsky method to television drama; among the theatrical directors in Bogotá, Fausto was the one who best knew what the Japanese man was talking about when he talked about Stanislavsky, and there was between the two of them a sense of shared tastes that could easily be confused with their political sympathies, so it was perfectly natural that Fausto should become his favourite disciple.

They were months of discovery. While the cameramen learned new ways of using their cameras (new angles, new framing techniques), and while the government was discovering the possibilities of the new medium to spread the message

79

of the dictatorship and the armed forces, Seki Sano had begun to train a whole generation of theatre people. He was intransigent with mediocrity and rigorous to the point of cruelty, and would not allow his students to have any less dedication or enthusiasm than he did. He easily became furious when his students didn't give him what he asked of them; more than once he threw his pipe and even his lighter at their heads, and once he grabbed a talentless actor by his shirt collar to drag him off the stage while shouting humiliating things at him. He and Fausto grew closer. He went to the Cabreras' place for lunch every weekend, and put up with Sergio and Marianella climbing up on his wooden leg for horse rides. In their spare time, he invited Fausto to watch other people's plays, but most of the time he would start to huff after the first scenes, and halfway through the presentation his patience would be exhausted.

"Come along, young man," he'd say to Fausto, not concerned that even the actors could hear him. "I can't stand any more of this rubbish."

Under Sano's attentive gaze, Fausto made his way into the jungle of televised space like an explorer with a machete at his belt: he adapted old novels and classics of the theatre to present live, direct to air, enduring the complaints of actors, who could not imagine their invisible audience. Television required a weekly piece, but for a director it would be miraculous to produce something decent in even a fortnight; so they designed a system in which Fausto would divide up the tasks between other directors, men with several years' more experience than Fausto, figures so important to the cultural life of the city that nobody would have thought them susceptible to feeling intimidated. But Seki Sano's presence made them uncomfortable:

maybe it was the Japanese man's reputation, or maybe it was the critical and sometimes sarcastic judgements the master might let slip on plays by the great and the good of Colombia, but Sano had become a problem, a real threat to the authority or pre-eminence that the others held.

And that is how the regime received the news – from one day to the next – that the Japanese director was proselytizing. Seki Sano had been a refugee in the Soviet Union and then in Mexico, that hot spot of the left, and none of that was going to sit very well with a country that had sent a battalion to the Korean War to join in the international struggle against communism. His convictions were Marxist and in his methods, to the great scandal of many, a materialist vision of the world could be glimpsed, though the truth was that Sano had never participated in politics. Little Sergio did not really understand why one day Sano stopped coming to lunch, but he would remember the efforts his father made to explain it to him: Seki Sano did not come because the dictator Rojas Pinilla expelled him from Colombia; and he expelled him owing to the denunciation of a group of artists, or at least that was always Fausto's theory. "A conspiracy of the envious," he said. An official notice gave Sano forty-eight hours to leave the country, and what saddened him most was having to abandon a staging of *Othello*, in a translation by the Spanish poet León Felipe.

Something was happening: the mood was no longer the same in Colombia. The veterans of the Korean War had brought back horrible stories about communists and their practices, about soldiers savagely tortured in deep caves or left in the snow to die of hypothermia or, if they were lucky, have their toes amputated. From the United States came news of a man called McCarthy, who was facing up to the red threat on his own. Seki Sano's expulsion was part of that, no doubt, but Fausto could not see the whole picture, no doubt because he was right in the middle of it: yes, these things were happening, but things weren't going badly for him. It was as if his destiny was running contrary to Colombia's, because now the violence was calming down and the two parties, who'd spent a decade killing each other, seemed capable of engaging in dialogue, as if their leaders in Bogotá had tired of playing war games with other people's soldiers. Meanwhile, the temperature in the theatre world was rising, and long-suppressed offences were beginning to surface. Fausto became the spokesman. Theatre people, he began by saying, had no rights in Colombia; the law considered the theatre a place of idleness and bohemia. On Luz Elena's advice he included a specific complaint on the part of actresses, since a woman who wanted to act had to ask her father or husband for permission. In a few weeks, the Colombian Circle of Artists had come into being under the suspicious eye of the authorities, and a few weeks after that was organizing its first strike.

Actors took over the television studios and broadcasts were suspended for a week. People turned on their sets and found nothing, and Colombians discovered a new emotion: fear of televisual emptiness. But then the government reacted, and Rojas Pinilla sent the police to the studios with an order: take the truck with the mobile unit out and drive it anywhere and make any programme, a matter of breaking the strike by the simple means of filling the screens. Fausto organized the striking actors, and one afternoon they met in front of the television station garage, where they formed a human chain to prevent the mobile unit being taken out. Luz Elena, who had joined the strike right at the start, was in the front row, and she was the one to hear most clearly the words of an army captain, in charge of controlling the situation, shouted at the top of his lungs. He was ordering the driver to put it in reverse and pay no attention to the actors.

"If they don't get up," he shouted, "we'll drive over them."

The first ones in the line of containment were all women. Luz Elena would later tell how she felt the exhaust pipe burning her arm at the very instant Fausto and the rest stood up to surrender. But they didn't surrender: when the squad tried to arrest them, the actors defended themselves with their bare fists, and Fausto took advantage of a moment of chaos to escape and hide in a neighbouring doorway with Luz Elena. He would always remember how, in the semi-darkness of their hiding place, excited from the incident, his wife's face seemed to shine with its own light.

Fausto won a new authority at the television station. Nobody understood how he got away with so many daring projects. One of them was *The Image and the Poem*, where Fausto would recite a poem, live on air, from his infinite repertoire, and as he listened to the poem the painter Fernando Botero would do a freehand drawing on a sheet of paper. In another he would broadcast chess matches between serious amateurs and actual masters. That had been a suggestion by the dictator Rojas Pinilla, who was a skilled player; nobody could have refused him, but they never expected it to be a success. It might have been around then that Uncle Felipe returned from Chile. He brought bad news: he was ill. He had already undergone cancer surgery and everything seemed to indicate that he was on the road to recovery, but the illness had broken his spirit. He moved into a hotel in central Bogotá with his wife and a little Pekinese dog, and there he spent his days remembering his best years for anyone who could put up with him, complaining about the Bogotá cold and saying that he'd return to Medellín the first chance he got. But his medical treatments wouldn't have allowed it even if he'd had the means to go. Each time Fausto went to see him, fulfilling a weekly routine he'd imposed on himself without anyone asking, he found him more bent over and less eloquent, but always with remnants of pride in his gaze, as if he were sure that others, when seeing him, were still seeing the war hero.

"How's it going, lad?" his uncle asked. "How're things in the theatre?"

"All's well, uncle," Fausto invariably said. "Everything's going really well."

On one of those days, Fausto found his uncle tired and sad, sitting in a wicker rocking chair beside his open scrapbook. The conversation didn't really go anywhere, although Felipe asked Fausto for information about what was happening in Colombia now that peace seemed to have arrived at last; but what the young man saw was a man in pain and not just bodily pain, but an almost palpable melancholy that suffused his expression. Fausto found out later that Felipe asked to have his dinner served in his room, because he didn't feel like seeing anyone, and ate the plantain slices and rice and powdered beef. Then he asked for the tray to be taken away, took his clippings out of their folders and arranged them on top of the bedspread. There was the news of his arrest and imprisonment for conspiring against the king; there was the false news of his death, disseminated by the fascists during the war, with his very recognizable photo and name. One cutting was more yellowed than the rest: in it his father, Antonio Díaz Benzo, appeared in his dress uniform, in an image from around the time he was sent to Guatemala. Then the pain flared up. They rushed him to hospital, and they surely would have operated again – for the third or fourth time – had it not been clear to the doctors that the man was beyond the powers of surgery.

Felipe Díaz Sandino died in the middle of the night, with his consciousness extinguished by drugs and with his sleeping hand between the hands of his Colombian wife. Fausto accompanied the coffin in the hearse along with his brother Mauro, and continued to accompany it in the Central Cemetery until the last of the few mourners had left. Then he went straight home. Sergio heard him arrive and lock himself in the garage. After a while he went to look for him, or at least that's how he remembers it, and he always said that there he saw him not just crying but in a state of collapse for the first time

V

The world seemed to transform overnight. Sergio would remember the afternoons his father arrived home early to listen to the radio news, an unusual thing because the Cabreras' radio – one of those huge cabinets that included a record player and was a piece of furniture, a very cumbersome one at that – was normally only used to play music. Fausto was enthusiastic and attempting to transmit his enthusiasm to his children. "The only sad thing is that Uncle Felipe is no longer here to witness it," he said. Luz Elena agreed. She skipped around the house, talking about the bearded ones as if she knew them and predicting that something similar was going to happen in the rest of the continent. Ever since January first when Fidel Castro entered Santiago de Cuba and the Second National Front of Escambray entered Havana, it was as if history had started over.

Fausto could not believe what was happening. Eighty-two Cuban revolutionaries, expelled from their country by a dictatorship, had returned to their island on the *Granma* sustained by a ferocious anti-imperialism; in spite of having lost two-thirds of their men, they had carried on fighting in the Sierra Maestra; they had confronted an army of 80,000 men under the bloodthirsty orders of the dictator Batista; and now they were legitimately in power, recognized by the entire world, including the *New York Times*, and had managed to convince a whole generation of Latin Americans that the new man was here to stay. The Cuban Revolution had firm supporters in Colombia, where the mid-century *campesino* movements, including those that had turned into violent guerrilla groups, got a facelift, and where a whole generation of students had begun to meet in clandestine groups to read Marx and Lenin and talk about how to bring here what had succeeded there. All that was happening in Latin America was what Fausto had dreamed of for his Republican Spain, his defeated Spain, the Spain that seemed unable to do with Franco what Castro and Guevara had done with Batista. Fausto felt, for the first time since he was called a Jew in the port of Ciudad Trujillo, that his exiled life was not a wasted life: that history, after all, could have a mission or a purpose. *Winds of the people carry me,* he recited in his head, *winds of the people sweep me along.* And how Fausto longed to stop being swept along.

One afternoon Luz Elena asked the children to come to her room, and without beating around the bush told them that Aunt Inés Amelia had stomach cancer. Sergio, who had witnessed from afar the death of Uncle Felipe, didn't need any more information, but Marianella wanted to know what cancer was and why her aunt had got it and what was going to happen now. Inés Amelia was only twenty-two years old. She was single and cheerful with a lively intelligence, and seemed to have affection to spare. In recent years she had become a beloved figure for Sergio and his sister, who went to see her in Medellín as if she were a second mother, and nobody had imagined that she could get sick with the same old people's illness that had killed Uncle Felipe. On the face of Luz Elena, who had watched and accompanied the deterioration, they could read a vivid anguish, or rather Sergio could read it, and wished he could do something to alleviate his mother's suffering. But for Aunt Inés Amalia, as with Uncle Felipe, there was nothing the doctors could do.

Luz Elena travelled to Medellín to be at her side during her last days, and when she returned to Bogotá, destroyed by grief, she brought a gift for each of her children. "It's like an inheritance," she said. What Sergio received was not just a gift, but an actual entry to another world: the Kodak Brownie Fiesta that his aunt had taken everywhere in her last months. Cameras were for adults, as they were expensive, the film was expensive, developing was expensive, and it was all so new that Kodak had published instructions for their purchasers, so they wouldn't waste money on piles of failed photographs. Each roll had twelve exposures: going to the laboratory was an adventure, since nobody could know what was going to come out on the prints, or guess which pictures had been spoiled by inexperience. So the pamphlets tried to be clear, and the same phrase was repeated in them and on the radio and in magazine ads: *Two or three steps back from your subject, the sun at your back and click.*

But Sergio did not agree: nobody – neither an instruction pamphlet nor an ad in *Cromos* magazine – was going to tell him how to take photos. He began by taking one with the sun on one side, then on the other, against the light and even at night, watched curiously by Luz Elena, who did not reprimand him for taking photographs that came out glazed or overexposed or almost dark, but also suggested new ways to violate the sacred instructions. Maybe it was out of affection, or maybe because the camera was a bequest from her dead sister, but Luz Elena supported those experiments with light with pedagogical patience, and sometimes it seemed that the wait – the eternal week between dropping off the roll of film at the lab and picking up the developed photographs – tormented her more than her son. "A week!" she said. "No, that's too much to expect of a child." During those days of waiting, Sergio prayed: he prayed that the photos would come out the way he'd imagined them, and he wrote down the disappointments in the same notebook where until now he'd kept meticulous track of his reading, his measured opinions on Dumas and Jules Verne and Emilio Salgari. *The one of Marianella in the window didn't come out well. The one of Alvaro and Gloria came out well. The one of the cupboard door did not come out well. The one of the black cat came out black.*

One night when he was bored he turned on the television, even though he didn't have permission, and he found his father and his mother, who were acting together in a televised play.

He took the photo with the feeling he was stealing someone else's moment and hoped his mother wouldn't notice when she sent the film to be developed. He was not in luck: Luz Elena arrived from the lab, called him to look at the photos, and it must have been the first time she had seen them, because when they got to the photo of the screen she started to cry.

"What's the matter, Mamá?" Sergio asked.

"Nothing, nothing," she said. "Nothing's the matter."

"What's wrong?"

"This photo is really good." And then: "Nothing's wrong, don't worry."

That's how he got his first hint that something was messed up in the adult world. But then he went with his parents to the television studios and everything seemed back to normal. They were doing *Aucassin and Nicolette*, a sort of comedy of courtly love that Fausto had adapted freely, and Sergio, when he saw the two of them rehearsing, dressed as medieval French lovers and looking at each other the way only lovers look at each other, he thought that no, he'd been mistaken: everything was fine.

Meanwhile, the country had marched firmly into the Cold War. Fear of the red threat floated in the atmosphere; in the political world, the blue of the Conservative Party seemed more than a tendency, it was a sort of antidote to worse evils. Sergio had begun to act seriously; acting had turned into a space of palpable happiness, for to move under the auspices of his father was to take on an entity, a materiality, which did not exist offstage, and was also to have his undivided attention. In front of the cameras, in the basement of the National Library where the first studios had been set up, and then in the station's new facilities, Sergio began to receive preliminary training in the virtues of the Stanislavsky method and apply them in import- ant productions. Luz Elena would have preferred him not to be in so many plays, nor such demanding ones, because the boy was already a lacklustre student before he had the pretext of television, and now rehearsals did nothing but aggravate the situation. They were more rigorous than anything Sergio had ever known, since the televised dramas were broadcast live and an error in front of the cameras could be catastrophic. The first rehearsals were held in an empty studio, the black floor of which was covered with marks and signals to orient the actors, and the day before transmission – in front of the cameras, with the set and props all in place – was the final rehearsal, when the air was filled with electricity and the actors staked their lives on their speeches. Unpredictably, Sergio responded well to the challenges. That was how he received his first serious job: the role of the boy in *The Spy*, by Bertolt Brecht.

The director was Santiago García, an architect turned theatre man. He had been through Seki Sano's academy, like

Fausto, and he was (like Fausto) one of the few the master had looked on with respect. He was a generous man who seemed to live for the theatre, as if nothing else existed in the world, and he had the rare gift of genuine modesty: he could tell people, for example, that he'd just come back from Paris, from seeing the opening night of *Waiting for Godot* in the presence of Beckett himself, and he wouldn't sound presumptuous or provoke envy. He liked aguardiente and he liked cooking and he liked asking other people about their lives, not just the parts they wanted to talk about, but their secrets as well. Fausto got along with him immediately, and within weeks they were preparing their first collaborations for television. After working together for months, discovering they admired the same playwrights and had the same ideas on what television drama should be like, putting on Brecht was a logical next step. Luz Elena only agreed once the Cabreras had had a dinner-length conversation about Hitler, Nazism and the swastika that Sergio would have to wear on his arm. In the play, Sergio's parents, a troubled couple, go into a panic when they discover their son has disappeared: maybe he's gone to denounce them. The son comes back later with a bag of sweets, but Sergio, who wanted to know why a child would do such a thing, did not share the fictitious parents' tranquillity: why would he betray his parents to a country's authorities? Luz Elena said:

"There are places like that."

What they couldn't have foreseen was the reaction of the press. "Colombian television has fallen into the hands of subversives," a columnist wrote under a pseudonym in *El Tiempo*. "Brecht is a communist here as anywhere, even if he disguises his Marxism as an indictment against something else. Are we

prepared to have the minds of ignorant Colombians poisoned with revolutionary theories that are destroying Christian values in other parts of the world? Where are those responsible for this harmful propaganda, and why do the authorities keep permitting them to do what they're doing with something that belongs to us all?" It was as if the country, this country that had generously taken him in sixteen years earlier, had transformed into a hostile place. Fausto had received his citizenship certificate by then – a paper covered in watermarks and signed by the president himself, which had moved him to tears – but Colombia seemed to be closing with one hand the doors it opened with the other. At the national television station, where he had led that first victorious strike when Luz Elena had been ready to be run over by a truck, Fausto now called a second strike to defend what he called "cultural programming". In recent times, publicity agencies had begun to lobby the ministry to be able to advertise more products in more spaces, but they weren't going to continue to invest their money if the programmes didn't interest anybody. Who wants to see an actor recite a poem that nobody understands while a painter paints lines that don't look like anything? Who wants to watch two unknown men, foreigners to boot, playing chess for an hour? No, no: Colombian television needs to modernize, commercialize, get out of the niche of intellectuals who speak for intellectuals. Colombian television needs to live in the world of real people, people on the street.

Their pressure soon began to get results, and the spaces that Fausto had invented and created as an heir of Seki Sano were taken off the air one by one, falling like sniper victims. One fine day Fausto woke up to realize there were none left: a whole life's work seemed to have vanished without a trace. The broadcaster offered him new, more commercial programmes, aimed at broader audiences, especially melodramas. "Why not do something by Corín Tellado?" someone said to him. "Everybody's doing those things. Do you know why? It's very simple: because everybody likes things like that." He had never felt out of place in Colombia, but now he was discovering that there was a first time for that as well. Fausto would later say that at the moment he made the decision he thought of only one person: Uncle Felipe. Would Uncle Felipe have let his arm be twisted? A civil war is not the same as a cultural battle, it's true, but principles are principles. Fausto refused the proposals with words that lived on in the family:

"We'll bear what's bearable," he said. "But I will not make drivel."

In mid-1961, Sergio was eleven years old and found himself lost in a precocious adolescence, ignorant of the political world, vaguely aware that an American astronaut had been put into orbit for the first time. The Cabreras had moved to a house on calle 85 at carrera 12. It was a gated community for well-off families, and their neighbours were cultured bourgeoisie who knew about Italian wines and medieval history and whose children walked with the Cabreras the few blocks to the same school: the French Lycée. It was not the most obvious choice for their parents, but Sergio would later understand how big a part Fausto's memories of the Lycée Pothier, back in the 1930s, when Uncle Felipe was a diplomat in Paris, had played in this decision. That ghost, who in some sense was more alive than ever, made his presence felt.

Sergio was not at ease in his world. He had started skipping class, and more than once he slipped away from the group before they got to school to wander the neighbourhood getting up to no good. He discovered the excitement of doing damage, an animal that showed up in the pit of his stomach before and after Sergio threw stones and broke the windows of neighbours' houses or the lowest apartments of the new buildings. His friends at the Lycée taught him to smoke. Sergio started buying his own packets, telling the shopkeeper they were for his parents, and returned to the schoolyard to generously share his cigarettes. Popularity had never been so cheap. The boys went out together to smoke in a corner, and in those moments it didn't matter that the rest of them were a head taller than Sergio, or that their voices had changed while Sergio still spoke in childish tones. With a packet of Lucky Strikes in his hand, Sergio was one of the gang. And there he was one afternoon, smoking in a corner, lost in the group with his packet in his hand, when his parents caught him. His mother issued the most extraordinary threat that came to mind.

"If this goes on," she said, "there'll be no more television."

That sentence, which so many children would hear in years to come, in their case meant something rather different: Sergio would no longer appear in front of the cameras. He could not have conceived of a worse punishment. It was a last resort for desperate parents, but they had good reasons: outside the controlled world of television, Sergio was messing up his life. He had begun to carry in his pocket a screwdriver he'd stolen from his father, and thus armed would walk around those residential streets removing the insignias from the luxury cars. One day he was removing his fifth Mercedes badge (a hard-to-find make in Bogotá back then, and therefore much appreciated by the young collector) when he was surprised by the owner. "Get in," the man said. "We'll go see what your father thinks about this." And he drove him home. Fausto thought that was indeed very bad and scolded Sergio in such a way that the owner of the Mercedes left the house feeling that justice had been done; but Sergio knew that nothing, not even this vandalism, mattered very much to his father: he had bigger problems to think about. After the departure of the irate car owner, Fausto demanded Sergio show him all that he had stolen. He didn't imagine that he was going to find a veritable cache of insignias. There were more than thirty: Volkswagen, Renault, BMW, a few worthless Chevrolets, the prized Mercedes. Fausto's disappointment was visible on his face, but Sergio did not expect the slap. Through the mist of tears, still feeling the heat of the blow on his cheek, Sergio heard his father say:

"You'll pay for this with your own money."

He didn't have to ask what he meant. His father took him all around the neighbourhood as if dragging him by the ear: they visited, one by one, all the little vandal's victims, and Sergio apologized to each and every one, and promised them all that it would not happen again, and he paid for the damage with the money he'd earned playing Brecht's boy informer. Sergio received considerable sums in an account at the Savings Bank, money that he was only allowed to use to develop his experimental photos. After paying for the repairs to all the cars he'd stolen insignias from, the account was almost empty. When Luz Elena found out what had happened she got so worried that one afternoon she waited for Sergio after school with some news: they were going to speak to a psychologist.

It wasn't something that happened back then, but Luz Elena understood that her son needed help and that neither she nor her husband was managing to give it to him. So there, three times a week, sitting in a comfortable armchair in front of a woman with plastic framed glasses and a tartan skirt and high heels, Sergio talked about smashing windows with stones, about cigarettes, about the stolen bits of metal, and then he'd receive a box of crayons and a sheet of paper. "Draw me a bird," the woman said. Sergio knew in some magical way that she was expecting to see crows or vultures, and what he did was draw sparrows and doves and inoffensive swallows and leave the session before his time was up. One of those days he had an illumination: "It's like talking to a priest," he told his mother. And it was true: nobody was more like the psychologist than Father Federico, who'd been in charge of catechism classes a couple of years earlier when Sergio should have had his first communion. The third-year pupils were informed that they'd go through something called "Preparation", a series of protocols prior to the rite, and that the first of their obligations was to make a list, as detailed as possible, of all the sins they'd committed up to the day of confession. "Since when?" Sergio asked. "Since you began to have the use of reason, son," the priest said. And he warned him that the list had to be very rigorous and include everything, from the most serious to the most venial, because God didn't like lies.

"Do you know what happens if you hide sins from the Lord?" Father Federico said. "The host turns to blood when you're about to take it. In front of everyone. Do you want that to happen to you?"

Sergio, who by then felt himself to be an unremitting sinner, owner of an interminable and shameful list of faults, felt trapped. He imagined himself dressed in his new suit at Sunday mass and joining the orderly queue to receive communion, and he imagined feeling how the host Father Federico placed in his mouth turned to liquid and the metal taste filled his mouth at the same time as the first drop of blood dripped out between his lips. He imagined the look of horror on his classmates' faces and the satisfaction on Father Federico's: now you see what happens when you lie to the Lord. So he went home and said:

"I don't want to do it."

"What?" said Fausto.

"I don't want to do my first communion. I'm not going to." And he added: "Unless I'm forced to."

But nobody forced him: there were no restrictions or punishments of any kind, only ambiguous explanations that seemed to be talking about something else. His father explained that the word *atheist*, in its original Greek, did not refer to those who did not believe in God, but those who had been abandoned by the gods. Could that perhaps be what had happened to him? Bit by bit Sergio began to accept that there was no other explanation: his God, the God he had prayed to for his photos that almost never came out well to come out well, had abandoned him. Sergio had become an annoyance to him, he thought, or he had found other more worthy or more urgent things to take care of.

The family was going through critical days. Perhaps the root of everything was in Fausto's employment problems, the doors that had closed on him in recent years, but it was obvious that something had broken in his relationship with Luz Elena. At least that was how Sergio felt, even though nobody had confirmed it, but too often he heard them arguing bitterly until very late at night: it was like being back in *The Spy*. His sister Marianella was too small to notice anything, but Sergio knew something was wrong. He had started to have suspicions one afternoon, after a long day of rehearsals at the studio, when he went with his father as he drove an actress home. Sergio thought they said goodbye too affectionately, and he noticed the cigarette the actress put out in the ashtray. Sergio saw that cigarette – that stubbed-out filter with lipstick that wasn't his mother's on it – as a threat. And for the next few weeks he would go down to the garage in the mornings, before the others woke up, to empty the smelly cigarette butts out of the ashtray of the Plymouth. Those infidelities, or rather the difficult task of hiding them, turned into part of Sergio's domestic chores, and it took a long time to realize that all his efforts were in vain, because the only thing more pigheaded than his father's promiscuity was his mother's talent for discovering it. One of those mornings Sergio went down too late, or Luz Elena decided to get up earlier than usual, and by the time he got to the garage war had broken out. But what Sergio never imagined, in his worst nightmares, was that he'd come home one day to the news that his mother was no longer there.

"She went to Medellín," Fausto explained. "She's going to live with your grandparents for a while. But you're going to visit her, don't worry. Every so often."

"How often?" he asked.

"Let's say every six months," his father said. "Travelling to Medellín is expensive."

"And my sister?"

"Marianella went too," Fausto said. "This way was best for everyone."

Sergio did not understand why this brutal change in the family should mean a change in his life, but that's how it was: after a series of secret decisions by his parents, in which he never participated even as an audience, from one day to the next Sergio went from living in his house and going to the

French Lycée to becoming a student at the Germán Peña boarding school. The place was only five blocks from home, but that wasn't a relief, more a source of anxiety: why hadn't his father wanted them to stay together, living in the same house? Why, if there was a crisis between his parents, had they allowed the whole family to be torn to pieces, instead of allowing the son the consolation of continuing to live with one of the two? Was it possible that Sergio was in the way? After God's desertion, was it now his family's turn? Just taking stock made him sad. Uncle Mauro, who had become a sales rep for Schering Pharmaceuticals, was always travelling; Grandpa Domingo had decided to close the Hotel Roca and move to Cali; Aunt Olga, recently married to the owner of a coffee thresher, rarely came to Bogotá. The clan was disintegrating.

The boarders at Germán Peña were all older than Sergio, boys from the Caribbean coast – from Montería, Sahagún, Valledupar – who came to the capital to finish their baccalaureate. Sergio, for them, was a curiosity, and not just because he was the son of a famous actor. At night, before going to sleep, his room-mates asked him the question that he'd been asking himself since the first day: why, if his house was five blocks away, had his parents sent him to a boarding school? Had he done something so terrible he wasn't allowed to go home? Sergio had to invite them to his house and introduce them to his father so they'd believe him once and for all. Those outings became a habit: several times a week, at snack time, Sergio would leave the school with his gang, smoke a couple of Lucky Strikes at the corner before getting home, and then they'd go in by the kitchen door and raid the fridge. In those moments, while his school friends ate whatever they could find, Sergio would go up to his room – his empty room, where his sister no longer was – and lie down on his bed for a few minutes and leaf through his books and put his head on his pillow that smelled the same as ever, just to remember the brief joys of normality.

It went on like that for months. Then, as abruptly as they had left for Medellín, his mother and his sister came back to Bogotá. There they were one weekend, when Sergio came home from school on one of his scheduled visits, sitting in the living room as if they'd never left; it confirmed this secrecy or clandestine commitment with which his parents had managed the crisis. Yes, his mother was back: but there was no way to know what hidden monsters were moving beneath the surface, nor was there any certainty that it wouldn't all implode at any moment, nor was Sergio sure the next time he came home from boarding school he wouldn't find the house locked and everyone gone. At those times he would have liked to count on God, since Sergio didn't know what was going on but was sure of one thing: everything was falling apart and there was nothing he could do about it.

That was when a new topic of conversation appeared overnight at the dinner table: China. Unexpectedly, the topics as they sat round the table revolved around Buddhism, the Great Wall, Mao Tse-tung and t'ai chi ch'uan. Sergio and Marianella learned that China means "central nation" and Peking "northern capital". They learned that in a country of sixty languages, everyone could understand each other thanks to their writing, as the ideograms functioned the way numbers work for us. Isn't that right, children, that we could understand the numbers in *Le Monde* even if we didn't speak a word of French? Yes, Papá. Isn't that so interesting? Yes, Papá. Sergio could not have known at that moment, but there was a precise reason for all that. A letter had arrived from Peking and their life was about to take a 180-degree turn.

The letter that came was from Mario Arancibia. Fausto and Luz Elena had met him years earlier, in Santiago de Chile, during their honeymoon-turned-tour of poetry recitals (or vice versa). Arancibia was a very talented Chilean baritone with left-wing convictions: around 1956 he had visited Colombia with his wife, the actress Maruja Orrequia, to give three concerts that didn't quite work out; and had ended up writing a couple of librettos for Fausto Cabrera. Television was not his natural medium, but his literary talent created a space and, later, other opportunities. He became very good friends with the Cuban technicians that Rojas Pinilla had brought over to get Colombian television off the ground, and within a few months of arriving in Colombia, Arancibia and Maruja Orrequia were travelling to Havana. He joined the Radio Havana team; she found work as an actress and presenter. And there they were, in Havana, on the day of the victorious entry of the bearded ones into the city. They decided to stay in Cuba and witness first hand the revolution, which was the most marvellous thing they'd ever seen, but they did not get to see very much, because in a matter of weeks the cultural attaché of the Embassy of the People's Republic of China sought them out.

The man had a somewhat exotic mission: to find Spanish teachers for the Foreign Languages Institute in Peking. The search was part of the great Chinese effort to understand the rest of the world, or to deliver to the rest of the world their propaganda or message, but until now their teachers had been

Spanish exiles who, after spending some time in the Soviet Union, had been sent to China by the Russians as part of their attempt to construct a new socialism. Now there were problems on that front: a few years earlier, relations between China and the Soviet Union had begun to sour; and one of the many consequences of those tensions had been the slow withdrawal of the Spanish teachers. The concerned authorities then began to look towards Latin America, but not just any country. Without any shame whatsoever, the cultural attaché explained that, in spite of being in Cuba, they didn't want Cubans, since everyone said the island's accent wasn't good for learning the language. The reason he was carrying out this mission in Havana was simple: of all the Spanish-speaking countries, only Cuba had diplomatic relations with communist China. He had arrived at the Radio Havana studios looking for the Chilean baritone to convert him into a language teacher, and the offer was so good that Mario had no hesitation in accepting. After slightly more than a year, when the Chinese authorities asked him to recommend someone else (if possible a Colombian, because people said their Spanish was the best), a single name came to mind: Fausto Cabrera. He was Spanish by birth, but was not contaminated by Soviet prejudices; more important was that he spoke Spanish like the gods, had studied the great literature of his century and knew how to transmit his enthusiasm. He was the perfect candidate.

Mario Arancibia's letter explained all this. Fausto remembered Arancibia had mentioned the same subject in a previous letter, but only in passing and only in a couple of lines; and that letter had reached Bogotá before the second strike at the television studios, when it seemed that things might be straightened out, so Fausto had not given it his full attention. Now everything had changed. Fausto replied immediately: he was interested, of course he was, he was very interested. He would have to speak to his family, as they might imagine, but he was sure they'd be interested too. His instructions to Arancibia were clear: put things in motion. A few weeks later an envelope arrived at the house on calle 85 with several stamps and colourful ideograms.

The official invitation was more than a lifesaver, it was like a declaration of love for Fausto Cabrera, who was then at the end of his tether. The Chinese government was offering him a generous salary in hard currency, travel expenses for the whole family and superior lodgings; as well as all that, they promised Fausto and Luz Elena, but not the children, a return trip to Colombia every two years. The terms seemed excellent. For Fausto, the idea of getting his family out of the crisis in which it was mired and the promise of a change of air that could maybe revive his relationship with Luz Elena were no less seductive than the double possibility of studying theatre in China while seeing Mao Tse-Tung's revolution up close. Uncle Felipe had talked to him about Mao, back in the distant days of the Spanish Civil War, and he had done so with admiration; as for the theatre, it hadn't been Felipe but an article by Bertolt Brecht, which had put the idea in his head that traditional Chinese drama contained infinite lessons, and understanding them was to understand a part of theatre – its political possibilities – that had yet to be explored in Latin America.

So one June night Fausto called a family meeting, and solemnly explained what had happened. A letter had arrived, he said; they were invited to China, on the other side of the world, to that exotic and exciting place they'd been talking about for weeks. He presented the situation as if he had no interest in it, getting his children excited with statements that weren't statements but invitations to adventure, telling them it would be the equivalent of going around the world, just like Captain Nemo's crew. But the family was not obliged to accept, of course: they could turn down this marvellous opportunity that nobody else in Colombia had, and they, Sergio and Marianella, had every right to refuse to do what none of their friends could dream of even in their wildest dreams. Everyone was free to miss unique opportunities, of course they were, and he, Fausto, was not going to force anyone to do anything. By the end of the meal, Sergio and Marianella were begging their father to accept, not to pass up this opportunity, so they could all go to the other side of the world. And Fausto, as if his children had just convinced him, or as if he was only doing it to give them pleasure, took Luz Elena by the hand and announced with the formality of someone forgiving a thief:

"Alright. We're going to China."

Shortly before their departure, the Cabreras travelled to Medellín to say goodbye to their grandparents. Everyone agreed that they were crazy: why would they want to go to China? Fausto, for his part, gave them instructions, for it was important that nobody, for any reason, told anyone that the Cabreras had gone to a communist country. And if people asked, the children's grandmother wanted to know. "Tell them we're in Europe," Fausto said. "That's it: that I was hired to teach in France." Then he pulled out a shiny passport and asked his in-laws to look at it. Printed on half a page a peremptory stamp indicated clearly: this document was valid for any country in the world, except for socialist countries. "This passport is missing something," Fausto said. "Do you know what it is? The visa. There is no Chinese visa. And do you know why? Because Colombia has no diplomatic relations with China. This is what I want you to understand. We're not just going to the other side of the world: we're going to a forbidden world. China, for all practical purposes, is an enemy nation."

VI

The Cabrera family flew from Bogotá to Santo Domingo, from Santo Domingo to Lisbon, from Lisbon to Paris. For Sergio and his sister, it was all a discovery and every new embarkation was an unprecedented adventure: they'd never been out of Colombia, and now, in a matter of days, they had to envision crossing an ocean with three stopovers in three different countries. Fausto's instructions were clear: in Paris he had to go to the offices of Xinhua, the Chinese press agency, where they would tell him what to do to get to Peking. For two days they wandered around Paris like tourists, knowing that they were not. For Sergio, this was like keeping appointments made in his French textbooks from the Lycée, but a certain clandestinity added something extra to the tourism. It was as if the family was living a new life. Luz Elena was a different woman here, far from Bogotá and everything in Bogotá that threatened her marriage. Fausto spoke French competently and told anecdotes of life in the 1930s, and Sergio discovered he was also able to communicate with people, free of the person he used to be. Here he did not have to be that disoriented boy, that poor student who disappointed his parents with his behavioural problems. Here he could be someone different.

The Xinhua agency was a narrow office, not very far from the Champs-Élysées. The correspondent who received them, a man with exquisite manners who spoke perfect French, invited them to sit around a low table and served green tea. He did not spare any ceremony: he steeped the tea in the teapot, heated the cups with water he then threw away and served the tea with both hands, all in the most rigorous silence. Meanwhile, Sergio took photos with his Kodak Brownie Fiesta. His father had forgotten his camera in Bogotá; Sergio, with his plastic camera, felt responsible for documenting their trip. He had already photographed the Eiffel Tower and the Arc de Triomphe, where, on his mother's instructions, he took a photo of the name Francisco de Miranda, the Venezuelan who fought for the independence of the United States and then for that of Venezuela and who had time, between those two wars, to place his life at the service of the French Revolution. Sergio documented the illustrious name; now he did the same with the tea ceremony. The correspondent was a type of person he would learn to recognize later: the Chinese bourgeois who, educated in China, became a communist, but never managed to lose his bourgeois manners, a certain sensibility, a flair for exquisite conversation.

"This is like *Remembrance of Things Past*," Luz Elena said. "But in Chinese."

The man explained that they would travel to Geneva, because that's where the nearest Chinese embassy was, and in Geneva they would receive the visas (on separate pieces of paper, so their passports would not be tainted) that would allow them to get to Peking. The route, the man informed them, would be via Moscow. However, Aeroflot only flew twice a week, so they would have to stop over for three days. He hoped that wouldn't be a problem. He hoped that wouldn't be uncomfortable for them.

To get to Moscow they had to fly to Prague and then take the Aeroflot plane that would take them to another world, a Martian world. Marianella spent the flight with her nose pressed against the window, scrutinizing the clouds, because she had heard her parents say they were going to cross an Iron Curtain and she was not prepared to miss such an event. ("But it doesn't exist," Luz Elena said. "It's just a figure of speech." "Not true," Sergio said. "Of course it exists. The Berlin Wall exists, the Great Wall of China exists. I've seen photos. I don't see why there can't be an iron curtain. It's simple logic." "Sergio, don't tell your sister lies." "Mamá," Marianella said, "they're not lies. I think my brother's right.") At a certain moment the captain said something in Russian over the loudspeaker and Sergio saw the passengers unbuckle their seat belts and stand up. Some raised their fists, others put their right hand over their heart, and all of them, hearing music crackling with static, began to sing. Fausto looked at his children.

"It's the Internationale," he said. "Everyone on your feet."

"Oh, Fausto, don't be silly," said Luz Elena. "Don't pay any attention, children. Sometimes your father acts crazy."

Fausto was overcome with emotion, even if he didn't join in with the rest of the passengers. The Soviets had been his heroes in the Civil War, and he always believed that everything that came out later – the Stalinist interventions, the intrigues against their Marxist rivals in the POUM, the murder of Andreu Nin in one of the *checas* – was nothing more than well-orchestrated slander spread by the enemy's propaganda campaigns; and although he'd never wanted to join the Colombian Communist Party, he had approached some of its members on various occasions, and envied their camaraderie and sense of mission. Now he would see Red Square, he would see the Kremlin; for, according to what the Xinhua correspondent had told him, the authorities would give them all a transit permit that would allow them to see the city, and Fausto planned to take advantage of it.

The reality was very different. Relations between China and the Soviet Union were going through a very bad patch, and the international communist movement, in the days when Fausto and his family arrived in Moscow, was already quite divided. Mao and his people defended the purity of Marxism–Leninism, while the Soviets had chosen to lower their guard and seek what they were calling pacific coexistence, which for Fausto was no more than a subtle rapprochement with the capitalist world. In a short space of time the adjective *revisionist* had become the worst possible insult. And even though Fausto, arriving in Moscow, was aware of the tensions and had begun to declare himself a follower of Mao, he could not have imagined the intensity of the belligerence that existed between the two countries. It became very clear to him as they left the Moscow airport, when the authorities drove the family to a nearby hotel that looked more like a prison camp, and told them that there, in a disgusting room, locked in – a padlock prevented them from opening the door – they would spend the three days of their stopover. They had no Soviet visa and without a Soviet visa they could not leave the hotel. It was that simple.

"But why?" Sergio asked.

"Because we're going to China," Fausto said. "And they don't like that."

"*But why?*" Sergio insisted. "Aren't they communists too?"

"Yes," Fausto said. "But the other kind."

It was three interminable days of enforced confinement. The only distractions were waiting for the food trolley, which was pushed to their door by comrades in military uniforms, and going out onto the balcony to look at Soviet buildings. Towards the end of the second day, they smoked the last of the Pielroja cigarettes they'd brought from Colombia, and Fausto had to beg their jailers to bring some tobacco. The last night, after everyone had gone to sleep, Sergio stole one of those cigarettes and went out to smoke it secretly on the balcony, under the noise of the planes taking off, watching the Moscow night through eyes smarting with the smoke. It was the most disgusting tobacco he'd ever tasted in his short smoker's life.

"Revisionists," he said to himself.

He stubbed out the cigarette and threw it into the street. And then he went to bed.

They arrived in Peking in the early afternoon, where a humid heat made their clothes stick to their skin. The flight from Moscow had stopped in Omsk and in Irkutsk, and there, because of a mechanical fault nobody explained, they had to spend a long and cold night. The Aeroflot staff ordered them off the plane; each passenger received a Cossack hat and overcoat at the door, and then they could go down the stairs and follow the queue to arrive in a hangar where the cold wind blew unhindered over a hundred camp beds. The hundred passengers from that infernal flight shared two bathrooms between them; Sergio locked himself in one of them, not to smoke Russian tobacco, but to ask himself, after the tobacco and the disgusting hotel and this freezing shed where he was going to have to spend the night, what were the actual virtues of Soviet socialism.

He slept during the whole flight that took them to Peking. He did not know that the untimely fatigue that weighed down his eyelids had a name, jet lag, but he felt as though he had been drugged. He woke up in time to see, through the window, a wheat field stretching away to the horizon. Theirs was the only plane on the runway. In the terminal, a building that was no bigger than the Germán Peña boarding school, there was not a single person who did not look at them as if they were members of another species. At the bottom of the plane steps a smiling, bowing group awaited them. A woman took one step forward and introduced herself in Spanish: they could call her Chu Lan, she said; she was the interpreter who would accompany them for the following days. The rest of them worked at the Foreign Languages Institute, Chu Lan explained, and had come to give the specialist's family a warm welcome. (*Specialist*, yes: that was Fausto's official position, that magic word appeared in his contract and opened all doors.) Then they realized the Arancibias had also come to welcome them. That changed everything.

Maruja was the first to come over, giving Luz Elena a bouquet of fragrant flowers wrapped in translucent paper and asking Chu Lan to take a photo of them all with Sergio's camera. Then, without waiting for the introductions to finish, she said:

"Well, let's go to the hotel now. You're going to die when you see the hotel, and I want you to see it in daylight."

She was right. After they had driven for half an hour along a straight road with no intersections that was flanked on both sides by monotonous wheat fields, the city appeared without warning, and then, when the green porcelain roofs of the Friendship Hotel appeared, Sergio understood he had arrived in a fabled place. The hotel had two entrances, both protected by armed guards whose presence never made much sense. It consisted of a large main building and fifteen smaller ones not visible from the street, but in all of them, each of which appeared to be the size of small citadel, only seven hundred foreigners lived. There had been many more in better times, for the hotel had been built in the early 1950s to house Russian contractors – engineers, architects – who came to transform the country of the Maoist revolution. After the confrontation between Mao and Khrushchev, the twenty-five hundred Russians had returned to their country as suddenly as they'd arrived, leaving their work half-finished and factories abandoned, and the Friendship Hotel had changed guests overnight.

The explanation was very simple. The government did not allow foreigners to have their own residences, so those who arrived in Peking as official employees went straight there. The only foreigners who lived outside the Friendship Hotel were diplomats and those who, having come to China when the Communist Party took power, had married Chinese citizens and settled there, in that poorer and harder world that began outside the gates of the Friendship Hotel: that world without an Olympic-sized swimming pool or tennis courts or friendly bellboys with the gift of being everywhere at once or taxis at the door ready to take guests wherever they wanted to go. All that gave the hotel an air of unreality that Luz Elena, as on so many other occasions, perceived more clearly than the rest.

"This is like a ghetto in reverse," she said. "Nobody wants to leave and everybody wants to get in."

And it was true that out there, in real-life Peking, the world was hostile. The Great Leap Forward, the overwhelming economic campaign with which Mao Tse-tung had undertaken the transformation of the ancient agrarian system into a society of communes, made such excessive demands on the peasants, and forced them to make such senseless efforts for such unreal results, that millions ended up starving to death while Party officials blamed the shortages on bad weather. Mao had ordered the collectivization of crops, forbidden private efforts and persecuted those who insisted on them with the worst of accusations: counter-revolutionaries. The results were disastrous. Thousands of landowners who rebelled against those idiocies were unceremoniously executed; hundreds of thousands of Chinese people died in forced-labour camps. When the Cabreras landed in Peking, all of China was still feeling the final lashings of one of the worst famines of its history, and Marianella suffered the immediate consequences: during breakfast on their second day in Peking she dared to say she didn't like the eggs, and her father roared in her face:

"Well, this is what the country can offer us, and you'll eat it whether you like it or not," he told her. "And you're going to eat everything they put on your plate, since they've been good enough to take you in."

Marianella could not understand how that country of disgusting food and incomprehensible people could be paradise for her father. Sergio, for his part, learned the new rules very quickly. He learned, for example, that you needed coupons to buy anything: cereal, cotton, oil, fuel. A person could have money, but without coupons it didn't do him any good: a shirt, for example, cost five yuan plus four cotton coupons. Five yuan was the equivalent of three days' worth of food at the hotel, which put what his parents earned into perspective: 680 yuan a month was a more than generous sum. "You earn as much as Mao," Fausto was told by a Party leader they met at a welcome banquet, and Fausto, who had no reason to doubt his word, chose not to confess at that moment that his family didn't get one salary, but two: for the comrade at the Foreign Languages Institute wanted to interview Luz Elena as soon as he met her, and that single interview sufficed to offer her a contract and 350 yuan a month. From then on, while Fausto taught classes in the university area, Luz Elena taught high school students, all children of high-ranking Party cadres. The two of them would arrive together at the Institute, a block of horrible buildings with soulless classrooms, parted without touching in the middle of a courtyard and met again in the same place after teaching, all under the curious gaze of hundreds of faces.

It was a life of luxury they'd never had in Colombia. The Institute housed them in two suites: Marianella, Luz Elena and Fausto slept in one; Sergio slept in the other, next door to the living room where the family gathered in the evenings to talk about their experiences. There was a small kitchen in the parents' suite, but they very rarely used it, since the hotel had three restaurants – one oriental, one western and one Muslim, which for mysterious reasons did not fit in either of the other two classifications – and there was never a good reason to cook. So Sergio spent the first days, before starting school, playing ping-pong with Marianella in the hotel club, teaching himself the rules of billiards, getting together with the new friends he was meeting – children of Argentinian or Bolivian professors, or Uruguayan poets who always carried a book under their arm, or Peruvian intellectuals who had arrived by chance and now wouldn't change places with anybody – to play chess or Go or kick a ball on the football pitch. It was soon no longer possible to swim, because summer was officially over and the hotel closed the pool. It didn't matter to Sergio. Sometimes it seemed, at the end of exhausting days, that there wasn't enough time for all he wanted to do in this fantastical place.

Not long after their arrival the four of them went out for their first visit to the city centre. An old Polish car took them to Wangfujing, the busiest street; the man waiting for them there, one of Fausto's colleagues at the Foreign Languages Institute, began by apologising for the discomforts they were about to endure. "What do you mean?" Fausto asked. "There are many people," the other man said. He spoke precise Spanish, but was difficult to understand. "Please, do not stop. There is nothing to see in the windows. Do not stop at windows, crowds will form. Walk, walk, do not stop." But they had not gone more than two blocks when Sergio, who had not understood the instructions or chose not to obey them, got distracted by some street entertainers. It was a sort of itinerant circus, poor and rudimentary, where a muscular man juggled steel bows with his mouth while a woman sang a strident song. When he got a bit closer, Sergio saw that the man had his teeth covered with metal. He told his parents, who had approached as well in spite of what the interpreter had said, and they observed the scene for a moment or two. Then Fausto said:

"Alright, that's enough. Let's keep going."

But they couldn't keep going. A multitude had surrounded them in a matter of seconds. There were more than two hundred people who hadn't been looking at the acrobats, but came over to look at them. They looked very closely, but Sergio could not interpret their expressions; some stretched out a timid hand to touch them, and one of them would have put a finger on Sergio's face if he hadn't pushed it away roughly. "What's going on, Mamá?" Marianella asked fearfully. The interpreter spoke to the curious onlookers, making gestures that might or might not be appeals for calm; and he must have done something right, because a corridor gradually began to open through the crowd so the Cabreras could move forward. A group of children pointed at Sergio and started shouting incomprehensible words. In her mother's arms, a little girl was crying. That was the last thing Sergio saw before they finally managed to leave the crowd behind.

"What were they shouting at me?" Sergio asked the interpreter.

"Who?"

"The children," Sergio said. "I want to know what they were saying."

The man hesitated for a few seconds before answering.

"Foreign devil," he said. "I'm very sorry. It is what they are taught."

Later, on their way back to the car, they passed a long queue that went right round the corner. In time Sergio would get used to that life where everyone queued up for everything, but that day he was surprised by the reason the people were waiting. They carried in their hands a small bamboo stick; Sergio asked for explanations, and the interpreter told him: "They are toothbrushes. They are getting them fixed. There are many things that do not arrive due to the blockade. Toothbrushes, for example." With use, the bristles had fallen out; this queue was to have new bristles attached. Sergio was walking so close to the people he could smell their damp clothes. Suddenly he realized they were all looking at him. It was a curious look, but there was also something displeased in it. Someone said something in Mandarin and someone replied. Sergio lowered his large green eyes, as if he knew they were troubling, and walked away in silence, trying to make amends for an imagined impertinence. And when they arrived at the Friendship Hotel and showed their ID cards at the gate and entered the protected world, Marianella said:

"Now I understand why nobody wants to go out. China is horrible."

"This is China too," Sergio said.

"Well then, the outside China," Marianella said. "I don't know why it can't be like ours."

After that Marianella got together with the Arancibias' son

and told him: "Teach me all the swear words." A few days later she could already insult her father without him being able to understand. Conflict with Fausto was constant, for the specialist's world was the opposite: the outside China was the model – "a paradise", he said and repeated – and the hotel was a substitute, a simulacrum or, even worse, hypocrisy. He was not wrong. In the hotel lived people of all nationalities, races, beliefs and ages, but, especially, people of all ideologies. Some had been sent by their governments and had not the slightest interest in the country or its culture, but others, many of them, were communists of various ideological lines. In the hotel Maoists coexisted with pro-Soviets, pro-Cubans with pro-Albanians, Yugoslavs with European communists, and everyone with the anti-Chinese foreigners, which is what they called anyone who criticized the government of the People's Republic. There were also, of course, anti-communists; and then, worst of all, the sinister blend of anti-Chinese anti-communists. Things didn't end there, of course, because there were also Spanish anarchists, Italian Trotskyists, the odd lunatic and no shortage of opportunists who were only there for the money. They had all been contracted by the Chinese government to help with language instruction, but some had ended up translating books and journals, dubbing films or broadcasting radio programmes in foreign languages. All worked in their respective languages. None, or almost none of them, spoke Chinese. None, or almost none of them, wanted to learn. And Fausto said:

"This isn't China."

In the middle of September private classes began. A schoolroom was set up in one of the function rooms of the Friendship

Hotel: someone put a blackboard in there so two private teachers, a man and a woman who took turns, could come and give intensive classes on Chinese language and culture to the two Colombian children. It was an unpleasant room, the light too white and the space too big; Sergio and Marianella felt confined and lonely, lonelier than they'd ever felt, until other new students began to join as the days went by and a small class, fewer than a dozen young people, eventually formed. That was now their whole day: classes ran from 9 a.m. to noon and from 2 p.m. to 5, six rigorous hours spent in a language of which neither Sergio nor his sister understood a single word. Six hours of listening to incomprehensible noises, trying to make the noises correspond to the drawings the man traced on the board and failing at the endeavour: that was how their days passed, frequently ending with headaches and protests and attempts at rebellion.

"I don't know why we came to China," Marianella said once. "We can't understand them at all. They can't understand us."

"Little by little," said Luz Elena.

"I want to go back to Colombia," Marianella said.

"So do I," Sergio said.

His father looked at him, not at his sister, and a sudden fury filled his face.

"Nobody's going anywhere," he said. "We are staying here for years, for your information. So it's very simple: either learn or you're screwed."

For Fausto, the journey had been a good move. His relationship with Luz Elena seemed to have started over, or at least left behind the burdens and confrontations that had threatened it in Colombia. After their experiences at the Foreign Languages

Institute, they would tell each other what they had seen in the street as if they were filing reports: a brave people enduring adversity with dignity and never allowing poverty to turn into destitution, and where the revolution had satisfied the most urgent needs of the people. Here, everyone had food, everyone had somewhere to live, everyone had something to wear every day. Did this not justify every revolutionary effort? Did this not prove that any sacrifice was worth making in the quest for socialism? One need only look at the enormous distance the country had travelled since the first days, when people were starving to death and nobody could do anything to prevent it. Yes, the Great Leap Forward had contained errors, had run into unpredictable accidents and the opposition of right-wing saboteurs that exist in all the revolutionary processes in the world, but Mao had his eyes on higher objectives. Fausto and Luz Elena agreed on this: there was a lot to learn here. For them, of course, but also for their children.

Conversations – at the restaurant tables, at midday and in the evenings, while the hotel orchestra absurdly played boleros, which Luz Elena loved – were filled with didacticism. Fausto told the children about his recent visit to a course on corporeal expression at the Modern Drama Institute; he told them how he tried to identify the director of the play, but without success, because they all worked as equals on the staging, and it took him a long time to discover that the director was the small man, dressed in the same blue overalls as all the technicians, who was fixing a spotlight. Every family encounter was full of these parables. Fausto had bought a Czechoslovakian motorbike from a specialist who was leaving China; one day, on his way back from the outskirts of Peking, the motorbike broke down. In a matter of seconds he was surrounded by dozens of Chinese men ready to do anything in order to fix the bike, and when they didn't succeed, they stopped a truck, loaded the motorbike and its owner onto it and took them back to the hotel. The next day, Fausto got the bike fixed at a nearby garage. He never managed to pay for the repairs, because a foreigner, and in particular if that foreigner had come to construct socialism, must never be charged for anything.

"That's how solidarity works," Fausto said. "Isn't that good?"

All the work he was doing taught him a new way to understand his art. At the Drama Institute he felt he was reading Brecht for the first time, as if he'd never understood him until then, and it gradually struck him as less and less possible that anyone could perform chamber theatre. When he went back to Colombia, he thought, his theatre would be made by the people and for the people. Now he understood what Brecht had felt when he discovered the actor Mei Lanfang. He had met him in Moscow, in the mid-1930s, and was immediately seduced by the possibilities of his way of understanding the stage: the revelation of the artificial mechanisms of theatre, the characters introducing themselves and even putting on their costumes in front of the audience, the effort the actors make so that the spectator, rather than identifying with the characters, stays distant from them . . . Each gesture was part of Brechtian alienation, and now Fausto was discovering where it had all come from. He felt like another link in the chain of theatrical tradition: Chaplin spoke of Mei Lanfang to Sergey Eisenstein, and Eisenstein spoke of Mei Lanfang to Brecht, and now Brecht was speaking of Mei Lanfang to Fausto Cabrera.

There weren't enough hours in the day for him. In addition

to his work as a professor of Spanish, and his visits to the world of Chinese theatre where he learned more than he taught, Fausto had agreed to direct dubbing at the Peking Cinema Institute. He spent hours in a recording booth while, on the other side of the glass, actors filled the Chinese mouths of the actors on the screen with Spanish words. Fausto had never worked in dubbing, but nothing was new to him: he knew how to direct actors and teach them diction and elocution and tell them secrets about how not to run out of air before reaching the end of a sentence, and more than once he received a mediocre actor and converted him, in the course of a shoot, into a new voice able to give a wartime speech.

One of the films they dubbed was a Chinese film called *Little Bell*, the protagonist of which was a boy. Fausto had no doubt: Sergio was perfect for the role. For twelve days they worked together in the studio, arriving together and going home together, and Sergio felt his father's pride again and began to live within it as he had in the television studios in Bogotá. They were long days with lots of downtime and many exhausting retakes, but Sergio immediately understood how that sorcery worked: he understood that he needed to act completely, even though he'd never be seen on screen, and there was something in the process that his timidity enjoyed: acting without anyone seeing him seemed like an ideal situation at times.

One day he noticed that the people in the studio were fluttering about more than usual. Sergio was trying to figure out what was going on when his father waved him over from the studio door, took him by the shoulders as soon as he was close enough and said in French: "This is my son." The man with him introduced himself as Franco Zeffirelli. He was

Italian, but he spoke fluent French; he was in the midst of a tour of China, courtesy of the Communist Party; he had just met Fausto a day or so earlier, and the two of them had hit it off, being the same age and both from countries with fascist histories and, most importantly, they were theatre men. Zeffirelli was interested in this Spaniard who'd lived in Latin America but was dubbing films in Mao's China; he insisted they go out for dinner, and during the meal told anecdotes about translating for English soldiers during the war, and Sergio enjoyed telling him he'd played the part of the boy in Brecht's *The Spy*, and he enjoyed the Italian asking him if he was going to be an actor. Maybe, said Sergio, but he'd also like to be a director, like his father. Zeffirelli let out a loud laugh, but Sergio realized he'd just put into words something he had already felt. In the world of cinema everything was familiar to him: it was like a house where he had been born, and which he'd never left. Being a director, that would no doubt please his father. What better reason could he have?

Sergio did not know when he began to understand what Chinese people were saying, but the experience was like emerging from the bottom of a swimming pool. It was miraculous: he talked and people understood him as well. He stopped pointing at the photos on the menus in the restaurants; when they showed a film in the theatre of the Friendship Hotel, he could read the Chinese version of the ad; the day the newspapers announced Kennedy's assassination, only Sergio could tell his anxious parents what had happened in Dallas, and in the days that followed he kept them up to date on what was known about the assassination and its connection to the Soviet

Union. Information arrived late, but it arrived, and it was in Sergio's hands (or his voice) to get it out of *The People's Daily*. That's how he told them that the new president, Lyndon Johnson, had declared his decision to defend South Vietnam. For the Chinese press, each and every one of his words was an aggression or a threat.

Marianella experienced the same discoveries. She picked up the new language so well, or her mouth connected so well with the demands of the impossible consonants and singsong vowels, that before she knew it she was more comfortable in Chinese than in her shaky Spanish. At the table, when they ate together, she would take out her hotel registration card and read the characters out loud, for the simple pleasure of feeling the sounds on her tongue. (As for the Cyrillic characters, stragglers from other political eras, there was nothing to be done with them.) She soon stopped answering to her name,

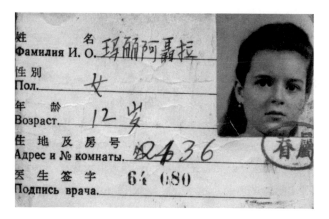

because the Chinese found it impossible or awkward to pronounce and baptized her in their own way: Lilí. She liked her new name, and began to sign her letters to her Colombian grandparents with it, and introduced herself when she met a new friend or their parents in the Friendship Hotel: "Lilí Cabrera," she'd say. "Nice to meet you." Sergio, meanwhile, had become friendly with the sons of another Señor Cabrera, a Uruguayan poet, who had turned into his accomplices and teammates. His father respected the poet, which was already an achievement, but it was impossible to know if the respect was owing to ideological affinities or their shared surname. The boys were called Dayman and Yanduy; both were half a head taller than Sergio, but they didn't speak Chinese as well as he did, nor would they ever. The four Cabreras celebrated Christmas with the rest of the students, and saw in the New Year, always aware that all that only meant something within the separate world – the parallel reality – that was the Friendship Hotel.

By the beginning of 1964, that had begun to trouble Fausto. The teachers had given their approval for Sergio and Marianella to start school, but Fausto had the inescapable impression that life in the hotel, unreal and contrived, was making his children bourgeois. The influences of that overly comfortable life, he thought, could contaminate their ideological purity, and he simply could not allow that. So he began to talk to them about those dangers; he presented a terrifying portrait of how much the Friendship Hotel resembled the capitalist world; and one evening he asked Sergio and Marianella if they would not prefer, considering the risks they were running in the hotel, to go and live and study at the Chong Wen boarding school. There they would receive a true education, like all Chinese children, not the distortion of reality they would get at one of the schools for Westerners. Sergio, who already knew what life was like at boarding school, who had already gone through the feeling of being a nuisance in his own home, thought of putting up some resistance, but he did not: because Fausto had already convinced Luz Elena, and when both of them agreed on something, it was not worth fighting. Marianella tried to rebel, anyway, and the argument was so major that a few days later, when the first snowfall arrived and the family went out to see snow for the first time in their lives, Fausto said to her:

"Not you. You stay and clean up your room. We didn't come here to live like pigs."

At moments like that Marianella wished her father would hit her, as he sometimes did her brother, instead of punishing her: a slap, a clean slap and out to see snow. She would have preferred that a thousand times.

One afternoon, shortly before school started, Yanduy, his Uruguayan friend, came to invite him to hunt sparrows. He carried an air rifle in each hand. Outside it was three degrees below zero, but Sergio knew that there was a plague of sparrows: they ate the wheat and rice seeds that belonged to the people. It was said that a few years earlier, in 1959, the plague had been so intense that people in the villages organized outings every day at noon, with the mission of making as much noise as they could. They set off firecrackers and shook rattles and banged gongs and rang bells and managed to make such a racket for so long that the sparrows began to die of heart failure, exhausted from not being able to rest. That year the harvests were saved from the sparrows; but the worms (which the sparrows ate) invaded and destroyed them, and the villagers had to return to the old system of scarecrows. Now in the Bamboo Park, stationed beside the people's communal plantations,

Sergio eliminated sparrows with sure shots. He had taken off his gloves for better aim and the cold hurt his hands, but he felt he was fulfilling a revolutionary mission. There, beside the frozen fields, he was training for a more arduous future, and walking back to the hotel, when an anonymous Englishman began to throw stones at him while calling him a murderer and shouting at him to leave the birds alone, he felt it again, and his chest filled with something resembling pride.

VII

"Let's see," Sergio said as he flipped through a book, "let's see if I can find the page."

They were in the restaurant of the film institute, which was so packed with people – men and women who would probably attend the opening of the retrospective in a few minutes – that they could barely talk. The place was as friendly as it was busy, and was presided over by the spirit of Marilyn Monroe, whose stylized image looked at them from the menu. Along the low ceilings ran five tubes painted with rings of colour that made them look like – Sergio thought, with first-hand knowledge – a coral snake. Sergio and his son Raúl were sitting in aluminium chairs facing a long wooden board that was more like a counter than a table, but instead of a bar across from them, they faced a wide picture window looking out on night-time in the Raval, where the downpour was just starting to ease and a few people walked by taking care not to slip. Raúl was engrossed in his own book, which Sergio had bought for him at the Filmoteca bookshop. "Choose whichever one you want," he'd said, and Raúl had passed over the art books, in spite of being interested in them, and the ones on the history of cinema, in spite of having grown up hearing about films, and had chosen a graphic novel, *Fight Club*, by Chuck Palahniuk, on the cover of which, disturbingly, a pair of open eyes looked out over a pair of closed ones. Sergio, for his part, had found a copy of *Mythologies*, by Roland Barthes, a book he'd read with enthusiasm in his youth, and immediately, as if from behind curtains of smoke, a passage had arrived in his head. Barthes' idea, he seemed to recall, was that the communist world, rather than a hostile place, was *another world*: different and most of all incomprehensible. And that was what he wanted to share with Raúl.

"It must be around here," he said, turning pages.

He looked at his son to try to see, reading his hermetic adolescent face, what he was making of the book. But Raúl, at eighteen, was no longer an adolescent; and what Sergio felt at seeing that, after sitting beside him for half an hour in the hard seats of La Monroe, was a happiness so intense it took him by surprise: happiness at being there, in Barcelona, after almost two years of distance, and happiness at seeing him grown into this handsome man a head taller than him, with a firm voice and sure look, full of opinions on everything under the sun. It was true that these opinions were a bit to the right of what Sergio would have preferred, but desiring his son to think exactly as he did seemed like one of the possible definitions of conservatism.

Raúl had arrived on the 16.40 flight, in the middle of a downpour that darkened the skies over Barcelona and delayed the traffic coming in along Gran Vía. The film centre people went to pick him up and brought him to the hotel while Sergio was finishing up an interview at a television studio, so Raúl was alone in the lobby, drinking a Coca-Cola, when his father arrived, shoulders darkened by the rain and his white hair as wet as if he'd just emerged from the shower. He barely had time to have a real shower and put on some dry clothes to go to the opening of the retrospective, so he suggested to Raúl that he wait for him there and he would be right back down. But before saying, sure, no problem, he'd play a video game on his phone, Raúl said:

"I'm really sorry, Papá. I'm really sorry about Tato."

Fausto never had an intense connection with Raúl, as they hadn't seen each other often enough, but he loved him devotedly, and he was always happy that his grandson could have in Spain the life that had been impossible for him. Whenever they saw each other, Fausto tended to retell a story for whoever was there – family, friends or perfect strangers – of what had happened to Sergio and Raúl in the Valley of the Fallen. "Let me tell you what happened to these two," he'd say; Raúl would roll his eyes and Sergio would get ready to fill in any information or detail for his father, who told the anecdote as if he'd been present. The protagonists of the story were Sergio, Lilí – the oldest of his three daughters, his first-born – and Raúl, who had been about to turn eight. Sergio had already separated from Raúl's mother, but he was still living in Spain, so his son came up from Málaga on the train to spend some weekends in Madrid. That weekend they'd decided to leave the city and spend the day on a boat, in one of those reservoirs that Madrileños call *pantanos*. As they were driving, Raúl saw the enormous cross at the Valley of the Fallen and asked what that place was and if they could go there.

"No," said Sergio. "Franco is buried there."

"And what's the problem?" Raúl said.

"What do you mean, what's the problem?" Sergio said.

"Everything this family has suffered is the problem. It's Franco's fault we had to leave Spain. All that Tato suffered, all that his Uncle Felipe suffered, was Franco's fault. Our family was shattered because of Franco. No, Raúl: we are not going there."

The day on the reservoir went by without anyone saying any more about the matter: Raúl must have detected something in his father's voice. But on the way home, seeing the cross again on the mountain in the distance, Raúl insisted that he wanted to visit that place. Before Sergio had time to react with another sermon about the broken family and the Civil War, Lilí said:

"Come on, Papá, what does it matter? We'll see the place for two seconds, Raúl will be happy and we'll go back to Madrid. There's nothing wrong with it. You can even explain things to him."

Minutes later they were there: for the first time in history, members of the Cabrera family were visiting the tomb of Franco. It was an imposing place, and Sergio had to remember the story of his relatives – Commander Felipe Díaz Sandino, Grandpa Domingo, his own father – to keep his emotions at a proper distance; on the other hand, he felt convinced that he was betraying the memory of his lineage, and he could not shake that conviction no matter how hard he tried. The dictator's tomb was a white rectangle on top of a grey stone floor, and in the centre of the rectangle rested three bouquets of flowers and a red and gold ribbon, the colours of the flag. Sergio walked past and went up two or three steps towards the altar and stared at the Christ figure at the back, trying to remember the last time he'd been inside a church. Then he heard a noise behind him, something like a shoe tapping loudly, and when he turned around, ready to frown at the guilty party, he saw his son stomping on the white rectangle while spitting obscenely.

Sergio grabbed his arm and pulled him aside. "Hey, what's the matter with you?"

"He's a bastard!" Raúl shouted. "It's all his fault! Because of him we had to leave Spain! My family was shattered because of him!"

And Fausto told all this with precise details, and, depending on the company, in his tale Raúl spat on the tomb or came out with insults that, of course, were not things an almost-eight-year-old boy would say, but those of a ninety-year-old exile: the insults that Fausto would have addressed to Franco if he'd seen him in his long-ago childhood. The only thing Sergio could add was the insipid tale of what happened later. How he threw Raúl over his shoulder and carried him out of the church before anyone noticed, how they didn't speak of it again on the way back to Madrid, how he found out later that Raúl had been telling the anecdote to his Spanish relatives, because he found his father's reaction funny. Sergio received a call from some concerned aunt worried about the bad manners he was teaching his son, the disrespect for the sacred, intolerance for other people's ideas. Sergio thought that Francoism, in his experience, was not very sacred. But he didn't say anything.

Leaving the hotel on their way to the Filmoteca, enduring the downpour that burst over the Rambla del Raval, he wanted to ask Raúl if he remembered that anecdote Tato liked so much, or, at least, if he'd been back to the Valley of the Fallen, but he guessed somehow that the amusing anecdote had long ago stopped amusing Raúl. Then they got distracted by the books in the shop, and from there they went to try to find a free space in the packed Monroe, and all that went before was no longer urgent. They were planning to have a drink while they waited: the organizers had invited them up to the offices, but Raúl wanted to stay downstairs, with the people, and Sergio wanted to stay with him. And now, in La Monroe, Sergio was looking for a passage in *Mythologies*, and was beginning to suspect it didn't exist.

"Ah," he said then. "Finally. Listen to this."

MARTIANS

The mystery of Flying Saucers was at first terrestrial: supposedly the saucer came from the Soviet unknown, that world as deprived of explicit intentions as another planet. And already this form of the myth contained in germ its planetary development; if the saucer of Soviet contrivance so readily became a Martian one, it was because in fact Western mythology attributes to the Communist world the very alterity of a planet: the USSR is an intermediate world between Earth and Mars.

"That's what China was back then," Sergio said. "For us I mean. 'Western mythology attributes to the Communist world the very alterity of a planet.' It's good, isn't it? I would have been about twenty when I discovered this book. And I thought, yes, that's how it was. That's what it was like to be in China at that time."

"All Martians," Raúl said.

"A bit, yeah."

"I had a different impression," Raúl said. "You told me something else."

"Something else?"

"I don't know. You've talked to me about China as if it were your own homeland."

"Not at first," Sergio said. "Anyway, it doesn't matter."

"But, Mars . . ." Raúl said. "Yes, it does matter. Mars, Papá. That's really shocking."

As was his habit, Sergio was sitting in the back row of the cinema. He always did that, not just so he could slip out without anyone noticing, but also to gauge the reactions of the audience and to take note of those who left. *Everybody Leaves*, the film that opened the retrospective, advanced on the screen with that rare autonomy that cinema has, detached from its observers or witnesses. Now, as he spied on Raúl's reactions – his laughter or interest or boredom – what always happened to Sergio was happening to him: what was going on up there, on the Filmoteca de Catalunya screen, ceased to be a film of his authorship, of movements which he had directed and of dialogues which he'd written or approved, and turned into an unfathomable mystery. On the screen images appeared and he could hear dialogue that was the same for everyone, but Sergio was sure that afterwards, when the film was over, there would not be two people in this theatre who had seen the same one. Not even Sergio had always seen the same film: sometimes it was a metaphor for a country, sometimes it was a domestic tragedy, sometimes it was the meticulous way men and women were mercilessly crushed under the steamroller of history: Cuban history, in this case, except that Cuban history was never just the history of Cuba: it was also the history of the United States, the history of the Soviet Union, the history of a war we call cold in spite of the fires ignited all over the continent: in Cuba and Nicaragua, in Guatemala and Chile, and also in Colombia. And in a certain sense it was still igniting them, of course. No, history was not a steamroller in Latin America: it was a flame-thrower, and it kept burning the continent as if the operator had gone mad and nobody was brave enough to stop him.

Everybody Leaves was a partial and capricious adaptation of a sad and beautiful novel by Wendy Guerra. The action takes place during the 1980s, when the Cuban Revolution was going through a new crisis. Nieve is the daughter of separated parents: a convinced revolutionary, who could have been a good playwright but has turned into a mere pamphleteer, and a sceptical mother now living with a Swedish man and missing the times when the revolution had more freedom and less authoritarianism. Against a background of a Cuba that doesn't really know what it wants to be, Nieve's parents begin a custody battle, but it is soon obvious that the confrontation has less to do with family than with ideology, and the only thing left when it is all over is a handful of destroyed lives and a heartrending image: that of the father, lost among the hundreds of Cubans who are leaving for the United States from the port of Mariel.

The film had been surrounded by controversy from the start. Sergio remembered the premiere in Havana in December 2014. Would it have mattered if he'd launched it in any other city? At the moment of deciding, Sergio would have confessed that he was also moved by the curiosity of seeing how a still revolutionary audience, or an audience in which there would surely be some convinced revolutionaries, would react to this problematic story. He had tried to film in Cuba, but the authorities, maybe because of the novel by a writer they'd never been too fond of, maybe due to reports of the novel's unfavourable portrayal of revolutionary life, kept a stubborn silence when Sergio requested the required permits; so the team had to fire up all the magic of cinema to convince spectators that scenes they'd shot in a neighbourhood of Santa Marta on the Caribbean coast of Colombia, or in some distant part of the Andes, had actually happened in Havana or the mountains of Cuba.

Not everyone in the cinema in Havana enjoyed that portrait of damaged lives. From his seat in the back row of the stalls, as always, Sergio could hear the reactions of the audience, because in Havana, for some reason, the audience in a cinema behaves like they did in theatres centuries ago: they encourage the characters, insult them, warn the hero that the villain is waiting for him around the corner. So the laughter and praise reached Sergio's ears, but so did the isolated protests and a few shameless jeers shouted over dialogue; and once, from the shadows bathed in the white light of the screen, he saw a silhouette who stood up indignantly, with an exaggerated fuss of hats or folded newspapers in a fist, marching up the aisle mumbling and stomping, the light shining from behind, standing out against the bright background. Before leaving, the silhouette exclaimed so everyone would hear:

"*Coño!* This is pure imperialist propaganda!"

When the film ended and the house lights came up, Silvia looked at Sergio with her big eyes wide open and a shy smile. "What a difficult audience, no?" Sergio spent a while talking to the people who approached him. He signed every film his fans brought (the plastic case or the disc that glinted under the lights); he smiled timidly at the praise, shook every hand that emerged from the crowd to greet him, always with that courtesy that seemed to apologize for the fact that his films didn't come into being on their own. That was when he remembered that the premiere, which was already marked out by the strange connection between the history of the film and the city where they were, was unique for other reasons as well: attending the projection of *Everybody Leaves,* sitting in different parts of the cinema, were the men and women who for the last two years had been seeking there in Havana, under the auspices of the Cuban government and the attentive gaze of the entire world, a negotiated end to the half-century of Colombian war. The guerrilla leaders were there, or at least a group of them, and also some of the government negotiators; they had watched under the same roof a story that spoke, with the ways and language of fiction, of a human reality that touched indirectly on the realities of their conversations and confrontations and irreconcilable disagreements. And now the guerrillas were coming over to say hello to Sergio, and it was almost comical watching them search for words to praise the film, when it was obvious they had not liked it at all: that it had struck them as unjust, untrue or counter-revolutionary.

One day earlier they had met for the first time. The guerrilla commanders heard that Sergio Cabrera was in the city and wanted to meet him. A casual conversation began in which they confessed to Sergio that they loved his films, that they watched them in their encampments, but that all the copies they had were pirated. They talked about *Time Out,* a comedy that imagined a truce between the army and the guerrillas with a single objective – to watch the Colombian national team play a football match – and one of the commanders made a joke protesting about the portrayal of the guerrillas. "They were toy guerrillas," he said. And the meeting could have gone on like that, in that light-hearted atmosphere, if they hadn't asked Sergio his opinion on what was happening in the peace talks. Sergio thought it would have been irresponsible to have all the commanders in front of him and not tell them the complete truth, so he did. He told them they'd been mistaken: that their image, among the people for whom they claimed to be fighting, could not be worse, and that their obligation was to do all that was necessary so that ordinary Colombians did not go on paying for this war with their suffering.

"You have caused a lot of pain," he told one of the commanders. "The only thing the people want is to see you in jail."

"Well, let's go to jail," the man replied. "But then we should all go. Because a war is not fought from only one side."

Sergio knew that, of course, and he knew how difficult it was to explain to someone who'd only suffered violence from one of the sides. In any case, it was strange to be presenting his film about a failed socialism there, in the Havana of the peace negotiations. The ghosts of the Cold War had shown up there too: in this same theatre where *Everybody Leaves* was premiering were the rancour, the resentments, the memory of the fears of a whole country, because these guerrillas who were going to see films a few seats away from those negotiators would not be here, in Havana, if history had decided to take a different route (if Fidel Castro had not triumphed on January 1, 1959), and in that case he wouldn't be here either, Sergio Cabrera's life had been marked by this Caribbean revolution. The ghosts, always the ghosts. For Colombians who had lived through this half-century of war, who had grown up among its terrors, who had provided the corpses, lost loved ones or embraced those who had and sometimes wished for someone else's death, someone who had killed or mocked their dead, for the Colombians who had not passed through the flames thrown by history with impunity, the ghosts were everywhere: there was no way to hide from them. They had even come this far: as far as a cinema in the middle of the Caribbean in the year 2014. How wilful history was, Sergio thought: it appears when we least expect it, as if playing with us.

The official premiere of *Everybody Leaves* took place the following year, in Bogotá on a rainy night. All four screens in a mall on avenida Chile showed it at the same time, and the spectators emerged from them commenting on what they'd seen, and Sergio waited at the entrance to the cinema, among hot dogs and soft-drink dispensers, to receive handshakes and kisses on the cheek and answer questions in front of the blinding light of a television camera. None of the people who greeted him, none of the journalists who interviewed him, could have imagined the immense effort he had to make to go through these formalities, because his head was elsewhere. Barely six months had gone by since Havana, but that trip seemed like an episode from another life: a life in which Sergio had felt at ease. When had that stopped?

As the weeks went by, as *Everybody Leaves* faded out of the country's listings like a hangover, Sergio had also been withdrawing from his own life. Silvia believed it was the same melancholy that struck him after finishing an important project, aggravated this time by the way the Colombian public had received the film. But it wasn't. And when she asked him what the problem was, if she could help him in some way, Sergio told her sadly that she could not help him in any way, because even he couldn't figure out where the problem was, what ghosts or demons were consuming him from within.

On one of those days he went to visit his father. Maybe because he hadn't done so since the celebration of his ninetieth birthday, which coincided with Sergio's preparations for presenting his film in Havana, or maybe because he hadn't paid him enough attention, Sergio found him hostile and gaunt. The reunion was a list of grievances. Fausto complained that Marianella didn't come to see him anymore: she had stopped years before. "She's been distancing herself ever since your mother died," Fausto said. "As if it hadn't hurt me just as much. It's like she fucking blames me. I don't know what I did to her." Sergio had always marvelled at his father's talent for not seeing what he didn't want to see, and let it pass in silence when possible, but this time he didn't manage to keep quiet.

"Well, have a think," he said. "I'm sure something will occur to you."

Towards the end of the evening, after Fausto complained that his own children judged him as if he were an enemy, Sergio, in a desperate attempt to change the subject and end the visit on a cordial note, told him what was happening with *Everybody Leaves*. It had been shown in cinemas for a disappointingly short time, it was true, but a lot of people had liked it since its preview showing in Havana. "Oh, good," said Fausto. "Must be because I wasn't in it." He said it in jest, but Sergio detected an underlying resentment in his words, a disguised grievance. Fausto had never given up the idea that his son didn't give him as much credit as he deserved in his films. "You never talk about me in interviews," he sometimes said, and Sergio talked himself hoarse trying to explain that he did but the journalists chose

to focus on other things. "I don't edit the interviews, Papá."
Now, with his aged voice that no longer recited poems (because
his memory could no longer summon up the lines), Fausto
looked at Sergio with a serenity that was worse than the
antagonism and said:

"Well, congratulations, but you know the truth."

"What truth is that, Papá?"

"That this film of yours betrays all that we believed in,"
Fausto said. "It's a slap in the face, Sergio Fausto, of everything
you and I did in this life."

When Sergio told Silvia about that episode, the only thing
he managed to say was: "My father is old." And it was reason-
able to think that his sadness stemmed from this acknowledg-
ment, the slow deterioration of the man he'd so admired for
so long, and thanks to whom he had experienced things of
which very few others could boast. But Fausto had put into
words something that others had thought since the screenplay
of the film began making the rounds to the usual hands:
friends, collaborators, producers, those who were all three at
once. One of those friends was Juan, a doctor who had been
through a thousand other battles with him and who one day,
after a consultation, explained why he could not accompany
him through this one. "I don't think this film should be
made." He said that the film would play into the hands of the
anti-Cubans and the imperialists, that it would tarnish Cuba's
image without gaining anything in return, that socialism always
had enough enemies to criticize its problems. "You're not
going to achieve anything with this film," he said. "Your friends
are not going to understand you making it, because they're
going to think it too critical, and your enemies aren't going

to understand either, because they're going to think it too indulgent. To put it in other words: you're fucked." His conclusion was blunt: "We don't wash our dirty linen in public." Sergio had heard that prescription many times, and had occasionally said it himself. But now something stirred in his chest and he had to ask:

"And what happens if nobody does the laundry at home?"

There was more than one conversation like that. Sergio searched in vain for a way to explain that *Everybody Leaves* was not a condemnation, and it wasn't even meant to be a questioning of anything, it was just the story of a little girl, Nieve, whose life goes off the rails as a result of a state interfering in the lives of its citizens, and that it resembled what he'd been through too closely to let it pass. Nieve in Cuba was what he'd been in China: a child at the mercy . . . But of what? He couldn't explain any of that, in part because the only way of doing justice to his Chinese memories had been to direct the film, in part because the only way to understand the film was to know his life through and through: to know it as nobody knew it: not his friends, not his children, not his wife.

But Juan's opinion stung. Sergio realized that those disagreements with the world wouldn't be so important, or would perhaps be more tolerable, if he had a project in hand. But even his work, which had always been a place where it was possible to feel he was in charge of things, now seemed to conspire against him. After he finished shooting *Everybody Leaves* at the beginning of 2014, he'd done what he always did between two films: a TV series. It was the story of the infamous doctor Mata, a lawyer in the 1940s who had committed twenty-eight murders with impunity and one more for which he was convicted. A serial killer: success was guaranteed. But the serial went over budget, and the network blamed the director for the excesses and the director blamed the network, and the dispute, which on occasion grew heated, left a chill in relations. So Sergio stopped receiving offers of work, and his pride prevented him from asking for or demanding any. It was like being dead while alive.

The days lost their structure. Instead of getting up at seven in the morning to look after Amalia, as he usually did, Sergio slept in late, recovering after a night spent watching films in the small family room at the opposite end of the apartment from the bedrooms. He told himself that watching the complete works of Bertolucci, for example, was a way of keeping his creative conduits open, but he knew deep down that his tank was empty. Silvia, for her part, took charge of dropping a smiling Amalia off at the nursery before going to her job at the Portuguese embassy, and once, returning home in the early afternoon, after picking up Amalia (who was still smiling, inexplicably satisfied), found that Sergio hadn't even opened the curtains. They began to live on contrasting schedules: he would be awake when she slept and vice versa; during those nights of insomnia, he would watch films or read books that had belonged to his mother or look in on Amalia or sit in the brightly coloured chair, beside her little bed with railings, watching her sleep with the conviction that he could spend the rest of his days like that. One evening, after several months of living in the strange solitude of those inverted schedules, in a sort of jet lag in the same house, Silvia said:

"I think we should talk to someone."

Silvia, who'd trained as a sociologist, had begun to study psychology since arriving in Colombia. This was not a dilettante interest: she had discovered Gestalt long before meeting Sergio, but only in her Bogotá life did she find the time that serious study demanded. Her mentor and guide, the therapist Jorge Llano, had quickly become a friend to both of them, and that was what allowed Silvia to put this proposal on the table: that Sergio should talk to him. Sergio couldn't see how it would help, but Silvia did not beat about the bush: it didn't have to be Llano she said, it could be anyone, she didn't have to have read all of Max Wertheimer to know that Sergio was going through a textbook case of depression.

"We'll look for someone," Silvia said. "Someone you like. But we have to do something, love. You're not well."

"I know I'm not well," Sergio said. "I don't need to pay anyone to tell me that."

"I know you know. But you don't know why. Or do you? Tell me: do you know why you're not well?"

"No," Sergio said.

"Well, there you go. And I think someone could help us find out."

But days went by without Sergio making a call, or arranging an appointment, or taking any steps in the direction they'd agreed. The inverted schedules continued, and at midday, when they managed to find the common space to eat lunch together, Silvia enjoyed hearing him talk about the Chinese films he'd watched through the night – "they didn't do things like that when I lived there," he'd say – but those areas of encounter in the middle of the day were rare and brief, and later, returning from the demanding routine of her work, her studies and their three-year-old daughter, Silvia could have believed she was living in her own country rather than Colombia, as a single mother rather than a married woman. The days felt long and, worse still, all the same. Silvia began to fall gradually into her own sadness until she no longer knew where hers started and Sergio's ended. That's how she explained it to him one night, after a dinner with friends in the apartment. They had all left by then and Sergio was washing the dishes, distractedly, as if absorbed by the play of light in the suds on his hands. Silvia, who had walked into the kitchen with a tray of empty bottles and leftover food, saw him and had the strange sensation that Sergio had absented himself. Minutes later, lying in a bed that had not been made that day, Silvia told him that she'd been thinking about it for several days, and maybe it was best if she went to Lisbon.

"It's best for Amalia, love," she said. "But it's also best for us."

Sergio thought her argument so precise, her quiet sadness so eloquent, that he didn't even try to object.

"How long for?" he asked.

She looked at him with infinite tenderness, but her gaze – the set of her mouth, which would have been mocking if it weren't so pained – told him: *You understand nothing.*

"It's not a matter of time," she said. "I'll go back to Lisbon and then we'll see how we can arrange for you to see our daughter. I love you, Sergio, and I know you love me, but I can't go on with this. I can't go on like this." And she concluded: "It wouldn't be good for anyone."

It was a cordial agreement, more like a diplomatic treaty than a couple's break-up. They went through the following weeks as if they were going away together, attending farewell parties at friends' houses and getting little Amalia ready, and maybe Sergio began to think that in that waiting time a miracle would occur. It did not: the departure day arrived. Sergio helped Silvia pack her bags, took stock of Amalia's things and was surprised again at how tiny a pair of leggings could be, that a whole body could fit inside this little undershirt with its pink bow on the neckline. He drove them to the airport and did not let them out of his sight while they checked in too many suitcases, and for the hour the three of them spent on the uncomfortable seats of a Juan Valdez café, while Amalia got crumbs from a giant muffin all over her face, he never took his hands off them, as if only that way, in contact with the two bodies that were going far away, could he believe that maybe it wasn't for ever.

Dawn broke radiantly over Barcelona on Friday morning. The wind had swept away the clouds and freshened the air, but was so strong that as they left the hotel, dazzled by the brightness of the day, Sergio and Raúl had to stop in the shade of a palm tree on the Rambla del Raval to put on their jackets. Sergio recognized the magnitude of the distraction that had overwhelmed him during these days, as he noticed at that moment for the first time the Fernando Botero sculpture that stood in the middle of the Rambla like a totem: it was an enormous bronze cat that somehow managed to have both empty eyes and a mischievous gaze. Sergio pointed to it.

"He was a friend of your grandfather's."

"The cat?" asked Raúl.

Sergio smiled. "When they were young," he said. "They did things together."

He told him about *The Image and the Poem*, the TV programme in which Fausto Cabrera recited lines of poetry while the young

Botero transformed them into charcoal sketches. The drawings remained in Fausto's possession, or rather Botero had forgotten them in the studios and never worried about collecting them. One day in this new century, when Sergio asked his father what had become of those youthful drawings by the man who was now the most expensive living artist in the world, Fausto responded that he'd sold them years ago, at a time when the Communist Party needed funds. And while they conjured up those moments, or while Sergio conjured them up, they began to walk towards the metro station. That morning, while they had breakfast, Sergio had asked his son what he wanted to do in Barcelona. He was well aware that his question was a testament to his disorientation: Raúl was not the same person he'd been two years ago, the last time they saw each other, and he had to foresee and respect his independence, not commit some fatherly faux pas that would ruin the weekend.

"What do you mean?" Raúl said.

"It's your first time here," Sergio said. "You have two entire days. You can go and see the city. I'm sure people have suggested places."

"I've come here to be with you," Raúl said. "That's what I want to do. Why don't you show me your Barcelona?"

"Mine?" Sergio said. "I don't know if there is such a thing."

He had been to the city many times, but always for work; and that, in his case, meant going from a hotel to a film theatre, from a cinema to a restaurant. He'd never been a tourist in this city: never, that is, since the summer of 1975. It was the year he returned to Colombia: after difficult times he didn't want to think about, after fleeing his own country like a criminal. He was coming from London; the ship stopped in the port of

Barcelona before crossing the Atlantic, and Sergio was faced with a dilemma: he wanted to see the city, but he had promised, out of respect for the memory of the family, not to set foot on Spanish soil until Franco was dead. In the end he decided to disembark and see, at least, the famous Sagrada Familia, which his father had talked about. And never, in all his visits to Barcelona, had he returned to that youthful memory.

"Perfect then," said Raúl. "Let's start there."

PART TWO

The Revolution in the Hotels

VIII

They lived a double life in Peking: hell at school and heaven at the hotel. At school they were only allowed to shower on Wednesdays, and the rest of the days they washed as best they could with little towels they wet in a washbasin. Luz Elena had obtained the favour of having them served a glass of milk, and Sergio and Marianella had to endure the taunts of their classmates who watched with undisguised disgust and said: "But do you know where that stuff you're drinking comes from?" Sergio lived through those early stages with true horror, as if the experience on Wangfujing Street had turned into the natural state of things, for his classmates did not just look at him with amazement and a measure of rejection (Party propaganda had taught them that Westerners were the enemy), but also enjoyed making fun of him. "Toad eyes!" they shouted at him. Sergio sat in the back rows, hiding in his own solitude, and took to reading novels. He was obsessed with Georges Simenon, and one day he'd been so absorbed in *Maigret and the Man on the Bench* that he opened it during a class, and, trying to hide the book inside a notebook, started reading. After a while a strange silence surrounded him. Sergio looked up and found the whole class staring at him disapprovingly: the teacher had gone out, leaving the door open. The boy at the next desk informed him: "He says that if you want to attend class, and for him to teach us, you can go and find him." The teacher asked him to present his apologies in writing and that they should include the offence to his classmates, whose education he'd put in danger with the egotism of his gesture.

Chong Wen was, in its way, an elite school set up for the children of absent parents: high-ranking cadres of the Communist Party, for example, or assimilated foreigners who had important jobs. Twenty or so students came, like Sergio and Marianella, from the Friendship Hotel, but they were the only ones who boarded there: the others returned to the hotel each afternoon, to enjoy the three restaurants and their luxurious rooms and their parents' company. Marianella envied them openly. "But what did we do wrong?" she said to Sergio. "Why can't we be with Mamá and Papá? What are they punishing us for?" Sergio, meanwhile, developed a solid camaraderie with the other boarders, built on resentment and the use of political language: they were the true proletariat; the ones who went home, despicable petits bourgeois. The magic lay in the way that Sergio became the link between the two worlds, and very soon realized the advantages this gave him. If some Chinese comrade wanted good shoes, Sergio could buy them at the Friendship Hotel shop; a pupil from one of the top years approached him one day, between two classes, and asked him quietly if it was true he could get Maotai. This was the most appetizing Chinese liqueur; it was produced in small quantities, or in quantities too small for such a big country, and it never reached the market (it was said that Party leaders drank all of it), but the guy with toad eyes had a way to buy it. It was like being back at Germán Peña and handing out Lucky Strikes.

On weekends, when Sergio and Marianella had permission to leave, Luz Elena took them for walks in the city. They liked to go to the antique shops on Liulichang Street, where the old bourgeois families that the revolution had swept away left their treasures, signs of their former opulence. Each shop was an inventory of times past, a memorandum of excessive wealth and a melancholy testament to the equality the revolution had imposed. Luz Elena looked at the shop windows sadly, because her imagination led her to think of those broken families, but she didn't want to contradict the message Fausto went on about whenever he got the chance: wasn't this world where all were equal marvellous? Wasn't this a marvellous world where, walking down the street, you couldn't tell the rich from the poor, because everyone dressed the same?

"Equal but ugly," Marianella said when she knew her father couldn't hear. "So, what's so great?"

But it was true: there, in the street of the antique dealers, everyone – men and women, children and old people – wore the same clothes dyed the same indigo blue. It was impossible to tell if they'd been rich in the past, or as poor as they were now, and of those aristocrats only lost signs remained: a certain elegant way of walking that could not be hidden, an inflection in the voice when asking for something, a commentary that revealed a glimpse of guilty cosmopolitanism. One day they had a close encounter with that disappeared world, and Sergio would never forget it. Every Sunday, the Bureau of Specialists, the organization in charge of receiving the guests at the Friend-ship Hotel, offered a tour of the city. For Sergio and Marianella, who had spent the week in the straitened circumstances of

Chong Wen, those few hours of going back to being Western tourists were soothing. Sergio knew that they were days of bourgeois contamination, of course, a risk for the mind of a young revolutionary, but he put a wool sweater over his shoulders and climbed aboard the bus with thirty others and went off to visit the Great Wall, or the Forbidden City, or the Summer Palace, and, there, with his arm around his mother, posing for a photo with his father, seeing them together again and far from the phantom of separation, he couldn't help but feel a repugnant happiness.

One of those guilty, bourgeois Sundays, they went to the Botanical Garden. In the morning, Luz Elena told the children: "Today you're going to meet someone special." She told them about Pu Yi, the last emperor of China. Sergio was enthusiastic about meeting a man who had been more powerful than a king, and arrived at the garden with his eyes wide. In the main room they were met by an ordinary functionary, in the same blue suit as everyone else, with the same hospitality in his manners, but who moved through his domain with a straight back and his head held high, as if searching for something on the horizon. He wore round glasses and a grin that could only be pride, even though he seemed extraordinarily clumsy (more than once during those brief minutes he tripped over something, and once he gestured and sent his own glasses flying through the air). He told them about the place and its wonders, and that's how Sergio realized the man was not just any functionary, but the person in charge of the garden. And then he understood: the man, in spite of his outfit and his trade, was not just a gardener. He was Pu Yi.

The former emperor did not say a single word about his

past, and nobody asked him a single question in spite of them all knowing who he was and what his previous life had been like: that session of tourism and gardening had been the closest thing to a pact of silence about a shameful past. Sergio had an inexplicable urgency to see him again, so he left the group and ran back to the place where they parted. And there he saw him, curled up among flowers, with a pair of garden shears in his right hand. In the other hand he held his glasses, and Sergio realized he'd taken them off to wipe his face. He could only see his profile and he was far away, so he couldn't see him clearly, but Sergio imagined that the former emperor was crying. The next day, back at school, he told one of the teachers about the visit. The teacher looked disgusted.

"A traitor," he said. "But he's reformed, the revolution has reformed him. He has admitted his crimes, recognized that his previous life had no value and he has repented for having lived it. And Mao has received him, because Mao is generous."

While Marianella locked horns at school – confronting her teachers and being duly reprimanded, steadfastedly refusing to learn the complex mathematics – Sergio had turned into a model student. By the end of the year, when exam time came, he knew the lives of the heroes as if he'd witnessed them and could repeat the revolutionary slogans; and he did so with pride, even though none of that helped him with the exams, since only two subjects were tested: Mathematics and Language. Sergio passed the maths exam with relative success, but nobody expected him to do as well as his classmates in the language exam. He knew that as a foreigner he would receive certain advantages – the privilege of a dictionary, for example – and then he found out that the exam consisted of only one test: the writing, in two hours, of an essay, the title of which the teacher would write on the board. It was a national exam, which meant that millions of Chinese students would be writing about the same subject all over the country. The teacher walked up to the board with the chalk in his hand, asked if everyone was ready and began to write. Sergio looked up and read:

I was born under the red flag with the five golden stars.

His first reaction was: That's not fair. I wasn't born here, I was born somewhere else, they can't ask that of me. He thought of protesting, asking for clemency. And then he saw an opportunity.

He corrected the title: *I was NOT born under the red flag with five golden stars.* He wrote: "No, I was not born under the red flag with its five golden stars, but now she shelters me and is therefore as much mine as my own . . ." And then he wrote that he had been born under a yellow, blue and red flag: the flag of a faraway country called Colombia. He explained the reasons that had brought him to this country, which had welcomed him with love and allowed him the privilege of continuing his education in a school like Chong Wen.

The essay, a youthful version of what the "international proletariat" was for Sergio, received the highest mark in the school. The teacher read it out in front of the class. The *People's Daily* published it alongside essays by other pupils selected from all over China, and the national radio station broadcast it word for word. At Chong Wen, Sergio, who was already popular as a trafficker of coveted things, had now become a trophy. Teachers and other pupils looked at him differently. Sergio was no longer the guy with the toad eyes, but rather someone who had come to construct socialism. Nobody asked him anymore, touching his hair, if he had to put rollers in at night to get it to be so curly. Nobody asked him anymore what colour he saw the world through his green eyes, because it was obvious that the world, for him, was the colour of the revolution.

Since the incidents of August, when two American ships were attacked in the Gulf of Tonkin, President Johnson had announced the escalation of the war in Vietnam. Bombing began after the attack on Camp Holloway, a helicopter base the US Army had built near Plieku, with a double objective: to get North Vietnam to stop supporting the Viet Cong and to raise morale in South Vietnam. This began a new stage in the war. The bombardments were the subject of many discussions at Chong Wen, and meetings and demonstrations were organized in support of North Vietnam, and the school gradually filled with posters denouncing the imperialist aggressions or demanding pupils' solidarity with their comrades, victims of capitalist armies. Sergio shared his classmates' indignation. As soon as the school created the Youth Battalion in Support of Vietnam, he joined, and shortly afterwards participated in the battalion's first mission: marching to Hanoi. It was a symbolic act, of course, in which the young people would cover the distance that separated Hanoi and Peking, but they would do so on the school track: at six kilometres a day, they calculated, it would take them three months to arrive. And that's what they did.

During the course of that year, daily life at the school changed. Sergio's year – boys who were all about fifteen years old – had begun to receive military training. Twice a week, Sergio went through a demanding training in the handling of firearms and the use of grenades, and learned hand-to-hand combat and how to charge with bayonets. They had target practice in a nearby yard, where, depending on the political climate in the city and the school, the targets were grotesque caricatures or enlarged photographs of Lyndon Johnson or Brezhnev or Chiang Kai-shek. During that year – that is, during the long march from Peking to Hanoi – Sergio discovered a fervour he'd never felt until then. Was he one of them? Yes, he had turned into an excellent student, and spent long hours studying the grammar and calligraphy of his new language, scrutinizing its secrets, investigating its history; and its history was also that of the culture that had taken him in, which was gradually becoming less impenetrable. Yes, all that was true, but Sergio realized that his studies and the manoeuvres, the grammar and the target practice, were only a means to something else. He wrote some private notes during those days: *The future is tangible. We breathe it, we dream it, we name it. The future belongs to us all and between us all we are making it. The future begins now.*

Shortly before the summer, when the students had walked to Hanoi, Fausto and Luz Elena travelled to Colombia. It was one of the privileges established in the contract for teachers: specialists could return to their country every two years with their spouse, though not with their children. So Sergio and Marianella were registered for a summer camp at the beach of Beidaihe, which in other times had been a bourgeois resort and was now the summer headquarters of the Central Committee of the Communist Party. Their parents were not away for long: just three weeks. But they were three active weeks that would mark the whole family for ever.

The first thing Fausto did when he arrived in Colombia was get in touch with the founders of the Party. Of course, what he called "the Party" had a longer name at that stage: the Marxist–Leninist–Maoist Thought Communist Party. The founders, among others, were two old acquaintances: Pedro León Arboleda, that tall man who had praised the poetic talent of the people of Medellín (and who was in some way responsible for the four happy years Fausto had spent there), and a certain Pedro Vásquez, who had joined a group of dissidents from the Communist Party when the differences between Peking and Moscow began to make coexistence impossible. A breach opened between the Muscovite line, the so-called *mamertos*, and the pro-China line, of which Fausto had become an involuntary ambassador. Fausto had lived a revolutionary life for two years, yes, and he had seen the successes of the Chinese revolution up close (and was prepared to keep quiet about the failures), but he was also bringing two important missives: one was an invitation to Camilo Torres, the Liberation Theology priest who had grown close to the Guevarista guerrillas, to visit communist China and see it first hand; the other was a documentary about China that Fausto Cabrera himself had dubbed into Spanish. In the documentary, Fausto also took charge of reading, in his deep voice, the writing of Comrade Mao – the famous 1934 letter, for example: "A single spark can ignite a whole field" – and reciting his poems with the same moving tones he'd used years earlier to recite poems by Machado and Miguel Hernández.

Soon dawn will break in the east.
Do not say "You start too early";

> *Crossing these blue hills adds nothing to one's years,*
> *The landscape here is beyond compare.*

Or this other one, "Mount Liupan", which Mao wrote after arriving with the Red Army at the end of the Long March:

> *If we fail to reach the Great Wall we are not men*
> *We who have already measured twenty thousand li*
> *High on the crest of Mount Liupan*
> *Red banners wave freely in the west wind.*

After several interviews with the leaders, the Party entrusted Fausto with a special mission: to develop some artistic and literary didactic material that would use the principles of their ideology (Marxist–Leninist–Maoist thought) and apply it to Colombian reality. That's how his militancy began. He contacted Camilo Torres. He explained the intentions of the Chinese and got Torres to receive him in his own house, on the south side of the Parque Nacional. Fausto arrived to see him with a journalist, the Colombian correspondent of a Chinese television station, because his intention was to record an interview with the priest and take it back to China. They spoke about Marxism and Christianity and Fidel Castro and Mao Tse-tung, and Torres was always equal to what Fausto had requested: a conversation *sans* cassock. "Yes, I knew you were in China," Torres said after they'd finishing recording. "You have to tell me what it is like." But he added that he could not accept the invitation, unfortunately: his commitments in Colombia, as much to his parishioners as to the revolution, were urgent and inescapable. "I have another proposal," he said. "Be my liaison with Peking. I'm very interested in making contact with China. Please do thank them for the invitation and tell them I would very much like to come and visit them. We'll do that later, when things have moved on a bit here. Yes, tell them that," he said. "As soon as I can I'll come and see them."

But he did not. Fausto and Luz Elena had returned to Peking and gone back to their life at the Friendship Hotel, and Fausto was immersed in the missions he'd been entrusted with by the Party in Colombia, when they received the news: Camilo Torres had died in combat – his guerrilla unit had ambushed an army patrol – in San Vicente de Chucurí. It was February 15, 1966. Sergio would remember it well, as he'd barely even heard of the guerrilla priest, and his father's grief took him by surprise. He hadn't seen him so sad since the death of Uncle Felipe, and that was the first clue that something invisible, but very powerful, had happened to him in Colombia.

Fausto had come back with his revolutionary vocation stronger than ever. Sergio saw him start a politico-military course, as the Chinese leaders called it, and spend the days studying the history of the revolution and Mao's thought. On Saturday nights he would often be waiting for Sergio with a text in his hand. "I need you to translate this for me," he'd say, and Sergio would notice an intensity in his gaze he hadn't seen before. There was no Saturday dinner or Sunday lunch when they didn't talk about what was going on in Colombia, about the Farc guerrillas, about the ELN guerrillas and Camilo Torres, and also the disagreements those guerrilla organizations had with the Marxist–Leninist–Maoist Communist Party. His father did still get up at five in the morning for his session of t'ai chi ch'uan, and did still get together with the friends he had at the Friendship Hotel – the Arancibias, the poet Cabrera and the ancient Castelo, a grouchy Spaniard whose chief occupation seemed to be asking when Franco would fall – but it was obvious that his head was elsewhere. Later, when he announced to his children the decision that he and Luz Elena had just made, Sergio thought he should have seen it coming.

It was a Sunday in March. Luz Elena had invited some of the directors of Peking University's school of languages to the Friendship Hotel. Sergio was at the hotel, as usual on a Sunday, and so was his sister. Luz Elena offered her guests coffee and they declined more vociferously than necessary, and then they explained that coffee was a stimulant and therefore a drug, and that a true communist never took drugs. One of them, younger than the others and with literary aspirations, talked of the writer Lu Xun, whose work he admired, and how Lu Xun had been a comrade many years before the revolution, a genuine socialist, and nevertheless he was famous for having enjoyed coffee.

"Proof," the young man said, "that bourgeois influences can reach the most committed."

Sergio was sitting with them, listening to them talk and occasionally participating in the conversation, and saw them out and said goodbye in his perfect Chinese. And when the guests had gone, Sergio told Luz Elena he was going to go and find his friends to play ping-pong for a while. "Well, that can wait," his mother said. "Your father wants to talk to you both." They went to find Marianella, who was listening to music in her room, and a few minutes later they were back down, in one of the many gardens, where Fausto was waiting for them with some papers in his hand. He told them the time had come to make a decision; that things had changed over the last few months, as much in China as in Colombia; and that they, Luz Elena and Fausto, had reached the conclusion that it was time to go back.

"But don't worry," Fausto clarified. "The time has come for us, not for you. You two are staying in China."

"It's better that way," said Luz Elena. "You've got your school here, which is really good, and opportunities you wouldn't have there. It's safe here, as well. It'll be better for all of us."

"If you agree," Fausto said, "I can get you a grant. So you can study at the best place."

"Where?" Sergio said.

"So you carry on getting the education you've been getting. You'll stay here and continue studying. Of course, there will be certain changes."

"Changes?" Marianella said. "What changes?"

"What you two have is a privilege," Fausto continued. "Not everyone can choose what they want to study, right?" Then he looked at Sergio. "If you want to study cinema, if that's really what you want, you have a place here: at the Peking School of Cinema. That's confirmed. Does that not seem like a privilege?"

"Yes, it's a privilege," Sergio said. "But what changes?"

They found out weeks later, when Fausto announced with a smile that he had obtained the promised grant, after much effort. Sergio and Marianella would finish their education in China, he told them, just as they'd requested; and Sergio thought it would be ungrateful to remind him that they hadn't actually asked for anything, it had all been their father's idea. But Fausto presented it all as if it were a gift he was giving his children. The China–Latin America Friendship Association, he told them, had awarded them an exceptional grant, and he was not exaggerating. "You are so lucky!" he said. "I would have loved this." The grant included the right to study at Chong Wen, a tutor in charge of visiting them once a week to see how everything was going, a monthly allowance of seventy yuan for food and minor expenses and a room each at the Friendship Hotel. But before they had time to be happy about anything, Fausto said:

"But we can't accept the room. This place has good things, but also lots of negative influences. Life isn't like this. You don't go through life signing a piece of paper whenever you want something, as if money doesn't exist. So I moved heaven and earth, called in all my influences and all my contacts, and got them to accept you somewhere else. It's much better. Much, much better."

A few days later they were visiting the Peace Hotel. It was an imposing, sixteen-storey building overlooking Wangfujing Street, right in the city centre, a few blocks from Tiananmen Square. The Communist Party had built it after the revolution, to host the International Peace Congress of 1950, and the administrators must have done something wrong, because the Party had sanctioned them by closing the hotel to the public. At that moment the hotel was uninhabited, but Sergio and Marianella would live there when their parents returned to Colombia. Sergio did not know what debts his father had called in or what strings he'd pulled, but that's how it was: that was the place the authorities had granted him for his children to stay while he was not there. "It's still weeks away," Fausto said. "We're leaving at the end of May. But there's a lot to prepare. We wanted you to know as soon as possible."

"I don't understand," Sergio said. "There's not going to be anybody else there?"

"Nobody else," his father confirmed. "You'll be the only two guests. The whole hotel just for you two."

Marianella still didn't understand. "But who's going to be with us?"

"Nobody," Fausto repeated. "The workers, of course. You are young people now, not children. If you need anything, if you have problems to resolve, the tutor will be available for that. And in any case, we'll keep in touch."

Then he reminded them of the procedure for writing letters to Colombia. They'd used it from the first day, since they lived a fictional life in Europe (their passports did not allow them to be where they now were); Fausto had made an arrangement with an Italian guitarist called Giorgio Zucchetti, who was coming to the end of his time in China and returning home. Giorgio had agreed to receive the letters the Cabreras wrote in Peking, put them in new envelopes and send them on to Colombia. This would go on working, Fausto explained, and the strategy was doubly necessary now that Fausto had joined the Communist Party and communications could not fall into the wrong hands.

"Write to us care of Giorgio," Fausto told them, "and be careful what you say. Everything is going to be fine."

"And what are you going to do?" Sergio asked.

Luz Elena had walked a short distance away and was looking at the gardens, as if she already knew the answer and it hurt her to hear it. Sergio thought she was crying and trying to hide her tears.

"We're going to unite with the people," Fausto said. "We're

going to contribute to the revolution." He paused and then added: "*Vive la vida de suerte*".

But he didn't finish the sentence.

The pool at the Friendship Hotel opened early that year; as in all the previous years, Marianella was one of the first guests to swim in it. She was fourteen years old and so rebellious that she needed to let off steam with physical activity, and the hotel swimming pool, with its seven-metre Olympic diving board, became her favourite place. So there she was, not swimming so much as doing contortions in a corner, when the Crooks came in. This was also a predictable event every spring, as David Crook, the father, was an expert swimmer. Fausto, who didn't give anyone more than his due, said that he could swim across the Jarama River with one arm tied behind his back. His wife, a blonde Canadian with a soft gaze who'd been born in China, was every bit as good as he was, and between the two of them had passed on the swimming bug to their three sons. That's why they frequented the Friendship Hotel, in spite of the mother and sons being Chinese by birth; their Western physiques allowed them to use the facilities, and there were none better in the city. That Saturday afternoon they walked into the pool area like a family of ducks, David first, then Isabel, and behind them, their sons in order of height: Carl, Michael and Paul. That's how it always went: they arrived, did their hundred lengths and left, and their intention not to mix more than necessary with the foreigners in that bourgeois oasis, where everything seemed to be for sale, was obvious: they came from a world apart, purer and more dignified. There were all sorts of legends told about David, but not even Fausto had been able to confirm them in their occasional conversations. It was known that he'd fought in the Spanish Civil War, and that was enough to win him more prestige than almost anyone else had. But David didn't talk about his life and the Cabreras didn't dare ask him to.

In any case, there were the Crooks that warm spring afternoon. Marianella saw them arrive – just as she had seen them the previous year, every weekend that the pool was open – but this time she felt something new or different was happening. It wasn't, of course, simple curiosity about the lives of their parents. What was it, then? Carl, who was about to turn eighteen, had become a creature of insolent beauty, or maybe Marianella was noticing it for the first time, and seeing him climb up to the diving board, look up, see him jump and spin skilfully through the air and slice neatly into the water, left her with a pain in her chest she'd never felt. She tried to speak to him later, when he was resting on the side of the pool, but the experience, she thought later, was very much like invisibility. The afternoon ended earlier than planned.

As the days went by, Marianella realized she hadn't stopped thinking about him. Carl was three years older than her and almost two heads taller, and besides, he had shown an insulting lack of interest in her, but none of that was a reason to be daunted. Marianella had seen him read whole books over a weekend in his spare time, passing his eyes over the pages not like one who reads, but like someone looking without interest through an album of photographs, and then get involved in arguments in English with the other teenagers in the hotel, who ended up tired of all they didn't know and went to play ping-pong. Shortly before the encounter in the pool, Fausto had tried to convince Marianella to read the *The Communist Manifesto* in an Argentine translation, as it didn't seem possible for his children to go on living without having read Marx and Engels; Marianella tried with her usual stubbornness, but it was as if she had left the Spanish language behind in Bogotá or, what was worse, in her eleven-year-old self's Bogotá. Now, guessing that it could be useful, she tried to read the book again and failed again. But then she had a revelation: Spanish was not her language, Chinese was. So she spent the week reading Mao at night, without telling anybody and much less saying why she wanted to read him, and on the next Saturday she strolled confidently over to Carl where he was resting after his hundred lengths and said:

"I need you to explain some points."

That's how they began to spend time together. While David swam a hundred lengths of front crawl, Carl explained to Marianella the difference between bringing the revolution about with the peasants and undertaking it with the proletariat, between ideological theory and revolutionary praxis, between the line of the masses and the Bolshevik model of popular participation in the Party. Little by little he began to discover that the fourteen-year-old Colombian girl, younger sister of that guy he didn't particularly like, was actually a force of nature, and that she lived in a permanent confrontation with the world: with her father, who watched over her as if he owned her, with her mother, who acted as if she favoured her brother; with the Friendship Hotel, whose residents had begun to strike her as mere capitalists who lived in an unforgivable contradiction. Was that a friendship? Yes, thought Marianella: the gap had been bridged and Carl no longer thought the

Cabreras were a bourgeois family like the rest of them. He invited her to spend time with his friends. He recommended books and she read them quickly and badly, memorizing enough to impress him. But she was the first one to be surprised when she realized she was reading Mao with genuine interest, and not just to earn some hours of conversation with Carl.

Fausto did not approve of this new relationship. "You're deviating," he said. "This is not what we came to China for." She did everything possible so that her rebellion would not go unnoticed. One of those weekends Carl invited her to go rowing at the Summer Palace, just the two of them, in that friendship that was slowly turning into something else. There they were, rowing a boat in the middle of the lake, when they saw Fausto, rowing his own, bigger boat with three students from his Spanish class.

"What are you doing here?" Fausto said.

"Boating, Papá," she replied. "Same as you."

Fausto did not make a scene, and Marianella never knew if his restraint was due to the presence of his students or the respect he had for David Crook. But at dinner that evening – at the Friendship Hotel's international restaurant, while the band played boleros in the background – Fausto took advantage of the fact that Sergio and Luz Elena had not yet come down to make a statement.

"You are not old enough to be doing those things."

"What things?" Marianella demanded brazenly. "What can't I be doing?"

"At your age a person has friends, but no more than friends. And I see that something more is going on here, and I don't like it."

"Well, it doesn't matter if *you* don't like it," she said. "It's enough that I like it."

"Don't be insolent," Fausto said. "Boyfriends are for eighteen-year-olds. So I don't want you to keep seeing that boy."

Marianella lowered her voice. "What is clear is that I learn more with him than with you."

"What are you saying?"

"That I'm not wasting my time with him, Papá. That he's the only exciting thing that has happened to me in three years of living here. You're going to Colombia. Why do I have to live by your rules, if you're on the other side of the world? You decided that we'd stay here. You decided that the Chinese revolution would educate us better than you could. And do you know what? I agree. Yeah, the truth is I couldn't agree more. Everything I need is here. Everything I need to learn, China can teach me."

Then she swore. But she swore in Chinese so Fausto couldn't understand.

Far away from there, far from the Friendship Hotel and the swimming pool where Marianella had met Carl Crook, far from Fausto Cabrera and his fights with his adolescent daughter, the country was shaking. The failure of the Great Leap Forward, with its millions of victims, had cost Mao Tse-tung the leadership of his party. The positions of power had stayed in the hands of his political enemies: the president, Liu Shaoqi, and the secretary general of the Party, Deng Xiaoping. But Mao, who still had the support of military leaders such as Lin Biao, of the People's Liberation Army, dismissed those who had criticized him and launched a strategy to recover power. The ideals of the revolution, he said, were in peril: threatened by traitors and revisionists, and it was necessary to protect them. In 1963, Lin Biao collected all of Mao's most important speeches and published them in a little red book that reached the hands of all the faithful. But it was not enough, or it wasn't yet. In the summer of 1965, while Sergio and Marianella were on the beaches of Beidaihe, Mao made the decision to take refuge in Shanghai, since the hostility towards him in Peking had become overt. From Shanghai he called for resistance: the bourgeoisie and the reactionaries were threatening the revolution. It was essential to protect it. It was time to go on the offensive.

It was a miraculous strategy. In April, with the first flowers, the *People's Liberation Army Daily* called on revolutionaries to defend Mao's thought and to participate actively in the Great Proletarian Cultural Revolution. That's how the movement was baptized. A session of the politburo in mid-May turned into a declaration in support of Mao Tse-tung, who was already back in Peking, and also contained accusations against the class enemies that had crept into the Party, and called them revisionists and counter-revolutionaries, and warned the public of a latent threat: a dictatorship of the bourgeoisie. Now the people had to defend itself, and for that the traitors must be identified, brought to light and punished mercilessly.

IX

Sergio knew something serious was going on when his comrades told him of their decision that day: they would not stand to greet their teacher. That was breaking with a sacred custom, the protocol that when the teacher crossed the threshold of the classroom, a monitor would shout in the voice of a military commander and the pupils would all stand up, face forward and salute. The teacher would inspect their clothing, their haircuts and the cleanliness of their faces, and confirm that the group was correctly ready to attend class. Two things surprised Sergio on the day of the rebellion: first, that that ritual of respect went to hell in the blink of an eye; second, that the teacher in question did not dare, not even with a raised eyebrow, to show his disagreement or protest. On one of those days, a classmate said to Sergio:

"You can smell it in the air. Something serious is going to happen here."

He was not wrong. Everyone in Peking was talking the same way: in the street, at the Friendship Hotel, at the Foreign Languages Institute. A few days after Marianella ran into her father on the lake at the Summer Palace, the Cabreras arrived at the Peace Hotel. Sergio and his sister settled into their rooms, one each, and marvelled again at being the only guests in a sixteen-storey hotel: how had their father secured this privilege for them? Fausto introduced them to Li, the woman who would be their tutor: a young militant convinced of the goodness of the Party and a guarantee of defence or protection against any bourgeois influence. When they asked her what was going on, her face lit up:

"Another step forward," she said.

The farewell took place a few days later. Sergio and Marianella went to the Friendship Hotel to hug their father and watch their mother cry and listen to advice and recommendations. Luz Elena gave Marianella a small bag with their leftover yuan – a generous quantity – and Fausto took an envelope out of his pocket. It was a bundle of pages of thin, almost translucent paper, which Sergio received in his two hands, like an offering.

"It's not for reading right now," Fausto said. "But soon. Promise?"

"We promise," Sergio said.

"I want you to know this," Fausto said. "I am proud of you both."

From the steps of the Friendship Hotel, standing under the green roofs, brother and sister watched their parents get into the taxi that would take them to the airport, and knew that the plane wouldn't take them to Colombia, but to Canton, and there they'd get a train to Hong Kong and then board an Italian ocean liner. They didn't take their eyes off the taxi as it drove away along the large white flagstone track that led to the avenue, between enormous cypresses and the occasional cherry tree lost among the magnolias that Luz Elena loved so much.

Then they returned to the Peace Hotel, to its echoing dining room and deserted corridors and spectral silence. By then they had begun talking to each other in Chinese, and in Chinese Marianella said:

"Very strange, don't you think?"

That night, after dinner, Sergio took the papers out of the envelope. "We promised Papá," he said to Marianella. "You promised," she said. "I didn't do anything." They opened the balcony doors, to let some air in, and Sergio began to read.

I am writing these lines for the following purpose: when either of you have some problem, some difficulty or setback, when the natural contradictions that always arise turn up, when you are not sure which line to follow with respect to an event, or you do not know what attitude to assume, or you are indecisive or have some doubt or wonder what your father would say about something or what your father would advise in this case, then you will have recourse to these lines; you can read the part that talks about particular things and that relate to the problem in question. Thus, it will serve you as a prompt, like a resource to be consulted, nothing more. It is not a magic wand or anything like that, it does not have an answer to everything, nor is it where you will find concrete solutions to specific cases or where everything is foreseen. No. None of that. Listen carefully: YOU TWO HAVE TO RELY ON YOUR OWN STRENGTHS. All the help you need you shall have, all the advice, all the guidance necessary. But this will be no more than a simple PROMPT. You have to be the ones to resolve your own problems, your own issues, your own decisions, in accordance with your basic moral and political principles.

I see revolutionary resolve in Sergio Fausto, revolutionary ideals, in a word, certain revolutionary consciousness, even when it is far from mature. I also see in him a great desire for progress and investigation. A sense, in general, of what is just and unjust, a certain maturity. All this together with great kindness. And these qualities have been demonstrated to us by deeds. He does have faults, which he will have to struggle against firmly to overcome – this is mainly owing to his bourgeois education – tendencies sometimes to abandon the struggle, bouts of pessimism, individualistic tendencies, a certain class egocentrism and feeling sometimes a bit superior. A series of very deep-rooted petit-bourgeois habits.

Marianella: sensitive and firmly resolved to reject evil, injustice and therefore exploitation and cruelty. Her very nature makes her basically revolutionary, as long as she has political and class guidance. She is lively, curious, kind and, when she decides to be, firm. She does not tolerate injustice. I have always thought, and especially recently, that Marianella will surprise us. She must overcome her insecurity and lack of confidence, which she has been overcoming in a very clear and telling way. She has to overcome other problems for which she will need to deploy all her willpower. These problems are the logical results of her petit-bourgeois education and mentality, such as her excessive idealism and also her individualism and subjectivism. That decadent, degenerate and bourgeois romanticism. (Here I must recommend that you try to reject all those books and magazines that you like, because they are true "poisonous weeds" which have caused and will continue to cause you incalculable damage. Do not forget this advice, as long as you do not renounce all that, your progress will be very difficult, as will your ideological

transformation.) To tell you the truth, in the last month she has
progressed quite a bit in this as well.

Summing up the positive on one side and the negative on
the other, both of you have more of the former than the latter and
it counts for more as well, taking into consideration the totally
petit-bourgeois antecedents and education you've naturally had.
Seeing your progress and the changes since our arrival in China
listed above, I can reach the conclusion that you can both be
trusted, that you can rely on your own strengths.

Now I'll try to tell you about different aspects that, as I
said, might serve as a prompt.

There were twelve pages, twelve long pages of foolscap
paper with forty-five lines on each, which Sergio read out loud
to Marianella and then took to his room to read again later.
His sister had not liked it at all: "Don't count on me to reread
that." It was all there, from how to tackle family problems to
a long discussion on the objective of their stay in China, as
well as financial business and good manners when writing.
There were twenty exhaustive points, which Sergio kept as an
instruction manual, and to which he returned countless times
during that strange summer, as the city began to boil.

What is the objective of staying in China? There might be two:
a) To study and prepare intellectually to become in the future a
"worthy man" as they say. This means trying to stand out, earn
money, fame, etc. All this, naturally, at the cost of the misery and
suffering of others, of the exploitation of man by man. b) The
other objective is to achieve a proletarian ideological and senti-
mental transformation and prepare to serve society, the people

and the revolution. Failure to enter the path of transformation means staying halfway down the road. To be a "revolutionary" with a bourgeois mentality means being a revisionist in practice. Going back to Colombia before having firmly begun that transformation would seem to me to have simply wasted your time in China, and not achieved the objective. In my opinion, if you enter into that well-grounded, authentic transformation, you will be ready for a possible return.

The first to react to Mao's call were the students. One day, after class, a group went round the classrooms with paper and ink. The *dazibao*, posters of aggressive propaganda in large characters, had begun to appear on the walls of the city a few months earlier, when the students of Peking University denounced the institution for falling under the control of bourgeois counter-revolutionaries. Mao, who had understood the power the students' support gave him, praised them in the press and contributed his own poster, a tacit attack on Liu Shaoqi and Deng Xiaoping. After that, the *dazibao* became ubiquitous. And now they had arrived at Chong Wen school. The students listened to the leaders' slogans and captured them with thick brush strokes, sometimes in arguments a dozen lines long, sometimes in a few ideograms. Sergio made several posters that afternoon and went to put them up on the walls himself. Later he found out that Marianella had also made hers. At school the atmosphere was electric. But the most serious thing happened the next day.

The drawing teacher, a thin, bespectacled man who all the pupils liked, had begun to discuss in his class the concept of aerodynamics. That's what he was talking about when he spontaneously compared the Soviet MiG, a combat plane designed in 1939 and produced in small quantities after the war, with the F-4 Phantom II, which McDonnell Douglas had brought into service in 1960. The two planes, Soviet and American, had participated in the Vietnam War, but the teacher had no reason to think of that when he praised the design of the Phantom II and dared to say it was better. An uncomfortable silence fell over the classroom. "But that is the enemy's plane," a pupil said after a moment. Sergio didn't know if he had realized his mistake, but the teacher tried briefly to defend himself: "Yes, it is. But its design is better. For example, it is faster. Why is it faster?" But his attempts fell into a void. The class was indignant. A murmur of disapproval grew ever louder. And that was when a pupil said: "If he prefers the enemy's weapons, he must be an enemy."

"Yes, he's an enemy," others said. "Traitor!" a voice shouted, and then: "Counter-revolutionary!" Before Sergio's eyes, the pupils advanced threateningly towards the man, who grabbed his things as best he could and left the classroom. But the group caught up with him in the corridor and cornered him against a wall. "You scorn our army," someone said. "No, that's not true, that's not what I meant," the teacher began, but to no effect. "Yes, it is true!" they shouted. "You scorn our heroes!" Sergio, who had followed the others, saw a grimace of fear on the teacher's face when the first gobs of spit landed on him. "Revisionist!" they shouted. "Bourgeois!" The teacher covered his face, tried to say something, but his voice was inaudible among the insults. Someone then threw the first punch, and the teacher's glasses flew through the air. "No, no," the man cried. Others punched him as well: in the face and body.

Then, as Sergio watched in terror, the teacher collapsed. Sergio had wanted to intervene, tell the rest that it was enough, that it was too much, but the power of the crowd swept him along and the words wouldn't form in his mouth. It was unbelievable: his classmates, the pupils with whom he had shared hours and days and conversations had turned into a ferocious, many-legged beast that was now kicking the vulnerable body of the drawing teacher. From his fallen body came faltering cries, moans and groans, but the kicking did not stop. And that was when Sergio, who had remained behind the others, saw himself make his way through his classmates and get in a kick as well. It was a timid kick, not to the ribs, but to the leg, and it was not followed by others. Sergio pulled back and after a while saw that the rest of them backed away as well, leaving the teacher lying on the ground, still, his arms covering his head.

He felt so guilty that the next day he hung his own *dazibao* on one of the walls at school, with a message of contrition: *This should not be done.* He knew that only his being a foreigner earned him a bit of tolerance, and otherwise he would have been considered a dissident or a traitor, and humiliated and beaten like the teacher. Yes, that should not be done; but Sergio had done it. His poster was ignored. In any case, the guilt remained; and the memory of the injustice he'd committed was so painful, and the impotence at the injustice was so uncomfortable, that Sergio did not speak of it to anyone: not to his parents, who luckily were not there, much less to his sister, who might have seen it all from a distance. Sergio found out later. Marianella had heard, as had everyone at school, about what happened to the drawing teacher, and when Sergio regretted what had happened – "Poor guy," he said – his sister's expression hardened.

"Poor?" she said almost with disgust. "Why poor? He was an enemy and he deserved it."

Marianella had begun to spend Saturday and Sunday at the Crooks' house. She would leave mid-morning and ride her bicycle through the streets crammed with Maoists, and arrive at the residences of the Foreign Languages Institute like someone coming home. They knew her as the daughter of a specialist who had taught there, but everyone knew that Fausto Cabrera had lived at the Friendship Hotel, and not everyone kept their negative opinions on that subject to themselves. The Crooks, luckily, did not judge her. They took Marianella in, not as their eldest son's girlfriend, but as if she were the daughter they'd never had, and they opened a space for her alongside Carl's brothers, so their apartment turned into her weekend home. It was on the ground floor of the four-storey, square, dark and ugly building where the professors lived. The place was too small for a family of five, or maybe that sensation was produced by the bookcases lining every single wall. Marianella had never seen so many books together in so little space, and in so many languages, and the first thing she thought was that her brother would be happy here; she, on the other hand, had so far solely taken an interest in books to get Carl to take her seriously.

The walls only left room for one small window, but that was enough for David. He said that before, during the first years in his post, the window looked out on a view of the countryside that refreshed the eye, but now they'd put up a building that barely left a glimpse of sky. The window faced west, and on summer evenings the setting sun would shine in for two hours, as if made just for him. "I don't need anything more," he would say. Sitting beside the window, in a Russian chair, he would greet Marianella: "Ah, the Republican's daughter." Sometimes he'd leave the seat free so Isabel could teach her to embroider; other times, especially if it was a Sunday, he would invite her to sit down and ask her about her family and the Spanish Civil War. Marianella told him about Uncle Felipe, of whom she knew nothing, except what her father had told Sergio, not her, in after-dinner conversations, and David listened to her with a fascination that did not seem feigned or paternalistic. And one of those days, a Sunday at the beginning of that violent summer, he began to tell her about his own years in the war. They weren't actually talking about Spain, but David had asked Marianella the first question all Westerners asked each other in Peking.

"And what brought your family to China?"

Marianella explained what she knew, and did so fully aware she did not have all the information. She spoke of her father's work in Bogotá: his life in the theatre and then on television, his clash with the market or what Marianella called the market: the forces that had wanted to convert an artistic medium into a machine to sell detergent. She spoke about her father's rebellion; of his refusal to lower himself to performing in cheap soap operas; of the accusations of communism in a country with a reactionary soul, victim of US imperialism. She spoke, finally, of the Arancibias, instruments of fate, and of the work her father had done in Peking until the moment he decided to return to Colombia. That was when Isabel interrupted.

"Wait a second. They left you here? Your parents are not

planning to come back, and they left you and your brother alone here?"

Marianella had never suspected her parents' decision might be questionable, much less viewed badly. Returning to their own country to work for the revolution: what could be more comprehensible for a family of convinced communists like the Crooks? But Isabel's silent judgement was hanging in the air of the apartment, and it was such an uncomfortable moment that Marianella sought a way to change the subject. The handiest was a reciprocal question.

"And you, David? Why are you here? What brought you to China?"

"Well, this will appeal to you, the Republican's daughter," David said. "I came because of Spain."

"From the war?"

"Dad, she's not interested in that," Carl said.

"Of course it interests me," Marianella said. "I'm very interested."

"In any case, they are old stories," David said.

"So are my father's," Marianella said. "I've been hearing old stories since I was born."

"OK," David said. "Well, maybe one day we'll talk about that. We have time, don't we? I think you're going to keep coming over here."

That evening the conversation moved from the apartment and its Russian chairs to the Institute restaurant. Marianella had understood – her instinct told her – that showing interest in David in front of his son was like reciting Mao, like having read the Communist Manifesto. She realized that Carl was looking at her differently: it was as if the temperature had

184

changed. That's what she was thinking when, as she returned to the hotel, riding her bike through the nocturnal streets where the Red Guards slept, she found Sergio waiting for her in the lobby like a worried father, and, like a worried father, he told her that this could not happen again.

"It'll happen whenever I want," Marianella said.

"But it's dangerous," Sergio said. "They are cutting off women's plaits. They'll take a person's shoes if they don't like them."

He was talking about the Red Guards, an extensive student organization who recognized Mao as their supreme commander and had taken on their shoulders the defence or strict application of the Cultural Revolution. Mao had welcomed them a few weeks earlier, in Tiananmen Square, when he made an appearance to wave to them in the olive-green uniform he hadn't worn for several years. It was said that he greeted more than a thousand guards personally that day, and even put on a red armband, which had become the movement's symbol. In Peking the Red Guards were a many-headed serpent, and it was never easy for young people – impulsive, inexperienced – to know whom to obey. It did not matter: they obeyed Mao; they carried their leader's speeches in their pockets at all times, in what they had come to call simply the Little Red Book. They were quick to resort to violence when punishing a dissident, anyone who had been accused of revisionism or counter-revolutionary behaviour; and, most of all, there were a lot of them, and they had started to arrive in Peking from every corner of China, lured by the idea of seeing Mao, even from a distance. And when they gathered in Tiananmen Square, they were so loud that Sergio could hear their revolutionary chants and the sound of their feet on the street from the Peace Hotel if he opened the window.

"They're not going to do anything to me," Marianella said.

"How can you be so sure?"

"Because I'm like them. I don't have long hair, or plaits, because I'm like them. I don't have bourgeois shoes because I'm like them. I'm from here, even if I don't look it. Same with my boyfriend, for example, same as his brothers and his dad."

"What did you say? Your boyfriend?"

"Well, yeah," she said. "Carl is going to be my boyfriend." And she added: "He lives in the same world as me. The world where he lives, that world is mine as well."

In the capitalist world it is common and even natural for people your age to have boyfriends or girlfriends. Why? In the first place the young have no ideals, no true worries, they spend their lives thinking only of that, dependent on that. It's the focus of their interest. It is a corrupted society that pins its greatest hopes on passion and sex. We already know the results: disgrace, solitude, anguish, terror, etc. What is the next step? Either jump in and marry young with no maturity, tying yourself down to duties that will prevent you from making the most of your life, your ideals, as well as later problems, or enter into an atmosphere around which the basic fact of life is that, gradually falling into a degeneration where the only important thing in life is sex.

The days went by and Chong Wen School did not go back to normal. After the drawing teacher other victims of the Cultural Revolution followed, or, to put it another way, more counter-revolutionaries received their well-deserved punishment. First was the doctor who was in charge of the infirmary, who, according to the students' accusations, had taken a small store of medicines home with her intending to treat bourgeois patients. Then came the turn of the principal, an older man whose loyalty to the Party had never been questioned, but among whose papers someone – nobody ever knew who – had found property title deeds. They were ancient titles for lands that had already been turned over to the state, and had no value. The principal alleged that he kept them as souvenirs, but the students agreed that he was waiting for the return of the capitalist and feudal system, and he was expelled from the school. The students did not just let him leave. They made him a dunce's hat that said *I Love Feudalism*, forcing him to wear it as he left the school and accompanying him for several blocks, so other Red Guards would point to him, laugh in his face (but with angry, hateful laughter) and come up to him to insult him.

By that time, Sergio was one of them. At the beginning of the Cultural Revolution, Chong Wen School had three distinct groups of Red Guards, separated by slight ideological differences, but one of them – the largest and the one with the most respected or feared young leaders – ended up devouring the second, and the rivalry with the third was only accentuated. In the midst of these power struggles, Sergio understood he could not remain apart; he wrote a long and spirited letter to request membership in the more powerful organization; a week later he received notification of his acceptance and was told when to report to a classroom covered in *dazibao* for a brief ceremony. There he was presented with his red armband, where a six-digit number, his personal code, seemed to shine under the name of the group. Sergio put it on his arm (it was too big: he would have to adjust it) and felt magically powerful, as if backed by an invisible but omnipresent power.

In June they suspended classes. Sergio began to go to Chong Wen only to make *dazibao* or write out a proclamation or join a demonstration in protest against something. The centre of Peking was another city, louder, more agitated, where it was normal to meet marching guards surrounding groups of accused, sad men and women who walked with their eyes glued to the broken ground wearing dunce's hats and signs around their necks. *I am a Class Enemy. I am an Infiltrated Capitalist. I wear this sign for living at the service of the bourgeoisie.* It was known that guards were sacking museums and temples and libraries to advance the destruction of what they called the "Four Olds": old customs, old culture, old habits, old ideas. The streets Sergio went along to get to Chong Wen (always by bicycle, almost always in his olive-green uniform) began to fill with portraits of Mao and posters with phrases from the Little Red Book. Sometimes the name that had been on a corner for as lomg as anyone could remember was suddenly changed to a new and revolutionary one, and Sergio had to pay special attention not to go the wrong way.

On one of those days, Sergio was on his way to the school when he heard shots fired, clearly coming from that direction. He got off his bike to be able to hear better and decide if it was dangerous to proceed. Yes, they were shots, and yes, they were coming from the street where Chong Wen School was located, but he carried on to try to get a closer view of the situation. When he turned a corner he bumped into a group of soldiers from the People's Liberation Army who stopped him roughly and demanded he go with them. Sergio, as happened in other situations, took a moment to remember that he was not Chinese, and realize that it might seem suspicious to the soldiers that a Westerner should be there so calmly and dressed as a Red Guard. "Are you a student at Chong Wen School?" they asked. "Why? Since when?" They asked for his identification and address, and with whom he lived and why he was in China, and Sergio answered as best he could.

"In the Peace Hotel?" a soldier said. "But that place is empty."

"It's not empty. We live there."

"But there are no guests there."

"There are two. Me and my sister. You can come there with me if you want and see for yourselves."

But he did not manage to convince them. And Sergio, for his part, did not manage to understand what was going on at the school, beyond the obvious disturbances. It was only later, talking to his group of Red Guards, that he could get a complete picture of what had happened. That morning, his comrades had decided to take over the school: carry out a coup d'état against the third group, who they considered mere puppets who defended the old hierarchies. It would all have gone no further than a dust-up among adolescents if the two groups of Red Guards had not attacked the headquarters of the China Militia, taking more than a hundred rifles and enough ammunition to last several days. Thus armed, they had begun a pitiless battle on the football field. Bullets flew in all directions. That's why the army was nearby: they had come to *pacify* the school. And Sergio, of course, seemed suspicious to them. He asserted that he was neither a spy nor an infiltrator, that he was a Red Guard just like the rest, but the soldiers seemed determined not to understand anything. Sergio was held for hours, without knowing where Marianella was and unable to let her know where he was. He had to wait until the confrontation had been quelled and the wayward Red Guards had surrendered their weapons before a group of them approached and recognized Sergio and explained to the soldiers who he was. He was an internationalist revolutionary, they told them, as were his parents. The Guards called the Association. Only then did they let him go.

That was the last time he was in the vicinity of his school. That evening, when he rode back to the Peace Hotel, his tutor Li was waiting for him, with a notification: from then on, owing to his being a foreigner, his admission to Chong Wen was forbidden. The same thing applied, of course, to his sister. Sergio protested, for his own sake and for Marianella's; he asked what had happened to proletarian internationalism, what use was wearing his Red Guard uniform in that case, and he complained that the authorities did not take into account his perfect integration into Chinese society, his mastery of the culture and knowledge of the language. "Well, it is precisely your command of the language," said the tutor, "that closes doors to you."

"I don't understand," Sergio said.

"You are a Westerner who speaks Chinese. You are a walking, talking information leak. And here everyone knows that the most important thing is to look after the message."

She was right, of course. Sergio wondered if he would ever stop appearing suspicious, if it were really possible to belong to this place that was not his. He began to pull back, in part to hide from the hostility of this city in turmoil. He spent the time locked in his room, investigating the books Fausto had left behind. So he read the twelve hundred pages of the complete works of Shakespeare in Luis Astrana Marín's translation: he read one play after another, from *Love's Labours Lost* to *The Tempest*, and then *Venus and Adonis*, *The Rape of Lucrece* and every one of the sonnets, and then he went back to the beginning to read the "Introduction for the Spanish-Speaking World". The days were long. In August, the Central Committee of the Communist Party announced its famous Sixteen Points, the mandates of which were scattered across the country by whatever means of communication Maoists could find, from the *PLA Daily* to the *People's Daily*, not to mention radio, comic strips and even pamphlets passed from hand to hand. The bourgeoisie had lost the war, but was still trying to infect the people with its customs and with its way of thinking. It was necessary to change the mentality and crush the ideological enemy infiltrated among us, it was necessary to transform literature and art, bastions of bourgeois ethics; it was necessary to banish the academic authorities of reaction and defend ourselves to the death from antiquated intellectual models. But that was happening out there, on the street, while Sergio was enjoying the work of an Englishman who'd died three and a half centuries ago. With the school closed, letting the days pass idly by at the Peace Hotel, Sergio began to sense that he was wasting valuable time in his revolutionary training.

Meals at the Peace Hotel, during which Sergio and Marianella sat alone in a gigantic dining room to receive the shameful attentions of a small army, were the only things that were repeated day after day. Or almost: every night, before going to sleep, Sergio would read a bit of Fausto's letter as a sort of private ritual, trying to give some shape to his days, looking for answers to his present situation. He seldom went out. He visited the Friendship Shop (which had no relation to the Friendship Hotel, but the idea of friendship was important to the revolution), a place in the diplomatic district where foreigners tended to go to buy things they could not otherwise find, or he invited Marianella on furtive incursions to the hotel that was their former domain, through the corridors of which their Latin American friends still moved, installed in a parallel reality, far from the tough realities of the Cultural Revolution. Their friends' amazement was limitless when Sergio showed them internal newspapers of the Red Guard organizations, where what was really happening in the country was reported and which he translated word for word.

"Is this all really happening?" they asked.

"And more things you don't know about," Sergio told them.

Sergio well understood that the military wanted to keep these things secret, since everything he was translating for his friends was a direct attack on the highest officials of the Communist Party and testament to the profound divisions that were splitting it apart from within. All that was grist to the anti-communist propaganda mill in any part of the world, and there, in the Friendship Hotel, the walls had ears. It was around then that Marianella started to look disapprovingly on the life in that unreal world of Olympic-sized pools and shops where you could buy liqueurs and orchestras that played boleros for nostalgic Latin Americans. She repeated the advice their father had left them: the hotel was a bad influence, real people didn't live like that. But she didn't approve of the Peace Hotel either, not only due to its luxuries, of which there were fewer, but because they were the only guests looked after by so many people. "It's like having servants," she said. One of those days

Sergio heard her come home – she had begun to go out on her own more often – and when he went to say hi, he found her dressed in the uniform of the Red Guard. When had she requested membership, which group had accepted her? Had she got Comrade Li's authorization? On her armband he read a date: June 15. The name of the group, the moment of their establishment? Looking at his sister, he thought of one of Mao's poems that their father liked. It was called "Militia Women":

China's daughters have high-aspiring minds,
They love their battle array, not silks and satins

Overnight Marianella had taken up the Cultural Revolution, or the Cultural Revolution had taken up Marianella. She grew ever more critical of the life they were leading, and she was constantly holding up Carl as an example. "That is a coherent person. He and his whole family. They could have lived like the bourgeoisie at the Friendship Hotel. David has received offers from the Institute. But they prefer to continue to live the way the rest of the Chinese people live, without privileges. We have a lot to learn from them, we who are here, with a whole hotel for just the two of us, like two little lords. We should be ashamed." The only thing Sergio could say in reply was: "And so why aren't they here? Why have they left at the most import-ant moment, instead of staying to fight like all of us?"

It was true. At the beginning of the summer, Carl had given Marianella the news: his family was going to England and Canada. Since 1947, when they had returned from a long tour of wars to settle in China permanently, David and Isabel had only left once. Now the Languages Institute had offered David paid holidays, and his three sons, at an age to make the most of a trip to their distant origins, had received the idea with such enthusiasm that nobody seriously considered the possibility of not accepting. It was a blow for Marianella. "And how long will you be gone?" she asked.

"I don't know," Carl said. "Four or five months. You don't travel that far to stay just a few days."

"And what about what's happening here?" Marianella said. "We're changing the world here. Doesn't that matter to you?"

"Of course it does," Carl said. "But the trip is now."

Marianella cried the tears of a lovelorn teenager, but told herself that there was nothing more counter-revolutionary than allowing yourself to be distracted by love.

X

At the beginning of September, after more than two months of unstructured life in the Peace Hotel, Sergio got in touch with the China–Latin America Friendship Association. He told them that his and Marianella's lives were quiet, that the Cultural Revolution was passing them by. He asked that they send them, him and his sister, to work on a commune until things went back to normal at school, but got no reply apart from a series of excuses; he asked that they be allowed to participate in the great revolutionary marches with the Red Guards, but the authorities responded that, for reasons of personal security, that was impossible. In general, the response of the Association was tantamount to sabotage, but Sergio did not have the tools he needed to rebel or protest. Defeated, he began to look for ways to fill his days. That was when he decided it was time to revive his French.

The Alliance Française was not far from the Peace Hotel. It was not one of the places that had begun to close out of fear of the Red Guards, so Sergio enrolled in some inexpensive courses that began at four in the afternoon. Most of his classmates were the children of diplomats, but there were also Chinese people from overseas, who tended to be privileged, having lived abroad, and they were never too shocked at phrases that were absurd or impossible in communist China. *Les enfants regardent la télé*, for example, or *J'achète des surgelés avec maman*. Later he wondered whether he had actually joined for the language courses, which were after all a bit basic for him, or for the right to attend the weekly film they showed. That turned into one of the things he most looked forward to in his routine. There, in the screening room of the Alliance Française, Sergio saw *Breathless* and *Shoot the Piano Player* and *Last Year at Marienbad*, which they showed over and over at certain intervals, and also Louis Malle's *Lift to the Scaffold*, not once, but many times. After one of these sessions, as he came out into the lobby of the Alliance Française, he thought he recognized a young woman he'd seen only once before, but those seconds were long enough to leave him with an impression of her beauty.

Her name was Smilka. She was a fifteen-year-old Yugoslav Sergio had met on June 1, when China celebrates World Children's Day and gatherings and festivities are held across the country. The city's big event took place at the Workers' Stadium: a huge party to which everyone was invited, and where there was a special zone for foreigners, from guests at the Friendship Hotel to children of diplomats. Sergio was not a child, nor was Smilka, but there they both were, taking part in the festivities with the negligence and also the audacity of teenagers. Smilka was with her sister, Milena, and Sergio with the Latin Americans from the Friendship Hotel. He was too shy to speak to her: he spent the whole day gazing at her from afar, and then, when it was time to leave and return to the hotel, he wasn't even brave enough to say goodbye. The months that followed were difficult – his parents' departure, political tensions at school, the move to the Peace Hotel – and the Yugoslavian girl disappeared from his thoughts. Until one evening, unaware they were in the same room, they both saw a Louis Malle film.

Sergio gathered his courage, walked over to her and asked, his heart racing, what she had thought of the film. They struck up a slightly awkward conversation full of shy smiles. And everything was going really well: Smilka was cheerful, and her French impeccable; she spoke appreciatively of the same directors Sergio admired and seemed willing to see him again. But then, at the moment when flirting turns to telling each other about their lives, Sergio asked what she was doing in China, and Smilka, unaware of the trouble she was about to cause, said that her father was the correspondent for a Yugoslavian press agency. Sergio heard an alarm go off is his head.

"Tanjug?" he asked.

"That's it," Smilka said. "You've heard of it?"

As a member of the proletarian youth, Sergio already had very well-formed ideas on the handling of propaganda and the dangers of giving out information to those who could use it to do harm. The great Western agencies – France-Presse, for example, or AP – did not have correspondents in China, which meant that most news got out through two media organizations: TASS, the Soviet agency, or the Yugoslavian Tanjug. In those days of Sino-Soviet tensions, everything that appeared on TASS was considered propaganda, disinformation or obvious lies; Tanjug, however, seemed to maintain a certain neutrality, so Sergio did not worry too much. But Smilka soon told him that her father was not only a journalist, but also belonged to the diplomatic corps.

That changed everything. Yugoslavia had been the first

country of the socialist bloc to break with Stalin and attempt an independent socialism, and had not only had partial success, going so far as to receive economic aid from the United States, but had also been among the founding nations of the Non-Aligned Movement. Sergio did not then know all the geopolitical details, all the intrigues and dalliances, but he knew the essential thing: Yugoslavians were bad socialists and accomplices to capitalism. Yugoslavians, in short, were a poisonous enemy.

The following week, when Sergio went back to class, he sat far away from Smilka and waved to her with studied coolness. If she was surprised or saddened by this behaviour, she did not let anything show on her face. A little while later, when the Red Guards' presence was at its height, Sergio received news that the Alliance Française was closing and classes were suspended. It would be many long weeks before he saw Smilka again, and it would happen under very different circumstances.

It is very important, decisive, to choose good friendships. The saying "You can know a man by the company he keeps" is very wise. The influence a friendship wields is decisive. Therefore, you must choose positive friends, politically, morally and intellectually positive. This doesn't mean they have to be perfect, no, but it is imperative that they be of an acceptable political level, that they are morally healthy and have a proletarian mentality, even when, naturally, they have defects, which you two can help them correct, and they you. If either of you has a friend contrary to the above, you should criticize them and make them see how harmful and dangerous they are. If they persist, you should help them in every way to stop keeping such company.

The street the Peace Hotel was on, Wangfujing, had become difficult. Pedestrian traffic was so dense that Sergio and his sister could take a whole hour to walk each block. The reason was very simple: Red Guards from all over the country, millions of young people dressed in olive green, were arriving in Peking to see their leader and, if they could not see him, to be close to Tiananmen Square and to Zhongnanhai, where the headquarters of the Party's Central Committee was. The youths had nowhere to sleep, and that had not been a problem in the summer, but now autumn was drawing to a close and the nights were cold. The Red Guards grew impatient and people said they had already taken over an unoccupied building nearby. Sergio found out that it was true, and not only that: they had also taken over schools and hospitals to have a place to spend the night while they declared their loyalty to Mao. One afternoon when Sergio and Marianella were returning from their Western world, with their heads covered in thick balaclavas to hide their features, they found that the crowd had reached the doors of the Peace Hotel. Sergio pretended not to understand when he heard one of the Red Guards say the place was empty and they should take it as well. If they did not, Sergio understood, it was because the Peace Hotel belonged to the Party, and these things were still respected. But he was scared, because anything could happen there any day. He talked it over with his sister and the two of them reached an indisputable conclusion: they could not stay where they were.

Seeing that they could not count on the authorities of the Association, who seemed more interested in protecting the youngsters in their charge than in allowing them to become revolutionaries, Sergio and Marianella took the initiative. Their efforts had results. They found out that the Bureau of Specialists, which before the Cultural Revolution had conducted tourism for foreigners, had organized an excursion to a communal farm. They asked if they could come along on the trip, and for days spoke to people, made calls, pestered, shouted, made themselves unbearable, ready to get what they wanted if necessary by exhausting all opposition. The communes were the heart and soul of the Great Leap Forward and, therefore, of Comrade Mao's vision of communist China. They were immense collective farms, places so enormous they were organized like small countries, but instead of provinces they had cooperatives. Sergio must have shown so much enthusiasm, or so much conviction about the importance of him and his sister getting to know those scenes of the proletarian revolution, that they ended up defeating the Association's resistance. In mid-November they arrived at the Popular Commune of Chinese–Romanian Friendship. The organization left Sergio sleeping with the men and sent Marianella to stay with a peasant household. The territory was so big, and they were so far away from each other, that Sergio didn't see his sister again for the rest of their stay.

The work consisted of picking cabbages for the year's great harvest. They started at seven in the morning, in the midst of a cold so intense that the cabbages were covered in frost. They cut them with care, to be sure not to damage them, and then, using their index and middle fingers as tongs, they removed the outer leaves, which had been ruined by insects and weather. What was left was a slender and beautiful object that was thrown into a wheelbarrow, and the wheelbarrow was taken to the gigantic warehouse where millions of cabbages were stored. Yes, it was true that their fingers froze and they had to wash their hands with warm water in a special sink so their skin didn't crack from the cold or their hands get so numb they wouldn't work, but Sergio had never felt so useful. Suddenly, faced with this reality he could touch and suffer with his bare hands, the world of cinema drifted away like a sly trick. At night, gathered with the rest of the pickers in a warm room, talking with the Latin Americans from the Friendship Hotel, who had also come, or taking turns to read aloud quotes from the Little Red Book, Sergio felt an unprecedented camaraderie, and during those moment he forgot that the food was horrible and the skin was going to fall off his hands.

For Marianella, meanwhile, the days in the commune were much more than the satisfactory fulfilment of a duty: they were truly transformational. The experience was so powerful that the first thing she did when they returned to the Peace Hotel was to write a letter to the China–Latin America Friendship

Association. She wrote in green ink on ten pages of translucent paper describing life on the commune, and each comma was an emotional comma, each spelling mistake trembled with fervour. *There are no words to express,* she began, *all the happiness and gratitude to the great people's commune where they took me in as if I were a member of family.* She was one of six young guests of an older woman who lived alone with a ten-year-old son, since her husband and older son had enlisted in the PLA. They got up at 6 a.m., and half an hour later they were walking out into the biting dawn cold. From the first day it was obvious she didn't have the proper clothing to protect her from the cold, but it did not occur to her to complain or ask for help: she noted: *The willpower of the other comrades doing* lao tun, *with no fear of getting dirty or tired, and the enthusiasm at the most difficult hours of the morning had to be seen to be believed. At those moments I sought refuge in Mao's wise words: 'Be resolute, fear no sacrifice, and surmount every difficulty to win victory.'*

At eight they went back for breakfast (*we fought to cook the noodles or chop the cauliflower, but since we could not all do everything, we swept the yard and took turns writing Mao's sayings on the board*), they had lunch at twelve and were back out in the fields, singing revolutionary songs, meeting with the commune workers, studying the Little Red Book during breaks from the exhausting toil. At night, after dinner, the six girls visited their host's mother-in-law. The granny was a stooped and almost blind woman who sat in a corner to tell them what the world was like before the revolution, and her stories were so sad that Marianella, although she made an effort not to cry, felt *a great hatred towards that exploitative class that fed off the pain and suffering of humankind.* Twice a week, Tuesdays and Thursdays, the commune took them to see a film outdoors. She didn't retain a single plot or any of the characters, but she knew that she would never forget the act of sitting on the ground, *on mats she would once have called uncomfortable* but that there, shared with her comrades, seemed *like feather cushions.*

In that month of hard work, saying goodbye was the most difficult of all. This time, when old Nainai took Marianella's hand between her own (small, emaciated, rough like badly dried clay), they both let themselves cry without saying a word. Marianella, from her seat in the bus that would take her back to Peking, saw the old lady take out a dirty handkerchief to dry her tears. *I have realized that the purest and most sincere class are the peasants.* On the bus she tried to explain this to her brother, but she could not find the words that now, facing the page, spilled out so fast that her hand could not keep up. Thanks to the labours of those days she was able to be a different person. *What kind of person? One who is preparing to faithfully serve her people. As Mao taught us: "Everything reactionary is the same; if you do not hit, it will not fall. This is also like sweeping the floor; as a rule, where the broom does not reach, the dust will not vanish of itself."* She signed the letter with her name in Chinese characters, and below, also in Chinese, these words: *The people and only the people can create the movement that can change the future of humanity.*

At the beginning of *My Universities*, the third volume of his autobiography, Maxim Gorky is on his way to the University of Kazan, after a childhood and youth of work and hardship. Nikolay Yevreinov, a student who had rented his grandmother's attic for a time and became his friend, was to blame. Yevreinov, certain that Gorky has an exceptional mind, has convinced him to travel with him to Kazan, his native land, to sit the entrance exams for the university. Days later, Gorky is there, living with the Yevreinov family, in a one-storey house at the end of a poor street. There are three Yevreinovs, the mother, who lives on her meagre widow's pension, and her two sons. "On her return from the market," Gorky writes, "I understood her plight. As she spread out her purchases on the kitchen table, I could see on her worried face the hopeless problem she had to solve – how to turn the meat scraps she had purchased into a meal to satisfy three growing youths, to say nothing of herself."

One morning, a few days after his arrival, Gorky goes to the kitchen to help prepare the vegetables. They talk about Gorky's intentions; she cuts her finger with a knife. Nikolay, Gorky's friend, comes in, and asks his mother why she doesn't make some of her wonderful meat dumplings. Gorky, to impress them, immediately says: "But this meat won't do for dumplings." The thoughtless remark enrages Madam Yevreinov, who starts to insult him, throws carrots down on the table and storms out, slamming the door behind her. "A touch of temperament, that's all," Nikolay says, with a wink, and Gorky, immediately regretful, realizes that neither of her sons is aware of how hard their mother works to put food on the table. It is a reality of hunger, or rather, hunger is the great problem every day. "But I understood the chemical feat and desperate economies she achieved in her kitchen," Gorky writes. "I understood the resourcefulness with which she daily deceived her sons' stomachs, and to find food for me too, a young tramp not particularly appealing in appearance and behaviour." And then: "This knowledge made every morsel of bread apportioned to me fall like a stone on my soul." He soon begins to leave the house earlier, just to avoid the Yevreinovs' meals, and to keep from starving to death he frequents the Volga docks, where he can earn fifteen or twenty kopeks a day.

Lying on his bed in the Peace Hotel with Gorky's selected works in his hands, reading *My Universities* as passionately as he had previously read *My Childhood* and *In the World* and also *The Lower Depths*, as well as *Mother*, Sergio realized that he had never, in his sixteen years of life, known hunger. What was it like, this world that Gorky portrayed with such realism? Did you not have to know these sensations up close to be a genuine revolutionary? Or rather, could you be a genuine revolutionary without knowing them? "And long stretches of hunger and yearnings made me feel capable of committing crimes," he read, "and not only against the sacred institutions of property." Sergio thought that his father had known hunger and had stolen capsules of cod liver oil. He, however, had led a life without want. Was that good?

The next morning, Sergio did not go down for breakfast. He didn't tell his sister anything and did not advise the restaurant, but simply stayed in his room reading. He did not go down for lunch either. As night fell, the phone rang: it was the receptionist, who was calling to find out if Comrade Cabrera was feeling alright. "I'm perfectly fine," Sergio said, and went to bed without eating. Marianella was surprised. She asked questions and he answered evasively. But she must have understood something, because she didn't insist further, not that night or the morning of the second day, when Sergio stayed in his room again. In those unstructured days that Sergio and his sister had been living since the beginning of their confinement, days without school or schedules or obligations, it was not so unusual for Sergio to spend the whole night reading and then skip breakfast in exchange for a few hours of sleep; but when he didn't come down for lunch either, those in charge of the hotel began to worry. It was around two in the afternoon when one of them came up with a doctor, and Sergio saw such anguish on their faces that he decided to tell them the truth: he was reading a book that described hunger in capitalist society, and had felt an urgent need to experience in his own body a sensation he'd never had in his life. The doctor and hotel worker listened patiently, and Sergio thought he had been direct and clear. But an hour later there was another knock on his door.

This time it was the tutor, Li. And she was not alone: she was with Comrade Chou, general secretary of the China–Latin America Friendship Association.

"We want to ask," said the secretary, "that you bring your strike to an end."

"I don't understand," Sergio said. "I'm reading a book, and I wanted to feel . . ."

"Your hunger strike," said Comrade Chou. "The Association asks with the utmost courtesy."

"But I'm not on strike," Sergio said.

Tutor Li interrupted: "We know that you have made requests," she said. "We know that you have made them several times. But it is not easy for us. You have to have patience. Everything will work out."

"We understand the circumstance," Comrade Chou added. "Please be patient."

They returned on the third day. They explained they'd held an urgent meeting and the committee had accepted the difficulties of Sergio and Marianella's living conditions.

"What difficulties?" Sergio asked.

"We understand that life in the Peace Hotel has changed due to the political situation," Comrade Chou said. "We know of your difficulties in going outside."

"We know the Red Guards behave with hostility," Li said. "They see the hotel almost empty and think they can stay here . . . Yes, we understand all that."

"And we have made a decision," Comrade Chou said. "The committee has made a decision."

"It's better that you not stay here," the tutor said. "You're going back to the Friendship Hotel."

Sergio took a second to understand what was going on: he had won his first hunger strike without even knowing he was on one. But then the same thing occurred to his sister and to him: what would their parents think of a return to the Friendship Hotel, source of so many bad influences?

"The Association is responsible for you and your parents know it," Li said. "The Association cannot run risks."

"It is," Chou concluded, "a matter of security."

That was how Sergio and Marianella returned to the Friendship Hotel. The workers at the Peace Hotel, who had had them as exclusive guests for almost four months, held a moving farewell for them, and only then did Sergio realize how much affection they had for each other. Comrade Liu, the manager of the hotel, promised them their rooms would remain at their disposal for ever. "They'll be here whenever you want to come back," he told them. "And we hope that will be soon." But a few days later he came to see them himself at the Friendship Hotel. He brought a box of books Sergio had left behind in his room (including the selected works of Gorky, which were to blame for the whole misunderstanding), and he also brought some news: the Red Guards had occupied the Peace Hotel, so Sergio and Marianella's rooms were no longer available. Comrade Liu was very sorry.

"It was a peaceful takeover," he added. "Don't let anyone tell you otherwise."

As for the Friendship Hotel, avoid going there as much as possible. Only for essentials: if you go there it must be for a concrete objective. Not to meet or keep in touch with the people who live there and make friends in that environment. Only in exceptional cases with elements you know with absolute certainty to be positive and in that case you should meet them elsewhere. If you prove with your deeds that you will not be swept up in the unhealthy ambience of the hotel and mix with people there, you can go there for specific events or to the pool in the summer, but don't make a habit of it either.

At the end of December, Sergio spoke to Smilka again. This time it was a telephone conversation with nothing fortuitous about it. Sergio remembered that in June, when he saw her for the first time at the World Children's Day celebrations, Smilka had exchanged a couple of words with Ivan Cheng, a boy with a Chinese father and French mother who lived at the Friendship Hotel, and it was easy to ask Ivan to get him her phone number. Sergio called with a trembling voice; he was surprised at how delighted she was to hear from him, and even more that she invited him over. But getting close to her was one thing; going to her house, where her father lived – a diplomat for a traitorous country that had moved away from socialism – was something else entirely. Sergio looked for excuses and gave evasive answers until Smilka suggested something else. The following Saturday she was meeting a group of friends at the International Club. "Why don't you come?" she said. He could not believe his bad luck. The International Club was an exclusive place for well-off Chinese and diplomats, and it presented two problems: one, Sergio was not a member; two, it was a terrible place, a symbol of bourgeois values, where foreigners led the same sort of lives they would have led in London or Paris without showing the slightest embarrassment on their faces. Fausto had always disparaged it, , and in even harsher terms than he used against the Friendship Hotel. In short, the International Club, where Smilka would be, represented all that Sergio had learned to detest.

Sergio accepted the invitation.

When the day arrived, he took a lot longer than he ever had before in deciding what to wear. He didn't have a lot of clothes to choose from, but there were still a few things his parents had brought from Colombia, so he spruced himself up as best he could and went to the International Club. The first thing was a curious thrill at seeing his name on a list of invited guests; the second, the amazement at having gone inside a forbidden place: it was like having sneaked into an opium den. But all his worries – about his clothes, about his ideology, about his socialist loyalties – evaporated when he saw Smilka, who was lovelier than ever. She had an open smile and a refined Mediterranean face: being with her was easy and exciting at the same time, and Sergio thought it was obvious they were already friends, but his invincible shyness wouldn't let him think of anything more. Smilka was with her sister Milena and with an English girl,

Ellen, who spoke excellent Spanish, because her father had been a diplomat in Argentina. And what was she doing in China, Sergio asked. She was the daughter of the United Kingdom's chargé d'affaires, she answered. And she didn't bat an eyelid.

From the start, the conversation at lunch revolved around the Beatles. Sergio didn't understand and couldn't contribute much, and after a while the rest of them noticed. "I know they exist," Sergio explained, or defended himself, "but I've never heard them." Silence fell over the table. He thought of Marianella, of her English friends and the music they'd introduced her to: he often heard Beatles songs coming from her room, and now Sergio regretted not having paid more attention. The records his parents had left were ones that they liked – Chavela Vargas, Atahualpa Yupanqui, Mercedes Sosa – but nothing coincided with the table's preferences. And then Smilka said that it was not possible, that a person couldn't go through life without hearing a whole Beatles album at least once. She looked at her watch and invited them all to go straight to her house so Sergio could fill the gaps in his cultural education.

Her house was nearby and they walked there. By then everyone knew that a Westerner couldn't walk heedlessly through streets full of Red Guards, and that, when there was no option, they had to follow certain rules. The two most important were: walk quickly and don't call attention to yourself. Sergio missed his armband; at the same time, thinking of his uniform made him ashamed. But he was resigned: now that he had been to the International Club, visiting the house of a Yugoslavian diplomat was simply descending to another circle of hell. So he went to Smilka's house, met her father and her mother, heard the Beatles – *Please Please Me* and *A Hard Day's Night* – and the Rolling Stones, and saw Ellen singing along with all the songs. And only then, when Smilka ceremoniously put on a new record and they all stopped talking and listened to that music of hard corners, those voices shouting incomprehensible lyrics, did Sergio find out that the reason for this gathering of friends, from meeting at the club to this moment, had been to arrive together at the British residence to see the film featuring the songs of the record they were listening to.

"Do you want to come and see it?" Ellen asked. "It's at my house. Don't you want to come?"

The situation could not be more compromising: every day the Chinese press talked about the aggressions of the British police in Hong Kong. There were often noisy Red Guards demonstrating in front of the British diplomatic mission. How could Sergio go to the diplomatic mission of capitalist repressers as a guest of the chargé d'affaires' daughter? Would that not be sinking very low? Could Sergio accept the invitation with a clear conscience, simply to spend a few more hours with Smilka?

Sergio accepted the invitation.

The chauffeur from the British diplomatic mission came to pick them up from Smilka's house. Soon Sergio realized, to his great relief, that the film would not be shown in the mission itself, but at the chargé d'affaires' residence, and this, at least, would avoid the probable demonstrations. And there they all arrived, at an enormous house with luxuries such as Sergio had never seen, with a screening room – with a 35 millimetre projector and comfortable seating for some thirty people – every bit as good as the one at the Friendship Hotel. It was a full-blown reception, full of men in white dinner jackets and women in hats and pearl necklaces, with the chargé d'affaires and his wife greeting the guests one by one, he shaking hands and she holding hers out to be kissed. Sergio knew at this moment he had made a pact with the devil. But he carried on, took a seat in the screening room, making sure he sat next to Smilka, and sat through the film like someone keeping a secret who is about to be discovered. Sometime later he would realize that he'd liked the Beatles film a lot – he liked the flippancy and the laughter, so different from the French films he had seen thus far, and he admired the work of Richard Lester before knowing who Richard Lester was – but he had watched it in a state of distraction due to Smilka's presence and the constant temptation to hold her hand.

He did not dare. And later, in the garden, while the others were having a drink, Sergio accepted a 555 cigarette and confessed his lack of daring to Smilka.

"How silly," she said. "Well, I'll dare then."

That's how an innocent romance began, stolen kisses and holding hands when nobody was looking, but nothing more. They always met in large groups with Milena and Marianella included, and often at the Friendship Shop, which was the closest thing they had to neutral territory. Like all the children of diplomats, however, Smilka was desperately curious about the Friendship Hotel, that legendary place where only foreigners lived and you needed a laminated card to get through the guarded door; Sergio had only to suggest a visit for some future date – to play ping-pong, for example, or to see a film, or even to get her hair cut at a more sophisticated salon – and Smilka's eyes would light up as if he'd invited her to an amusement park. They only saw each other at weekends, not only because Smilka was fifteen and lived with her parents, but also because Sergio had begun, after insistent requests, a real, socialist and proletarian job, at Peking Tool Factory Number 2.

Although it did not last long, a little more than a month, for Sergio this was a genuine apprenticeship. Factories were universities of life, as Gorky explained so marvellously, and Sergio was finally in one. He learned how to use a milling machine, and later a lathe, and discovered that he was better on the lathe: it was a monster of an intense green colour like the iron of shipwrecks, and Sergio came to know its corners and its cranks and handles and levers (each of its moving parts and all their hidden dangers) so well that he could have operated it with his eyes closed. He learned to get along with his co-workers, just as he had for a shorter time at the commune, but without the frozen hands at dawn and without the torture of the bad food: there, in Factory Number 2, lunch and dinner were prepared on site with fresh ingredients. The cold stuck to the iron lathe on those late winter days, and Sergio was forced to work in a woollen hat; and if the heating cut out, as everything cut out so often during the Cultural Revolution, it was not infrequent that he would go to sleep wearing gloves, even though the presence of other humans warmed the air in the barracks. On weekends he returned to his Western life and seeing Smilka, innocent kisses and naive jokes. And one of those Saturdays, at last, he invited her to the Friendship Hotel. They went up to the rooms and out to the tennis courts and walked in the gardens talking nonsense, and ended up in the hotel club, which Sergio thought was a vulgar place compared to the International Club. But it was a memorable day, after all, for the simple fact of having seen Smilka – her girlish smile, her lively hands – excited by this behind-closed-doors world she'd so often imagined.

So then, due to the many circumstances and aspects we've analysed, we see how unsuitable it is to have a boyfriend or girlfriend. If you want to achieve the objective of not wasting your time in China, you must not get into such relationship troubles. Until you are mature and trained, this kind of thing is not suitable at all. I repeat: friendships yes, good friends, but no complications. You must not try to absorb your friends or be absorbed by them. Do not throw yourselves passionately into friendship, but just in a natural way.

The following Monday, Sergio was back at the Number 2 Tool Factory, working in the mill, when a comrade called him to say a woman was waiting for him at the door. He started to fantasize that it might be Smilka, but when he went out he recognized the tutor, Li. "I need to talk to you," she said, and took him by the sleeve and led him to a small, uncomfortable meeting room, identical to rooms in factories all over China. "Sit down," Li said, and then she asked him: "Do you have something to tell me?" Sergio knew immediately what they were talking about, even if she hadn't begun to speak, but he was not ready to reveal more than he had to. So he waited. He felt for the first time what his friends at the hotel had frequently described without his believing them: paranoia, the need to look over his shoulder, the conviction that someone was listening in on his phone calls. No, Sergio had said every time the subject came up, that was not possible: nobody can spy on fifteen hundred foreigners speaking all kinds of different languages. And that's what he was thinking when the tutor Li began to speak of Smilka, adding her surname and her father's occupation, and told Sergio that the girl could not return to the hotel.

"You should be ashamed," she said to Sergio in an almost maternal tone of voice. "Her father is a slanderer. He has libelled the revolution in the press. He has libelled our chairman."

Sergio tried to downplay the matter: "But she's just a friend. She just came to the hotel for one afternoon."

"No," the tutor said. "This must not happen again. Wait here."

Sergio watched her leave. He didn't know how long he sat alone in that meeting room, looking at Chairman Mao's double chin; when she returned, Li seemed to be dragging Marianella. Sergio understood that the tutor had gone to pick her up from the hotel and explained the whole matter to her, but she wanted Sergio to be present at the moment when she reprimanded her again for her negligence, for not having kept an eye on her brother, for having allowed him to get involved with the wrong people. She ordered Sergio not to see that girl again; she accused Marianella of failing in her revolutionary duty. When she wanted to know what her fault was, the tutor answered:

"Your duty was to denounce your brother, and you did not. And the Party does not know if it can still trust you."

XI

As they walked across the park towards calle Mallorca, away from the Sagrada Familia, Sergio ventured to comment that the visit had disappointed him. The construction they'd seen looked nothing like the one he remembered, and he was willing to bet that Gaudí, if he came back to life, if he rose out of his tomb bearing the bruises and scars from the tram that killed him, would stand in horror in front of the most important project of his life and say: "But what have they done to my church?" Sergio knew that nostalgia carried too much weight in that opinion, remembering that visit in 1975 when he first set foot in the country that had expelled his father. Now he was seeing the pond that looked straight out of a nativity scene, the pedlars, the streets of Ensanche lined with endless rows of shady plane trees; he was seeing tourists so numerous they blocked the entrance to the church and got in the way of pedestrians, not individual tourists but enormous herds emerging from huge buses that cast their square shadows across the pavement. And he said to Raúl:

"It's just that I was remembering something different."

He remembered walking along the narrow streets of Ensanche one day in 1975 and coming upon the cathedral as he turned a corner, a form unlike anything Sergio, at twenty-five, had ever seen before. He remembered a day of clear skies, very similar to the one above them now: this sky that kept them from getting on the metro or even into a taxi. It was true they had to get back to the hotel, find a restaurant to have lunch – but not just anywhere, rather a place that celebrated the fact of being here, in Barcelona, together, a father and son talking about everything and nothing – and to have a couple of hours to relax before the evening session at the Filmoteca. But calle Mallorca still had the smell of recent rain, or the smell the rain had brought out of the trees, and Raúl kept asking questions about his grandfather; and Sergio, as he answered them, realized he'd talked a lot about his father over the years, told many times the fabulous stories of a life that had not been like other people's, and how strange it was to be telling them now, when that life was over. So, talking about Domingo, Fausto's father, who had been Uncle Felipe's bodyguard, and Josefina Bosch, Domingo's Catalan wife, and the dog Pilón, who was frightened by the bombing raids, they reached the Paseo de Gracia and began to walk down towards plaza Cataluña. They were approaching the plaza when Raúl asked: "And where did Tato live? Where did his family live?" Sergio said he didn't know: it had to be in one of the neighbourhoods bombed by the Italians, because that happened very close by, but Fausto had never said precisely where their Barcelona apartment was.

"He said they could see Montjuic from the roof," Sergio said. "But he didn't remember anything else. Not surprising: he was thirteen years old, but he was just a kid. The bombings must have been in '38, I think." Then his memory lit up. "But I knew someone who was in the worst of it. Well, I barely knew him, your aunt knew him much better. Because he was her boyfriend's father, a boyfriend she had in China. His was another one of those lives. Like Tato's: those lives that tell a bigger story, I don't know if you get my meaning. Or maybe it's not that they tell a story, but that history sweeps them along. Sometimes I wonder if that's what brought them together: being the children of people like that leaves a mark. Of course, I don't know if one realizes such things at that age. Your aunt was fourteen when she met Carl Crook, I was sixteen, Carl seventeen: what could we know about life? We lived alone in a hotel, we came and went as we wished, and thought we had everything under control. But we did not."

David had been here. In the days of the standoff in Barcelona, his tall, ungainly silhouette had passed this way. Sergio, all of a sudden, could easily imagine him in these streets, walking down the Paseo de Gracia, walking across this plaza: an Englishman like so many Englishmen fighting in the Civil War. A whole generation who saw Franco's uprising, who saw what was happening in the rest of Europe and reached the conclusion that the struggle against fascism would be lost or won depending on the fate of the Republic. David Crook was twenty-six years old when that began, and it seemed obvious to him that he should lend a hand. How could he know that it would change his life? The strange thing, for Sergio, was realizing all that he now knew about David Crook that he didn't know then. All that he hadn't known living in China, seeing the Crooks every week, seeing Carl and his brothers Michael and Paul, hearing people talk about adventurous David and the courageous Isabel, daughter of missionaries; all that he had learned over the years, in conversations with Marianella and with Carl, reading the memoirs David had written and published in his old age: you learn a lot in half a century. The strange thing was that it was all surfacing now. Was it possible that Sergio's mere presence in Barcelona, that banal geographical concurrence of a body and a city, should cause this return to the past? No, it was no doubt more complicated. *This is going to be a real retrospective, after all,* Sergio had said to the director of the Filmoteca. But he could never have imagined he would apply such dedication to remembering those long-lost people, their stories and words. His father, if he could read his mind, would seize the moment to recite Machado, *We make the path by walking it and turning to look back,* and Sergio had to wonder if that was what was happening to him now, if he was seeing a path he would never set foot on again. When you were the son of Fausto Cabrera, poetry tended to intrude at the most unexpected moments. And there was not much you could do about it.

In the summer of 1936, David Crook attended a lecture in Oxford where a Spanish man spoke passionately about the fascist uprising; in October, while working on a left-wing student magazine, he met a communist poet who arrived in the editorial offices with a bandaged head: he had just been wounded in Spain and had now returned to recruit combatants. Around that time Oswald Mosley, the aristocrat who had founded the British Union of Fascists, negotiated commercial accords with Hitler and had his photograph taken with Mussolini, organized an anti-Semitic march in the East End of London with his Blackshirts. David was Jewish, and the East End had been his father's neighbourhood before he had enough money to move to a Gentile part of London and begin the slow gentrification of his family. So he joined the crowds that stood up to the fascists and shouted a slogan imported from the Spanish Republicans, the sounds of which filled his mouth in spite of his not understanding the words: "¡No pasarán!"

David's father, son of immigrants from Tsarist Russia, had made a modest fortune selling furs to soldiers fighting on the Russian front during the Great War, but the post-war depression had ruined his business. In any case, David grew up privileged near Hampstead Heath, where the family had a governess and three servants, where every park hid a tennis court, and through the streets of which in other times had walked Karl Marx, who liked to take his family on Sunday picnics. In March 1929 he arrived in New York with the intention of going to university like a British aristocrat, but seven months later, when the stock market crashed, his world capsized. After years of seeing hunger on people's faces, queues to buy bread and desperate children selling apples on every corner, and of work cleaning furs and pushing carts for the Jewish furriers, he was experiencing a slow transformation, the result of his reading and chance encounters, and finally, when he joined the League of Young Communists, the only surprise was that it hadn't happened sooner. That was the young man who returned to London, who participated in the anti-fascist demonstrations and at the end of the year turned up in Covent Garden, at the headquarters of the Communist Party, to sign up for the International Brigades.

It was not as easy as he had thought. For the recruitment officer, a young man of proletarian origins, David was nothing more than a bourgeois adventurer, and the Party was making great efforts to send people who were prepared: this, although many only realized when it was too late, was a real war. When he learned that the *brigadistas* left from Paris, David pawned his Bar Mitzvah cufflinks in Regent Street, and on the second day of 1937 he was entering Spanish territory from Perpignan. He spent a few days in Barcelona and then was on his way to the International Brigade's headquarters, in Albacete, where he got a few weeks' training in the use of a Lewis anti-aircraft battery, an old wreck that had seen better days fighting in the Great War and then the October Revolution. At the beginning of February, around the time the Republican government decreed equal rights for men and women, something happened to him.

His company had received intelligence that the fascists were going to cut off the route between Valencia and Madrid. Their intention was to reach the road to Barcelona, and that would have been a catastrophe for the Republicans, so the *brigadistas* headed towards the valley of Jarama, to join up with those who were trying to prevent the disaster. When the airplanes flew over, everyone was ready, except David, who was surprised by the bursts of fire while relieving himself between some bushes. He thought his life was going to end there, in Spain, with his trousers around his ankles, before he'd had time to do anything to change the world. At that moment he was in luck. Together with Sam Wild, a working-class comrade much more competent than he was, he positioned himself on a hill to defend it, because he seemed to understand that everything depended on it. He never saw the enemy, but someone shouted in English: "It's the Moors!" After hours of combat that had taken the lives of several *brigadistas* and many more fascists, David and Sam heard the order to retreat and dragged themselves to the other side of the hill, collecting abandoned rifles and a box of ammunition along the way. Then they thought they saw something move not far from where they were. Before they could take cover, another burst of gunfire came out of nowhere: a bullet wounded Sam, two hit David in the leg and another ruptured his canteen.

The darkness protected him. Thirty years later, talking to Marianella in his apartment in Peking, David's voice broke when he remembered the moon that night, which he still described as if he could see it through the window: a moon in the shape of a sickle that was hanging in the clear sky and whose faint light shone on the bodies of the dead. At dawn, after a night spent half-conscious, lying on the hard ground of the hill, he heard the stretcher bearers coming to pick him up: his friend Sam had got as far as the front to notify them. An ambulance took him to Madrid; and on that same day, as David travelled with his thigh destroyed by lead and fearing amputation, the battle of Jarama, which lasted forty days, involved sixty thousand combatants and killed two thousand five hundred *brigadistas*, began. His wound on the hill – which much later would become known as Suicide Hill – saved his life. Two-thirds of his comrades died there, and many of them were better trained than he was. He always thought that, had he gone into that battle, he probably would not have survived.

His convalescence in Madrid was useful. He read Dickens and Jack London, and also *Reminiscences of Lenin*, by Krupskaya, whose generous opinion of Trotsky took him by surprise. Someone told him about the Hotel Gran Vía, where English-speaking journalists got together for meals, and as soon as he could walk – on crutches, of course – he headed over there, less for the food than for conversation in his own language.

In the basement restaurant he met Martha Gellhorn and Ernest Hemingway, in whose room on one of the top floors he spent an evening drinking wine and philosophizing about war while shells whistled past. He met Stephen Spender, who struck him as the epitome of an insufferable Oxford intellectual, and a Canadian journalist with whom he fell instantly in love. The woman lived with some compatriots in the transfusion centre directed by Norman Bethune, the doctor who had designed a system to collect blood donations in Madrid and take them in mobile units to the front lines. And David was there, in the middle of his wartime romance, when a Frenchman who had heard him badmouth Trotsky one night approached to ask him, in a whisper, if he would be prepared to carry out a special mission. "It's for the movement," he said.

"For the movement," David replied, "I'll do whatever I'm asked."

They arranged to meet at the Hotel Palace with two other Soviet comrades, and then at Gaylord's, and then again at the Palace, until they were convinced they could trust him. David, for his part, had always trusted the Soviets: it seemed clear to him that France and Great Britain had turned their backs on Spain with the cowardly argument of non-intervention, while Moscow had been able to recognize the transcendence of the moment. It was with Soviet rifles that they had fought in Jarama, and Soviet experts who had arrived at the Republican front to show the Spanish how to operate Soviet tanks. So David would have accepted any mission they assigned him. But the Soviets were reticent and they dispatched him with a single sentence.

"We will summon you when we need you."

Back at his battalion he learned of the death of Sam Wild,

whose leg wound had become gangrenous, and he looked at his fate as if in a mirror. During his convalescence he had time to think: he thought about the Canadian journalist he'd fallen in love with; he thought briefly of leaving the war and going to live with her; he was ashamed of his selfishness. In the grand scheme of the defeat of fascism and the victory of the socialist revolution, not only was an individual death not tragic, it was the necessary condition for victory. In April they sent him to Albacete, to a training school where he learned infantry tactics and map reading while cleaning the latrines, and then to Valencia, to receive orders from the Soviet consul while eating a plate of paella. It was the mission he'd been waiting for, so he took his orders and his money and on April 27 arrived in Barcelona. It was a city in turmoil.

"They met him in a hotel on the Paseo de Gracias," Sergio said. They were across from the Café Zurich, where tourists were soaking up the midday sun. Sergio gestured vaguely towards the opposite corner of the plaza. "In Barcelona the Republicans were confronting each other, and in that hotel David sat down with six people who were discussing in three languages what they were going to have him do. And then they explained that his orders came directly from the secret police."

"And what did he have to do?" Raúl asked.

"Spy on the POUM," said Sergio.

The Workers Party of Marxist Unification had the reputation of being a nest of Trotskyism, and had become a formidable anti-Stalinist force in the war. David understood or accepted that all this, combined with their alliance with the anarchists, represented a threat to the Republican victory.

Siding with the POUM there was also a British party, the Independent Labour Party, which met at the Hotel Continental on the Ramblas. "And here's where you come in," they told David. He got a room there. His mission was to introduce himself as the correspondent of a British weekly, make friends with the Trotskyists and Independent Labour Party members and inform the Soviets on their activities and contacts.

"Come on, I'll show you," Sergio said.

They crossed the street, skirted round the metro entrance and past the Canaletas fountain. Suddenly Sergio picked up his pace, and when he stopped, a few metres further down the street, they were facing the Hotel Continental. The narrow door, the iron awning and white glass, the modest balconies: unlike the rest of the buildings in the area, with their luxury handbags and golden lights, the facade of the Hotel Continental seemed part of another city, more frank or less ostentatious: a vanished city. They crossed the street and went into the lobby, where an overly large chandelier hung, as if the building around it had mysteriously shrunk.

"He was here," Sergio said. "David Crook was here."

"Well, it wouldn't have been exactly here," Raúl said.

"Of course, it wasn't the same lobby," Sergio said. "But imagine. Imagine him coming in from the Ramblas, in the wartime city, into a place that had become a sort of British headquarters. People coming and going, comrades saluting each other, bringing good news and bad news."

Among the guests was a tall, ungainly writer who the comrades thought suspicious, as they knew his name, George Orwell, was not his real one. David saw him coming and going with his wife, Eileen Blair, and, while taking notes on his movements, began to frequent the ILP offices. In a few days he had already managed to take advantage of siesta time to steal documents, photograph them and return them to their folders without anyone noticing. In the middle of May, the police arrested a group of POUM supporters, among whom were Georges Kopp, a Belgian soldier who had joined the cause, and Orwell's wife. The Soviets saw an opportunity: they pretended to arrest David, whose mission in the cells was to get as much information as possible out of the detainees.

"He spent his days in jail trying to hear something of interest," Sergio said. "David spoke to Kopp, but didn't get anything. He spoke to Eileen Blair and was surprised that he could get along so well with someone who was so wrong. After nine days they let him go and David returned here, to the hotel, to watch Orwell from a distance while outside, in the streets, people had started killing each other. Here, in plaza Catalunya. And that was when David came back into the picture."

The anarchists had taken over the Telephone Exchange, and were spying on or cutting off or intercepting communications between the communists and the Republican government; when they tried to recover the building, a pitched battle burst out in the middle of the plaza, and in a few hours the streets of Barcelona became the stage for confrontations that would have seemed like drunken brawls if there hadn't been barricades and dead bodies in the streets. After those days of violence, an Austrian named Landau, a leading light of international anarcho-communism, managed to take advantage of the confusion to go into hiding. David had known him: he was blond and congenial and cultured, a man who under other circumstances might have been a genuine friend and not simply his objective or his prey. Finding him became the Soviets' top priority. David never really knew why that man was so important, but he found himself from one day to the next contacting other anarchists, whose trust he had won in jail, to get the phone number of the missing man.

It was not difficult. With the help of the communications office, the Soviets could use that number to find out their victim's address, which turned out to be a luxurious villa in the same neighbourhood as their consulate. They just needed someone to identify him, David found out that Landau went out into the garden every afternoon to read for hours, in full view of anyone walking past on the street, and decided to do exactly that: hand in hand with another spy, pretending to be a couple, he walked past the villa, saw Landau and recognized him beyond a shadow of a doubt. In a matter of days, the man had disappeared. When David asked what had happened to him, his immediate superior gave a prectiable explanation: he had been captured and put on one of those Soviet ships that brought food for the Republicans. He was never heard from again.

"At that moment, David had no doubts: the anti-Stalinists were the enemy," Sergio said. "It would take him many years to realize that not everything was as he thought it was."

During the following year, David witnessed the slow failure of the Republic. Sometimes it seemed barely perceptible – like water withdrawing from a shore – and sometimes it seemed it arrived in crushing blows, as when he found out that the Nationalists had entered Bilbao or that the Spanish bishops, in an open letter, had come out in favour of Franco and called the uprising a crusade. The POUM was defeated, and its leader,

Andreu Nin, captured and imprisoned, and the security forces in Barcelona began to persecute its members; meanwhile, David continued his espionage work, almost always insignificant, and his Stalinist convictions were confirmed more each time, for it seemed clear to him that the Soviet Union's commitment was the only way to avoid defeat. Around that time he chanced to read the book *Red Star Over China* by a certain Edgar Snow, about the revolution that was taking place in that distant country. It was a true epiphany: for days, walking around Barcelona, David was daydreaming of a man called Mao Tse-tung, his Long March, the twenty-three heroes who had confronted the enemy on an iron bridge. Something important was happening there, he thought, while here the perspectives were not encouraging: they had lost Zaragoza; the north had fallen. One of those days, walking along the Ramblas, David saw Sam Wild, his comrade on the eve of the Battle of Jarama, and he thought it must be a hallucination until Sam recognized him too. The news of his death had been a misunderstanding. David was delighted, but the relationship was contaminated: the spy had put on too many masks to be able to speak normally.

The months went by. In March 1938, while Italian planes bombed Barcelona, David was summoned to the safe house on calle Muntaner where the Soviets collated their intelligence work. It was a rainy night. Before he had time to sit down, the Soviets took David to a limousine waiting for them on the other side of the street, and drove around the city in no particular direction while two fat Russians congratulated him on the work he'd done so far. At the intersection with calle Mallorca, one of them asked:

"Wouldn't you like to carry on your work in Shanghai?"

Of course, neither of those men had any way of knowing that David had read *Red Star Over China*, or that he kept thinking of the communist capital of Yanan, but it took him no more than a block to accept. In May he arrived in Paris; he spent some weeks learning Russian in the Berlitz school, since his trip would take him through Moscow. The excitement of seeing the city of his ideological passions did not last long: plans changed for reasons that were never explained to him, and David travelled weeks later than planned, and not by way of the Soviet Union but by ship from Marseilles. He had time to return to London to say goodbye to his family, and although he did not tell them the real reasons he was going to the other side of the world, he was glad he had paid that visit, because it was the last time he saw his mother. She died a short time later, at the age of fifty-six, convinced that her son had been hired to teach literature in China at St John's University.

So, he arrived in Shanghai as an agent of the Soviet Union. His first mission was to spy on Frank Glass, an intelligent, likeable and well-read journalist, an admirer of Trotsky and convinced anti-Stalinist, who met his colleagues in a pub for Westerners that they all referred to by the name of the little street it was on: Blood Alley. With time, David Crook would come to think that those days of living at the YMCA, working as a spy, his false identity as a professor of literature, had just been an accident that allowed him to discover his true life. Having read Malraux and Pearl Buck did not suffice to afford even a glimpse of this country that was developing before his eyes, and Glass seized the opportunity to indoctrinate him. He suggested that David write an article on the similarities between China and Spain; David accepted, mostly in order to shield his alibi, but in the process he discovered, or thought he discovered, that this country, in the midst of the war with Japan, was not so different from the Republic: both were suffering bitter defeats at the hands of fascist aggressors while the rest of the world seemed to look away. At Glass's recommendation (or indoctrination) he read Arthur Koestler's anti-Stalinist writings and the testimonials of rebellious or disenchanted Soviet spies. In his daily life he was moving closer to China and further away from the Soviet Union, and his handlers must have noticed, for one day, when he arrived at the French Concession house where he submitted his reports, David found it empty. The Russians had left: they had abandoned him. Nobody ever explained why.

Without his spy's salary, David suddenly found himself in a precarious financial situation. He asked for a raise; the rector of St John's told him that would only be feasible if he joined the Anglican Mission. "I'm afraid that's impossible," David said. "You see, I am an atheist." He began to look for options: he took a second job at the University of Suzhou, in a part of the city that turned into a red-light district at night, but after a few months the opportunity he'd been waiting for fell into his lap: a post at Nanjing University, in the interior of the country, which would at last allow him to leave Shanghai, that city of artifice, and venture into the real China. When St John's offered him the chance to teach a summer course, he thought it would be a good way to get a little money together for the journey to Nanjing, and in a matter of days he had prepared a seminar on Satirical Literature. He told his students about Aristophanes, Rabelais and Don Quixote, and he put up with complaints from the most puritanical among them, who asked, in the middle of a session on *Gargantua and Pantagruel*, if it was obligatory to read it, if it was really necessary for the book to be so vulgar.

By the end of the summer, David had arrived in Nanjing. The days were strange: every morning, at half past eleven, the Japanese bombarded the area, and the schedule was so rigidly observed that the university had implemented a system of alarms to warn of the bombing raids an hour and a half ahead of time. Classes were taught according to the bombs, which was no more arbitrary than any other routine. He began to attend meetings of a study group that taught him about Chinese reality, and then he found out that some of the participants were members of the Communist Party. He also learned that Norman Bethune, the doctor who had served with the Republicans in Madrid, had arrived in the province of Shanxi at the beginning of 1938; he had joined the communists led by Mao, but towards the end of 1939 he cut his finger while operating on a wounded soldier and died of septicaemia in Yanan. David considered the possibility of going to see what was happening there, but all his friends advised against it: the blockade by the Kuomintang, the Chinese Nationalist Party, was impregnable. It would have been a suicidal journey.

So he carried on teaching at the university. One afternoon he was marking some papers when Julia Brown, the daughter of Canadian missionaries, and his colleague in the English department, walked in. "Julia, you've changed your hair," David said. But Julia was not Julia, rather her sister Isabel, a woman so beautiful that she always had several suitors, but with such a strong personality that they all gave up. David bought a second-hand bicycle just to go on rides with her, and in the summer of '41, along with four other friends, they travelled into the mountains and the province of Xikang, and for several kilometres they overlapped the route of Mao's Long March. The trip lasted six days. They talked about the Jewish religion that he had rejected and the Christianity that she was beginning to question. She had been born in Sichuan to Western parents, and in six days of mountainous tracks she led him through the labyrinths of the Chinese mentality better than any of the people he'd met over the past three years. When they returned, David shaved and went to ask Isabel to marry him. It would always seem incredible to him that she had said yes.

Raúl said he was going to walk down the Ramblas as far as the statue of Columbus: he wanted to see how the sea reached Barcelona. Sergio went up to his room to rest a little, for in half an hour they would come to pick him up for a radio interview; however, instead of closing his eyes and trying to have a siesta, which was what his body was requesting, he ended up making use of the internet connection to call Marianella. It was just after nine in Bogotá, and she had been working for three hours. She had recently begun to bring an old project into being: a method for learning Chinese. Sergio was enthusiastic about the idea, so they talked about that for quite a while, and then Marianella wanted to know how everything was going in Barcelona: how was his reunion with Raúl; how things were going at the Filmoteca. "We were talking about the Crooks," Sergio said. "These days have been strange, you know? I've thought a lot about Papá, of course, but then I end up talking to Raúl about David Crook. I didn't imagine that this trip would do this to me. I mean, I didn't come here for this. I came to show my films, to see my son, but not for this. I didn't come here to talk about things that happened eighty years ago to someone we knew fifty years ago. I didn't come here to talk about all the uncomfortable stuff, all the things you don't like to talk about. But here we are, and Papá has just died, and Raúl is with me and asks questions, so tell me: how do I answer them? Tonight we're going to watch *Time Out*, for example. It's impossible he won't come out with more questions. I've never been scared of that, you know. But there are things a person would like to forget, aren't there?"

"You're telling me," Marianella said, before hanging up. "I've spent my whole life trying."

After speaking to Marianella, he opened WhatsApp and tried to chat with Silvia.

He wrote:

I feel awkward insisting so much on recovering your love. It's not my style, as you know better than anyone. I feel as if I'm forcing you to act contrary to your emotions and that doesn't seem right, and although I know, as you told me the other night, you might tell me to forget about winning you back and romanticism, I feel like I'm feeling my way in the dark. And fortunately you haven't told me that, because while it's true that I'm ready to be very patient, it's also true that I need you to be patient too, so that every day, every night, every second, every word can play in my favour.

He wrote:

I hope I'm not making you uncomfortable, I want you to know that everything I'm doing, I'm doing with all the emotion I have left, because I don't want, if these attempts at winning you back fail, to be left regretting that I wasn't convincing, assertive or dramatic enough. Anyhow: not having tried everything before giving up. But if I don't persist, who will?

He wrote:

I want you to know there are moments when I lose hope and think I'll never get your love back, your caresses, your care . . . And there are other times when I'm angry and think all this is unfair, that my punishment is disproportionate to my sins, and I want to ask for a reduction. As if we were in Bogotá's plaza de Paloquemao or on the Silk Road.

And then: Send.

XII

The Crooks returned from the West at the end of November: all except David, who took advantage of their stay in Canada to undertake a lecture tour of the United States, from coast to coast, with the mission of explaining to the capitalist world the wonders that were happening in China. He had witnessed in recent years the collectivization of agriculture, the death of feudalism and the birth of the People's Republic, and he wanted to spread the good news the length and breadth of that country, which was so powerful and so in need of reform, so rich and so unjust, so civilized and so savage. That's what Carl told Marianella: "Nobody understands what's going on here. That is part of our mission: explain to the world what the Great Proletarian Cultural Revolution is." She could not have agreed more. She spent the end of the year dividing her time between the Friendship Hotel and the Crooks' apartment, talking non-stop about Mao Tse-tung and the Little Red Book. Later, when David Crook came back from his propaganda tour, she talked to him and admired him even more.

David immediately joined the struggle, but he complained about what he'd encountered at the Institute. The professors and students were divided into rival factions; David and Isabel found themselves forced to choose one of the revolutionary groups. They were all in agreement on the defence of Mao's thought, but their enemies were different. "Our enemies define us more than our friends do," David said. "Tell me who attacks you and I'll tell you who you are." One of the groups had pointed out and denounced the members of the Red Flag Battalion, who David knew well: they were honest and devoted comrades for whom both he and his wife would have walked through fire, so David went to them, even though only out of a sense of justice, and asked them to accept him in their group. It was not as easy as it would have been earlier, because the Cultural Revolution had brought an unprecedented mistrust of foreigners. It seemed implausible to David that a word like that could be used to describe him: a foreigner, him? He'd been living in China for decades, his children had been born in China and so had his wife, he had worked for the revolutionary cause, and four years earlier, when the communist world was in confrontation – the true schism, between the Chinese and the Soviets – he had unequivocally chosen Mao's side. How could they consider him a foreigner?

He joined the Red Flag Battalion. He denounced the Soviets for whom in years past he would have given his life; he shouted slogans in the street and recited Mao's Little Red Book; he composed *dazibao* that defended Vietnam and attacked Liu Shaoqi. He participated in the denunciation of an old worker who had become a minister, although he never really knew why he had been singled out or what he was accused of, he committed himself to the group's drive in a disciplined way. His own behaviour struck him as unusual, for he normally hesitated, questioned and informed himself before making decisions, not to mention engaging in activism: he had left far behind the blind faith of his childhood. But there, swept up in the songs of collective action, he thought it was unworthy or disloyal to raise objections to an event that was shaking the world. At the birth of a new culture, who could complain that the inexperience of youth might commit certain excesses? Yes, he did find the loudspeakers spitting out Mao's latest instructions all night long disagreeable, but only an affluent old man would complain that the Cultural Revolution was interrupting his sleep. And he, at fifty-seven, was not that. He still had several battles to fight.

Meanwhile, the factory work had come to an end. Sergio and Marianella, together again at the Friendship Hotel, wondered if there was some proletarian workplace they could go to together, as Marianella was not prepared to stay idle. The disappointment was enormous. The Association had nothing to offer them, and Sergio had the impression that nobody was making much effort to find anything. After all, two young foreigners, children of an absent specialist comfortably installed in five-star rooms, must have been the least of their worries. The only answer they received was the advice not to go out, as Westerners in the city were still suffering persecution and attacks from the Red Guards, and Sergio's reminder that they had been, or even were still, part of one of those organizations seemed to count for nothing. Nobody had told them expressly they could not still be members.

"Fine, but that would have to be explained," one comrade told them. "And Red Guards are not the type of people who listen patiently to explanations."

He was right. So Sergio and Marianella faced another spell

of enforced idleness, but this time, unlike at the Peace Hotel, they were not alone: since the schools had closed during the excesses of the Cultural Revolution and all the kids at the Friendship Hotel were just as idle, their parents saw no alternative but to improvise a school for them in one of the conference rooms. They called it Bethune-Yanan. Their teachers were philologists, historians, philosophers and even a mathematician; their activities had also been paused by the Cultural Revolution, so it was not difficult to divide up the subjects to continue their children's education, as if it were an emergency measure in the midst of a pandemic. One of them, a Colombian historian called Gustavo Vargas, took over a conference room in the hotel to set up an exhibition on the National Liberation Army, the ELN, the guerrilla army Father Camilo Torres had been fighting for when he was killed. Marianella went to the exhibition out of curiosity, but did not allow herself anything more than that: the ELN had chosen their side in the revolution, and it wasn't that of Mao Tse-tung. Later, one evening with the Crooks, she talked about the school and mentioned its name. Isabel told David; David smiled with the air of someone remembering something. That night was special for Marianella. Isabel taught her how to knit and David told her anecdotes; the Crooks celebrated her fifteenth birthday with ravioli; Carl kissed her and told her he loved her, and she told him she loved him too.

Gradually the young students at the Bethune-Yanan school, all Western residents of the Friendship Hotel, decided to take their commitment one step further. That's how the Rebel Regiment was born, for all practical effects, an organization of foreign Red Guards, all dressed in green, all with their red armbands with luminous yellow lettering, who came together under the authority of the most radical and committed parents. David Crook, of course, was one of them. Sometimes with him and sometimes on their own, the youths of the Rebel Regiment met in a room the Friendship Hotel provided with no objection, a small dark space, which was equipped with a mimeograph ready to print revolutionary pamphlets, where the regiment met to plan the future and listen to music and have long ideological discussions, in which Marianella was much more ardent than her boyfriend. At one of those meetings, however, Carl was chosen to represent the group at a huge event in support of the Cultural Revolution. Together they wrote a speech condemning and repudiating Liu Shaoqi; they called him a traitor, counter-revolutionary and capitalist scum, accused him of allying himself with Deng Xiaoping to bring about the failure of the People's Republic. Carl gave the speech in the open air, in a stadium where ten thousand people shouted and clapped and booed when the enemies' names were pronounced. And Marianella, a few steps away from the microphone, had never felt so in love with Carl or so proud of their regiment.

Around that time there was a great argument in the halls of the Friendship Hotel. The centre of the conflict was the traffic lights. They had changed; it was a decision by the Red Guards, and the Rebel Regiment could not stay on the sidelines. It was about recognizing that the colour red, symbol of the Guards and of the Cultural Revolution, could not continue to indicate that people should stop, since for all of them it was the colour of progress. From now on, red would mean advance; conversely green would become the signal to stop. Groups of Guards divided up the streets, screwdrivers in hand, to make the necessary changes. When he was bored, Sergio went outside and found a corner just to witness that unusual chromatic inversion, feeling a shiver each time a car accelerated when the light turned red, each time the young revolutionaries took advantage of a green light to show their posters or cross the street, in the midst of one of their marches, surrounding the accused. He would have liked to go out with his camera and document the whole matter, but he knew perfectly well that it was a terrible idea: at the very least, a Westerner taking photos would be considered a provocation and the incident would end with the confiscation of the roll of film and maybe even the camera; at worst, with dangerous accusations of espionage and a free night in some dark police station courtesy of the Department of Public Security. On one occasion he made fun of the whole matter in front of the tutor, Li. He thought she would laugh along with him, but instead he met with the severe expression of someone who has received an insult.

"What meaning do colours have?" she asked. "You do know that the red of our flag symbolizes the blood of our heroes, don't you? The blood of millions of comrades who gave their lives for the Republic. Think about what a revolutionary feels when he sees that someone else, in another country, has decided on a whim that the colour red, the colour for which we are ready to give our lives, should become an order to stop. And if we accept it, if we accept that red should be the signal for cars to stop, we would also have to accept that pedestrians should stop at red . . . at pedestrian crossing lights. And we are not just pedestrians, we are revolutionary combatants! And we cannot accept foreign interference in the Revolution!"

*

Three months went by like that. Three months of theoretical discussions in the Friendship Hotel, three months of classes with brilliant anthropologists and mathematicians and translators that gave Sergio the sensation that life was passing him by, three months of spending his free time on games of ping-pong or billiards. During that time Smilka tried several times to get in touch with him: she phoned (but Sergio asked the operator not to put the girl's calls through), wrote him a letter (to which Sergio did not reply, despite feeling he was being unfair) and even came to the hotel and asked for him at reception. "Tell her I'm not here," Sergio asked the receptionist. After a few weeks, Smilka gave up. The last time they saw each other was sad. The Bethune-Yanan Rebel Regiment had organized a day of protest outside the British diplomatic mission, and there were Sergio, Marianella and Carl shouting slogans against the Six Day War (which on the *dazibao* appeared as "aggression against Arab countries by Great Britain, the United States and Israel"), when a luxury car passed through the gates and the group of Red Guards. It was driving fast enough to keep the demonstrators from thinking of trying to stop it, but even so Sergio managed to see, pressed against the back window, Smilka's beautiful face, on which apprehension, disappointment and sadness all ran together. They never saw each other again. Better that way, Sergio thought, and he might have believed it to be true.

At the end of June, but not as a response to their requests, the Association organized a revolutionary trip. The beneficiaries were the children of international communist leaders – the children, in other words, of high-ranking guerrilla commanders in Laos, Cambodia and Vietnam – but Sergio and Marianella were on the list from the start, as if their father, on the other side of the sea, was still pulling the strings of their lives. This was not proletarian work, and it wouldn't help them progress in their intention to truly live like the people, but it was closer to the revolution than the bourgeois routine at the hotel. Two buses left for the south, and the passengers of both chanted slogans and walked up and down the aisles and laughed rudely for kilometres, like on any teenage outing. They made stops in Ruijin, the place where the First Red Army began their march in 1934, led by Mao and Zhou Enlai, and then they visited Shaoshan, the hamlet in Hunan where Mao was born in 1893, and along the way they had time to visit the War of Liberation bases.

It was not a simple trip, as the Red Guards frequently closed the route, alarmed by the spectacle of a bus full of privileged young people, all potential counter-revolutionaries. They ordered them off the bus with insults and sometimes went so far as to assault them, and things would have been worse if the leaders' children hadn't intervened. They asked Sergio and Marianella to get off the bus and pointed to them as if they were criminals in a line-up, but not to accuse them of anything, just the opposite: they used them to defend themselves. "They

are Latin American comrades," they said. And that, apparently, was the incontrovertible proof that it was not an outing for bourgeois Chinese but a gathering of international revolutionaries, even if some of them were still children.

The trip lasted just over a month. When they returned to Peking, driving through streets on red lights, Sergio and Marianella found the hotel deserted. It was the most humid August in many years, and the families who lived at the Friendship Hotel had gone to endure the heat elsewhere. The place was like a ghost town. Sergio began to spend the days shut up in his room, reading and rereading *How the Steel Was Tempered*, a novel by Nikolay Ostrovsky that became his only bridge to the unreachable proletarian future. Marianella reproached him for his stillness. "The revolution is for people who act," she said. "What are we doing stuck in here?" One night she caught him reading Ostrovsky's book and he looked so absorbed, so far away from the world around him, that she took a photo of him, as if she wanted to preserve the evidence of a crime. Sergio

didn't even notice, because he was playing music at full volume: he had found an old recording of *Don Giovanni* at the hotel shop and a more recent one of *La Traviata*, and had bought them without a second thought, even though Mozart and Verdi were already names outlawed by the Cultural Revolution.

Shut up in his own room, Sergio lost track of the number of times Marianella saw Carl in her room. Sometimes he stayed overnight; Sergio would meet him when he went down for breakfast, and then, in tense conversations, he found out all that had happened with the Rebel Regiment in their absence. While the Cabreras were travelling on a bus with other teenage revolutionaries, the regiment had organized demonstrations to protest the arrests of Chinese journalists in Hong Kong and the anti-China actions of the Burmese government, agreed to send a telegram of support to the proletarians of Wuhan and were now preparing to celebrate the centenary of Marx's *Das Kapital*, which would fall in September. Marianella felt that she had missed so many things by going on the trip and, at the same time, that nothing important had happened. In the midst of the convulsions on the other side of the hotel gates, her life had been paralysed. Carl seemed increasingly in love with her; for her, however, it was as though she were waiting for life to happen, a life that was nowhere to be seen.

One hot afternoon, the Rebel Regiment met to examine their achievements over the summer. The adults were not there, but all the young people – Carl, Marianella, Sergio – and also the most active foreigners: Shapiro, Rittenberg, Sol Adler. It was Adler who read the report on the attacks the regiment had begun to receive from other Red Guards. It was a precise list that she passed, mimeographed, from hand to hand:

The Regiment's leadership was conservative

The Regiment has blocked the Cultural Revolution among foreigners for a year and a half

The Regiment (old authorities) wants to control the movements of Asian-African-Latin American women

The Regiment wrote poems against itself to win sympathy

"This is all ridiculous," Marianella said. "Outside comrades are working for the revolution, and here we are fighting over stupidities beside an Olympic-sized swimming pool."

"They're not stupidities," Carl said. "The attacks are serious. They are putting up *dazibao* on the university walls, Lilí. They are attacking Jews, all Jews. We cannot allow . . ."

"But that's here, Carlos," said Marianella, who sometimes called him by the Spanish translation of his name. "That happens in the Friendship Hotel."

"Well, my father was attacked right here," Carl said. "With his own name, besides."

He was referring to a *dazibao* that had appeared a few days earlier at the entrance to the Friendship Hotel's international dining room. The authors, it seems, were a group of Arabs who did not look kindly on the participation of so many Jewish people in the Cultural Revolution. David had defended the presence of Westerners, and the Arabs responded with a question that was a play on words using an old English phrase: BY HOOK OR BY CROOK? Marianella did not understand.

"They mean that my father is unscrupulous," Carl said. "That he'll do anything to get what he wants. I'm not saying they weren't ingenious, but it's an attack, and it's personal, and it's serious."

"That may be so," Marianella said, "but it doesn't matter.

Here we are, in a hotel with a pool and dance halls. Here is not where things happen. This is not proletarian life here, Carlos. This is not real life."

The first day of September, Sergio lost patience. He had stopped counting the number of times he'd written to the Association, but he could make an inventory of the visits from the comrades, always very sympathetic, always very understanding, who took note of his grievances – about his frustrated studies, about contact with the world of workers – and then they asked for some days to consider a response that never came. Now he could wait no longer. He took the grey case out of his wardrobe, and from it the typewriter his father had left, an Olivetti the capitals of which skipped, and set it up on the table. He fed a blank piece of paper into the roller and wrote: *Comrades*. Then, on the next line: *China–Latin America Friendship Association*. And then he let loose.

> *In view of the difficulties we have found in communicating with you, we have had to resort to writing a letter by means of which we want to raise some points we feel need repeating, as well as some criticisms of your treatment of us. We think it best to begin with the root of the problem. Therefore, we want to remind you of the objective we have been pursuing by remaining in China. From what we have observed with respect to this problem, you have a mistaken point of view. This can be seen in the way you've treated us.*

Yes, that was good, Sergio thought. Then he listed the reasons that had led him and his sister to stay in Peking. There were several, but they could be summed up in one: to achieve a radical change in their petit-bourgeois concept of the world and an ideological restructuring – that was the word Sergio used: *restructuring* – to acquire the consciousness of the proletarian class and, when they returned to their country, be able to better support the revolutionary struggle of the Colombian people.

And we have stayed in China to study precisely because China is the centre of the worldwide proletarian revolution, because it is the Marxist–Leninist vanguard of the world in the current era, and therefore the most appropriate place for young people like us to be educated and nourished by the thought of Mao Tse-tung, which is the highest level of Marxism–Leninism in our era.

That was good too: "the highest level in our era". But then, after the praise, he had to raise the tone.

We are aware of the following teaching of Comrade Mao Tse-tung, and we believe that you must also be aware of it: "We who have conquered victory in our revolution must help those who are still struggling. This is our internationalist duty." Do you people consider that in your treatment of us you are fulfilling that teaching of Comrade Mao? The simple fact of our being here does not mean we are fulfilling the objective previously stated in this letter. The fact that we are here, under your care, is in itself an internationalist act. But, does it satisfy the requirements of help expressed by Comrade Mao in the previously cited passage? We think not. How does one acquire a political education? Is it acquired by being permanently enclosed between four walls, without actively participating in the life and political struggles of the masses of the people? No. Absolutely not! How can one acquire a consciousness and a position in the proletarian class without merging with the proletarian masses?

Then he went on quoting Mao:

To acquire a true understanding of Marxism, it must be learned not only from books, but also principally through the class struggle, practical work and intimate contact with the proletarian and peasant masses. Have you satisfied this desire? Have you made the slightest effort to initiate our political training in the way Comrade Mao teaches?

The answer was no. Sergio listed the various moments he had gone to the Association to ask for their help without receiving anything but refusal, evasion and silence, or in the best of cases the tired argument of "safety" (Sergio used a pair of quotes here that seemed to double over with irony). *All your refusals have gradually been crushing our faith that you might help us to achieve the objective of our stay here.* This was now an accusation and quite a serious one. Instead of calming his rhetoric, Sergio decided to pile on even more pressure.

Everything indicates that the line you've applied to us is extremely mistaken and is not the proletarian revolutionary line of Comrade Mao. Everything indicates obstruction of our political training instead of facilitation. Do you people perhaps not realize how important it is for us to be able to begin our ideological transformation and our political training? Do you not see the Colombian revolution's need for young people who are politically firm in their proletarian class position? Have you not noticed our desire to become people of that class? Do you perhaps want to see us take an erroneous path? Do you perhaps desire to see us degenerate towards revisionism?

We are asking for some concrete solutions: we request that you give us the opportunity to integrate with the revolutionary Chinese masses to learn from them, whether in a factory, a people's commune, a school or an institution of translation until classes resume. Although our greatest desire – which we beg you to do everything possible to bring about – is to receive military and political training with units of the People's Liberation Army.

There it is, he thought, now I've said it. This was the moment to bring out all the heavy artillery.

We rebel against the application of a reactionary bourgeois line in our treatment! We protest at the treatment we have so far received on the part of the Association! We demand the fulfilment of the Marxist–Leninist principles of the international proletariat, as taught by Comrade Mao Tse-tung! We demand a concrete response as soon as possible!

Sergio signed the letter, certain he was taking a step into the void. Such a list of complaints could only have two results: either they would listen and give them what they wanted, or they would get in touch with their parents to send them back to Colombia for having turned into a burden. During the next visit from the tutor Li, Sergio placed the envelope in her hand without saying a word, with the solemnity of someone handing over an urn of ashes, and he waited.

Four days later he was moving, together with Marianella, to the Peking Alarm Clock Factory.

They arrived early in the morning, when the air was still cool. Comrade Chou, the Association's secretary, had picked them up at the Friendship Hotel, and on the way explained two or three things about the place where they'd live from now on. It was an important factory: despite the modest name, it produced sophisticated machines for petroleum exploitation and high precision devices for the aeronautics industry (Sergio, when he heard this, thought briefly of the drawing teacher from Chong Wen School). For the Party, Comrade Chou said, the Alarm Clock Factory was of strategic importance, and the Cabrera siblings should feel fortunate. Not everyone had the privilege of working in a place like this.

The Management Committee received them with a small welcome gathering. The members of the Association were there, greeting people with the pride of mentors, and several workers, representatives of each of the divisions. A photographer documented the moment: he moved Sergio and Marianella as if they were cardboard cut-outs, taking them from group to group, making sure to photograph them with all those present. Sergio thanked them in silence for the brief ceremony, useful only to add some glitter to his arrival. Mao said somewhere that there should be no difference between the Chinese and foreign revolutionaries, and this is what Sergio expected. He wanted to be one of them. He wanted to be one of the crowd.

In brief speeches, the managers thanked them for coming to China to help in the construction of socialism. Others praised the solidarity between peoples and the internationalist spirit of this moment. Comrade Chou addressed the managers of the factory to tell them that the young Cabreras were the children of Colombian revolutionaries, that their parents had been specialists at the Foreign Languages Institute and that they had returned to their country to prepare the ground for the revolution there. "That is why they delegated the enormous responsibility of educating their children to the Chinese people," said Comrade Chou, visibly moved. "And the Chinese people have fulfilled that responsibility with dedication and commitment." He paused and continued: "For their first days, the new arrivals will tour the whole factory. I ask all the section heads, the people in charge of each workshop, to welcome them with comradeship, give them your time, support them and teach them your trade." When the meeting was over, Sergio approached one of the managers of the factory and explained that in the other factory he'd learned to operate a lathe, and he'd learned well, and that was what he'd like to do here. He thought he was doing the right thing, claiming a skill and showing enthusiasm, but the manager looked at him severely.

"You are not here to do what most amuses you," he said. "You are here to do what is needed."

He turned and left. It was Comrade Wang. He was not only one of the managers of the factory, but also a man respected by the workers: he had a sort of natural authority that he could not have hidden if he tried, and he spoke with few words and obscure sayings that did not use revolutionary slang and would have awakened suspicion or mistrust if anyone else had said them. It was obvious he had not been impressed by the arrival of the two young Westerners who were now telling him what to do out of the blue, and over the next few days he seemed to be avoiding them. For Sergio these were exhausting days: not just because of the physical work with machines he'd never seen before, or the tension of trying to do what was asked of him correctly, but the effort of understanding a language that was neither street nor school. He wasn't sleeping well, besides, because the daytime temperature was already starting to drop, and the nights were so cold that they had to put hot water bottles in their beds. They went round the whole factory during the first days, visiting every warehouse and workshop, doing a sort of reconnaissance mission. Then they visited the design section and it was like being back at Chong Wen (the drawing boards, the rulers and compasses, the fine-leaded pencils). Finally, they arrived at the maintenance workshops, where Sergio felt more comfortable: it was an enormous warehouse full of milling machines and drills and presses and lathes where they could barely talk over the noise, and in the air of which floated the dense smell of metal filings. Yes, this was his environment, Sergio thought, he would move around there like a fish in water. But then he was introduced to the head of the workshop: it was Comrade Wang.

"I see you got what you wanted," he said. Sergio noted the informal mode of address; he also noted the deep voice, unusual in China. "You like what you see?"

"I do," Sergio said. "But I promise I won't be amusing myself."

Wang didn't smile. With a serious look, but without the slightest trace of solemnity or arrogance, he said: "The taller the bamboo, the more flexible its trunk must be to allow its leaves to touch the waters of the river."

He put an arm around Sergio – only then did Sergio notice that he was half a head taller than the man – and took him around the workshop. He told all the workers they met that this was their Colombian comrade, that his name in Chinese was Li Zhi Qiang, that it was the duty of all of them to make his stay among them a happy time, and they all responded with bows of varying degrees and smiles that seemed sincere. Finally, they arrived at a lathe that had no operator: it was bigger than the one at the Number 2 Tool Factory; it was also a more complex mechanism. Comrade Wang put a hand on the handle, as big as the steering wheel of a car, and stroked the machine with the other hand as if it were a faithful horse.

"From now on, and for as long as you want, I shall be your teacher," he said. "From now on, and for as long as you want, this will be your lathe. We're going to take good care of it."

And then the lesson began.

Your attitude towards China, at the very least, should be one of gratitude. You should think that it is China that is giving you everything necessary so that you two can become revolutionaries who can serve your people. They are doing this out of their extraordinary proletarian internationalist spirit. In reality, you have no right to demand anything. Request what you need, yes, but always in a very polite and comradely way. When you find that something is not going well (and always and only when you're absolutely sure this is the case) and you can see the solution, you should provide the necessary observations, for this type of criticism is also a help to the Chinese people. You must be aware that it's natural for there still to be some things that don't work perfectly, that have defects or errors, but in principle, fundamentally, there is a basic correct Marxist–Leninist policy.

*

Every morning, after breakfast and before beginning their working day, the labourers met in a room free of furniture, in front of an enormous photograph of Chairman Mao adorned with flags and garlands of artificial flowers. And then they appealed to him out loud: that he guide them on the correct path so that what they produced would be good; that he allow them to fulfil the plans made by the directors; that he protect them from industrial accidents. The same scene was repeated at the end of the day, before dinner, with the same workers as in the morning, and ended with the same combative shout: "Long live Chairman Mao!" One day, during lunch, Sergio talked to Marianella about it. He asked her if those rituals did not seem strange to her or even a little uncomfortable: if they didn't seem to resemble Catholic mass. It turned out that Marianella had said something similar to her foreman.

"What?" Sergio said. "And you didn't get into trouble?"

Quite the contrary. Her foreman was an older man who had taken her under his wing as if he had to protect her from something. At first, Marianella had been sent to the section where they sealed clocks that were already put together, and for days she specialized in tightening a tiny screw, always the same one and always with the same tool, until she got sick of it all: the tiny screw, the tool and the clocks. And she said so: "I'm fed up." Her foreman, instead of reproaching her, immediately transferred her to the workshop where they cast the bases for the clocks. They were slow machines that didn't demand a lot of attention, so Marianella made use of the time and her self-confidence to get to know her foreman better. That's why, when she found herself repeating memorized phrases of Mao's in front of his portrait, she did not hesitate to say:

"This is like the Sacred Heart of Jesus."

"What are you saying, Comrade Lilí?"

"In my country, they do this with God. And I've never liked it."

Her foreman's only response was to invite her to his home one evening, two poor rooms in a grey concrete building. He lived with his wife, whose wrinkled face brought back images for Marianella of the grandmother at the commune, who cooked without speaking while the foreman showed Marianella the walls of the tiny place. Not one more portrait of Chairman Mao could have fit on them, and where there was not a portrait there was a framed saying, like a smaller and more venerable *dazibao*.

"If my walls fall down from the weight, let them fall," the foreman said. "Mao has given me everything. I have work and food thanks to him. Japanese soldiers killed my parents. That was less than twenty years ago, but it seems like another lifetime. I know I am not going to die in a war, because China is powerful now. And if I had to die for my people, I would do so with pleasure. If Mao asked me to die for the nation, I would not think twice. Look, miss, the difference is very clear: you, in your country, have a dead God. Our God is alive. Why shouldn't we talk to him?"

Marianella thought he was completely right.

Sergio, meanwhile, noticed that Comrade Wang did not participate with the same enthusiasm in the sessions, and did not shout slogans with the same vehemence. After a few weeks he noticed that the morning greeting had changed: "Long live Chairman Mao! May he live for many years!" the workers now shouted, but Comrade Wang's deep voice could not be clearly heard. Sergio raised the subject during a break between two intense jobs. His foreman, who by then had begun to ask him to call him Lao Wang (it was like saying "old man Wang": a term of address denoting confidence), signalled that they'd talk later. And when they left the workshop, when he was sure nobody could hear them, he began to talk about what was happening with Chairman Mao. He spoke of the portraits hanging all over the factory, in all the cafeterias, in all the dormitories; he spoke of the photos that all workers carried in their pockets; when they didn't carry photos, they carried badges with the chairman's image on them, and photos or images were invariably carried inside the Little Red Book, which the workers consulted during their breaks. Lao Wang summed up the situation in a few words: "They are turning him into a Buddha."

Sergio had seen Red Guards sleeping in the street and enduring the cold in order to have the possibility of glimpsing Mao on his balcony in Tiananmen Square. He had seen millions of them arrive from all over China to be closer to the leader, even if they were five blocks away from him and even if the only contact they had with him were the anthems they sang endlessly. There was something twisted in those excesses. Chairman Mao himself had harshly criticized the cult of personality surrounding Stalin, which contaminated Soviet socialism for many years, and pointed out how harmful it could be to the development of the proletarian revolution. Sergio found the morning and evening rituals frankly annoying, but he made sure no-one ever noticed. By the beginning of November the slogan had changed again: "May Chairman Mao have an infinite life without end!" the workers said or shouted in unison in front of a full-colour portrait of Mao. One day Lao Wang said to Sergio: "The salute to the Emperor was not much different." There was a genuine sorrow in his voice, and Sergio understood the feeling very well. He had already noticed that other things functioned badly in the revolution, and the cult of Mao was not the only symptom.

He had been talking to the workers. In their downtime, at meals, on walks between one workshop and another or between the dormitories and the workplace, they told him things that seemed like spontaneous conversation, but were always said in low tones. Now Sergio understood why the Association had had so much trouble finding a place for the Cabreras to work: the factory was one of the few that had not closed in these critical times. The workers told him about strikes all over the country, constant sabotage by the workers themselves, such a critical lack of raw materials that sometimes there was not even coal to heat the barracks, where people slept when it was ten degrees below zero outside. Hearing them it was impossible to distinguish any tone of complaint: they all recounted these things as if they were talking about a natural disaster. What could they do? Yes, Comrade Li Zhi Qiang, the country was suffering: there was famine in Heilongjiang, outrages in Daoxian, where the Red Guards, our comrades, had murdered thousands of compatriots. In any case, they asked Comrade Li Zhi Qiang not to repeat what they had just told him. Please, comrade, never tell anyone that we said this!

Then they told him about the comrade who had made an imprudent comment criticizing the strikes; they had accused him of being a capitalist, and his punishment, as for all those suspected of capitalism, had been to clean the factory toilets without help from anyone.

Comrade Li Zhi Qiang promised never to say a word.

Sergio had forgotten those conversations a couple of weeks later, when he and his sister arrived back at the Friendship Hotel and found a message from the Association: their parents wanted to speak to them; they had to call Colombia. They asked the hotel operator to place the call on Saturday morning, at around ten, and the next day the telephone in his room rang. It was his father. "How are you?" Fausto asked. "How's everything going?" Fausto explained that he and Luz Elena had been talking, and the two of them had reached the conclusion that it was time for Sergio and Marianella to return to Colombia. "Of course, that will be when you've finished everything. But we think it's time for you to come back. Do you agree?" Sergio thought for a moment, listening to the static on the line. *When you've finished everything.* The phrase was cryptic, but it would have been unwise to mention over the phone the plan they'd hatched: to receive military training with the People's Liberation Army. It was a privilege reserved for very few, and the participation of foreigners was kept strictly secret, for no Chinese comrade would be pleased to learn that a Westerner was taking a place that one of them could have had.

"Yes," Sergio said at last. "If we don't do it now, the revolution will be carried out by others."

"Well, that's that, then," Fausto said. "Start preparing for the trip. Now you'll need to get some things. Have you got a pen and paper?"

Then he gave him a series of instructions. Neither Sergio nor Marianella had travel documents, as four years earlier when they'd arrived in China, Sergio and Marianella were still children and travelled on their parents' passports; now they needed their own individual passports, and to get them they'd have to deal with the paperwork at a Colombian consulate. France and China had recently renewed diplomatic relations, and Air France had a weekly flight between Peking and Paris. So Fausto would send the passports by post, along with their birth certificates, and Sergio would travel to Paris to exchange them for new ones. The Association, Fausto said, would take care of purchasing the tickets and reserving a hotel, and give him sufficient spending money. Since Sergio needed something to wear (he'd outgrown all the clothes he arrived with four years earlier, and everything he'd acquired since was Chinese), Marianella asked Carl to lend her brother a pair of jeans, and Carl arrived at the Friendship Hotel one day with a pair of Levi's, as it said on the label, that he'd picked up in Canada. Sergio thought it strange that an item of workers' clothing was all the rage among the Western bourgeoisie. "Happy Christmas," Carl said. "Two months ahead of time."

They would remember that phrase – and that date – because of what happened later.

On one of those autumn mornings, David Crook was crossing the campus of the Institute towards the office to collect his post. The ground was covered in stones, because the confrontations between the different factions had intensified, and a group of Red Guards were keeping watch around the classroom they'd turned into their centre of operations. At that moment, some other students emerged from the shadows, their heads covered by helmets that looked like military ones, and aggressively demanded that David hand over his camera. "Camera? I'm not carrying a camera," he said. "Liar," one of them said. "You are a spy. A foreign spy." They took him to a room on the second floor, took his briefcase, and asked him to empty his pockets. "You have no right to hold me," David told them. It was night when they took him downstairs, and forced him into the back seat of a car too small for him and the two Guards accompanying him. After a half-hour drive they arrived at the headquarters of the Peking garrison. By then, David had realized those kids were not playing games.

Two hours later, a young man who looked like an officer arrived to tell him he'd have to spend the night in custody: they had found suspicious material in his briefcase. He thought of the texts he was carrying: two of Mao's latest instructions, which the Red Flag Battalion had received but had not broadcast yet. Would that be what seemed suspicious to them? Yes, they were official documents, and yes, they were in the hands of a foreigner: it was not improbable that might arouse suspicion. David protested, but again it was in vain. The guard took him to a cell barely big enough for a rickety old bed. There he spent the night, and the following day, and the next night as well. When he tried to look out through the barred window, the guard growled. David understood he was only to look within, to better meditate on his guilt. On the third day a green van transferred him to another place, across the city, and two weeks later, in the middle of the night, they put him back into a vehicle to cross the city in the opposite direction. What he found was disheartening: a tiny, damp, dark cell, adorned only with a poster calling for the suppression of counter-revolutionary elements. The next day, when he asked for permission to go to the toilet, a guard accompanied him to the other side of a cement courtyard, and David thus discovered that he was in a sort of complex of brick buildings that had not always been the improvised prison they'd now become. In the distance he saw the red star of the Military Museum, which was lit up at night, and David grew accustomed to looking for it whenever he went to the toilet, every night of every week of every month, to remember that out there the world still existed.

XIII

Sergio landed in Paris in mid-December 1967. According to what Comrade Chou had told him, an official from the new Chinese embassy would be waiting for him at the exit from Orly airport. It seemed like a clandestine mission: in his parents' passport, where his name was listed, there was also an express prohibition in huge letters against travelling to any communist country, including the People's Republic of China; in other words, Sergio had to hide his airport of origin from the consular authorities. But his clandestinity did not last long, as an immigration officer, seeing his passport, took him out of the queue and began to interrogate him, and at the first opportunity Sergio had explained everything: that he was coming from Peking, that he did not have his own passport and that his intention was to get a new one at the Colombian consulate in Paris. It was a proper interrogation, lasting three intense hours, in a windowless office, during which the French officer could not understand why Sergio refused to phone his own consulate. "*Mais, pourquoi pas?*" the gendarme shouted. "*Mais dîtes-moi, monsieur! Pourquoi pas?*" And Sergio could not explain that his father's most explicit instruction had been that one: do not tell the Colombians that he was coming from China. When he finally left the airport, the official had left, and Sergio had to pay a taxi to take him to the Chinese embassy. The comrades who were expecting him took him out for supper and then to the hotel they'd reserved for him. There, in a narrow room, he left his heavy suitcase and went straight back out, because an acquaintance was waiting for him.

His name was Jorge Leiva. He was thirty-eight years old, though his receding hairline made him look older. He had finished his law degree, but, when it came time to return to Colombia and put into practice what he'd learned, he decided to stay in the city where his favourite poets had written their poetry and write his own poems there. To get by he had sold vegetables in Les Halles market and sung tangos in a bar called the Veracruz, and now he worked in the Fnac shops on Sébastopol. He had a profound link with Sergio: the simple fact of having lived in Peking, where he had acquired his political convictions. His older brother also lived in Paris, and his name was not important for being that of a prestigious cardiologist, but for his clandestine activities as secretary of the MOEC, a workers' movement looking for a way to arm itself to wage revolution in Latin America. In fact, the reason Sergio's suitcase was so heavy was political: comrades in Peking had sent Leiva and his brother several dozen copies of the Little Red Book. The night of his arrival in Paris, after meeting Leiva at the Fnac and walking with him to his attic apartment on rue de Lille, Sergio thought the same thing he would often think over the next several years. He had chanced to be born at a time when everyone, everywhere, by any means, had a single objective: to bring about revolution. How lucky he was to be alive.

Sergio spent the night there, in the low-ceilinged room,

halfway between the docks of the Seine and Boulevard Saint-Germain. The poet Leiva offered him two square metres of his apartment, and Sergio immediately accepted: it was better to save his spending money than to waste it on a hotel. The next morning, very early, he went to the Colombian consulate. His nervousness had woken him; as he walked, it grew more intense. As he crossed the river, a gust of wind blew in his face, but Sergio was thinking of how much depended on this procedure. He was going to ask the consul for a passport to allow him to return to Colombia and join his father, who was now working for the Communist Party; he had just spent years in a forbidden country that his own country considered an enemy. In that state he arrived at the Colombian consulate. A receptionist took his documents and asked him to sit down. Sergio began to regret this journey: what if they refused to give him a passport? What if they took away the one he already had, for having used it to travel to forbidden places? And what if Marianella had to stay by herself in China, unable to travel, without her own passport and also without that of her parents? And what if the consul was in the know about the activities of Fausto Cabrera, a well-known actor who frequently appeared in newspapers and who had never hidden his left-wing sympathies?

At that moment the consul came out. He was wearing large glasses with a little chain that encircled a turtleneck. He welcomed Sergio with a smile and invited him into his office, and there, while someone went to get a cup of coffee, he looked over the documents Sergio had brought and asked a single question, addressing him informally as if he were a friend's son: "So, what were you doing in China?" And when Sergio stood up to explain (he never knew why he had felt it would be better to give his explanations on his feet), the blood rushed from his head, his world went black, and the next thing he saw was a group of six agitated hands trying to fan him with magazines and handkerchiefs. Someone thought he must be hungry; someone said they should give the poor kid a few francs.

Sergio left the consulate with the consul's sympathy, some money in his pocket and an encouraging response. Yes, they could expedite the passport, but they needed more than birth certificates: it was essential to have his father's express author-ization, certified by a notary. He called Colombia from the first phone booth he came to (and marvelled at how easy communication was here, compared with the torment of Peking), asked for what he needed and gave the address of the poet Leiva. Then he went to the hotel, picked up his things and took them to the attic apartment, and from that moment on he spent his time waiting.

"My trip has been prolonged," he told Leiva.

"Good," he replied. "Interesting things are happening here."

He spent the first few days walking along the Seine, looking at cheap books in the stalls on the quay and tolerating the permanent drizzle. He often wondered why everyone looked at him with such curiosity, until he realized that his Levi's caught Parisians' attention as if a cowboy had just moved to the left bank. Several times he walked to the Louvre to look at Italian paintings or to the Orangerie to see Impressionist pictures while the cold seeped out of his skin. He went into churches to sit and read on a pew in the back, near a stained-glass window; he'd take refuge in Saint-Julien-le-Pauvre, for example, or in Saint-Germain-des-Prés, reading an essay on China by Simone de Beauvoir or one by Roland Barthes about many things, and hours would fly by. The book by Barthes was called *Mythologies*. Sergio read it in four hours on a cold morning and found it so interesting, and talked about it so enthusiastically, that Leiva said: "Well, take it with you as a gift and shut up about it." The money they gave him for no reason at the Colombian consulate also bought him cinema tickets and in a theatre on rue Racine he saw Luis Buñuel's *Belle de jour*. But then he discovered the Cinemateca, which not only let him see less recent films that he knew only by reputation, but was also one of the cheaper ways to pass the time. And then he remembered what Leiva had told him: "Interesting things are happening here." How right he'd been, although the interesting things he'd been talking about were not necessarily the things that were happening to Sergio in the depths of his consciousness.

In Paris, in the streets and film theatres and bookshops by the Seine, Sergio discovered a world, news of which barely reached the country of the Cultural Revolution. Mid-morning, after Leiva had gone to work at the Fnac, he'd walk along Saint-Germain or by the river, depending on how cold it was, he'd stop for a coffee somewhere and then go straight to the Trocadéro. Soon the columns of the building were as familiar as the ceilings of the attic apartment. There, in the Palais de Chaillot, he saw several Hitchcock films (and liked *Rear Window* best of all), he saw several of Kurosawa's (*Rashomon*, *Red Beard*, *Seven Samurai*), he saw *Modern Times* and *The Great Dictator*, he saw *Citizen Kane* and he saw *Casablanca* and he saw *Johnny Guitar*. He came out of the Cinemateca onto the esplanade when night had already fallen over the Eiffel Tower and began walking back. Those forty-five minutes of solitude became crucial to Sergio: he would still be feeling a sort of mental excitement, an electricity that kept his eyes open, and he did not want to lose that emotion too quickly, didn't want the images to disappear, those luminous images he continued to see on his retinas while he walked, as clear as if he was projecting them himself on the sky or on the river.

He spent Christmas with Leiva and his brother the cardiologist and a handful of women and men with hair much longer than his who wanted to know everything, absolutely everything, about China and about Mao and about the Cultural Revolution, and wanted to know if the proletariat was as happy as they said, and as heroic. "Is it true?" they said. "Is it true they are breaking with the feudal past, with thousands of years of history? Is it true that can be done?" Sergio thought about the men and women humiliated in public, heads bowed, metre-high hats accusing their wearers of complicity with capitalism, signs hanging from their necks with other charges in large characters – despots, landowners, enemy sympathizers, elements of counter-revolutionary gangs – and remembered the museums and temples ransacked by the violent crowds and the news of executions in the countryside, which only a very few ever found out about. He remembered all that and felt for mysterious reasons that he could not talk about anything, or that they wouldn't understand if he told them what he knew.

"Yes," he said. "It's true. It can be done."

He saw them again a few days later, at a political meeting that Leiva had organized in his attic apartment. Something had changed. This time they weren't asking with insatiable curiosity about life in China and the truth of Maoism, but were more circumspect, or maybe they'd just had less to drink. They were talking about Robbe-Grillet, whose novels were on everyone's mind, and someone remembered that in *Far from Vietnam* Godard said he'd never liked Robbe-Grillet much. And they laughed, but they did so while looking at a quiet Frenchman watching the scene from a cushion, sitting in the lotus position, leaning against a wall. The Frenchman smiled and said: "Godard is so wicked." It was Louis Malle. Sergio gathered all the courage in his arsenal to tell him he'd seen *Lift to the Scaffold* at the Alliance Française in Peking. What he didn't tell him, however, was that he'd gone back to see it again no fewer than six times, and that it was one of the films to blame for his taking seriously the absurd idea of being – one day, in a distant future – a film director.

Maybe it was strange, but the city seemed more familiar because everyone was talking about the war in Vietnam as if it was happening to them. Of all the films he saw in Paris, while he counted the days an envelope could take to arrive from Colombia, the one that made the biggest impact was *Far from Vietnam*, which he went to see as soon as possible after hearing the comments and jokes the night of the gathering. It was a documentary made by five New Wave directors (Godard, Agnès Varda, Alain Resnais, Claude Lelouch and Chris Marker), a fashion photographer turned film-maker (William Klein) and a veteran Dutch documentary director who over the years had become a hero of the international left: Joris Ivens. Sergio went to see the film in December and was so impressed that he went back in January, after the holidays, to feel the same indignation as before and at the same time the same astonishment, for he had never imagined that this could be done with cinema, or that cinema was capable of giving us such wonders. He heard Godard repeat the words of Che Guevara, when he urged that in Latin America "two, three, or many Vietnams" should flourish; he saw Fidel Castro sitting in the forest, wearing his olive-green uniform with black and red diamonds on the epaulettes, saying that the armed struggle was the only option for the Cuban people, and that in his opinion, given the conditions in the immense majority of Latin American countries, there was no other path for them than the armed struggle. Vietnam had demonstrated, Fidel Castro said, that no military machine, no matter how powerful, can crush a guerrilla movement supported by the people. The United States Army had failed against the heroic people of Vietnam, Castro said. Today, nobody doubted it. That was one of the great services the people of Vietnam had provided to the world.

Sergio walked out into the night still thinking of the last words of the documentary, which announced exactly this: he was going to walk out into a world without war, far from Vietnam, where it was easy to forget that this reality existed. In those few words, in their melancholy and their apparent resignation and the denunciation of a world without solidarity, Sergio found the most eloquent protest he had ever seen, including the marches in which he'd participated as a student at Chong Wen. And it also seemed to be the most efficient, if the efficiency of a protest was judged by the level of violence it provoked. The second time he went to see the documentary, Sergio felt something strange when he sat down, and he noticed that not only his, but all the seats around him as well, had suffered vicious knife attacks. Later he learned that the perpetrators were members of Occident, a fascist group that went around Paris confronting demonstrators, and one of their commando operations was to enter the cinemas that showed *Far from Vietnam* and slash the upholstery to shreds.

The film did not seem any less admirable seen on a torn screen, and it was obvious that he was not alone in his admiration: the streets of the Latin Quarter, in that cold January, were filled every day with demonstrators against the war who seemed to have just come out of the same cinema. They shouted slogans and echoed its protests. They were almost always students, and often from the Sorbonne, so Sergio could not have been surprised when, accompanying Leiva, he arrived at a demonstration in front of the Mutualité and recognized, among the crowd, several familiar faces. The French friends who had interrogated him about the Cultural Revolution were there, waving signs that Sergio didn't manage to read, shouting slogans with their comrades. The whole scene felt familiar. Sergio had seen similar sights in Peking: irate youngsters protesting against the old authorities. He wondered if something like the Cultural Revolution could happen here. Months later, when the first news about the May '68 events reached him, he would feel a confusing pride at having detected the way the situation would develop, and having done so thanks to his years in China.

Leiva invited him to another demonstration later. It was exactly the same as the previous one: in the same place, with the same students shouting the same slogans, with the same police observing them unblinkingly from behind their shields. It had stopped raining but the sky was still cloudy, and there were shiny puddles on the pavement that looked like mercury until a boot stepped in them. The demonstrators held up their signs: PAIX AU VIETNAM HÉROÏQUE and JOHNSON ASSASSIN were written on cardboard or sheets. In front of the Maubert pharmacy, the police seemed to be waiting for the protestors to attack first. And then it happened: a stone hit one of their shields, and then another, and then another, and an uproar of battle deafened Sergio. The police charged them, and the crowd writhed like a whip, and someone beside Sergio fell, perhaps injured by friendly fire. Sergio and Leiva were lucky to have arrived late, because most of the wounded were falling in the centre of the demonstration. Both of them ran off, trying to cover their heads, and lost track of each other in their flight. They met up again later, in the attic apartment on rue de Lille. Sergio noticed that Leiva's eyes were shining.

Around the time the papers arrived from Colombia, with thousands of stamps and authentications and even the signature of the Minister for Foreign Relations, Leiva showed Sergio a new poem:

> *The great war-leader Sun Tzu*
> *moved his faint-hearted soldiers into combat*
> *Brave was his scimitar*
> *One day*
> *he made the Dynasty's concubines wrestle*
> *until they were ecstatic*
> *Great was his valour*
> *when pierced by a thick dart*
> *he stood up saying:*
> *"Let them put roots in me"*
> *Later*
> *a tree grew from his guts*
> *and the warrior now*
> *gives shade to the wayfarer.*

"I don't know what title to give it," he said. "But I think it's on the right track, don't you?"

Sergio flew back to Peking in the middle of February. It seemed like he'd managed a miracle, but there, in the pocket of his coat, was his passport; it was more incomprehensible still that the consul had given him his sister's as well. He was also bringing two litres of Coca-Cola, in order to share with Marianella what could not be found even in the Friendship Shop (it was the drink of the enemy). When he arrived in Peking, he didn't go directly to the Alarm Clock Factory, where the bottles would have caused a scandal, but made a stop at the Friendship Hotel, intending to put them in the fridge in his room. He was thinking of his sister, who had taken David Crook's arrest very badly, and wondering how she would be now. He thought those days would not have been easy for her, sharing Carl's anxiety about the uncertainty of the accusations, and maybe for that reason was surprised to find the walls of their room papered with posters drawn by Marianella. *Hurrah for the military course of the Communist Party*, one of them said. *Hail the People's Liberation Army of China. Long live the revolution in Latin America.*

He lay down with the intention of taking a short siesta before going to find his sister at the factory. In recent months he had spent so much time lying down that he had decided to use the ceiling the way other people used walls, and he had pinned up his maps of Colombia, of China and of the world, to memorize them during his leisure hours, marking with coloured drawing pins the places he'd been to, even fleetingly. He looked at Peking, then at Bogotá, and tried to trace an invisible line marking the trajectory they would take to where his parents were, not eastwards, which seemed the most sensible route according to the map, but rather by way of Moscow and Europe. But the posters his sister had drawn overpowered his unfocused attention, and Sergio would remember them days later, when he discovered the nickname, not entirely kindly, that their friends at the hotel had given Marianella during his absence: the Revolutionary Nun.

From Marianella's diary:

1968.1.11

Today I found out that the People's Daily wants to talk to me about participating in a production of a film with other foreigners. I feel I shouldn't participate because my father is doing clandestine work in Colombia and my job in China is to study the thought of Mao Tse-tung so when I return I'll be able to take on the task of my father and other comrades; in China I should be learning from the great Chinese people, to be loyal to the thought of Mao Tse-tung, to take the thought of Mao Tse-tung to Colombia. My father is currently in a very dangerous situation in Colombia, the Americans are looking for me and my brother, which is why I don't think I should participate in the making of this film. Perhaps the purpose of the film is propaganda, but I don't think I've studied the works of Chairman Mao enough. I believe the reason I have such good relations with the workers is because I've learned from Chairman Mao, but that's not enough. All the progress I've made is the result of the help from my comrades. I must always be honest, not too proud of only this small progress. I shall always learn from the masses with humility, I shall always be the little student of the masses and strive to progress further!

我还要跟这样的同志经常
连系，更使我能为我祖国和世
界，为全世界人民的大事业！

李

1968.2.4.

朋友初学的榜样。我也是非常难
理在就是这样。心 妈妈知道：我们
这个问题因为直去看长华希及各种
……我欢的。求千西万妈妈谢我们心血
所说些我们的思想，帮我 一个不
……为我们觉，为我们祖国人民和全世
大的 掌 声 感谢伟大的中国人
民就这用为爱为义而自争斗！
的！越老人家的思想是指引我们
直是我们心中最红最红的红太阳！！！
……更好做力伟大思想 到到我的
情店官，因为它是最大的政理我前
理！！！我若有我最爱给！把可
……很伟大思想！我 着 博伟
……消 因为它是最大政
……信我吧！我也 ……
民 站来的人就是最坚强的
要为做个正确的……吃工

王连军

张斗到底！永远做群众的小学生，

昨天晚上爸爸回到北京了，我心
怕的。他 苦了爸爸妈妈的信使看见
泪有 望 着爸爸的，妈妈是个资产
阶级人，所以就把我们流在中国
使我们有一个无所事事思想 为了代价
事。她要求我们革命但他自己不去求
认为革命 也 亚就不当跟她这样为
过了艰苦…很艰苦的道路。我哥
现方 的帮助你就要说：我决定走
……革命很艰苦的道路使我以前不
需要的是战争，现在我很高兴 很
要些斗到底！这个虽也很不好说
我不完了决心，但是我还需要帮助
好的斗私改我没求的地步。我帮
为阶级服务，你们把 我吧！
好最好的帮助！你们给我们这条
求，你们想不到多大的帮助！！！
……我不明白的东西，爸爸 很类
地慢之地 前 明 地先
……很艰苦的，但是我很

1968.1.28

Today is my day off, everyone else has gone home for Spring Festival, but not me, I'll spend this holiday in the factory. I think the best thing I can do in these days is something of service for the people. I see that the bathrooms are dirty, so I decide to spend the afternoon rest period cleaning the bathrooms. People make fun of me and say that I must be a "capitalist". But I don't think this is a task only for capitalists, we must serve the people, we are the custodians of the people, so we must do these kinds of jobs. I told my comrades who had mistakenly said that. Should everything we do not be at the service of the people? In the future we must do more mundane tasks. Small jobs, ordinary work, and speak in less florid phrases.

These holidays I'll spend here, in China, wherever I am will be my home. Today I am in a socialist society, in a big revolutionary family, living in the epoch of the great Chairman Mao Tse-tung. What happiness! In the future, I shall carry the red flag of Mao Tse-tung Thought high, and I'll serve the people with my heart and soul to achieve more and greater achievements.

1968.2.14

I have just returned from my friend Carl's house. I was profoundly saddened to see that my comrade now finds himself in this state. I wonder: has he changed or have I? And with this question in mind, I returned home to see what Chairman Mao has to say. In the last instance, I think I'm the one who has changed. I thank my comrades, the factory workers, a thousand million times. I am grateful for their help in reforming my ideology, they helped me to establish a proletarian ideology that will help me serve our party and the people of my country for ever. With my greatest respect, I am grateful to the Chinese people who have taken me in as a comrade in arms in our common fight for communism.

*Oh, great Chairman Mao! Your ideology has thrown a brilliant light
on my heart. Oh, beloved Chairman Mao! You really are the reddest red
sun of my heart!!!! I am determined to always obey your words! To take
your great ideology to Colombia. To propagate it, because it is the
greatest truth, our Colombian people will never turn away from it!!!
Chairman Mao, I love you most! I can do without my father and mother,
but I cannot do without your great ideology!*

1968.2.16
*Last night my brother returned to Peking, and I was so happy to see him
. . . He brought letters from Papá and Mamá. Tears ran from my eyes
after reading them. Especially the letter from my mother. My mother is
bourgeois, but she did not want us to follow in her footsteps, which is why
our parents left us in China, to study the thought of Mao Tse-tung better,
to acquire the proletarian ideology, so we'll be able to serve the proletariat
of our own country. She wants us to bring about the Revolution, but she
doesn't want to bring about the Revolution herself; she believes socialism
is good, believes that one day Colombia can be as great as China, but she
has always said that she doesn't want to follow this difficult and arduous
path. Now, in the letter my brother brought, she says:*

*"The only help I can offer you is to tell you that I have decided to follow
you and the people on this long and arduous path that I didn't want to
take before. Now I see that what we need is the armed struggle, now I am
happy and very resolute! I believe in myself, I shall fight to the end! It
is difficult to say all this, but I think you'll understand. I have made my
decision, but I still need help, I need care and love. I still need to struggle
against my egotism to reform my defects. I must struggle constantly
against my own interests to serve the proletarian class. All of you can help
by criticizing me! This will be the best help you can offer! We received
the books with quotes of Chairman Mao that you sent us! You wouldn't*

believe how marvellous they seem to me!!! I'm studying them with your father every day. He patiently explains the parts I don't understand. And thus we advance little by little. I understand clearly that this will be a long and arduous path, but I am progressing with determination. The further I go, the stronger I feel. I feel my strength will never run out!"

After seeing my mother's resolution, I felt very strong, I felt happy! We are a revolutionary family, all four of us, four revolutionary "bolts", even if we're very small. I feel a great joy in my heart.

At the beginning of April 1968, not long after Marianella's sixteenth birthday, they packed a few basics, according to the instructions they'd received, and prepared to return to Nanjing. But before the trip they had time to find out that David Crook had been transferred again, after almost six months of confinement, and that his situation did not seem to be improving at all. The charges against him were still not clear, but in his letters he said they hadn't even continued interrogating him. Isabel sent him an English translation of the complete works of Mao, a bilingual edition of the Little Red Book and a small radio to improve his pronunciation of Chinese, but she was his only correspondent: never, in all that time, had David received any news from the comrades who were, supposedly, in charge of his case.

His letters were courageous, but full of distress. In them he said he was thinking of their sons and worrying about their safety; that he was thinking of Isabel and imagining if the guards imprisoned her as well. He told them what he could in those letters – he wrote them in Chinese, because English might arouse suspicions – and Carl told Marianella with tears in his eyes. Marianella heard from him that the interrogations had started again, and again David defended himself with the truth, and that he was certain again that they were accusing him (although they never said so) of being a British spy. All the sessions with his interrogator, a veteran of the Korean War for whom David never lost respect, ended with the same words: "Crook, you have been extremely dishonest this afternoon. Go back to your cell and think about what you've said. And next time tell me the truth." He asked him about his life, his family, his job and his convictions. In his letters David said, as much for his wife and children as for the officials who would read them: "But I am telling the truth. I am telling the whole truth."

"And what can he do if they don't believe him?" said Carl.

Marianella had a surprising revelation in that instant: Carl was weak. She loved him – more than that, she was in love with him – but she had to surrender to the painful evidence that her boyfriend did not share either the intensity of her commitment or her profound sense of mission. Otherwise he would know that the Party did not make mistakes: if David was in prison, there must be a good reason. She did not tell him that in those words, but she knew that Carl was asking for more than she could give him. In long conversations about David Crook's fate, Carl leaned on her, cried with her, complained to her of the profound injustice that the Cultural Revolution had committed, and she could only think that her time in China was coming to an end.

The Communist Party had a Central Committee and the Central Committee had a Military Commission and the Military Commission had a Latin American Department, and in the Latin American Department there was a section that was in contact with the Colombian Communist Party. That was the imprecise and tortuous path that Sergio's and Marianella's names had travelled until arriving there, at the training camp bigger than some European countries, to share military training with another fifty-odd apprentices. All of this was a privilege. While Sergio and Marianella were training in Nanjing, hundreds of Latin Americans who were doing the same thing elsewhere – in Albania, for example – would have secretly preferred to be in China. But the selection process was long and complex, though they never really knew the criteria.

Each of them had their own room, on the second floor of a house built on the edge of a road. Next to the room, each apprentice had a small study, and on the floor below, which was much bigger, were the barracks of ten professional soldiers, young people in their early twenties who would be their companions and in time would turn into their small guerrilla unit: comrades for whom Sergio was prepared to run any risk, even if they were just the fictitious risks of controlled drills. In his or her room, each trainee had a gun rack with eight different types of firearms: M1 Garands, Mausers, FAL automatic rifles. When they finished the course, the Cabreras learned, they should be able to dismantle and assemble all eight guns blindfolded.

For two weeks they rose at dawn, dressed in the military uniform of the People's Republic and took their places in the classroom facing a blackboard and an instructor, to fill their heads with theoretical knowledge. As the days went by, the theories grew more complex and the strategy instructors more demanding. It was a technical apprenticeship: they did talk about politics sometimes, but only to remind themselves of Mao's campaigns or what Chairman Mao had written about military strategy, and the indoctrination that Sergio had known at school had disappeared completely. The blackboard filled up with maps where troop movements were decided and where it was a question of dots of one colour surrounding those of another, and it was shocking to think that those geometric figures would represent for some of those in the room a reality made of death. Between classes, if he pricked up his ears, Sergio could make out Latin American accents – Chileans, Argentines, Mexicans – but he never came into contact with them. He spoke Chinese with his sister; also with the instructors. He liked that clandestinity.

In the afternoons they had more physical training. Sergio and Marianella spent two hours each day in the polygon, familiarizing themselves with all the rifles they had in their gun racks, but also with fragmentation grenades, mortars and bazookas, and even .50 machine guns, which could fire 250 rounds a minute. The Chinese knew about the guerrilla war in Vietnam, and their course included rudimentary instructions on how to make traps with branches and leaves, how to use a river for an ambush, how to make a bayonet with no other tools than a knife and the forest. Sergio learned how to camouflage, to run over loose logs, to cross raging rivers without getting his gun wet and without getting pushed off balance by the current; he learned to shrink his own silhouette to be less of a target for the enemy and to know how many enemies he was facing just by the sounds; he learned how to distinguish the highest-ranking enemy officer in combat when there are no insignia, because his strategic value is much higher than a soldier's. He learned to dry sawdust to get the humidity out of it and mix it with ammonium nitrate to make explosives that were no less powerful than dynamite, and he learned to drive a tank, and take it where he wanted and use its gun, and destroy armaments they didn't need or couldn't carry, to keep them from falling into enemy hands. And in the middle of all that he learned that cowardice, more than a character defect, is a strategic error: whoever is frightened does not fire, and therefore becomes a target. In other words, the one who fires is keeping others from aiming at him. That mentality was crucial: more than one had died because they had gone into combat without having absorbed it.

But then came the operations, and they came without warning. One night, around nine, Sergio found a note on the door to his room that said in Chinese characters: *Report for patrol at 0300. Route 32.* He did not sleep well, in part from knowing something was going to happen to him, in part from worrying he wouldn't wake up. At the appointed hour he was there, at route 32, a badly-lit, tree-lined dirt path. He knew he was in the middle of a training exercise and his life was not in danger, but that didn't keep the anxiety from lodging in his chest: something was going to happen to him, but it was impossible to know where it would come from or what form it would take. Every shadow was a threat and every rustle of leaves made him turn sharply, raising his rifle to aim into the darkness. The moon was a piece of glass and time stood still. Sergio would also have preferred not to continue advancing, because his own footsteps, it seemed to him, might be masking a more important sound. He hated the gloom and hated the breeze and hated his own inexperience.

He didn't know how much time had gone by – it could have been an hour, it could have been two – when some trees fell on top of him from both sides of the road, armed and with helmets and with faces painted green and brown. He managed to shoot one of the enemies, but the rest were on top of him too quickly, and the rules of these operations were clear as to the minimum distance to shoot from: blank cartridges could do damage up close. Sergio found himself surrounded by four trainees who were pointing their weapons at him, and had to surrender. It was true what he'd heard: blanks don't kill, but the noise they make destroys your nerves as if they were real.

The eve of their departure, when they had finished the course and were considered graduates, their instructors organized a dinner in their honour. The six men who taught the classes or were responsible for their training were there, and also some of their classmates. There were farewell speeches and Sergio and Marianella replied with gratitude, and then one of the leaders took them to a side table: there, in wooden boxes, were two grenades that they had made themselves in the days they'd learned to work with cast iron. The instructor asked them each to sign the one they'd made. They planned to keep them as mementos.

Afterwards they invited them into an office. Under a portrait of Chairman Mao, they handed them each a piece of paper: they were codes they must memorize. One of the instructors explained that those codes would allow them to get in contact with the Military Commission from any Chinese embassy anywhere in the world. Sergio did not really know what he would need it for or when he might use that code, for his immediate horizon was to return to Colombia and put himself at the service of the revolution, but he memorized the eight numbers and destroyed the piece of paper. And then he went to pack his things, because they'd been told that very early the next morning a military car would take them to the airport for their flight back to Peking. Sergio opened the windows of his room and let in the warm July air. He could hear the soldiers getting ready for bed downstairs. He thought, while he folded the same clothes he'd arrived with four months earlier, that what was happening had the taste of inevitability: in a certain sense, Sergio had not decided alone: all this had already been written by someone else.

The last days in Peking were filled with anticipatory nostalgia, but also a sense of purpose that neither of the siblings had experienced before. The evenings were for sad farewells with their friends from Chong Wen School and the Friendship Hotel, and during the long summer days Marianella went to the Institute residences to visit the Crooks. Sometimes she found Isabel making enquiries by telephone or talking to Party officials to try to get her husband released; other times she didn't find her, because Isabel was in some other part of the vast city showing documents or begging in front of a uniformed man with no other proof than her biography and no other weapon than her worry, and even so she had the generosity of spirit to ask Marianella about her own life and even suggest she bring her brother along one of these days, because Isabel would like to meet him. Marianella made up some excuse. She did not want Sergio inside the Crooks' house, as if he might steal something or contaminate a purity.

One of those afternoons Isabel told her what had happened while Marianella was in Nanjing. In the days leading up to May first, International Workers' Day, Isabel and David had hopes there might be a solution in sight, since the Party leaders celebrated the foreign specialists' presence in China every year on that date. "If your father were here," Isabel said, "they would be inviting him to banquets and parades and things like that. I'm sure it happened to him every year, just that you don't remember." But May Day approached without any invitations arriving for the Crooks; not to banquets or parades or ceremonies of any kind in the Great Hall of the People. The days passed without her petitions for clemency receiving any attention whatsoever, and before the holiday, on a night like any other, David was transferred again. Isabel knew this would be the last time. "And that's not good?" Marianella asked. No, that was not good: in fact, it was the worst news in the world. David had been sent to Qincheng high security prison, the place enemies of the people were held. Everyone agreed: it was quite possible never to leave Qincheng prison.

That afternoon Carl and Marianella went out for a bike ride, and almost without realizing it ended up at the Summer Palace, taking out a boat and rowing to the middle of the lake, where they had once had an uncomfortable run-in with Fausto. "This is serious," Carl said. "Dad shouldn't be in there. It's not fair. After all he's done for China. It's just not fair." He had stopped rowing, and the water stilled around the boat. They were alone.

"Don't go," Carl said. "Stay here, stay with me."

Carl had taken off his jacket to row. Marianella looked at his swimmer's arms – a thick vein ran from the edge of his short sleeve – and that face that took on a certain childlike sweetness when they were together. Yes, she thought briefly, she could be happy with him: she could stay in Peking, as David and Isabel had done, and build a life there. It would be a socialist life, a life in service to her ideals; but it would also be a life far from her country.

"You know I can't," she said. "I have to go, it's all decided." And she added: "My people need me."

From Marianella's diary:

> *Again I write*
>> *With the caress*
>> *That sentiment can write;*
>> *You know I think so much of you.*

> *Again I write*
>> *With the revolutionary passion*
>> *That binds us,*
>> *To tell you: until victory!*

> *So I tell you,*
>> *Because now I am going,*
>> *And maybe it will be the last time*
>> *We can write to each other:*
>> *I'll remember you all my life.*

> *Again I write to you*
>> *And you'll know you'll not hear anymore from me,*
>>> *But you'll receive my love every day*
>>> *And this great passion, great courage,*
>>> *Great firmness that binds us!*

On the first page she wrote: Peking, May 1968. And then: To Carlos. She put the notebook in a brass box along with her Red Guard armband, the three booklets of her diary in Chinese and a bundle of photographs that Carl had taken in recent months: there she was with her brother, walking along a path during a mountain hike; or her alone, one night, with teenage timidity not looking at the camera, wearing the brooch with Mao's face on her blouse. It was nice to think of Carl remembering her like that.

The box would be her parting gift.

Sergio went to visit Lao Wang at the Alarm Clock Factory. He was one of the few people who knew of his training in Nanjing, as they had kept it secret: the idea that the communist army was training Westerners could not sit well among the workers, even if they were Westerners who were committed to the revolution. He told Lao Wang that he was going back to his country and explained the reasons; Lao Wang did not look at him, he pronounced a tai chi master's precept and said the doors of China would always be open to him. Sergio spent the afternoon

writing out, in minuscule Chinese characters, the most important lessons of the military course, including the formulas for
making explosives. After he finished he looked for the long
letter from his father, which he always kept with him, and reread
a few fragments. It had turned into his instruction manual for
those last months, and sometimes he was struck by the notion
that in the letter, magically, all the questions Sergio might ask
were answered and, what was more surprising, in the same
instant that he asked them. At that moment joining the
Colombian guerrilla force was not among his plans, he was
thinking more of putting himself at the service of the revolution
from the city, but he felt prepared for anything: his body told
him so, having been cared for and trained in anticipation of any
requirement, and his mind told him so, for in those four months
he had reached a sort of reconciliation with the possibility of
death. It was the first time he'd felt it, and there, in his second-
floor room, Sergio accepted that revelation as if it were an
ambush: he knew it was going to happen, but not when or
how, and now that it had happened, what was left was relief.

*And finally I'll tell you that I shall live my life on the lookout for you
both, always thinking of you, happy to know you're marching always
forward, that you belong to a glorious generation which will radically
change the face of the world, that you will be members of a fairer, healthier
and therefore much happier and more prosperous society, which you'll
both serve wholeheartedly. That you'll contribute to bringing this about
in your homeland in the small support you're able to give the revolutionary struggle. Thinking all these things I shall be happy, very happy,
knowing I have a son and daughter worthy of that society that will
change the world. What greater happiness could a father feel?*

287

XIV

Their arrival in Bogotá was not free of incident. Pope Paul VI was coming to visit Colombia and his plane would land a few hours after theirs, so the airport was teeming with people. But that wasn't the problem, it was more the fact that Sergio had hidden his notes on the manufacture of explosives in the cable compartment of his tape recorder, and by very bad luck this was the only thing the customs officers confiscated; and although it was not too serious – even if the authorities found the document, they wouldn't be able to read it – Sergio felt that he had lost important information. They slept in Bogotá and the next day flew to Medellín, where their parents, on the instructions of the National Directorship of the Party, had settled since their return. The leaders considered Medellín to be better than Bogotá, given its proximity to the headquarters of the leadership in the Sinú Valley, and that Fausto should set up what he would call his headquarters there. For Sergio, everything was strange: people speaking Spanish, the fact that the Spanish sounded familiar, his family greeting him as if he were the same innocent boy who had left, and not a man who knew how to use all kinds of weapons and was ready to change the world. It was also strange that his parents were leading a double

life of which Sergio, until now, had no knowledge; but correspondence, no matter how coded, did not allow them to talk
about certain things, or rather, there were certain things that
could only be explained out loud and in person. But that's how
it was: neither his grandparents nor his aunts and uncles had
the slightest suspicion that the Cabreras had not been in Europe
for five years, or that they were not the theatre man and
housewife – a little rebellious and headstrong, it's true: living
in Europe changes women – that they were in their visible lives.

Luz Elena had begun working from the start with women's
associations in underprivileged neighbourhoods. She helped
them to get funding, acted as their advocate with better-off
people, and suggested the possibility that having masses of
children was not the same thing as serving God. During the
last months of her life in Peking she had spent her salary on
Liulichang Street, and when she came back to Colombia she
had enough antiques and furniture and artworks to mount an
exhibition; and that's exactly what she did in the Zea Museum,
not just as a cultural enterprise, but also as a tactical facade.
Fausto, for his part, had been doing theatre work since his
return, more than two years ago now, but he no longer wanted
to put on anything by Molière, or even Arthur Miller or Tennes-
see Williams, but had become obsessed with the idea of
collective creation. Chamber theatre was done by and for the
bourgeoisie, the concept of an author was egotistical and retro-
grade, and he had learned in China that the stage could also
be, *must be*, a weapon to bring about change. Meanwhile, the
Party had named him political secretary of an urban cell, so
the theatre would also serve to camouflage his activities.

The trigger was a polemic he found himself involved in

shortly after returning to Colombia, when Santiago García invited him to participate in a festival of chamber theatre. García was that student of Seki Sano with whom Fausto had done a marvellous production of Brecht's *The Spy*; he had become the Director of the Casa de la Cultura, a quality company he'd set up in a beautiful house on calle 13, in the centre of Bogotá, and was now starting to win over the public's appreciation with impeccable stagings. García's invitation was a way of welcoming back a colleague who had been away, but Fausto quickly seized the opportunity for his own interests: in an open letter he turned down the proposal, saying that chamber theatre was not appropriate for these times, that they should be making popular theatre in Colombia, that anything else was reactionary and elitist. Then came an exchange of articles and letters and opinion pieces in which directors such as Manuel Drezner and Bernardo Romero Lozano defended the simple but intolerably difficult mission of putting on good plays and doing it well: was that not an artist's obligation? The debate lasted several days. Finally, in what was an odd way of getting the last word in, Fausto embarked on an ambitious project: FRECAL. Behind this unappealing acronym was the Frente Común en el Arte y la Literatura, which was meant to be the first openly Marxist art and literature movement in Colombia.

Fausto set out to put into practice all he'd learned of the new Chinese dramatics. He put on a long play, *The Invader*, which told the history of Colombia from the thesis of the eternal exploitation of man by man. He put on plays about the revolt of the *comuneros*, that eighteenth-century popular uprising, and about the life of an ordinary worker who betrays his own class in the twentieth century; but none of them were successful, largely because ideological convictions did not always go hand in hand with artistic talent, and Fausto seemed much more interested in the former than the latter. Actors who did not side with Marxism were branded reactionaries. Playwrights who suggested an exploration of love and infidelity were written off as bourgeois counter-revolutionaries, denizens of an ivory tower. When the sectarianism of the Front, which had now started to refuse people of the left if it was not the correct left, was thrown in his face, Fausto defended himself by quoting César Vallejo:

> *A cripple passes by holding a child's hand.*
> *After that I'm going to read André Breton?*
>
> *Another trembles from cold, coughs, spits blood.*
> *Will it ever be possible to allude to the profound "I"?*
>
> *Another searches in the muck for bones, rinds.*
> *How to write, after that, about the infinite?*
>
> *A bricklayer falls from a roof, dies, and no longer eats lunch.*
> *To innovate then, the trope, the metaphor?*

Deep down he had doubts, but he did not confess them, for doubt and uncertainty were a revolutionary's worst enemies. What he had seen in China seemed crystal clear: a nation that was starving to death a few years earlier was now alive. How can we not have a revolution? And if we accept this premise, how can we not put everything, including art, into declared service of this cause? Who could think that the beauty of a scene or the euphony of a phrase was more important than the liberation of a people? It was true that Fausto had no experience in the tasks the Party put on his desk, and it was true that his idealism led him to condemn valuable people when he didn't see the commitment from them that he expected. But the objective was clear, and they weren't going to get there by half-measures. Fausto had founded the School of Scenic Arts in Medellín, and there, in the same empty hall where they rehearsed plays, his cell began to meet for long political conversations in which they decided the fate of the less orthodox. Later, when the school's facilities also became the editorial room for an ambitiously named pamphlet, *Revolution*, it was clear that the border between politics and theatre had disappeared for good.

Luz Elena, for her part, took on more and more responsibilities. The leadership assigned her as liaison to the leaders of other revolutionary movements, and she suddenly found herself crossing from one side of the country to the other in the family car, braving mountain roads entirely on her own to cross the border into Ecuador and reach Quito, where the Party had centralized its funds that were arriving from all over Latin America, and especially from Chilean Marxism–Leninism. She began carrying large sums of money or important documents, because the Party had more confidence in her than in anybody, but she suspected that the fact she was a woman encouraged that trust, and thought that any day, were she not the open and transparent person she'd always been, she could have disappeared with the movement's money and started up a new life wherever she wanted. Those clandestine trips took place once a month, and Luz Elena, who had embarked on them apprehensively at first, gradually began to enjoy them: they were moments of solitude, independence and even silence she'd never had since she'd married Fausto, because every hour of every day over the last twenty years had gone into arranging the routines of her husband and their children. Apart from these three people, nobody knew about her trips, so she didn't feel too guilty about devoting time to herself that she could have been devoting to others. She decided where to spend the night, in Cali or Popayán, and arrived alone at a city hotel and withstood the receptionist's looks, which were curious when not frankly disapproving. "You're not a hooker, are you?" one man asked as she filled out the registration card. In any case, the Colombian leaders saw more daring in her than in many guerrilla fighters with rifles over their shoulders. Later, when the time came to choose an alias, the political secretary made a bad pun:

"Such a valiant woman must be called Valentina."

And so it stuck.

This was the situation that Sergio found when he arrived from Peking. Two days after his return, Fausto was already asking him to come to the School of Scenic Arts to work as an assistant director, and sometimes as a temporary director. He was still physically exhausted from the trip and his sleeping and waking hours were still out of kilter, but Fausto demanded that he get up early to start work. One afternoon, after a heavy lunch, Sergio fell asleep in the middle of a company meeting, and Fausto accused him in front of everyone of lacking commitment and asked if he had come back to Colombia to become totally bourgeois. They were putting on a collective creation with the title *The History We Were Never Told*, which someone had proposed without fearing the staging might be unequal to the task. It was obvious to Sergio that the play held no interest, or that its only merit was as propaganda, but that was not why he'd fallen asleep. In any case, his father's accusation was unfair, owing more to a moment's nervousness than anything else, but it stayed with Sergio like a skin irritation: he had already begun to serve as a member of an urban cell, and the altercation, which seemed to revolve around the theatre, was actually calling his revolutionary commitment into question. And that he would not allow. He would show his father that his revolutionary vocation was intact.

When they saw each other, almost always around the dining table, the Cabreras did not talk about how their days had gone. Luz Elena had been in Medellín's poorest neighbourhoods, in Pedregal or the north-eastern communities where a woman like her could run more risks than they imagined. Sergio had been working at the Popular Theatre of Antioquia or in one of its satellite groups, writing the play they would perform in collaboration with all the actors, and secretly printing pamphlets for the Party on a Gestetner mimeograph machine, very different from the one in the meeting room of the Friendship Hotel where the Rebel Regiment used to meet, but Sergio learned to operate it as if it were a lathe in a Chinese factory, setting the bands of type himself as if it were silk-screen printing. But the Cabreras didn't talk about that either. It was like a pact of silence, but it was strange, because it would have helped them all a lot to share this new life they were experiencing. From a certain point these gatherings happened less frequently, not only on account of the obligation of secrecy or prudence, but also because Sergio had gone to live with a group of comrades from the cell.

What he didn't tell anybody was that in his free time – and some times that were not free – he sneaked off to the cinema to watch films. He would evade his obligations to see any old thing, just for the pleasure he had always found in the darkness of the theatre, in front of a luminous screen where the whole world happened. One of those days he discovered a film by Luchino Visconti, *The Stranger*, and he spent four days in a row inventing clandestine missions to go back and see it again. One sunny afternoon, as he returned from a mission that was not invented but genuine, he saw a poster for a matinee with an image of two young lovers embracing. It was *How Do I Love You*, an absurd melodrama the only virtue of which, at that moment, was the simple fact of having Gigliola Cinquetti songs, which Marianella liked so much. Carried away by fleeting nostalgia, overwhelmed by guilt (a revolutionary like him could not be interested in such kitsch), Sergio bought a ticket. His enthusiasm didn't last long: twenty minutes in, after Cinquetti had sung her first song, he'd already given up. But when he got outside, while he was waiting for his eyes to adjust to the intense daylight, he heard someone say hello: "What are you doing here?" It was two of his housemates.

"Talking to a contact," Sergio said. "I can't say any more right now, comrade."

Sergio was one of the most active members of his group. He was making a monthly trip to Bogotá to pick up munitions, medicine or documents: these were undercover trips, like his mother's, during which he was in considerable danger. He stayed with his Uncle Mauro, who was not a Party member, but did sympathize with his brother's ideas; and at those moments they shared a formidable understanding that there was something they could not talk about and therefore there were questions it was not worth asking. So much the better: Sergio realized he did not know much about what was happening to him, as if he were moving through a jungle blindfolded. He didn't know, for example, that anonymous voices were having secret conversations during those days about his future and that of his sister Marianella, and their destiny was decided without them really knowing how. At some informal encounter, someone said to Sergio that it was about time he joined the guerrillas and he had answered: "That's what we came for." But at that moment the conversation had no consequences, and they didn't talk about the subject again until one Tuesday morning, when a call came that Sergio answered as if he were talking about somebody else. It was a coded conversation, because everyone knew that the telephones were bugged, but what Sergio heard was crystal clear to him. They told him to come to a café in downtown Medellín, warning him, of course, not to mention the meeting to anyone: not even his parents. Sergio would say a long time later that the meeting lasted the length of time it takes to drink a coffee, but its consequences would last the rest of his life.

He arrived at the café, around the corner from the Hotel Nutibara, and waited a few minutes, during which he was sure the person he was going to see was already observing him from somewhere. After a while a labour leader with whom he'd exchanged the odd word, but didn't know much about, sat down across from him, and before they'd barely said a polite hello, was already giving him instructions, a few very specific instructions: he had to buy a hammock, a machete and a pair of rubber boots; he had to pack one change of clothes; and then he had to wait for the call.

"I'm going now?"

"You're going tomorrow, comrade," the man said. "Because we believe you're ready."

Sergio felt ambushed: stupidly, because there was nothing unexpected about that meeting. Joining the guerrillas had been his destiny for a long time by then – as if some force had made the decision in his place, as if his consent had not been necessary – but he never thought it would happen so soon. He listened to the rest of the instructions as if in a dream: the bus station at a precise time, the name of the village of Dabeiba, the importance of telling no-one of his departure. He left the café feeling frustration and contentment blending in his gut, along with the bothersome intuition that the decision had not been his alone. He walked to the corner of the Nutibara, where he had seen a shop selling handicrafts for tourists, and went in without thinking. Imagining that one hammock was much the same as any other, he found a large, comfortable one with bright stripes, and did not have the presence of mind to realize that a double hammock was a terrible idea, as it was not only twice the size, but twice the weight he'd have to carry on his back. Incredibly, he also found a decent machete there, and in the shop next door he could buy a pair of La Macha boots, shiny and black and smelling of fresh rubber. He bought two of everything, because he had to think of Marianella as well. He called her that afternoon.

"We're going tomorrow," he said.

"Where?"

"Where we have to go."

There was a second of silence on the line.

Marianella said: "And does it have to be now? Can't we talk it over once more?"

Sergio was scared, because that was not his sister's voice, not the voice of the convinced militant, the Revolutionary Nun. It was the voice of a little girl.

"No, we can't discuss it," he said firmly. And he thought he had the definitive argument when he added: "And anyway, I've already bought everything, and we can't return it."

He spent a difficult night in the safe house. He couldn't even talk to his comrades and room-mates, who would have understood better than anyone and could even have given him advice on what to do. But the order from his superiors was clear.

To better comply with the departure instructions, he agreed with Marianella that they would arrive separately at the bus station. He didn't know what time she left their parents' house, or how she filled the long hours that opened out before them until their trip, but Sergio experienced that morning as a first test of his revolutionary discipline. He had breakfast with his room-mates and took a shower and dressed as if for an ordinary day, keeping the silence as ordered, and then he packed his things. He included a pair of boots he'd brought from China – high and made of fine leather – thinking they'd come in handy: if they were good enough for the Chinese PLA, which ran the country, why wouldn't they be good for the one here? He ate lunch without appetite and then went to the station. On his way there he had a feeling he'd forgotten something, and it took a great effort to realize that the emptiness, as palpable as the absence of his house keys in his pocket, was the sadness of not having said goodbye to his mother, the infinite sadness of not having hugged her to share the possibility they might never see each other again.

From Marianella's diary:

March, 1969
It's all clear. I wrote to Mamá. I'm taking her smiles and her goodbye kisses with me. I know she was crying inside, but Mamá is the most understanding person on earth, the noblest and fairest. I tell her I'm happy, and I will soon be totally out of the hands of the minions of capitalism proudly serving on my new front with the guerrillas. I feel I will have then lessened the distance that separates me from her and Papá because we will be serving the same cause.

Comrade Juan brought a large quantity of medicine that I must carry with me at all times. It's called Aralen. He says it fights malaria and I have to take one tablet every day, as that disease is fierce in this part of the country. Its name sounds terrible, and I don't want to find out what it feels like.

March 7

Since secrecy is absolute, I have devoted myself entirely to reading. Yesterday I tried to have a conversation with Ester, Juan's companion, but it was futile. We speak very different Spanish. I told her I'd rather have short hair because it would be more comfortable and hygienic in future circumstances, then she kindly offered to cut it for me and I accepted. While the murder of my long hair was going on I had to allow a little vanity in the face of objective reason and then, when I looked in the mirror, I smiled.

Only a few hours to go and sometimes I feel like I'm in an abyss. There is something that scares me. How many times Mamá and I accompanied other comrades going in. The early morning hours closed in by those precipices where the car could barely pass. We commented how terrible but how admirable it was; and now it's my turn. And I am decisive, onward I go!

The bus left at just after five one rainy afternoon. Sergio didn't know that part of the city very well, and didn't manage to figure out in which direction they were going or what route they were taking out. He was thinking about other things, as well: they had told him that two other militants would be travelling on the bus for the same reason as them, and he tried to take advantage of the patches of street lighting to figure out who they were. Can one see revolution in the face of a young man? Is the urge to change the world etched into the features? Three rows behind was Marianella, as they'd been given strict instructions not to sit together, and when he looked at her he thought maybe the other two were looking for them as well. He thought briefly that this trip meant the indefinite postponement of a life in cinema, but he felt ashamed of those bourgeois preoccupations; he thought it was very possible he would never return from this trip, and he wondered where the projects of those who die before they get started go, and again felt a dull sadness, but this time it was contaminated with guilt. How would his mother be taking it? How would she have received the news that her children had gone to join the guerrilla army without saying goodbye? And his father, what would he have thought? He was pondering these things when night closed in. He discreetly looked for Marianella, who was now sleeping with her face against the window, and closed his eyes, thinking he should probably get some rest too. And then he fell asleep.

It was a journey of eight long hours. He would not remember clearly what happened along the way or their arrival itself, when a man and a woman who didn't introduce themselves by name or ask how the trip was came out to meet them and helped them get their heavy bags off the bus. Then the other two comrades were revealed. One was a young black man with a shaved head and hard features; the other had a sort of natural authority, and when he greeted Sergio and Marianella it was obvious he knew who they were. When they began to walk, skirting the village as if undecided whether to enter it, it was eleven at night. They came upon a nocturnal demonstration, or let it catch up to them, but as the people approached, Sergio realized it was not a demonstration but a religious procession.

"Of course," he said to his sister. "It's Holy Thursday."

They hadn't realized that till then. The guerrillas motioned them to join the procession, to blend in, and they walked along with the procession for quite a while. The Christ figure was up front, far away, but they could see his varnished head shining when they passed under a lamp post. Then one of their hosts, the man or the woman, signalled: "Here." They all left the procession like people getting off a moving train, and began to walk through the stubble of a recently harvested field where it was difficult to move without getting one's feet caught up in the stalks. Then they came out onto a path made by pack animals over many years of secret traffic. A man was waiting to serve as their guide. They began to follow him: seven silhouettes advancing, without a word, in the darkness.

They walked all night. Day broke slowly, under a light drizzle, but the sky cleared suddenly when the sun appeared above the mountains, and vegetation such as Sergio had never seen burst into view on either side of the trail. Nobody else stared at the bright bromeliads, or at the mercury-coloured yarumo trees, or the size of some of the leaves the water streamed down as if from watering cans, and Sergio realized that expressing his surprise aloud would be inappropriate, and even more ridiculous would be telling them that all this reminded him of his visit to the Botanical Gardens of Peking, where he'd seen the last emperor of China as close as he now saw his comrades. No, none of that could be put into words; but Sergio knew that the sensation of discovery he had had that morning would never leave him. Maybe that's why he was in a good mood when they arrived at the camp, where a dozen guerrilla fighters were starting to untie their hammocks from the trees. The same twelve showed up a short time later, summoned by a figure of authority. It was Comandante Carlos, who was not only the best surgeon they had, but also a member of the Central Committee and the General Staff of the guerrilla army. Carlos assembled the guerrillas and proposed that they welcome their four new comrades. Before he began, he asked Sergio what he would like to be called.

"Sergio," said Sergio.

"No, no," Comandante Carlos said. "I'm asking for the name you're going to have here. Your sister is going to be called Sol."

It was Marianella's first name. When she was little, when her father wanted to punish her, he called her Sol Marianella, and that was the name she had chosen for this new revolutionary life. But Sergio, out of shyness or surprise, couldn't come up with a suitable name for himself, and Comandante Carlos did not want to wait for him to make up his mind. He spoke of the new arrivals with words that they had surely communicated to him just a few minutes earlier, and then he introduced them. The young black man was Comrade Pacho; the other, who had inspired some intangible respect, was Comrade Ernesto; he had been a community leader in the department of Quindio and later received military training in Albania. Then Carlos pointed at Marianella and said her new name, and almost in the same breath, as if he had decided beforehand, he introduced Sergio with two short words: "Comrade Raúl."

PART THREE

Light and Smoke

XV

On the screen of the Filmoteca, a caricature guerrilla unit confronts a laughable police force, all silly characters that seem straight out of a Berlanga comedy. There's a loud-mouthed sergeant, some overly solemn revolutionaries, an evil idiot Gringo, a sanctimonious but lucid priest, a cynical arms dealer and an Andalusian in a short flamenco jacket and wide-brimmed hat driving a busload of prostitutes around the war zones. Sitting in the back row between the aisle and Raúl, Sergio wondered the same thing he always wondered: how much of what is told would get lost on the long road from the illuminated screen to the spectator's darkened seat; how much would get lost in the cultural gap. The main story of *Time Out*, that crazy film, revolved around a football match, and in that, at least, there was a sort of universal language, a narrative Esperanto. The national teams of Argentina and Colombia were going to play a qualifying match for the 1994 World Cup, but the antenna had been blown up by mistake and the battalion's only television was broken into pieces; so the soldiers and guerrillas agreed to a truce to repair an improbable appliance and manufacture an antenna out of tin foil and forget, for ninety minutes, the war they were waging. It was a fable with love stories and a happy ending; Sergio had known from the start that this film had to be in the retrospective, but he had also chosen it to be shown during his few days there in person. A few minutes before it began, while people were making their way to their seats, one spectator had approached to ask for his reasons. Why not *Ilona Arrives with the Rain* or *The Art of Losing*, which were wonderful? Why *Time Out*? In reply, Sergio only had to point to Raúl:

"Because when it first came out, this guy was a few days old," he said. "And, with his eyes closed, the poor kid didn't understand too much."

It was true, but only partially. Yes, he wanted to be with Raúl the first time he saw this film, which had been born at the same time as him, on the big screen; he wanted to remember the strong emotions of the year 1998, when Raúl arrived in the world at the same time as Sergio went into politics. It had been a brief stay in the Colombian House of Representatives, and what Sergio remembered was the conviction, while he edited *Time Out* in moments stolen from the campaigns, that this would be his final work, a testament in every sense. At that time it did not seem strange that the preoccupations of cinema and politics, although they had such different packaging, would end up being reduced to two stubborn and eternal words in the Colombian vocabulary: war and peace. The film opened on December 25, a sort of Christmas present for a country that was sinking in a sea of blood. The guerrillas were killing, the paramilitaries were killing and the army was killing, but in the fantasy on screen the enemies gathered and hugged each other because their football team had put five goals past their rivals. At that time, when everyone seemed to think Colombia was a ruin, the attempts at peace failed one after another, and sometimes it seemed to Sergio that failure was less an accident than a true vocation: that the country was not made for living but for killing. And making this film had been an act of barefaced optimism. Now eighteen years had passed since the film was released, and reality had decided to come and give it a second life.

A few weeks earlier, at the end of September, when Octavi Martí wrote from the Filmoteca to ask Sergio for the definitive list of films to be shown in his presence, Colombians were on the brink of making the most important decision of the Republic's two hundred years of existence. It was a vote, an unprecedented referendum, concerning a three-hundred-page document. "Except that it's not a document," Sergio had said in an interview. "It's a new country." It was the Havana Peace Accords. Since the end of 2012, the Colombian government and the Farc, the oldest and perhaps the most pernicious guerrilla army of the continent, had been meeting in Cuba to seek a way out of a conflict that had now been going on for more than half a century, had left some eight million victims dead, injured, displaced, and the infernal dynamics of which had produced levels of cruelty sufficient to provoke serious doubts about the mental health of the whole country. Similar attempts had been made in the past, always with disastrous results, and the words of a guerrilla leader , who stood up from the table after the failure of the 1992 negotiations held in Mexico, were famous: "We'll see you after another ten thousand deaths." Many more had died since then in this degraded war without the world finding out about it. But all that had now changed.

The entire planet had followed the four years of negotiations. At one point or another, everyone who had anything to say about the dismantling of a festering conflict had interceded: the Irish who negotiated the Good Friday agreement, the South Africans who negotiated the post-apartheid peace, and even the Israelis who negotiated the Camp David accords. When the news came out in Havana that the parties had reached an agreement, Sergio could not stop thinking that the impossible had happened: a country accustomed to war was going to turn the page and start again. All they needed was the Colombian people to approve the accord at the polls. But that was just a procedural step, of course, a formality: who could imagine a country in such pain would refuse to bring the war to an end?

So, that September afternoon when he sat down to choose the films that would be shown while he was there, Sergio realized that the Barcelona retrospective was going to take place in a new world: a world with one war less going on. In other words, he thought that there, in front of the Barcelona audience, he would have the privilege of going on stage after the screening of *Time Out* and pronouncing words that had been unthinkable before. He would say: "This comedy about an absurd peace has just been shown for the first time in a world where a real peace has been achieved." Or maybe: "This film was made eighteen years ago in a war-torn country. Today, while we are watching it here in Barcelona, the country of the film has found peace." Or some similar phrase, sweetly sensationalist, idealistic but not innocent. These were his thoughts as he included *Time Out*, sent the email and turned to the task of living through that long week leading up to the Sunday referendum.

They were difficult days, but not only because of the

importance of the political moment. In fact, life seemed to leave Sergio little time to appreciate the magnitude of what was about to affect everyone, as he barely had enough energy to deal with what was happening to him. At the same time as he was responding to the Filmoteca's requests – compiling archival material about his life and work, accepting some interviews and gently declining others – he was up to his ears in preparations for a TV series on the life of Jaime Garzón. It was an exhausting job that required more hours than there were in a day. Sergio went back and forth across the city to scout locations, sometimes undertaking arduous investigations to discover the real spaces where the real life of his character had played out, sometimes inventing fictitious spaces and trying to imagine the story superimposed onto a house, a street, a restaurant Garzón had probably never set foot in. How difficult it is to imagine the story of a real man who we've actually known! Another part of the day was spent auditioning actors: trying to find a boy Garzón, an adolescent Garzón and an adult Garzón, over the course of interminable hours in the producer's office, under bright lights that tire your eyes after a while. Sergio heard lines he knew too well to be surprised by them: he looked into other people's faces and other people's bodies searching for the ghost of an old friend. And while all this was happening, not for an instant did he stop thinking about Silvia, feeling the emptiness of her absence and wondering if their marriage had failed irremediably.

During the week he spoke to her every day, almost always in the morning, and then used any free time to write long WhatsApp messages that were like letters from a prisoner: a prisoner who hadn't lost his sense of humour. In those

messages they seemed to be sharing everyday life, and sometimes it would have been possible to believe they were living
in the same city. Sergio never wrote without the conviction
that *this* – the brief word that contained the enormity of their
situation – could be mended, if only because of the evidence
of how much they loved each other or, rather, because they
loved each other too much not to end up together, if only out
of pure stubbornness. The idea of not living with his daughter
Amalia again tormented him to the point of depriving him
of sleep. He had begun to hate the stupid silence of the
mornings without her, and the messages also helped him in
the middle of the day: to receive a photo of his daughter pulling faces, or an audio message, or even a video with Amalia
spinning on the living room floor with a naked doll in each
hand, while in the background childish voices were speaking
incomprehensible Portuguese on the television.

Meanwhile the country, oblivious to his matrimonial
troubles, having nothing to do with his difficulties in finding
a house for Jaime Garzón, advanced towards the date of the
referendum. Then an NGO requested he make a twenty-second
video in defence of the peace accords. "We are living in the last
moments of the war," he said. "I don't know if people realize."
But maybe it's normal and predictable that people don't
realize. Why should it be any different, Sergio thought, if none
of these people he crossed paths with really knew what war
was like? There was a lot of talk about this in those days, in
the opinion columns and on the talk shows: an enormous rift
had opened in the country between those who had experienced
the war first-hand and those who had seen it on the television
news, or read about it in the magazines and newspapers. And

that was not the only disagreement. You just had to go outside to feel the tension in the atmosphere, a climate of confrontation that was new for Sergio because it was happening in the placeless place of social media. He, who had never ventured into those worlds of electrons, occasionally received supernatural reports that arrived from an unrecognizable country. It was said that the Havana peace accords were going to abolish private property. It was said – but who said? – that, if the accords were approved, Colombia would turn into a communist dictatorship. Fausto Cabrera, who had lost interest in almost everything since his last visit to China, spending all his days indoors and speaking to nobody apart from his wife Nayibe, emerged from his silence one afternoon when Sergio was visiting.

"They said the same thing when I was thirty," he said.

"About the communist threat?"

"And when I was fifteen as well, now that I think of it. That little trick seems so silly, but it has worked many times."

Sergio listened to the aspiring actors who tried to imitate Jaime Garzón, and wrote messages to Silvia full of secret codes like a love-struck teenager, and all the while supernatural reports kept arriving from that other country with a parallel existence. A taxi driver who took him downtown asked how he was going to vote on Sunday. "I'm going to vote Yes," Sergio said. The driver looked at him in the rear-view mirror.

"Not me, chief," he said. "Because they haven't got the right."

"The right to what?"

"They're going to pay the guerrillas minimum wage. And you know where that money's coming from? Our pensions. I've been working my whole life, and what for? To pay those sons of bitches not to kill us anymore? No, I'm not falling for that."

It wasn't true, but Sergio had no trouble understanding the sentiment. He didn't say anything, because he realized he didn't have the tools to convince the man. It was his word against Facebook; it was some passenger's poor argument against the authority of Twitter. Something similar, but much more alarming, happened on the Saturday before the referendum. Sergio had to leave the city to look for a town that looked like Sumapaz, where Jaime Garzón had been mayor in his youth (using the real town, which was a four-hour drive away on mountain roads, was unworkable), so the producer assigned him a white van with a visible logo on the side and a driver, a short man with a moustache who needed a thick cushion to raise him high enough to see over the steering wheel. The traffic on the way out of the city was already dense as was to be expected on a sunny weekend day, so Sergio, anticipating a long trip, decided to be the first to ask this time: "So, how are you going to vote tomorrow?" A shadow fell over the man's gaze.

"I know what side you're on, Don Sergio," he said almost with sympathy. "But I'm a Christian. You can't ask me to accept that aberration."

"I don't understand," said Sergio.

"We've talked a lot about it at my church. And peace is one thing, but this cannot be. This is an attack on the Christian family. Tell me the truth, Don Sergio. Is that what you want for your children?"

There was no more conversation as they drove towards Salto de Tequendama, or during the waits, while Sergio walked through a town and then through the next town to see which one looked more like the original. But that evening Sergio was trying to write a long WhatsApp message to Silvia when his phone vibrated. In the video was Alejandro Ordoñez, who had just left his post as attorney general. He had always seemed like a religious fanatic to Sergio, one of those true extremists, who for years had been using the immense power of his position to sabotage everything that defied his *lefebvrista* morality, from abortion rights to gay marriage. And there was Ordoñez in this video, accusing the government of using peace as an excuse to "impose the ideology of gender". "Think carefully on October second," the man said in his ominous nasal voice. "You are deciding your children's future. You are deciding the future of the Colombian family." He never quoted the lines from the accord that would destroy the family; he never referred to the exact paragraph in the accord that would ruin the future of Colombian children. But that was not necessary, apparently, for the video to reach the pastors' sermons. Sergio thought: Something's going on here. With that idea, which wasn't enough to become a concern, he went to sleep.

Sunday started off cloudy. Halfway through the morning, Sergio began to walk from his apartment on calle 100 sixteen blocks north to Hacienda Santa Bárbara, the shopping centre where his polling station was. They said the city would be a party, but on carrera Séptima, where a few parents waved banners bigger than their children and the honking of cars cut through the quiet, it was as though the party had not yet started. From a distance he caught sight, as always when he walked through this neighbourhood, of the Feliza Bursztyn statue on the lower slope of the Eastern Hills, and now, as he approached the Cavalry School, his memory was bringing things to mind he had not been seeking, like a cat who leaves the offering of a recently caught mouse outside our door. Right there, in some part of the facilities that stood on both sides of the avenue, Feliza Bursztyn had spent the worst hours of her life. The year was 1981. At five in the morning on a Friday (Sergio remembered the time and the day, but not the month: July? August?), a group of soldiers out of uniform, members of the army's intelligence services, forced their way into her house, searched it from top to bottom and, having found nothing, arrested her on some vague accusation of collaborating with the M-19 guerrillas. The abuse lasted for eleven hours: eleven hours of answering absurd questions while blindfolded, tied to a chair in the military stables: eleven hours of fear. As soon as they released her, unable to prove anything or considering the lesson complete, Feliza ran to seek refuge in the Mexican embassy. A few days later she left Colombia. Six months later, not yet fifty years old, she died of a heart attack in Paris. Sergio could not say that Feliza was his friend, as he hadn't met her more than four or five times, at exhibitions and gatherings of acquaintances. That's why he was surprised that the news of her death hurt him so much. Now he was remembering that shock, that news, that death.

So this was also one of the war zones, he thought. Bogotá was like that: a person walked along distracted, thinking their own thoughts, and on any corner the violent history of the country could jump out and hit them in the face. As he left behind the military facilities where Feliza had been interrogated and manhandled thirty-five years earlier, Sergio thought that a few blocks south, on that same avenida Séptima, was the monument to Diana Turbay, the journalist kidnapped by Pablo Escobar and killed during an attempt to rescue her; and even further south was the social club where the Farc put two hundred kilos of C-4 explosives in a small car and blew it up in the underground car park. Thirty-six people died. And if you kept walking without turning you could reach the corner of avenida Jiménez, the place where Jorge Eliécer Gaitán was assassinated with three shots in 1948. Many said that there, on that April 9, it had all really started. Yes, thought Sergio, the Colombian war was a long avenue; and if it were true that it had all started with Gaitán's death on carrera Séptima at the corner of avenida Jiménez, now Sergio was arriving at a shopping centre on the other side of the city, a hundred blocks north on that same street, to finish the war by putting his vote into a cardboard box. He showed his ID, put an X where he had to put one and folded the paper to put it through the slot, but at the moment of doing so he noticed that people were talking about him. Someone had recognized him, and when Sergio was given back his documents and was about to leave, he heard the voice of an older woman who said:

"He's one of those who want to hand the country over to the guerrillas."

Hours later, after having lunch on his own in the solitude of his apartment without Silvia or Amalia, he went over to Humberto Dorado's house. He was an actor who'd worked with Sergio since his first film, A Matter of Honour, in which he'd played a butcher who has to kill a schoolteacher over a matter of honour, and then he was Maqroll el Gaviero in Ilona Arrives with the Rain and the priest in Time Out: their friendship had lasted almost thirty years with very few surprises, and perhaps for that reason the idea of being together when they announced the approval of the accords was so appealing: it was the most surprising thing that had happened to them.

"Who could have imagined it?" Humberto said. "I thought Bogotá would have subway trains before the country had peace."

Sergio had brought not one but two bottles of an extraordinary Rioja, gifts from a producer from Madrid that had been sleeping in wooden boxes for seven years waiting for a worthy occasion; Humberto, a whisky drinker, had put his own bottle on the glass table. And so the hours went by, with talk of future projects while the television emitted its monologues without anyone paying attention, like a guest nobody talks to, and showed ominous images of the Caribbean coast, where a hurricane had prevented hundreds of thousands of citizens from getting out to vote. Towards the end of the evening, when they began to announce the first results, it was obvious things were not going as they had hoped. The Bogotá sky grew prematurely dark and the phones began to buzz as messages arrived from all over the country. At one point Humberto, whose sweet nature was legendary, threw the remote control and said to no-one:

"What a fucked-up world."

That night Sergio did not sleep well, and the next day he was outside at first light, trying to clear his head in the cold morning air of Bogotá. The streets were deserted. Sergio walked up to Séptima, took a photo of Feliza's sculpture and sent it to Silvia. "This country is hopeless," he wrote in a rage. The first news reports were saying that the peace accords had been defeated by a margin of fifty thousand votes: the number of people who go to a football match in El Campín stadium. Sergio thought what had happened was much more mysterious, and more serious, than a political defeat. But what was it? What did the rejection of the accords say about Colombians?

What kind of future was coming down on this divided country the referendum was leaving in its wake, a country at loggerheads, where families had split, friendships had broken, a country where people seemed to have discovered new and powerful reasons to hate each other to death?

The same questions were still pestering him days later when he arrived in Barcelona, as he gradually found out that what happened in Colombia had not stayed in Colombia. All the journalists asked him about it, all conversations tried to touch on the subject, because nobody could understand how a country that had been at war for fifty years could have voted against ending it. Sergio said exactly that to a journalist from *La Vanguardia* who had asked him about his long-ago years in politics. And in justification of those years, he said: "If a person despises politics, they end up being governed by those they despise," he said. "And why did you give it up?" the journalist asked. "Because of threats," Sergio said. "I began to prepare to debate. I was on the Military Affairs Commission. But I had been in a guerrilla army, albeit thirty years earlier, and that did not amuse the extreme right, which was killing people left, right and centre in those days. And so I got death threats." "The 'No to reconciliation' must have hurt," the journalist said next. "Well, it's a lie that won," Sergio said. "A few days ago, one of the strategists of the campaign explained what tools they'd used. And it's very sad." He was referring to a news item that had been like an earthquake, one more reason for confrontation in a country that was already fighting with itself. Speaking into to a live microphone of a national newspaper, during a completely legitimate interview, the director of the campaign against the accords had declared, without raising an eyebrow, that his strategy had been designed to exploit the rage, the fear, the resentment and anguish of Colombians. He put his objective into short form:

"We want people *berraca* when they're going out to vote."

"What's *berraca*?" the journalist asked.

"Angry, but much stronger," Sergio said. "Like we all are at this moment."

Now, on the Filmoteca de Catalunya screen, *Time Out* – its vaudeville war and fairy tale peace – was reaching its end. Sergio was seized by a strange melancholy. Maybe it was the concurrence of the two events, the rejection of the peace accords and Fausto's death, or maybe the added circumstance of the wreckage of his marriage; in any case, there, in the auditorium, sitting next to Raúl, so close that their shoulders were touching, Sergio felt fleetingly that the affection of his children was the only solid thing left in his life, as all the rest – his father, his marriage and his country – had suddenly broken down, and all he could see was a panorama in ruins: the shell of a bombed-out city.

That's what he was thinking when people began to applaud and it was his turn to go on stage. He discovered he was not in the mood for the question and answer session; he wished it was already over. He wanted to close his eyes and open them to find himself in his hotel room, turning on the television, looking for an old film to watch with Raúl. By the time he sat down on a tall stool, in front of a black microphone that had materialized in the time it took him to get there from the back row, a man in a red jacket – one of those new puffer jackets, that looked like a eiderdown – was waiting, standing up among the audience like a single poppy in a field. A moderator welcomed them in

Catalan and briefly introduced Sergio, whose presence honoured them, and spoke with gratitude of the great sacrifices Sergio had made to be at that retrospective of his work. Sergio recognized the young man who had picked him up at the airport the day he'd arrived from Bogotá: the skinny bearded youth who that day had worn a convict's T-shirt, and tonight wore a wrinkled lumberjack shirt. Sergio said hello, thanked the Filmoteca for the invitation, opened the bottle of water awaiting him on a small round table and took a sip. He was going to point to the man in the red jacket, but the moderator had already given the wireless mic to someone else. A woman of about sixty, with grey hair and red-framed glasses, spoke to him familiarly, as if continuing a friendly conversation the film had interrupted.

"Your father just died, Sergio," she said. "I'm so sorry."

"Thank you," Sergio said.

"I wanted to ask: was he an important figure in your filmmaking? And what did he think of *Time Out*?"

"He liked it," Sergio said, laughing his brief timid laugh. It was a nervous gesture he'd always had, that stifled laugh that led into his sentences like knuckles knocking on a door before a person walked in. "And he liked his role, which was not easy. To answer the other question: yes, he was very important to me. Without my father, I never would have gone into filmmaking. He taught me how to act, back in the 1950s. He taught me how to direct an actor. He has been such a huge presence in my life that he's in almost all my films."

"I read an interview you gave the other day," the woman said. "You said there that you'd been with the guerrillas in your country. Did that help you make this film?"

"Well, it helped me to know what I was talking about.

This film is a caricature, but to make caricatures it's best to know the real model. In any case, the guerrillas I knew didn't resemble the ones in the film. I went into the guerrilla force in 1969. Everything was different. We truly believed that armed struggle was the only way."

The woman was going to say something else, but Sergio looked away and his gesture was enough to make the moderator look for the next question. Sergio noticed that the man in the red jacket had not sat down during the exchange: he listened to the dialogue standing in his place, as if wanting to make sure they didn't forget about him. But his turn had not come yet: the microphone was passed from hand to hand in the opposite direction, as if floating away from him on the waves of people and ended up at one edge of the auditorium. Sergio put a hand to his forehead, like a visor, because the silhouette was just below a strong light that dazzled him. The effect was beautiful: the light formed a corona around the head of a woman – it was another woman – like the aura of a virgin by Leonardo.

"I just have one question: did you shoot anyone? Did you use firearms?"

A murmur rippled through the crowd.

"Well, yes," Sergio said. "That's what happens in those situations: you either shoot or get shot." There was a hard silence. "Look, I'm not a person who believes in violence, but at that stage of my life we were led to believe that armed struggle was the only way. Now the country has changed, of course. It's now possible to participate in politics without resorting to armed struggle. However, it is still a profoundly unjust country."

"Can I ask another question?"

The audience murmured again.

"Sure," Sergio said.

"Would you make the same film today? I mean: what film would you make today?"

Sergio sat back in his chair.

"I might not make a comedy," he said. "All film-makers know that the public prefers comedy: comedies stand a better chance of success at the box office. But most Colombian films in recent years have not gone in that direction. It's a country undergoing a dramatic war, with problems of corruption and drug trafficking, and it would be suspicious if Colombians made complacent films . . . I've always been interested in what went on in the cinema of socialist countries. They showed us wonderful places, true paradise, and the day the Berlin Wall came down we discovered it was all a sham: that they had the same problems as us, perhaps even more serious. Those propaganda films, cinema at the service of the state, camouflaged reality. I think Colombian cinema doesn't do that. Maybe we believe that the only way for things to change is by showing them. That's what's happening now with the peace process: it's the only way to make peace, by scratching the wounds."

He regretted it as soon as he'd said it. It was not the wisest idea to raise the subject, but now it was too late to backtrack: the woman had seized on the opportunity.

"Now that you mention it," she said, "I would like to know your opinion on what just happened in your country. With the failure of the peace accords, I mean. Could you talk a little bit about that?"

"I think we should let someone else have a word, if you don't mind," Sergio said. The man in the red jacket still stood at his place with an almost vegetable indifference. The moderator had also noticed him, and now gave him his turn. The man waited for the slow-travelling mic to reach him. He seemed to have all the time in the world, and was showing his patience with that singular expression of those so convinced they are right that they put up with any aggravation without complaint. He was young, despite his bald head, but as soon as he started to speak Sergio recognized the same solemnity he'd seen so often in so many places.

"Señor Cabrera," he said, "you were a guerrilla fighter, and, as you said, 'you shot so you wouldn't get shot'. But in this film you decided to mock the war. Why?"

Sergio took another sip and let out his brief laugh.

"Well, I don't agree," he said. "It was not my intention to mock anything. The film is a comedy."

"But it is also a mockery," the man said. "It mocks very painful things. Is that why you make films, to mock things that are very painful for many people? Colombia has many problems, and one of those problems is the guerrillas. And you seem to take that lightly."

"Yes, guerrillas are a problem," Sergio said. "But they are also a symptom: a symptom of the many problems the country has. Colombia is still a very unjust country, despite having made progress."

"Well, excuse me," the man said, suddenly haughty. "But if the country is so unjust, why don't you go back to the jungle?"

"What?"

"Why don't you take up arms again? Or are you not willing to risk your life for those ideas you have?"

Sergio sighed and hoped nobody had noticed. It was not

the first time he'd received attacks like this. Why was he so annoyed all of a sudden? Yes, these had been long days of strong emotions, but all that was behind him: his father's funeral, condolences he'd replied to briefly and those he had left unanswered. Sergio began to tell a story, or to speak in the tone of someone telling a story, not someone defending himself against a malicious question.

"You can't imagine how difficult it was to make *Time Out*," he said. "Do you know why? Because it occurred to some friends of mine around that time to form a political party. And they asked me, no, they *begged* me to stand for election. What I was interested in doing was to carry on making my films. It was what I'd wanted to do my whole life, and I was finally getting it right. But friends have the capacity to convince a person. And it's not because they're friends, but because they know our weak points. They knew mine. They talked to me about a sense of duty, of my responsibility as a citizen, things like that. And then I found myself with a problem: my friends were right. So I accepted. I was shooting the film far from Bogotá, in places that were difficult to get to, because the story happens in the jungle, as you've all just seen. And on Saturdays I flew in a tiny bush plane, terribly afraid it would crash, and I went to campaign in the poor neighbourhoods of Bogotá. My luck was so bad that they elected me."

Sergio laughed and the audience laughed along with him. He looked towards the front rows and saw Octavi Martí, not leaning back in his seat but forward, following his words with eyebrows raised. He went on:

"I was vice-president of the House of Representatives. Imagine. Me, who just wanted to make films! My film-making was interrupted, and yes, it was as if they'd cut off my hand. But my sense of duty . . . My citizen's responsibility . . . That's all blackmail."

Sergio fell silent for a moment. He took a gulp of water, then another. Then he said:

"The threats began to arrive a few months into my term. I'm not talking about unfriendly letters, no. I'm talking about condolences with my name on them arriving at my house, spattered with red ink as if it were blood. They came with small coffins, as small as a child's toy, if there are children who play with coffins. And in the coffins, inside the tiny coffins, came a piece of meat that was beginning to smell rotten. I wasn't the only one to receive threats: my mother also got some, and my sister. My son Raúl, who lives in Marbella, is here today in the audience to watch these films: obviously he has nothing better to do." People laughed again. Some looked left and right, trying to pick out Sergio Cabrera's son. "Raúl does not remember this, but he spent the first two years of his life playing with the armed bodyguards the government assigned to protect me. I have photos: my son riding his tricycle followed by a smiling man in a tie and shirtsleeves, a pistol in his holster . . . Anyway, after the threats, everything was left in the hands of the police intelligence department, who treated us very well. One day we were summoned to a minister's office. Well, I was summoned, and when I arrived I found I wasn't the only one. There was Jaime Garzón, a wonderful comedian. He fronted the best political satire show on TV in those days, and it turned out he had also been receiving death threats. I wasn't at all surprised. We talked about it. It was explained that we were much appreciated in the country and it was very unlikely that anyone would dare to harm us. But one day, not long after that conversation, they dared. They killed Jaime Garzón."

He took a drink of water. Utter silence.

"Then they called me in again and told me, basically, that things had changed. That I should forget all the reassuring messages: that my life was in danger and the best thing to do would be to leave the country. My sister and mother had to go too. They went to Guyana and I spent several years living in Madrid. My film-making went to shit, of course, and I lost money, and I lost my place as a film director and had to reinvent myself as a television director. I was able to do that, and having directed *Cuéntame cómo pasó* is one of the most rewarding things I've done. And that's why I feel so indebted to Spain."

He stopped talking there, and it was as if someone had interrupted a transmission. The man in the red jacket seemed confused, and said:

"Yes, but I asked—"

Sergio cut him off in a different tone of voice. "I know what you asked. And this is my reply: I believe in peace, even if this one is not working, and I believe we have to keep seeking it. If I've told you all of this it's so you can see – so you all can see – that I have always defended my ideas with my life. Tell me something, señor, can you say the same?"

"OK, let's leave it there for today," the moderator said, hurrying onto the stage. People in every part of the auditorium started shouting. Someone said they had a question, but in vain, because the moderator had switched into Catalan and was reminding everyone they'd be showing five more Sergio Cabrera films over the next few days. He hoped they had enjoyed

Time Out and wished them all, in the name of the Filmoteca de Catalunya, a pleasant evening. Thank you very much.

Here and there could be heard, scattered, reticent, the last of the day's applause.

That night, when Raúl had fallen asleep in the next bed, he wrote to Silvia. *I think demonstrative gratitude has never been one of my characteristics,* he told her, *but I am grateful, I always have been even if in silence, in secret, as if it embarrassed me. And I don't know why, because I could shout out loud all my gratitude for so many things that have happened to me in my life: my children, who I adore and feel adored by, my professional successes that have been numerous and frequent, my luck, without which those and other things would perhaps never have happened.* He looked up, because a quiet snore came from Raúl's pillow. *But most of all, I feel grateful to destiny for having met you. And this is not something that occurs to me now in the middle of this tempest we're going through, no, and you know it, this is something I've told you a thousand times. I have told you softly in a whisper, out loud in letters and in messages, and I'm telling you again with my whole heart: I have been a very lucky man. And I want to continue to be.*

XVI

Forgetting his own name was easier than he would have thought. Comrade Raúl got used to his new identity at the same time as he did to his new life, taking on its demands, correcting his earlier mistakes, so naturally that he never needed to ask Comandante Carlos why he had chosen that name for him. Having carried the double hammock for long distances, after enduring Marianella's private protests, he traded it with a *campesino* for a single hammock to give to his sister and did the same with hers as soon as the opportunity arose. He also traded the machete, which he'd bought in the tourist shop in Medellín thinking it was the best one since it was the biggest, for in the jungle he'd realized that the bigger something was the more hassle it caused. In a lodge by the River Cauca, a mule driver happily traded his smaller and more manageable one, but felt the exchange was unfair and added a Swiss army knife.

He was already completely Raúl when they reached the camp in the flood plains of the Tigre. In a few weeks they had climbed mountains where the air was thin and descended to this hot, humid valley where the pores opened and skin felt sticky and the world's smells had changed, because the vegetation grew and rotted in every square metre of the tropical earth.

By then the long days trekking through different terrains, more difficult than anything he'd seen in China, had inflamed one of his knees so much he could barely move it. Comandante Armando welcomed them with honours they hadn't earned and ordered a healer to be brought for Raúl, who received warm cloths and massages with cacao ointment and wondered why he was getting this privileged treatment. Armando, whose name inspired a messianic respect among the guerrilla fighters, was a man with a kind face and olive-coloured skin, like that of the Indians of India, and seemed made of nothing but muscles and bone. When the healer had finished his work, he asked Comrade Raúl for his documents and any money he was carrying: all that was no longer necessary. He took the ID with a disused name; he didn't read it out loud, but what he did read was Comrade Raúl's date of birth. "Damn," he said, "today's the comrade's birthday." He gathered the rest for an improvised celebration in which the guerrillas sang to Raúl, with English words they didn't know the meaning of, and he thought under better circumstances they would even have lit some candles for him. The whole scene seemed to belong in another story.

His knee got better as the days went by and he got used to walking the long distances, or rather he tolerated them better, in spite of occasional pains and inflammation that he treated with ointments. If he sometimes forgot about the pain, it was because of the need to be alert to other training, other precautions, or just because the heat distracted him. What surprised him at first was the emptiness of those places. The troop moved for days across deserted mountains, although they frequently found abandoned huts as evidence of life in earlier times. What Mao recommended in his military writings was very different: revolutionaries should distance themselves from the enemy's nerve centres, yes, but always going in search of the people, because only among the people is it possible to build a support base. In Maoist military thought, creating a solid base of support was like liberating a country: that way you could draw borders, create sovereignty and begin to conquer terrain, as you can only start to win the war when there are territories where the enemy cannot move around at will. He mentioned it first to Marianella, speaking in Chinese so nobody would understand his probable heresies.

"I was thinking the same thing," she said. "But we're not going to teach them how to do things."

"And why not? Why can't we teach them?"

"Because we're not from here. You and I are from somewhere else, even if it doesn't seem like it."

It took many weeks – of obedience, wariness and humility – before he felt he had the right to remember out loud the teachings of Chairman Mao and ask if that was not the reason for combat: the creation of a place for a guerrilla base that could later turn into a base of support. Should they not have more of a presence where people lived? "Oh," said Armando. "The comrade has opinions." Gradually they told him the story of Pedro Vásquez Rendón, the journalist who had been one of the founders of the Popular Liberation Army, the EPL, two years earlier. He was the one who chose the zone where they began operations, between the Cauca and Sinú rivers, building schools and health centres in small villages in the San Jorge plains. They indoctrinated the young people and converted the old, and not much time passed before the army had noticed the appearance of a new guerrilla group. Then the campaigns of enclosure and annihilation began. The first failed, but several commanders died in the second, Vásquez Rendón among them. The army took dozens of *campesinos* out of the zone: the ones who didn't leave with the army left with the guerrillas; those who didn't leave with either side emigrated to other villages or to the cities. They could not stay in their houses, because the San Jorge plains were now considered territory under the influence of the EPL, and anyone living there was considered to be a guerrilla fighter or supporter. That's how the zone was depopulated until only the most stubborn or those who had nothing to lose remained.

All this was explained to Comrade Raúl. He was in a detachment of about fifteen people, but these debates were as loud as if they were being conducted by a much larger group, and someone often had to interrupt to remind them that the army might not be as far away as they thought. The conversations took place at night, while the guerrillas ate dinner, generally after the comrades had peppered Raúl with questions about life in China and the Red Army's military training. The first question they asked him was whether China was really as far away as they'd been told, and Raúl thought at first that the best way to answer was to look up at the sky when a plane was flying over, one of the many on their way to Panama or the United States, and say: "If we were on board that plane, it would take more than a whole day." He realized his explanation was not a good one when one of the older guerrillas, whose grey beard did not entirely hide his harelip, said: "So it's not that far. One day is closer than the sea." Raúl had to overcome his aversion to the limelight to explain the speed of a plane and the distances covered, and once, trying to convince them that there were two possible routes to reach China, he even found himself forced to remind them that the Earth was round.

In those moments he felt two things at the same time: first, that his presence there occasionally had a tangible value; second that he was a weird creature, a circus freak. The comrades had never met a guerrilla fighter who had studied in the schools of the Bogotá elite and then been to Europe, and who could talk about Russian literature, Italian opera and Japanese cinema in Spanish, French or Chinese. It was Raúl who explained, for example, that what they'd heard on the radio was not a lie: a man had reached the moon in a spaceship. The comrades had gathered around the radio, a transistor with knobs constantly coming loose, as they did every night, to listen to the day's news. But that night, something special was going to happen and they all knew it. The jungle filled with the static of the broadcast. In excited voices the presenters said that a human being had stepped on the moon, that he was called Armstrong and the spaceship was called *Apollo*; but the comrades did not care that the name was that of a Greek god, and when they looked up at the moon in the clear sky, they pointed out that it didn't look like anyone was up there. Raúl was alone in his astonishment. "Man on the moon," he said to nobody. "It's like something out of a novel." The comrades did not seem impressed. One of them asked if the engine of the rocket was like a car's; another wanted to know if you had to study a lot to make that journey, or if anyone would be able to do it from here on in. Then one of the youngest settled the night's argument.

"This is complete bullshit," he said. "A gringo lie. Pure imperialist propaganda, comrades."

And Raúl tried to say that no, it was true, but then he

realized he was defending the gringos, and chose to retreat into an inoffensive silence.

After a few weeks, Armando made a decision: Comrade Sol would be deployed to the President Mao School detachment, a place for the preparation of young militants where there were more women and they felt more comfortable. "So she won't be the only woman in a group of men," he explained. Raúl would have liked to tell him that this woman, at the age of sixteen, had better military training than most of them. But he did not. He watched her hoist her backpack and join a group of guerrillas without even waving goodbye, and he wondered how his sister would fit in with those local girls who wore make-up every day and could not avoid some degree of vanity even when aiming a rifle. As well as Sol, Pacho, the young black man who'd come on the same bus from Medellín, and two other comrades of those who'd welcomed them, Jaime and Arturo, were going. They liked Sol. Arturo, a *campesino* with indigenous features and a teenager's moustache, adopted her as if they'd grown up together.

Raúl, meanwhile, stayed with Comandante Armando, acting under his orders, learning from him. Thus began a routine of improbable monotony. The days were made up of repeated moments that seemed like copies of the same times on the previous day, and the day before that as well. Working with the *campesinos*, meeting the commanders, building a school or health centre: the days always began and ended at the same times. The other detachments must have been bored too, because the women were seen more and more often talking to the men. That was frowned on: despite the commanders having their spouses, whether having brought them from their previous lives or having met them in the region, the EPL manual prohibited *guerrilleros* and *guerrilleras* from looking at each other as if they could be anything more than comrades in the cause. However, one of Sol's comrades had started smiling at Raúl and resting a hand on his arm when they met.

"How's my blondie?" she'd say. "Come on, look at me with those green eyes."

She was called Isabela there, but Raúl never knew her real name. She was local, evidently, as she spoke with the same accent as the *campesinos* and moved with the ease of one who has grown up in these parts and only finds it strange that others have come to occupy them. She was a year younger than Raúl, but she talked as if she'd lived two lifetimes, or at least as though she had a pressing urgency to start living them. One afternoon, while Raúl was chopping down weeds with his machete as a commander had requested, she crept up behind him and crouched down to help him, leaning against his body, and Raúl felt her breasts so clearly he could have drawn them. More contacts followed: brushing up against him as they walked side by side, insinuating looks in front of everyone. It was just a matter of days before something else happened.

So he was not surprised, or at least not totally, the night that Isabela stole over to his hammock in the darkness, without using a torch or making any noise, and in one dextrous movement lay down beside him. Raúl had not had a woman's body so close in a long time, and he knew he would regret what was about to happen, but two fears combined, that of disciplinary measures and the last vestiges of Christian morality, and landed on him simultaneously.

"No, we can't do this," he whispered. "Go away, comrade. Go, we can't do this."

He did not need to see her face to feel first her confusion and then a concise, efficient, concentrated form of contempt.

Guard duty was what he most detested. Guard duty was staying still at night to be the easy target of all the mosquitos in the world. The guerrillas relieved each other after one-hour shifts; that eternal hour was measured by Raúl's watch, and he soon realized that every comrade moved the hands of the watch five or ten minutes ahead to shorten their turns, so the last one on duty ended up having to guard for all the accumulated extra minutes the others had made disappear. The only thing he could do during those detestable minutes, apart from scratching his bites and trying to distinguish his comrades' snores from the sounds of animals, was think. He thought, for example, about Pacho: he had been killed in combat near Caucasia, and the news caused Raúl a nightmare he hadn't anticipated. He'd barely known him; he'd shared his first hours as a guerrilla with him (in the bus from Medellín, although at that point they hadn't met, and then walking from Dabeiba to the camp), but not much more. Why did it affect him so strongly? "Must be your first death," Armando said. Raúl thought of Uncle Felipe and Aunt Inés Amelia. But those were deaths from another life; they had died for another person. "Your first," Armando continued, "but he won't be your last. Don't worry, you get used to it."

He also thought about Isabela, and regretted having turned her down and fantasized about what might have happened, and then regretted it again. He was sure of one thing: he'd behaved correctly. He had understood that revolution was inseparable from a certain puritanism; he knew that Lenin had copied communist organization from early Christianity, and an inviolable prohibition hung over relations between men and women. Isabela seemed not to have heard of that. Or maybe the prohibitions were not as strict for everyone. Yes, that was also possible: that Raúl was an overly rigorous soldier, as if trying to compensate with his discipline for the sin of his origins.

Raúl thought about all this.

And he also thought other absurd things.

Was it possible that the Party had simply given itself a medal? After all, if two youngsters like them, bourgeois and privileged, had travelled to communist China and received military training from their army and returned to join the ranks of the EPL, if all that could happen in Colombia, the revolution was not only alive, but had all the cards to triumph. Couldn't the same thing happen to them as happened to Father Camilo Torres? The priest, a bourgeois from a liberal family, would have been much more useful in the city, but ended up dying uselessly in his first battle. And for what? Gradually Raúl began to glimpse the possibility that it had not really been necessary for either him or his sister to join the guerrillas; but as soon as those thoughts appeared, he banished them with the old trick of shame, and carried on without questioning himself and by convincing himself that his secret doubts were the remnants of a reactionary life. In any case, he never freed himself from the nagging certainty that he had something to prove, and that his comrades looked at him warily, as if he wasn't entirely one of them.

Every week there were two meetings Raúl attended with his two masks: the member of the Party cell and the rank-and-file guerrilla fighter. The cell did analyses and self-criticisms, and

Raúl realized that his presence there made no sense if not for the privileges of his father, who had managed to become an authority figure in Medellín: not only for practising as a sort of ambassador for Maoism in Colombia, of course, but also for the simple circumstances of being white and European. In the assembly of soldiers, however, Raúl was what he'd always wanted to be: one of many. The assembly of soldiers was a tradition implemented by the Red Army during their marches, a weekly session in which men have the right to criticize each other and even their commanders. Sergio had always been proud of that moment when combatants were all equal, with no distinction of rank, origin or race. But now that proletarian equality was not turning out as he had imagined.

Among the commanders, one in particular seemed to look at Raúl as if he were carrying imported grievances from other lives. His name was Fernando, and he was not just any commander: he was one of the founders of the EPL. He was forty-five years old at that point, more or less, and his life had been long enough to study law in Bogotá, to join the Communist Youth of Colombia and to begin to compete in athletic trials at national level. He was such a good runner that Independiente Santa Fe, one of Bogotá's two football teams, signed him for their athletic division, where Fernando trained so well that he won four gold medals in the 1950 National Games. When he was expelled from the Communist Youth for Maoist tendencies, Fernando founded a new party – that is: the Marxist–Leninist–Maoist Thought Communist Party – and began to serve in the EPL, and his ideological debates with the other founders soon became the stuff of legend. He was an intransigent man, quick and aggressive with his words, who was capable of branding one of his peers a petit-bourgeois revisionist for not agreeing with him on a point of doctrine, and who had also won the respect that physical strength wins: Fernando marched faster than the others, endured the longest distances better, and not even the worst of trails were a problem for his legs. As the days went by, Raúl learned to recognize in him the intensity of sectarians, which he already knew well from other experiences in other latitudes, and he thought it was a bad thing that this man had him in his sights.

He was right. Fernando was annoyed from the start that Comrade Raúl was reminding them of Mao's teachings to criticize Central Command's military decisions, and he said so out loud at one of the cell's meetings, but also managed to repeat the accusation at the assembly of soldiers. Raúl tried to respond to the accusations, even though what was expected of him was not a defence but a self-criticism, and he also did so by repeating the attitudes that had motivated the charge: by quoting Mao. Mao's military teachings talked about a guerrilla base, which is the source of the base of support, which is the territory where the guerrillas exercise a form of sovereignty. Raúl said, with pride, that he had known that situation to which they aspired. And what he was seeing here, in Colombia, was very different.

"Here we call a base of support what is still a guerrilla base," he said. "And I wonder if we aren't deceiving ourselves."

The silence was the harshest reply possible. Then came Fernando's cutting voice: "This is not China, comrade, in case you hadn't noticed." Someone further away added an incomprehensible phrase between gritted teeth, but Raúl caught the word *boots* and heard the laughter of the others. It was not hard to know what that was referring to: weeks earlier they had found out that Comrade Raúl was carrying a pair of high boots of fine leather that he'd brought from China, and explaining that they were Red Army boots did nothing to help the situation: they told him straight out that leather was useless in the jungle, because you couldn't cross the river in them and once wet they would destroy the feet of the strongest man, and they began to cut the boots into pieces, saying that on the other hand they were good for making cartridge belts.

"This guy thinks he can run the guerrilla army," Fernando said to nobody in particular, "because he's just arrived from China."

He stood up and the meeting ended. Raúl felt his years of devotion to Maoism and his revolutionary vocation deserved a different answer, but he didn't say anything, not that week or in the following ones. Fernando's ill will remained. He made it known at meal times, which in those days consisted of banana soup at midday and at night, and he made it known during the intelligence sessions, and he made it known the day he realized Raúl had a compass in his hand. "That's not from around here," he said. Raúl explained that the Red Army had given it to him the day he finished his military training: a sort of graduation present, so to speak. "Graduation present, how nice," said Fernando. He put the compass in his pocket, turned around and walked away without another word. Raúl never got it back, and he couldn't complain, of course. The commander was the authority, despite the efforts the EPL made not to reproduce the codes of militarism, and only with effort and submission and commitment, thought Raúl, could he deactivate a powerful man's dislike. He was very careful not to mention the matter: he did not tell Comandante Armando, who had taken him under his wing from the start, much less his father, who one day, to everyone's surprise, arrived at the camp on the Tigre plain.

His visit was so unexpected that Raúl thought, when Armando gave him the news, that something serious had happened in the family. He thought briefly of his mother, thought she was dead, thought that would be the worst news in the world. That was not it. It seemed Fausto had been at a council meeting of the Public Services Union of Antioquia, one of the places where he operated as a promoter of theatre and man of culture, when some union member interrupted the conversations to reveal to everyone his most recent discovery.

"I want to denounce this Señor Cabrera," he said, "as a political secretary of the Communist Party."

Fausto had been outed. The army and police were looking for him, and would have captured him if he hadn't hidden for twenty days. It was so unexpected that he couldn't even say goodbye to Luz Elena, but was simply swallowed up by the earth and the earth vomited him up twenty days later on the shoulder of the road to the sea, in the direction of Dabeiba, with a castaway's beard and the same clothes he'd been wearing the day he'd gone into hiding. At four the next morning, after spending the night in a house on the outskirts of the village, he went up a trail that damaged his ankles, arrived at a sugar mill on the highest point of the ridge and walked to another house. Thus, from one refuge to another, guided by a scout, he ended up reaching the zone after seven days that felt like many more. He'd been lost, had blisters on his feet and embarrassed himself by getting frightened by a *churrusco* caterpillar, but there he was, near the River Sinú, joining the EPL's National Directorate. Just before he arrived he ran into a guerrilla fighter wearing a jacket that looked like one his son had brought back from Peking.

"A gift from Comrade Raúl," the man said. "What a great guy, you know?"

So that's how he learned his son's name, and that's what he called him when they met. Raúl had come out to welcome him with his sister, and Fausto hugged them both with so much emotion that Raúl had to struggle not to cry. By then Sol had become the military secretary of the President Mao School detachment. She was in charge of the initial training of new recruits: a position of immense responsibility for someone so young. Fausto gently took off her Chinese cap, stroked her tied-back hair and took his leave with the guerrillas' slogan: *Combatiendo venceremos* (Fighting we shall win). Then he hugged Raúl, contravening several rules by doing so, and introduced himself with his new name: "Emecías, at your service." He talked about the importance of what they were doing, of the pride he felt for his two children and the luck of being part of that family. "It's not common, for sure," he said in an exalted tone. "It's not common for a family to fight together for the same cause, with the same weapons, on the same front. We are privileged. This is not of this world, but of the one to come, the one we're all bringing into being. There will be those who say we are mad, of course, but I say: what beautiful madness."

A few hours later they heard the helicopters. At first it was just a fluttering sound, and Fausto did not have the training to recognize it, but he noticed that the camp began to move and alerts sounded from every direction. It seemed like three or four, but soon the uproar was so noisy that it was difficult to talk on the ground. The commanders agreed that somebody, one of their own, must have betrayed them, because otherwise they couldn't understand how the helicopters had found such a secure camp. Men moved as if their itinerary were marked with signs on the ground; Fausto, however, didn't know what to do or where to go, but simply listened uncomprehendingly to the troops' instructions. He saw Raúl go by, handling his rifle, and wanted to ask him, but then he felt a hand on his arm and heard a voice say: "You come with me, comrade." And he found himself suddenly being swept up as if by a wave into the dense jungle, far from the tarpaulins, where Comandante Armando was leading the retreat. In the end, in the midst of the agitation, Armando had time to go over to Fausto and wordlessly point something out. Fausto turned and saw Raúl very far away, waving a hand in the air to say goodbye. Fausto waved back.

"Don't worry, comrade," Armando said. "Comrade Raúl will catch up with us later."

The whole manoeuvre took less than two hours. The guerrilla fighters abandoned the zone barefoot, so they wouldn't leave trails, and dispersed in different directions to sow confusion. Those who had come from the city went back there. Fausto did not go back with them: he would have to spend months in the jungle before it was safe to return. He was forced to stay with Armando and the main body of the military force, more than fifty men experienced in the fiercest combat who were pulling the group back and defending the rear guard. He didn't know how long he walked not knowing where he was going, advancing into the depths of the jungle on an empty stomach, but he was sure the escape lasted for more than an entire day before he was reunited with his son. He learned that Raúl had been assigned to containment duties, and he admired him and feared for him but had no opportunity to tell him so, because the troop was busy with other jobs. They had detailed a search party to go out hunting, because the comrades were starving, but the team had returned empty-handed. Then a comrade brought back some good news: not far away, by the stream, a three-metre-long boa was sunning itself, having just eaten. Two men killed it, but it took ten of them to skin it, remove a small capybara from its belly, clean it of cartilage and begin to cook it. Fausto was given a bowl of greasy soup so dense that chunks of meat floated on top, and he could not bring the first spoonful to his lips without feeling he was going to vomit in front of everyone. Raúl, who was eating beside him, gave him a reproachful glare so pitiless that Fausto ate the rest of his soup without a word.

This time they said goodbye aware they might very well never see each other again alive. Raúl did not allow himself a moment's hesitation. He felt observed at every turn: the containment group would leave under orders of Comandante Fernando, who knew very well who the Cabreras were, and Raúl perceived his vigilant eyes from some part of the jungle trying to find an attitude – a hug, a tear – to reproach in the next assembly. But the hug and tears came from Fausto. "Take care," he said. "We'll see each other when we can." The questions of civilian life – Where are you going? For how long? When will we see you again? – had no meaning or value in the jungle. As he left Fausto, Raúl hated Fernando, hated his presence as judge or informer, because he would have liked to speak to his father about what was happening in the city, and especially about Luz Elena's clandestine work. He still had questions in his head when he walked away with the other members of the containment group – Ernesto, the one who had done the military course in Albania, and a scout – all walking a few metres behind Comandante Fernando, confident of being under the orders of a good strategist who knew the army's techniques well, but aware of the risks they were going to be running in the days to come. Raúl was by now moving through the jungle as if he'd grown up there: his knees had got used to the terrain and no longer gave him trouble; he had stopped looking at the ground as he walked, as he did at first, for he'd been made to understand that he'd never see a snake before stepping on one, and it was best to trust to fate, or hope the snake would get out of the way first.

The soldiers who'd disembarked had set up four posts on the high points of a large area, the size of a large city. That's what had landed in the helicopters: an operation to retake the zone. The task of the containment group was child's play, but the four guerrilla fighters were risking their lives at it. The objective was to trick the army into believing that the guerrillas were still there. The strategy was to lie in ambush near the water sources and then attack one of the posts, which were generally high up in the mountains: that gave the soldiers a vantage point, but at the same time made it difficult to return fire, for those firing from above lose a visible horizon, and it is very difficult not to shoot into the ground. The containment group attacked twice a day; they did so using more ammunition than necessary, to give the soldiers the impression that the enemy was numerous, and then advanced toward the next post to repeat the manoeuvre. Raúl had never been under such persistent fire as from those desperate soldiers who could not see their enemy, and he always thought it nothing short of miraculous to reach the end of the day unscathed.

The operation lasted three weeks. Disoriented or confused, and in any case unable to figure out where the enemy was or how many men they were facing, the soldiers abandoned the zone. From then on, Comandante Fernando and comrades Raúl and Ernesto devoted themselves to rebuilding the detachment. They welcomed men who came from nearby areas and re-established alliances with the *campesinos* of the zone. It was an arduous task, and Raúl had every reason in the world to think that his performance during the containment strategy, as well as the reconstruction of the detachment, could have earned him Comandante Fernando's sympathy, or at least neutralized his ill will. The truth was very different.

From Sol's diary:

Undated
There are days when I don't entirely understand myself. I put in order the organizational plans and the tactics to follow, but normally it is difficult to plan the following day. I understand that my confusion is not unconnected to the sudden not just physical but, principally, psychic change I'm suffering. The truth is, I am not prepared for this. Why do I feel these moments of emptiness I can't manage to calm and that confuse me? Today is definitely not a good day for me.

We are spending the night in a tent, too sophisticated for this jungle. I will go and hang up my hammock later to see if I might glimpse the moon through some gap in the trees.

Undated

We have not been able to move from this mosquito-plagued spot. I curse the absurd circumstances that one after the other we have gone through more due to Central Command's leadership than our lack of guerrilla experience. And here we are twiddling our thumbs without getting any answers. It seems like we're sitting here waiting for death.

Undated

I haven't had any rest for 66 hours. When we crossed the Río Negro I began to limp due to a slight dislocation of my right ankle. When the sun began to set we thought we would camp and that's when the shooting started and in a second we dispersed; trying to cover the retreat of the main group who went into the jungle, Jaime crossed the path and began to fire. Arturo and I tried to advance to take the troop from behind when a bullet pierced Arturo's jaw while I was trying to stand up having tripped over a root. When I tried to go and help him I felt a bullet smash into my right thigh. We had to get out of there. Jaime motioned from afar to point out the route we should take.

I have spent the longest night of my life at the side of Arturo who was losing a lot of blood; I feared he would die due to my incompetence. Without lowering his arm that was leaning on my shoulder he started to become groggy and between my wounded thigh and dislocated ankle, I decided not to move and wait to be rescued. Jaime went to advise Fernando and they came back for us. That happened when the sun had already crossed a quarter of the sky and I had gone through moments of anguish and tears.

Three days have passed and we are feverishly trying to save Arturo's life. Arturo must live!

*

The harassment started during those days, while Sol was recovering from her thigh wound and Arturo was evacuated to a *campesino*'s house where it would be decided whether it would be better to send him to the city. Sol was sitting in her hammock, with her legs hanging over the edge, when the shadow of Comandante Fernando came out of nowhere, silhouetted against the distant and weak firelight. He began to ask her if she was alright, and she said yes: tired, hungry, but fine. He asked her if she'd been scared, and she said no, not scared, because she'd been trained for things like that. "Anyway," she added, "thanks very much. You saved our lives, Comandante." Then Fernando came closer and put a hand on her leg. "You're very pretty, comrade," he said. She was so surprised she didn't know what to say, and her body suddenly seemed to have no grip or support, floating in a hammock unable to react, so a long second went by before Sol managed to jump down to the ground without hurting her injured thigh. "Fernando, don't say things like that," she said, "that's not allowed." "You're right, comrade," he said. "I promise it won't happen again."

But he came back the next night. "Is this how you treat the man who saved your life?" he said. "Don't you want to thank me?" It had rained and the air was saturated with humidity, and every face was shining; as Fernando approached, the atmosphere was permeated by the smell of his armpits. "Fernando, this cannot be," Sol told him in a low but firm voice, trying at the same time not to be heard by anyone else and not to have any intimacy whatsoever in her tone. "Have you got a boyfriend?" Fernando asked. "Where? In China or Medellín?" The scene was identical to the previous night: the final hours of a long day, Sol sitting in her hammock with her boots dangling in the air, the man's body too close to her knees. Yesterday he had stretched out a hand and rested it on her thigh; today he came so close that she felt his crotch against her knee. She rejected him again, but Fernando seemed not to understand; or he seemed to have no doubt that her rejections were not sincere: the bourgeois guerrilla girl playing hard to get, wanting to be begged. He tried again and Sol turned him down again.

The days went on. The injured thigh healed fully: the body has this incredible talent. Sol noticed that Fernando had stopped approaching her, as if he'd forgotten her completely.

One afternoon, while she was teaching the alphabet to a class of *campesino* girls, Sol felt a heat that was not the tropics. That night, however, she was woken by an intense cold, and it was several seconds before she realized that it wasn't cold that was overwhelming her there, in the midst of the steamy jungle, but such strong shivers that her body was shaking her hammock. It was the highest fever she'd ever experienced. She spent entire days lying down, unable even to raise a hand to take the water her comrades offered, weeping silently from the violence of the headache, which wasn't a stabbing pain but as if the blood in her brain was hammering from within. She sweated so much during the night that she had to change her shirt, and once they had to put her hammock in the sun all day to dry it. It never occurred to her to ask for medicine of any kind, but someone looked in the cache for chloroquine tablets and returned with the news that they'd run out. Two feverish weeks went by before the arrival of another dose, and Sol went through them as if she were fording a river, swinging from vulnerability to rage and from despair to paranoia, losing her notion of time and also her trust in those around her. When she began to recover, they told her: "Comandante Fernando was here visiting you. You were so sick you didn't even notice."

"And did he come close?" Sol asked. "Did he get close to my hammock and did you let him?"

Nobody knew where these questions were coming from, and maybe it was better that way. She had been rebuffing Fernando with friendly words for many weeks, so he wouldn't get offended, and, most of all, so the rest of the women wouldn't realize what was going on, because everyone's reactions were unpredictable. But now, recently recovered from the illness, the idea of that man approaching her defenceless body produced something very similar to revulsion. He could have touched her if he'd wanted to. Sol thought maybe he had: how would she know? Would her body show the trace of an intrusive hand? Disgust, that's what she felt.

The last intrusion took place shortly after her convalescence, when Sol had resumed her active life. A comrade whose face she didn't retain, but who had been nursing her, gave her the news that she was anaemic; she sometimes had difficulties breathing, but could feel her health improving every day, and Sol thought she was getting back to normal. Then Fernando came back: at night, with the firelight illuminating him from behind, with his voice changed by what he'd come looking for. "Now then, when are you going to give me a little kiss?" Later it would seem strange to her that in that moment of extreme weakness she should feel stronger than ever. "Stop fucking with me or I'll leave," she said, "that's the last time I'll say it." Fernando took a step back. "Oh, she's getting feisty on me."

She turned her back on him and walked away, and for a couple of seconds she was sure the man was following her. But when she reached her hammock, half expecting to turn and find his face disfigured by desire, momentum she had not anticipated took over her hands, and in minutes she had packed her back-pack with enough food for the following day. It was strange that she did these things without being entirely aware of doing them, moved by repudiation and not by reason, and at the same time she felt more in charge of herself than ever.

She walked for an entire day without really knowing where she was going, driven by the need to put distance between herself and Fernando. She reached the house of some *campesinos* she knew and spent the night there, and the next night she spent in another house; she went along like that, from house to house, until she reached a village called Tierralta where she could find a bus to Medellín. She had to rely on the charity of the *campesinos* to get the fare together, and managed to get a mountain man to trade her Chinese canteen for a large muleteer's poncho to hide her uniform. When she arrived at the Cabreras' Medellín apartment, three days had passed, and her mother had to help her up the stairs because Sol had no strength left in her legs. The doctor who Luz Elena urgently called in, a family friend, saw her and marvelled that she was still alive.

"Her haemoglobin level is down to four," he said. "It's a miracle she can even walk."

"If you knew where I've come from," Sol said.

"Where?"

"From far away," Sol said. "From very far away."

XVII

One night, already in his hammock, Raúl heard the unmistakable sounds of a mule train going past. He raised his head and saw some other curious heads peeking out of other hammocks, and saw, in effect, two men not wearing uniforms leading mules towards the huts of the Central Command. They went behind the tarps and Raúl lost sight of them, but he had enough time to see that they were carrying full loads, and the next day when the mules were gone, he knew that the cargo was for an exclusive beneficiary. Since it wasn't the first time it had happened, he had no trouble imagining or supposing what had gone on, and he gradually confirmed it over the course of the day: what the mules had brought was for Central Command, and the regular guerrilla fighters would not see any of it. On other occasions the air had filled with smells as soon as the mules had left, and there, in the middle of the jungle, Raúl didn't know whether to be indignant about the commanders' privileges or worry about the possibility of a jaguar, attracted by the aromas of ham and chorizo, coming to visit them. This time, perhaps to avoid suspicion, Fernando called everyone together. He explained that provisions had arrived, mostly medical supplies, and then he called four soldiers by name and took them apart from the rest. Raúl and another three were ordered unambiguously to build a cache to store the things.

"And make sure it's well hidden," he said. "Nobody needs to know where it is and nobody needs to know what's in there."

It was the rainy season, so the construction took a bit longer than planned, as the earth excavated in the afternoon would be washed back down into the hole in the morning, but the men carried out the order diligently and without comment. After they finished, they stored vanilla and cinnamon and two months' worth of *turrón*, two gigantic boxes of Maggi stock cubes and various medicines. Nobody said anything afterwards. They knew that anything they said could be used against them at the next assembly, as had happened to Raúl a few weeks earlier, when one of the comrades asked him to criticize himself; since he didn't know what to say, someone spoke for him: "Five months ago Comrade Raúl questioned the tactic of forming a base of support again." Raúl was astute enough to realize it was a quicksand accusation: the more he defended himself, the more he would sink. So he accepted the accusation, ascribed it to his inexperience and let the incident fade from view.

Days after putting together the cache, Comandante Fernando came over to Raúl. "Comrade," he said, "we need to hold a *convite*." It was one of his favourite ideas, although nobody had been able to demonstrate its utility. Comandante Fernando was convinced that the best way to build the support base was using the forms of primitive communism that were already present in *campesino* society. "There it is in its pure form," he said excitedly when he explained the idea, "there is the source." The *convite* was a whole ritual: a *campesino* who needed a hand (to till his land, to build a trough or a stable, to roof a house with palm leaves) would get a day's labour from all the members of the community, and in exchange would hold a banquet in gratitude for the solidarity and to compensate his neighbours for their efforts with a moment of relaxation. In this case, a man needed to clear some stubble from a field to plant rice, an easy but exhausting task that consisted of walking up and down across the whole field with a machete to get rid of the weeds and bushes. They called a machete a *rula* there: it was longer than most, almost a metre in length, and heavier, because its sharp blade had to cut the bushes without undue strain on the arm.

Raúl slung his rifle around his back, as he'd seen people do in China, and got down to work. The *rula* was bigger than the machete he'd bought in Medellín the first day, which had been the biggest in the shop. He had never used a tool of such proportions, so heavy that it seemed to have a life of its own when it fell on the stubble, and maybe he was marvelling at its power or perhaps he was saying something to a comrade, but a mixture of inexperience and distraction deflected the machete from its course. The blade hit Raúl in the shin, cut through his trousers, sliced cleanly through his flesh, only stopping when it hit bone, and when Raúl crouched down to check the seriousness of the wound he saw so much blood that, had it been someone else's, he would have thought they were playing a bad practical joke. The hem of his trouser leg turned black in seconds. Something told him that could not be good, and the alarmed faces of the *campesinos* confirmed his premonition.

They took him to the nearest hut and laid him down in a hammock, behind the hut, on a dirt-floored patio. "Lift your leg, comrade," they said, "raise it up high, higher than your head." Someone said ground coffee, someone else said no, chewed tobacco, and someone else suggested a herbal poultice, and since they could not agree they applied all of it at once. Nothing had any effect: the blood kept gushing out, soaking through the poultices and running down the white skin and landing on the ground in a persistent drip. Then one of his comrades, whose voice Raúl didn't recognize, said: "We'll have to cauterize it." Only a couple of seconds had passed when Raúl felt an atrocious searing on his leg and later he had a strange conviction: if he had not fainted from the pain, it was from the surprise that not even red-hot iron worked. He kept bleeding, just as copiously. Then, in a moment of lucidity (or in a window of insight that opened in the middle of his wooziness), he called the comrade who had put the iron on his wound.

"Run back to camp and look for the cache," he said. "You need to get me some coagulant before I bleed to death."

It was a medicine imported from Spain, scarce and hard to come by, which had arrived on the back of a mule in three little red boxes with aquamarine labels, and which had the reputation of being able to stop the most obstinate haemorrhages. Raúl asked for a piece of paper and pencil and drew a few rudimentary lines that indicated the precise location of the cache. But before the comrade returned with the little red box and an unused syringe, Raúl had lost consciousness, and the last thing he managed to see was the pool of blood that had formed on the dirt floor, just below the hammock, small but so deep that a dog had come over and was lapping it up.

He woke up again twenty-four hours later. He was so weak

that he could not even sit up and he still felt faint and dizzy and his aching head felt very heavy. "This must be what people feel when they're dying," he thought. He knew he would not be able to walk back to camp, but it was also impossible to stay with the *campesinos*: the presence of a guerrilla, not to mention the fact of having helped him, would put them in mortal danger. But he didn't even have the strength to speak of his own destiny, so he put himself in the hands of others, and a few hours later opened his eyes to find he was floating on an improvised stretcher, crossing a field of stubble, and when he opened them again he was no longer near the stubble, but in a field hospital, and the haemorrhage had completely stopped and the implausible intuition that he would go on living had appeared.

He did not attend the next soldiers' assembly, as he was not well enough, but he was at the one after that. And the first item on the agenda – the agenda that Comandante Fernando had in mind – was to single out Raúl. "The comrade committed two serious offences," he said. "First, revealing the location of the cache. Second, using everyone's medicine for his own benefit. And all for a little cut." Then he fixed his black eyes on him. "Let's have it, Comrade Raúl," he said. "The troop awaits your self-critique."

Raúl stood up. "Comrades," he began.

But Fernando cut him off. "Where is your sister, comrade?"

"What?"

"Comrade Sol. Where is she?"

"I don't know what you mean, comrade. She . . ."

"Comrade Sol deserted a while ago," Fernando said. "So don't go defending her now, comrade. But let's hope your family learns that such things come at a higher price out here." He turned to everyone. "You realize, right? Comrade Sol betrayed us. I can't take responsibility for the punishment she deserves."

That's how Raúl found out about his sister's decision. He immediately knew something serious had happened, for the Revolutionary Nun would not leave everything without good reason. But what could it be? He tried to find out on his own, asking here and there, but his worry hit the wall of the guerrillas' secrecy. Although it was also possible, of course, that nobody knew anything.

Raúl then started to endure one hardship after another. One night he woke up with a malarial fever, and was in bed for two weeks, shaking and shivering through nights of insomnia, feeling like his brain was pounding on the walls of his skull. When he was barely emerging from those frights he noticed a dull pain in his heel. It was night, and shining a torch he got a good scare: under the white light he found a sore the size of a coin, and his comrades had to get in touch with Comandante Carlos to find out how to treat that. "What a fucking drag," he heard someone say. "City boys pick up everything." The situation was so critical that they had to take him to a field hospital, a row of homemade beds made out of planks covered by green tarps, where only his Philips transistor radio kept him company. During the days of fever, he hadn't even thought of turning it on, but now his worry was not his temperature but his loneliness, and the Philips turned into a priceless palliative. (His mother had sent it for his twentieth birthday. How long ago was that? Three, four, five months? He couldn't remember for sure. Time no longer had consistency, as if the humidity had rotted it from within.) The Philips was the size of a large book with an antenna two hand-spans long, so ostentatious that Raúl, upon receiving it, had known immediately what he had to do.

"It's everyone's," he announced. "It's for the whole detachment."

But his comrades took a long time to take advantage of the offer. Raúl put the radio in the middle of everyone at dinner time to listen to the national news on RCN or Radio Caracol, and later he took it to his hammock. One night, looking for news stations, he came across an opera being broadcast by the Radio Nacional. It was *La Traviata*, which he loved. Raúl lowered the volume as much as possible, less to keep from bothering others than to hide, leaned his ear against the speaker and closed his eyes. It was a rare moment of tranquillity: through one ear he could hear the sounds of the jungle – the breeze in the leaves, a frog in the distance – and through the other a toast from an excited tenor. He hadn't reached the end of the aria when he felt a pain in his ear. It was Comandante Fernando, who had snatched the radio and was now turning up the volume so everyone else could hear it.

"Look what bollocks the comrade's listening to!" he shouted. "What is this music?"

"It's opera, comrade," Raúl said.

"No," Comandante Fernando said. "It's bourgeois music. And using the radio that belongs to everyone." Maybe he had an intuition at that moment, because he opened the battery compartment and recognized the batteries they had bought for the camp. "And with communal batteries, as well. Who gave you permission to take them?"

"Nobody, comrade."

"Is that right?"

"Yes, comrade."

As punishment, Raúl had to cook for the whole detachment for a week: they brought him coypus or tapirs split and gutted, and he skinned them and turned them into something they could put on their plates. After that moment of humiliation, Comandante Fernando ordered Raúl to always carry the radio. He would have done so anyway, because he felt it was his, but the fact that it was everyone's (and that its weight increased that of his backpack) converted that schoolboy reproach into an actual disciplinary punishment. The marches they went on during those months were not too demanding, but the weight of the radio made them strangely longer, and not even the nocturnal sessions, in which smaller groups of comrades surrounded Raúl to listen to a news bulletin, mitigated the ridicule he'd suffered days earlier.

But now, in the field hospital, when not even the obligation to stand guard occupied his nights and the physical inactivity had turned him into an insomniac, the Philips radio was his only companion at certain hours. He listened to the news of that repetitive country that existed in the cities, where President Misael Pastrana took power amid allegations of fraud, and supporters of his opponent, the very same military officer who had brought television to Colombia when he was a boy, Gustavo Rojas Pinilla, attacked buses full of passengers and burned down shops and stoned the offices of the major newspapers. Over the radio Raúl heard that Vietnam was still being bombed, even though the United States Senate had repealed the Gulf of Tonkin Resolution, and one day in November he learned with satisfaction that a socialist had been elected president of

Chile. He found the station that played opera and occasionally, when he was sure nobody would hear, he allowed himself a few minutes together with some voice he was unable to identify and that took him out of the jungle and then brought him back with a mixture of guilt and relief. Everything was equally far away – Verdi and Cambodia, Allende and Pastrana – in a world that there, in the field hospital, had no relevance.

In Raúl's memory, those radio days were associated with the arrival of the vampire bats. Nobody knew who first raised the alarm, but from one day to the next the patients in the hospital, men with broken bones or suffering from tropical fevers, began to complain of something biting them during the night. They realized that the bats flew around the tarps in the last minutes of daylight, swift silhouettes that men managed to see fleetingly against the indigo sky, and later attacked their bare arms, necks and legs immobilized by plaster or bandages. The attacks took place once the men were asleep, so they barely felt the bite, and only later noticed the reddening; if they were awake, however, the bite was as painful as many needles breaking into the skin at once. Not even the locals remembered such a long-lasting plague, and none of them took the matter with as much stoicism as Raúl, who counted twenty-five bites before his condition allowed him to start back to camp. On one of the last days of his convalescence he had a conversation with a comrade that left him concerned, and he wondered if it was possible that the bats' fangs, which could transmit rabies, might also transmit certain forms of anxiety.

That comrade's name was Alberto. He was a student leader from Montería, skinny and cheerful, and endowed with a mysterious energy when he spoke: mysterious because it didn't come from the timbre of his voice, which was rather sharp or nasal or both at once, but rather from the conviction of his phrases and his well-timed humour. Raúl was fond of this young man who had never left his city until the moment he joined the guerrillas, who laughed at anything and spoke with the intensity of those who have had an epiphany. They had become friends over time, if such a thing existed in the detachment, and they used to talk in the dead times with the fascination of those who know deep down they are similar: Alberto liked football, and he found it unbelievable that there could be a Colombian who didn't know who Caimán Sánchez was, and didn't support any team, as he fanatically supported the Barranquilla Juniors, and spoke about football in the same exalted tones, Raúl thought, as his father spoke of Brecht or Miguel Hernández.

Anyway, after the attack of the bats, which lasted for nine fearful nights, Alberto, in his own camp bed, began saying things that seemed like they were coming from another person. He was recovering from a case of malaria similar to the one that had laid Raúl low, so soon afterwards that he sometimes accused his comrade of having infected him. "But it's not contagious, don't talk rubbish," Raúl said once, from one camp bed to the other, his words passing over those of other comrades. "I don't know, but it's very suspicious," Alberto said. "You come down with it, then I get it. I don't know." Raúl didn't take him seriously, mainly because he had other things on his mind: his leishmaniasis, which had destroyed the skin over his Achilles tendon, leaving a painful scab in place of the red sore; the humidity that destroyed his cigarettes and his writing paper, which tore at the least excess pressure of his Parker pen as if someone had thrown a glass of water over it. But later he began to worry about the bats' teeth, wondering if it was true that they sucked blood and could kill a cow, and when the bats left, as unexpectedly as they arrived, he also wondered if they caused fever: and the question, in the middle of the silent night, was feverish in itself. On another similar night, Alberto called out to Raúl:

"You awake?"

"I'm here, comrade," Raúl said.

"Do you know what I like best about the night?"

"No. What do you like best about night?"

Alberto said: "It makes the green disappear."

Raúl liked the metaphor and told him so, but then immediately asked what he meant. No, Alberto replied in an offended tone of voice, it was not a fucking metaphor: at night, when the lights were off, the eyes could rest from all the green harassment: the green of the jungle, the trees, the grass, the green of the green uniforms, the green of the tarps and the canvas of the bags and the tents: all that green that overwhelmed the view and make him feel trapped, imprisoned in a jail without walls. "So much green, comrade, so much green everywhere," Alberto said. "Fucking shut up, and let us sleep," said another voice, and Alberto's voice – fevered, tremulous, weakened – obeyed immediately. Raúl stayed alert, lying there in silence but looking at the dark night, the black night that made the green disappear, the black night in which the bats no longer lurked. He stayed still, without turning on his radio, to see if Alberto would say anything else. But he didn't hear anything. A gentle breeze blew, so rare that Raúl, distracted or consoled for those seconds of unexpected relief, fell asleep.

Two days later, Comandante Carlos said he could go back to the base camp. But the hike was farther than his body could handle, since his Achilles heel meant he could not walk without opening up the sore again in his rubber boots; so the commander agreed they should stop for the night in a *campesino*'s house, the home of a couple of guerrilla sympathizers and parents – this should not have been said, but Carlos said it anyway – of a comrade. There Raúl would spend the night, to divide the journey in two, and the next day he'd return to camp even if he had to hop on one leg. Raúl asked about Comrade Alberto.

"Oh, he's staying for a few more days," Carlos said.

"What's wrong with him?" Raúl asked.

"He needs rest," Carlos said. "The comrade's not well, and the last thing he needs is combat."

"Is it dangerous for him?"

"Well, yeah," Carlos said. "But for us too."

They arrived at the house at dusk: the time the bats came out. It was a humbler house than Raúl had expected, but at the same time better equipped, for it was obvious that commanders used it frequently. The owners were a young *campesino* couple – or they looked young in the fading light – who walked barefoot on the dirt floor. They welcomed Raúl with the gravity of people fulfilling a mission that was beyond their means, gave him stove-top coffee, sat him in a kitchen smelling of recently burnt firewood and then led him to their bedroom, the window of which looked out on a mango tree and the poultry yard, with hens vaguely visible in the gloom. "The comrade will sleep here," the woman said, pointing to the double bed. "No, no," Raúl tried to protest, but without success. The couple's satisfaction was evident: that a guerrilla should sleep in their bed, this accident, seemed a kind of sacrament. While he arranged his things – he was so weak that lifting his backpack required superhuman effort – Raúl learned from those proud voices that two of their children had taken up arms. He was about to ask who they were when he noticed there was another person in the house, outside the room, who then appeared at the threshold, beside the owners.

"Hey, handsome," said Isabela with a sarcasm that could cut stone. "And this miracle?"

So one of the children of the owners was not a son, but a daughter: the only woman Raúl had desired in the long year and a half of his *guerrillero* life. He had desired her, but he had also rejected her advances. Regret had arrived too late, like a friend who forgets to give us a message, and now, having her there under the same roof (or the same mango tree) and with the whole night ahead, Raúl realized that in these last months his prejudices had entirely vanished, or at least had weakened enough for him to pay no attention to them. At night, when Isabela brought him a banana leaf with rice and plantain and something resembling meat, but a sad, unconvincing meat, Raúl asked her to stay and keep him company while he ate. She sat on the bed frame and looked at him from that distance as he tried to maintain some impossible manners while stuffing rice in his mouth. "Is it good?" Isabela asked. She had matured in those few months: her black eyes seemed bigger, and her voice, which had welcomed him with harshness, had now recovered an involuntarily seductive tone, and in any case the whole situation – there, safe from the view of other comrades, in a place without risks – was like a reminder of the interrupted intimacy of other days. She, of course, read Raúl like a book.

"Oh, no," she said. "Look, handsome, this is not then. We can't do that now."

"Why not?"

"Because Comandante Fernando noticed and he told me. He said he saw me and that it's not allowed, that I should be careful."

"Well, he's not here," Raúl said, not recognizing himself in his own words. "He's jealous, that's what he is."

"Well, that may be, but what can you do?" Isabela said. "I don't want to get into trouble."

He wasn't entirely surprised, because he had seen the commander looking lustfully at Isabela, but he nevertheless took this news as an intolerable interference. So even there, in that imprecise territory that was other people's private lives, Comandante Fernando, whose tyranny Raúl had always accepted, exercised his control. He didn't know when he began speaking, or perhaps he was speaking like someone unaware he is thinking out loud, or perhaps he let his frustrated desire get mixed up with other dissatisfactions. "And if I decided to leave, would you come with me?" It was idiotic to say something like that, but Isabela's eyes opened wide again and looked up at him as if illuminated. It was just a moment: Raúl knew he had put into words an impossible idea, and it was only because the idea had been lurking in some part of his emotions and had come out as soon as it saw an opportunity. Was desertion – the most terrible crime a guerrilla fighter could commit, and that his sister had committed without Raúl being able to find out why – possible? No, it was not possible; and now Raúl felt that not only had his conscience committed a terrible crime against the revolution, against everything he had pursued for years and all that his parents had pursued, but he had run the risk of infecting someone else, malarial mosquito, rabid bat.

"We'd better forget we ever had this conversation," said Isabela.

Raúl agreed. But days after returning to base camp, in a soggy notebook that acted as his diary, he wrote a confession, without melodrama, but feeling an intense guilt: *I've spent a couple of days thinking that I would perhaps be a happier young man if I were dead. I am tired of always hoping to pass an exam, an elusive exam for which it is not possible to prepare. There is always something that makes me feel guilty and inept for the revolutionary struggle, I always feel the suspicion that, in spite of all the efforts I make, I do not manage to offer the commanders and especially Fernando the fervour they expect of me. I think they actually distrust my submission and everyone's in general, and they give the impression that they believe that only dead guerrilleros can be trusted. Maybe I've never been trustworthy and as things are I don't think I can even trust myself. With increasing frequency defeatist ideas pass through my mind. Pessimism gains ground and the illusion of a victory, a victory of our ideas, is ever farther away.*

The story of the lighter began in a letter. Raúl had begun to find serenity in his correspondence with his mother: he didn't tell her of his misfortunes, not wanting to worry her, but he did allow himself to suggest his dissatisfaction, which in his head had taken shape with these words: "I think I got on the wrong bus." So the censor would not suspect anything, he had to disguise it when he wrote. "Do you remember that time in Tokyo when I got on the wrong bus?" Luz Elena, incredibly, decoded the message, and then responded with words of affection, trying to lift his morale any way she could in long letters that became a haven of humanity and, at the same time, reminders of the same guilt as before. What right did Raúl have to melancholy or doubt when his mother, there in the city, was leading a clandestine life of daily danger, running countless risks every day, never allowing herself a word of disapproval or complaint? Luz Elena was a courageous woman, but you would have to be her son to also see her fragile side, which did not sit well with the austere demands of conspiracy. In the letters that reached the camp, the urban guerrilla militant talked with tender words to the *guerrillero* shouldering a rifle, and told him that she had made a decision to send him a gift. She was not going to accept no for an answer; she'd already asked permission of the commanders and Comrade Alejandro had already given it. "Tell me what you'd like," she wrote. "But please, *please* don't tell me you don't need anything."

Raúl had no trouble deciding: he wanted a butane lighter. He had bought one in Rome, during the week's stopover he and his sister had made on their way back from Peking, and in the jungle he realized it would be enormously useful. So much there depended on being able to light fires and light them well, but the humidity penetrated the heads of matches and inevitably ruined them, unless a person warmed them for lengthy minutes between thumb and forefinger, the heat of the hand drying them from inside. He asked Comandante Fernando when he could send a letter to Bogotá – but he didn't mention his mother or her tender words or gifts of any sort – and discovered that post would be going out in two days. That night he wrote the letter: he asked for the lighter, told a couple of anecdotes about camp life and surprised himself by saying at the same time how happy he was at being able to fight for his convictions and how the same suspicion as before was close: "It seems there is only one way to get them to believe in a person: to die." He did not use forbidden words – commitment, revolution – but the message was there. He did not ask the question he had wanted to ask her for months and that would continue to spin around in his head for many years to come: at what point do parents reach the conviction that the revolution can educate their children better than they can themselves? He handed the letter to the comrade in charge of the post and forgot the matter.

But the following Thursday, at the beginning of the soldiers' assembly, Comandante Fernando stood up and said he was going to read something. He didn't have to say more than four words for Raúl to recognize them the way we recognize our face in someone else's photo. The whole detachment listened to the letter he'd written to his mother, but not in the tone that the sentences had in his head, but with the vicious sarcasm Fernando imposed on them. Each word came out of his mouth twisted into something else, and not even the most hypocritical sentences, which Raúl had written with that part of his mind that knows he is watched, were safe from the sarcasm. "Perhaps with a lighter it would be easier to start a fire on rainy nights, and that would not only help me, but would be a great relief to my comrades." In the commander's reading, that blatant attempt at solidarity came out sounding like a vague affectation.

When the commander had tired, or when his joke got old, he put the letter back into the envelope he'd taken it out of in front of everyone and said:

"Comrade Raúl thinks the problems of this guerrilla army can be solved with a little butane lighter. What do you guys think?"

In any case – and to the great surprise of Raúl, who had given up the whole thing as a lost cause – the letter went to Bogotá. A month later his mother's reply arrived. Comandante Fernando crossed the camp, one morning of murderous sunshine, to hand it to Raúl personally. The envelope had been opened; the paper was torn on one corner, mutilated by a careless censor. "And this came as well," he said. He opened the palm of his hand, and there was the lighter, a silver German Ronson with a striated surface: striated like Fernando's hand. "But you know what, comrade? Maybe it's better if I keep it."

One night they were awakened by gunfire. The whole detachment was awake and mobilized in seconds, all with their rifles raised even though their eyes were so filled with sleep they would not have been able to aim at anything. Like someone stepping into a dark room from bright daylight, Raúl had to wait a few instants before he could distinguish shapes clearly, to recover his sense of location and perspective, and only then did he recognize Comrade Alberto. Raúl, who last saw him at the field hospital the night of the conversation about the green, had kept his distance since hearing he was back. He had heard rumours about him; it was said that his cheerful personality had disappeared, as if it had been a disguise he'd taken off; that he'd arrived back from the hospital an embittered guy, and he no longer talked about football or told stupid jokes or laughed with those guffaws the commanders reprimanded him for. Well, they didn't have to worry about that anymore; Alberto had stopped laughing, and now spent all day complaining and grumbling and insulting absent enemies, in a sort of invincible and permanent fury.

Apparently, Alberto had woken up in the middle of the night, and without anyone hearing him had found a San Cristobal carbine, had walked a few steps away from his hammock and had begun to fire it. Carbines have a strong recoil, and there, vertical on the bark of a tree, were the impacts of the bullets, none at the height of a human being. But the incident was enough for the rest of them to agree: Alberto, who put up no resistance when they approached to take the carbine away from him, had become a danger. Comandante Tomás issued an unpopular and painful order, and before dawn Alberto was chained to a tree. When Raúl went over to talk to him the way they used to talk, to ask him if something had happened or to calm him down with the promise that the situation was temporary, he saw that his eyes were no longer looking at him, or rather, they were no longer fixed in place as they used to be, but moved in a disorderly way, marbles rolling around inside a glass jar. He opened his mouth and revealed his yellow teeth: a grimace of effort, as if he were trying to lift something very heavy. "What's wrong, comrade?" Raúl said. Alberto took a minute to find the face that had asked him the question.

"They want to kill me," he said.

"Who?"

"All these revisionists," Alberto said.

They left him there, tied to the tree, shouting randomly that they were all traitors. But he never directed an insult at Raúl:

it was as if he didn't see him, and that was surely why the detachment allocated him the task of feeding the poor demented comrade. Raúl took him food and asked him if he was well, and Alberto said no, he did not feel well, that the revisionists wanted to kill him, that this food was poisoned. With time he grew more violent, and no longer said that they were going to kill him, but that he was going to kill all of them. Sometimes he started to talk about Chairman Mao, whose lessons had been forgotten by or were unknown to the commanders, and Raúl would not have felt so moved by his madness had he not seen in it one of his own possible fates.

The tree to which Alberto was chained appeared one morning with neither chain nor prisoner. Raúl didn't know how it all happened, but he asked.

"He had to be removed from the zone," he was told.

And they didn't say anything more.

Sol returned to the jungle after seven months of living in hiding in Medellín. It had taken time to resolve all the problems, including that of convincing her mother that this was the best way. Sol underwent a blood transfusion that seemed to enter drop by drop, in a long and clandestine process that would have been impossible without her mother's help. The process – Operation Haemoglobin, Luz Elena called it – included trips between the apartment and the hospital where Sol travelled in the boot of the car and kept her fingers crossed there would be no police checks, and wondered what her fate might have been if her mother had not had the surname she happened to have. So this was what it meant to be middle class: the possibility of walking through a whole city with impunity, the guarantee that doors – those of a hospital, for example – would easily open for you. Nobody, in all those days, asked her mother any questions about her daughter, or the reasons she'd fallen ill: she was Luz Elena Cárdenas, one of the Cárdenas family that everybody knew, and if she asked for a favour, that favour was granted without a word. None of the doctors suspected that Luz Elena, smiling her thousand-carat smile, paying for the hospital services with her ample chequebook, was at the same instant Comrade Valentina, secret courier of the urban guerrillas, mother of two EPL combatants and wife of a revolutionary Maoist leader.

During those clandestine months in Medellín, Sol realized that the guerrillas had begun to look for her. She noticed strange presences at the corner when she peered out of the window. Her mother showed her letters from her brother: "If you hear anything from my sister, tell her the commanders here are furious. She should take care, they could carry out reprisals." She knew it, of course, and knew very well what that meant. "I have to go back," she said to Luz Elena one morning. "If I don't go back and clear things up they'll pursue me for the rest of my life." Luz Elena screamed at her as if she were a little girl, called her irresponsible, went from forbidding her to begging, but deep down she knew Sol was right. If she didn't go back to the jungle to make amends for her desertion, not only would she have to look over her shoulder for the rest of her life, but the whole family would be left on the wrong side of the revolution. They both started to make contact through clandestine channels, and one comrade led them to another, and that one to another, and so on, until they were given definite instructions. They should go to Cali, to a clandestine apartment in the north of the city, and wait there to be contacted. They arrived in Cali by bus, found the urban cell and settled down to wait. Four months of uncertainty passed before a comrade called Guillermo, military secretary of the Valle sector, appeared. He came on behalf of Comandante Armando.

"He spoke very highly of you, comrade," Guillermo said. "Armando values you. I don't know why, but I do what they ask."

"Where are we going?" she said.

"To raise ducks," he said. "While we wash off that stain you're carrying."

XVIII

The day they went out to hunt cattle, Raúl had woken at dawn with an idea stuck in his head: he had to tell his mother the truth. For days he had lived with anguish in his chest, wondering how she would take the news that her son wanted to leave the ranks of the EPL. That's what he wanted to explain: he felt he was living a lie. The mimeographed pages of the guerrilla newsletter *Combatiendo venceremos* had circulated through the camp, and the latest issue described a world where the guerrilla zone was a true support base and the Party controlled the justice system, ran the economy and had an army capable of defending its sovereign borders. None of that resembled what Raúl saw every day: the guerrilla zone where he lived was far – very far – from becoming that invincible source of popular power. He had not told his mother, not only because none of the phrases he had in mind would have passed the censor, but on account of the more primitive fear of disappointing her. He felt ridiculous seeing himself like that, a guerrilla fighter hardened by combat and well trained in tactics and strategy, a grown man who would soon turn twenty-one, worried about what his mother would think. Oh, but she was not just any mother: Comrade Valentina had become indispensable to the urban commandos, and her work had won her the Party's respect and admiration. She had lived her clandestine life with integrity and carried out dangerous jobs without ever losing her facade of a nice middle-class lady, and now Raúl was going to shake up her life with his uncertainties and disillusionment?

Well, yes: that was exactly what he was going to do.

He had decided that morning, while walking with twenty-five other guerrillas towards the open fields where they could find cattle. They were holding a plenary session of the Party Central Committee in the zone at the time, and there, in a camp expanded for the occasion, the commanders of the eight detachments that operated on the Tigre plains had gathered. It was a beautiful area with wide-open skies and spacious lands bordering on impenetrable jungle; it had belonged – each of its many hectares – to grand landowners, and their cows were still there, gone wild, as wild as the jaguars that threatened them, as the tapirs and peccaries the guerrillas went out to hunt when they could. Raúl and his comrades were on a mission that morning of getting meat for the camp, enough for the hundred and fifty guerrilla fighters who had arrived from far and wide to protect the Central Committee's plenary, and they had been walking for an hour, looking for the wild cattle, when they saw six cows calmly grazing in the distance. The men circled around the area to get downwind, so their scent would not alert their prey, and advanced in a low crouch until the cows were within range of their M1 rifles. Raúl counted eight shots and saw two of the animals fall dead on the spot. The rest dispersed, but one more had been wounded. Half the hunting squad had to follow it for half an hour before they were able to finish it off; the others, meanwhile, stayed with the first carcasses to begin to butcher them. When they returned to camp, each one carrying a big lump of fresh meat on their backs, they were received as heroes.

These were times of relative peace, and that was why they had been able to organize the plenary, but everyone knew the army was only a few kilometres away, in Tierralta, and they could not let their guard down. That was why more guerrillas than had ever been seen together had come into the zone: to repel any unexpected attack with sufficient force. That was also why the commanders had dispatched small patrols throughout the area to alert them to any movement of enemy troops. And that afternoon, after the beef had been grilled over charcoal, after the most copious lunch the troop had eaten in months, Commander Carlos called Raúl to assign him a job: he should take command of a small detachment of five guerrillas and set up a checkpoint on the outskirts of Tucurá. That was where a difficult stretch of the trail began, a sort of natural trench that opened in the marshy ground, which the guerrillas had travelled, but which the army, if they were clever, could use to surprise them.

"Go there and close that route for me," the commander said. "In eight days I'll send relief."

That very night they were dug in, and stayed there for another five nights, suffering the bites of gnats, in silence, for in the darkness it's impossible to know if the enemy is near and any movement, even that of a hand slapping a bug, could give them away. Those hellish nights were followed by days of repressed sleep and resentful muscles, but what frightened Raúl most was the tedium of the dead time: his head would get to thinking, and then the questions would start to come:

wouldn't he be better off in an urban cell? Wouldn't he be more useful to the cause leading the clandestine life his mother was leading, maybe using theatre as a front, instead of stuck in something he no longer believed in? The armed struggle had turned into an obscene ritual: winning the trust of the *campesinos* to carry out war operations, and contemplating how the victims of those operations, in the long run, were the same *campesinos* whose trust they'd gained. No, this could not be revolution.

On the sixth day, something happened. Provisions were running low: the quiet produced the illusion of hunger, and the tins of tuna and condensed milk were running out prematurely, so Raúl went to see one of those trusted *campesinos* and put some money in his hand.

"Rice, beans and sugar," he said. "Come when it gets dark."

The man arrived punctually that night. He handed Raúl his purchases and the change, and left without accepting the invitation to eat with them. While his comrades started soaking the rice and the beans, Raúl unpacked the raw sugar loaf, which came as usual wrapped in a sheet of newspaper, and something caught his attention. As he spread out the torn page – the newspaper was *El Espacio* – thinking it was impossible that he'd seen what he thought he'd seen, he found a photo of his mother looking at him in full colour from the shaft of light from his torch. From the elegant woman's half-smile, her well-coiffed hair and her flowered blouse, one might think that the image had come out of a society magazine, but the caption destroyed any such comforting thought: *Two members of the EPL's urban network arrested in Bogotá.* Raúl read the text for confirmation of his fears, and found the two names: the woman was, indeed, the former actress Luz Elena Cárdenas; the woman was, indeed, the wife of the noted theatre director Fausto Cabrera.

Raúl felt his mouth go dry. He had been trained for years in the art of keeping quiet and hiding in plain sight, and had to summon up those instincts so as not to give himself away to his comrades. But he kept the cutting and later, lying in his hammock, he managed to take out his torch and read the rest of the article. Luz Elena was imprisoned in the Brigada de Institutos Militares and would be subjected to an oral court martial. She had not fallen alone: she was with someone called Silvio, a guerrilla in the urban network who did not appear in the photo because his arrest was not scandalous. The oral court martial was a recent tool the state of siege had made available to judges in the fight against subversion that enabled them to judge civilians with military laws. His mother's sentence, the article said, would be at least eight years in prison, and could be much more generous.

Generous, thought Raúl, and hated the world.

He shone the torch on the date at the top of the page, March 10, 1971, and thought that in three days Luz Elena would turn forty-two in a prison cell in Bogotá, without either of her children, without her husband, without anybody. And while he tried to reconstruct the situation and imagine possible actions, more or less illusory ways of rescuing her, Raúl understood that the only thing that could worsen his mother's misfortune at that moment, what could destroy the little morale she might have left, would be to receive news from her son of his discontent. There, concealed in the jungle, stuck in his hammock as if the world were ending, Raúl realized that all his previous plans – having a political confrontation with the commanders, asking for a discharge or deserting if necessary – had just then gone to shit.

Two days later the relief arrived. Raúl had an annoying hunch, when he received his comrades, that everyone already knew what had happened: he noticed something in their changed voices and their evasive looks. This was confirmed when he got back to base camp, when the same people who had cheered his arrival the day of the cow hunt now wouldn't even look him in the eye. It was not surprising that they should know all about it, since one of the camp's routines was to begin the day listening to the radio, and both national broadcasters would have gone into detail about that piece of news. The strange thing was that nobody said anything to him. It was an absurd situation in which they all pretended not to know, thinking Raúl didn't know, and Raúl, who already knew all about it, pretended not to know that they knew. Later he discovered that Comandante Fernando had been the first to find out. He had quickly called the whole troop together and announced the capture of Comrade Valentina, Comrade Raúl's mother, and immediately ordered them not to say anything to him: it would be Central Command who would take charge of giving him the news.

It was all shocking: the secrets, or rather the ethics of pretence hiding pretence, duplicity and hypocrisy, that had become as natural to the combatants as their uniform, and that once, for example, led them to the ridiculous situation of spending a week searching for a cache of food and weapons: they'd hidden it so well, and protected it with so much secrecy, that nobody could find it when they needed it, and in the end they had to accept that the jungle had swallowed it. Yes, it was shocking that Comandante Fernando had decided to break the sacred rule of hiding combatants' family ties, that he had claimed the right to break the news personally and that now he seemed to do all this with a certain mean-minded satisfaction, as if the incident served to teach someone a lesson. If this man had broken the rules of compartmentalization, Raúl thought, those rules without which the double life of a guerrilla no longer made sense, he must have a good reason. That was the least frightening explanation, for the other, which Raúl had not completely ruled out, was as simple as it was terrifying: if Comandante Fernando wanted to be the one to give him the news, it was merely out of *Schadenfreude*. Perhaps he was kidding himself, but that was what Raúl saw in Fernando's face when, the day after returning to camp (and not immediately, as the urgency of the situation or simple solidarity demanded), the commander summoned him.

"Well, comrade," he said. "I imagine you've already heard."

Raúl didn't want to give him the satisfaction. "Heard what, comrade?"

"Of course you've heard," Fernando said. "Well, the revolution carries on. That's what I wanted to tell you."

"I don't understand, comrade. What did you want to tell me?"

"That this isn't going to stop because they caught someone. I imagine that's clear."

"Very clear," said Raúl. "But can I ask you something?"

"What's that?"

"I want to let my sister know. How can I do that?"

"Oh, your sister," Fernando said. "Leave your sister alone, she's a big girl."

"What's that supposed to mean?"

"If she doesn't know, that's her problem. As if I didn't have other things to think about."

Comrade Sol, ignorant of her mother's capture, had settled in at her new posting. Guillermo had taken her to one of the so-called patriotic fronts, rural properties that served as facades for guerrilla work, and where they grew crops or raised animals. Guillermo's patriotic front was south of Pance, a district in the Cauca river valley; it was a small farm in the foothills of the Andes, just high enough to be above the unbearable heat of the valley, two hectares surrounded by a barbed wire fence, tangled with feathers. Behind the house was a poultry yard with a flock of Muscovy ducks, which amused Sol enormously, who started calling them Muscovites, and when she was in a good mood, would throw corn to them while saying:

"Time to eat, revisionists!"

The other four comrades didn't seem to get the joke, but Guillermo would roar with laughter. Sol realized at those moments that she'd been lucky: of all the secretaries of all the detachments she could have been sent to, how many would have understood her situation as well as this man? He was kind, and his face wasn't weighed down by shadows the way the faces of so many comrades were, that sort of languid solemnity. Sol liked talking to him. Even though it wasn't necessary, she apologized for having run away and made an effort to demonstrate repentance, but also explained the hostile situation that had existed on the Tigre plains, with Comandante Fernando, and she did so in terms that were not ambiguous: "If I'd stayed, he would have raped me." Guillermo said: "I understand, comrade." And it seemed to be true. Or maybe his comprehension was the result of orders and suggestions from Armando, who everyone respected. And Sol had to wonder: what did Armando see in her and in Raúl that led him to treat them with more deference? Were they perhaps the beneficiaries of their father's position of power? Fausto, after all, was still the direct contact between communist China, home of the real Mao, and the revolutionary army of Colombia, where Mao was but a rumour, a collection of sayings: a figure made of words.

Half the week, or sometimes more, they spent away from the patriotic front, in a detachment that was camped at El Tambo, a day's walk south. It was a group of a dozen comrades who were doing intelligence work around Popayán, the department capital, and also indoctrination work in the region's small villages. Guillermo stayed in Pance, with the revisionist ducks, while four comrades, one of whom was Sol, covered the distance talking to the *campesinos*, doing propaganda work, lending a hand to build schools, making their presence felt in the zone: in short, constructing the base that Mao talked about. They stayed four days in El Tambo and then returned to Pance, to the duck farm, and Sol returned to her conversations with Comrade Guillermo, and from one day to the next she began to notice that she missed him when she was out with the detachment. It wasn't simply that there were comforts at the patriotic front that were unthinkable out there, such as a bed and a shower. This Guillermo saw her with fresh eyes, and when she talked of her bad experiences, he seemed to stop what he was doing (he never really did, but he gave that mysterious impression) to pay attention to her while he stroked his caricature rancher's moustache.

Sol began to dislike the moment she had to leave for Pance. The work at El Tambo camp was harder, but it wasn't about that, because there was also time for ideas. Every week they received a pamphlet called *Peking Informs*, and every week, during the political assembly, they read the articles in the pamphlet as if it were the Little Red Book itself. For Sol it was like being back in the clock factory, not with hundreds of workers, but with a dozen comrades. All they needed was a portrait of Mao hanging from a ceiba tree. On one occasion, after a reading of *Peking Informs*, Sol mentioned that one May Day, when she was living in Peking, she had seen Mao from five metres away. She thought the memory would make a good impression, or would at least provoke exclamations or questions, however what followed was silence. Eventually, one comrade said:

"You know what, comrade? Don't talk such shit. We're not so well travelled here, but don't fucking take us for idiots."

Sol would not have thought in just a few months she would have aroused such resentment in a comrade. The man was the detachment's military secretary. His name was Manuel; he was small but tough and he seemed to stand on tiptoe whenever he was about to speak. He was, also, the only one in the detachment who seemed to *have studied,* which was how the rest of them talked about anyone who had been to school. He was from Turbo, on the Gulf, and his accent was a strange blend of Antioquian mountain-region dialect and coastal Caribbean Spanish, so everything he said sounded to Sol like falsification or pretence. There was something about him that reminded her of Fernando. Sol, whose *nom de guerre* meant sun, thought she'd identified it when a comrade, the night before an operation in Popayán, asked how long it would take them to get there, and Manuel made a pun that was not without wit:

"With bad weather, six hours. With Sol, twelve."

It was his way of exercising the power he'd been given, and Sol understood that and put up with the insults. But later, when she first wrote a letter and asked who she should give it to and when the post went out and they told her that all correspondence went through Comrade Manuel, she was less accepting. Every time she wrote letters to Luz Elena that received no reply, moving the pencil mechanically over the soggy paper, asking routine questions and sending routine hugs, she did so with the certainty that what she sent had to get by several obstacles: interception by the enemy, of course, but also censorship from Manuel, who would read each line with his ideological magnifying glass, trying to identify the fateful moment when this comrade, who threatened to go astray, or had already gone astray inside, could contaminate someone else with her own weakness. Sol envied her brother's ease with Spanish at those moments. For her, it still felt like a foreign language, a vague reminder of her childhood, and she did not manage to use it fluently. In these letters, besides, she was obliged to use codes and allusions and insinuations and cryptic keywords, and while she had always thought that such caution was justified to prevent the police or army from intercepting their communications and acquiring information they could use; now there was a new reason, and it was to escape the gaze of her own people. Like in the mornings, when she had to hide to wash her body and change her clothes. That had not been the case at the President Mao School.

Things fell apart without any warning whatsoever. It

happened on a humid morning, when they were holding a soldiers' assembly, and the comrades spent a long time discussing the most important thing that had happened to them so far in their lives as combatants: the IV Plenary of the Colombian Communist Party (M-L), which was about to be held on the Tigre plains. All the members of the Central Command would be travelling there in the following days, and Comrade Sol's detachment should prepare, like all the rest, to cover the thousand miles: depending on their luck, climate and buses they could use without running risks, the trip could take between five and fifteen days. Sol thought of her brother, who might be hearing the same speeches in similar soldiers' assemblies, not from a small and peripheral detachment in the south of the country, but from the centre of the world: the very place where it was all going to happen. That was when Comrade Manuel, who was running the assembly, stood up with a pamphlet in his hand and said:

"OK. Now we're going to read *Peking Informs*."

Sol never knew what made her lose patience, what long list of grievances overflowed at that moment, and she was more surprised than anyone to hear herself speak with such disdain.

"Oh, no more of that crap," she said. "I'm not sucking up any more of that *Peking Informs*."

There was an incredulous silence among the comrades. The figure of Manuel would have been comical had it not been so obvious that he felt insulted.

"Careful, comrade," he said.

"Sorry, comrade," Sol said, "but that's how it is: I can't take another single word from *Peking Informs*. With all due respect, what the fuck does it matter to us what happens in Peking?"

"You seem to be forgetting where you are, comrade," Manuel said. "This is a guerrilla army of Mao Thought. This is the Marxist–Leninist–Maoist Communist Party..."

"I do know that," Sol interrupted. "With all due respect, comrade, don't explain Mao's ideology to me. I defended Mao's ideology three blocks away from Mao. I drank in Mao's voice from loudspeakers for entire nights in the city where Mao lives." Then she brought a horizontal hand up to her forehead. "This cap I'm wearing, do you know what it is? It's the cap of Mao's Red Guards. And do you know why I have it? Because I was one of Mao's Red Guards! So I have every right to tell you this: I've had it up to here, up to Mao's fucking cap, with reading *Peking Informs*."

"This cannot be allowed," one comrade said.

"A bit of respect," another said.

"Calm down, comrade," Manuel said. "We are going to take steps."

"What steps and what shit?" Sol said. "Look, comrade, what I want to say is very simple: we are not in Peking here. Isn't it about time we informed ourselves about what's happening here in the valley, rather than in Peking? All this *Peking Informs* and we have no fucking idea what's going on in Colombia. I think that's more important, don't you?"

Commander Manuel closed the meeting. The rest of the day Sol stayed isolated from her comrades: she had awakened unknown emotions in them, and instinct told her it would be best to give them time to get the measure of their anger. She distracted herself cutting up the meat of a peccary they'd hunted the day before and that was now salted, and as she did so she was reminded of something her brother had said in the days of the alarm clock factory, something that he knew because Lao Wang, his master there, had told him. It was this: during construction of the Great Wall in the times of the Ming dynasty, the authorities discovered that nothing frustrated the workers more than the feeling of being stuck on an infinite job. They then had the idea of relieving the entire workforce after every *li*, a measure equivalent to half a kilometre, so the builders worked under the illusion of a final day or a job finished. "It's important that your path has an arrival point," Lao Wang had said to her brother with that tone of a Buddhist philosopher, and her brother imitated the tone when he repeated the words. And now Sol remembered Mao's military writings, where he said that revolutions should be planned as a prolonged war. Would this guerrilla war, Sol wondered, be her own Wall of China?

Two days later – two long days during which she was repudiated, banished, alive but dead – they summoned her to a meeting of the detachment. They pointed to a log and asked her to sit there, and the rest of them eloquently occupied the space facing her. This was a trial, Sol understood, and it was confirmed when Commander Manuel read the sixteen charges they were bringing against her after careful deliberation. They accused her of disrespecting the figure of Mao, of ideological deviation, of rejecting the armed struggle, of being against China, and, therefore, of being pro-Soviet, Stalinist and a sympathizer of the ELN. They called her counter-revolutionary and reminded her of her bourgeois origins. They told her that all these charges they had made deserved punishment and the punishment would be very severe, but before sentencing they were going to allow her an opportunity for self-criticsm. Sol, who had listened to the monologue with a feeling of unreality that was no different from fever, thought of Guillermo and his Muscovy ducks and wished she were back in Pance right now, immediately. She stood up to leave, and the last thing she said before starting to walk away was:

"No self-criticism at all. Not with this bunch of imbeciles . . ."

She had spun all the way around and was walking away from the guerrillas when she heard the shot. She felt herself thrown forward, as if an enormous force had punched her in the back, and she fell face down on the ground, with a 32-calibre bullet in her body, surprise at feeling no pain and a fearless certainty that they were now coming to finish her off.

Raúl's camp was already preparing for the great concentration of Central Command, and the commanders and secretaries of other detachments began to arrive in the zone. Sometimes Raúl had to take on security jobs, and he liked that, because that way he could think of something other than the fate of his mother, imprisoned in Bogotá's Buen Pastor in unimaginable conditions (or the imagining of which produced only hair-raising scenes) and unable to get news to her loved ones. They assured him that Valentina was going to have the best lawyers, that the most important thing was to keep morale high, that she was committed to the cause and the Party was going to help her in every necessary way. One morning Raúl went to see Comandante Fernando, to ask him if someone was looking after his mother's case, if the Party was doing what it should and had promised to do, and he found out that Fernando was no longer in the camp. He had gone to explore a new zone, but among the comrades people were saying that what was new was a girlfriend in Bijao, and he was visiting her.

But then time passed and he did not return, and that was not normal. The guerrillas heard that he had gone to northwest Antioquia, a combat zone, and an uncomfortable rumour began to hang around the detachment like a stray dog: Fernando had committed a serious disciplinary breach and Central Command had sanctioned him harshly. People said he'd been demoted, others spoke of expulsion, and some even mentioned a firing squad. This was not plausible: in spite of the opinion Raúl still had of him, Fernando was one of the most respected figures in the guerrilla force, and for many it was not impossible that he would end up leading the Party. There was speculation in low voices about the nature of his misconduct: a woman, insubordination, a military fault? In his absence they spoke of him in the past tense as they do of the dead, as if he were already history, and that's how Raúl began to see some of the reasons for his misunderstandings. Fernando, who years earlier (it was rumoured) had been expelled from the Communist Youth for his pro-China tendencies, had once got involved in a life-or-death debate with Pedro León Arboleda, whose influence over the Party was notorious. Arboleda defended a single vision of the Party: militarization. Comandante Fernando, however, maintained the importance of working with the proletariat, which he called the Bolshevization of the Party, and the problem that was now overwhelming them, the reason things were not working, was singular: far from Bolshevizing, the Party was suffering a real petit-bourgeois invasion. It was impossible for the commander to see Raúl without thinking that there, in those green eyes, in that education with violins and French words, with fine radios and butane lighters, lurked decadence and the inevitable death of the revolution.

One night, Comandante Armando asked him to take charge of an important mission. It was a matter of taking some urgent and secret Party documents, on which, to judge from the commander's tone, more things than he could name depended.

"Forget everything else," he said. "This is important. Go with Ernesto. Leave first thing tomorrow."

Comrade Ernesto. Raúl had arrived with him on the same bus, along with his sister and Pachito, their dead comrade; and he had carried out the containment manoeuvres against the army with him after the scattering of the National Directorate in Sinú. But that could not be called friendship: Ernesto was one of those men who look like they've never laughed, or whose sense of humour seemed to have disappeared in combat. He was so difficult to have a conversation with that his life, even after two years of sharing a cause and a camp, was still the blank slate it was on their naming day, when Comandante Carlos introduced him as a popular leader from Quindío who had trained in Albania. Then again, Ernesto had always given him a strange sense of confidence, ever since the first moment: there are people like that, with whom we wouldn't have a drink but with whom we'd trust our children. Raúl asked:

"Where do we have to go?"

"Orlando knows," the commander said.

"We're going with Orlando?"

"The guy knows the zone as well as the jaguars do. He

knows how to get to the handover spot. I can't tell you any more, comrade. For security, understand?"

"Yes, comrade," Raúl lied. "I understand."

They left at first light. Orlando walked ahead, showing them the route, and behind him went Ernesto and Raúl. They kept a distance of twenty metres between each other in case of ambush; that procedure gave them a chance of not all falling at the same time, but it also made the trek more arduous, because each one of them walked as if he was on his own. Each of the three carried his rifle across his chest and his backpack of provisions, but Raúl also carried the other pack, the one with the documents, so light it seemed like a joke that its dispatch required an escort of three distinguished combatants. The sweat soaked their clothes from morning onwards, but it wasn't hot: it was the humidity of the air they walked through that made every step an effort, feeling as they inhaled through their mouths what one might feel when leaning over a pot of boiling water. But in his legs and his lungs, and also in his feet that were no longer torn to pieces inside the rubber boots, Raúl noted his experience, the hundreds of kilometres covered in those years of marches; he realized that the jungle no longer felt like an inhospitable place, and a twinge of pride passed through his chest. He looked up. A canopy of dense leaves closed above them, high up in the tops of the tall trees, and did not let the slimmest ray of light in. The only way to get your bearings was to follow the guide.

The guide. From his silent rear guard, Raúl watched with admiration his goat-like gait, which seemed to open the path for the others to pass. Orlando was a *campesino* who had been in the guerrilla army since the very first years: the founders had co-opted him there, in the zone, and gradually trained him until he became a detachment chief. He was an astute and cunning man, so quiet he seemed to be from the interior, and he had two scars on his torso, one from a machete and the other from a bullet, which was the private history of his violence. It was said that in the early years, when the pioneers who would become the guerrillas had recently gathered, he had confronted a veteran of other wars who ordered him to address him by his title of commander. "I am going to call you by your name, and if you don't like it, you can fuck off," he had said. "If I'm supposed to salute every bloody bastard, I might as well join the army." He was punished for his bad language, but the leaders admitted the rationale of his protest. Since then he'd done nothing but rise through the ranks under the leaders' satisfied gaze and especially Fernando's, who saw him as a Bolshevized ideal. He'd had a wife and two children in his old life and, although nobody knew where they were, people said Orlando visited them without permission, always sure of the leadership's complicity.

The first night they camped without incident. But the next day Orlando started muttering something, and his intention to protest was so transparent that his grouchy murmurs reached Raúl with total clarity, despite the forty metres between them. When they asked him what was wrong, Orlando complained that they weren't advancing at the planned pace; at this rate, he said, they'd never make the meeting place on time, and they'd run the risk of not being able to complete the handover, that the urban contacts would return to their bases if they didn't find them or – worse still – decide to wait and allow themselves to be caught by a military patrol. That was how

Raúl found out that all this time they had been exerting them-selves much less than necessary. He had felt so satisfied with the pace that the humiliating possibility that Orlando had slack-ened his pace to wait for them had never even crossed his mind: that he'd slowed down to allow these two boys, who for all their foreign training were still creatures of the city, to keep up.

"With all due respect, comrades," he said, "you've still got a lot to learn."

They decided to go out onto the *camino real*. This was a wide track between clusters of houses and villages built in colonial times, now used by traders and mule trains to supply the local shops. The guerrillas were expressly forbidden from using it, for they were unprotected there, easy targets, and they left an obvious trail for anyone who wanted to follow them. But they would advance more quickly and make up for lost time. At that moment Orlando was sure there was no other way to reach the point he'd planned to camp that night, and if they didn't stick to the itinerary, there was no way they'd reach the meeting to hand over the documents either. So that's what they did, and for an hour, the last of daylight, they walked those open spaces where they could see the sky and where the air circulated better, and where they didn't have to think about the snakes that might be hiding under the fallen leaves at every step. They camped without lighting a fire, so they wouldn't attract anyone's attention with the smoke or the smell of smoke. That night Raúl dreamed of his mother in prison.

In the morning, after eating, they did what they called a *conspiritivo minuto*. It was a security ritual: before leaving any camp, the men chose a rendezvous in case of confrontation or accident, and sometimes, if the group was a large one, they also established a watchword to avoid shooting each other in the midst of uncertainty. Comrade Orlando, the only one of the three who knew the area and, most of all, who could find the destination on the map in his head, fixed the encounter spot in the exact place they were leaving. They covered their traces and left, leaving the required distance between each other, seeing the other set off and counting their steps like relay runners. They advanced along the edge of a small stream, a thread of water that made its way through muddy banks, zigzagging around smooth rocks that looked like submerged hippopotamuses, and after an hour flowed into a more copious stream, flanked by steep banks three times the height of a man. They had not walked a hundred steps there, beside the fresh water that sparkled smoothly and murmured in a friendly whisper, when the shots rang out.

Raúl's first reaction was to take two steps back and aim his rifle to return fire. He was outside the ambush and so he began to fire towards the vague green space where the shots were coming from. In the midst of the chaos he realized that Ernesto had run back to escape the ambush, and saw him scrambling up the sheer bank somehow and knew he should do the same. The shots whistled past, and Raúl thought that each second underlined the miracle that none of them had wounded him, as he saw them hit the ground or the stones or the broad leaves that barely moved, as if they hadn't been struck by a bullet but just flicked. He got to the top of the bank and disappeared into the trees, running in a crouch back the way they'd come, and then he saw Ernesto, unarmed, running a few metres ahead of him: as he escaped, his rifle had fallen down the bank. Together they reached the rendezvous, but they took the precaution of concealing themselves away from the precise place, a few metres above, on a slope from which they would be able to see Orlando arrive without running the risk of being seen, while they established, simultaneously and in silence, that they were still alive and didn't have even a scratch.

But Orlando never arrived. They waited for him longer than was prudent. They waited for whole minutes, even after hearing the unmistakable noises of machetes and axes chopping down trees and hacking away branches. They knew very well what that meant, and it was soon confirmed: the blades of a helicopter, which would land in the clearing the soldiers were making could be heard in the distance. Evidently a patrol had picked up their trail on the *camino real*. Orlando had made a mistake, and now he would not arrive, and despite Raúl still holding out a vague hope, the most sensible thing was to accept that the guide was either dead or captured. It must have been about five in the afternoon, which in the jungle is almost nightfall, when they thought the noises were coming closer. Maybe it was a false impression, Raúl thought, like in that childhood game of closing his eyes so his sister could tickle his bare forearm, and he had to guess the moment her fingers reached the inside of his elbow. Then they heard a voice. They didn't manage to understand the words, but they knew they couldn't move: escaping at night and without Orlando might not only alert the soldiers' attention, but would also send them into a nightmare scenario. So they stayed huddled where they were, in absolute silence that was also the silence of fear, while night fell and darkness swallowed the tree trunks and the green that had driven Alberto mad, and in a matter of minutes they could no longer see the palms of their own hands.

How much time passed? Fifteen minutes or perhaps an hour: impossible to know. All of a sudden they realized they were hearing the noises of the jungle again; the patrol had gone by or given up. Finding their way in the jungle had always been difficult, like being on the open sea, and finding their way in the jungle at night, without even being able to look up to see which direction the sun was hitting the leaves from, was impossible. Raúl and Ernesto remembered that in the morning they had walked with the sun ahead of them, so as soon as there was light they would try to go in the opposite direction: with dawn at their backs. They ate something, confirmed they had enough supplies for the day's walk back and took turns to sleep a little while the other stood guard. And that's how they spent the night, always fearing the army's return, aware that in this part of the world everyone knew who Orlando was: capturing him alive was halfway to having a map to the camp where some of the most important men of the guerrilla army were gathered. Raúl, for the first time, hoped that Orlando was dead.

They were already both awake when they heard, from far off, the sound of a helicopter. They began to leave with a sort of irritated resignation, guessing the route back, maintaining the twenty metres' distance even if at times it seemed absurd, catching each other's eye to confirm that a rock or maybe an anthill looked familiar, or that a stream was the same one they'd walked past going the other way. The helicopter kept flying over them: of that they were sure, even though they didn't see it. If they tried to find it in the sky, they saw nothing on the other side of the green canopy, except glimpses of blue and perhaps the silhouette of a marmoset leaping from one branch to another, but they heard the demented throbbing of the blades, and if that wasn't enough, even when they couldn't hear it anymore they seemed to still hear it. "That motherfucker's still up there," Ernesto would say. "We've been walking for a day and he's still there, as if he can see us. And who knows, maybe he can. They know we're here, comrade." And Raúl: "I don't hear it." And Ernesto: "Sure you do. There's that noise. It's still there." And Raúl would listen carefully, separating the noise of his footsteps from the rest of the world and there it is, there's that noise, that helicopter was still there, like a hellish bumblebee, whereas the departure point, where they'd camped with Orlando the first night, was nowhere to be found.

"Shit," Raúl said. "We're lost."

It was impossible to know if they'd been walking in circles. All the trees were the same and the sun had got lost in the sky. Raúl thought of the compass he'd brought from China, a gift from the Red Army on the day of his graduation, and again cursed Fernando, who had taken it without explanation, not confiscating someone else's property, but as if preventing with this arbitrary gesture the penetration of the guerrilla army by the bourgeoisie. He committed the error of mentioning it without talking about what happened: "I had a compass." "Well you should've brought it, dickhead." It could have set off a fight if they hadn't both realized immediately that the jungle was getting to them. That afternoon Raúl reached into the backpack for a tin of condensed milk, and his hand came out empty. Ernesto confirmed that his provisions had also run out, which was not surprising: the excursion had already lasted two days longer than planned.

They lost all sense of time. Ernesto moved his head as if he'd heard a sound, but then kept walking: no, it had been nothing.

Then he stopped again. "What's that?" he asked with his eyes wide open. "Hear it? An animal." But Raúl didn't hear anything. Stubborn, wilful, the jungle had begun to play with them. The hallucinations took the form of a black jaguar or made the noise of the damned helicopter. The hunger of the third day – or the fourth, there was no way of knowing – forced them to dig the toothpaste out of their packs, a matter of deceiving their stomachs, but a few hours later Raúl felt an intense burning in the centre of his torso, as if the mint had opened an ulcer in his oesophagus. They looked for roots to eat, some edible sprouts that were not uncommon in the region, but in vain, and when they reached a stream they'd never seen before, they realized their sealed stomachs would not even accept a gulp of water. The jungle, which was conspiring against them, hid the snakes, hid the capybaras, hid the rivers where they could have fished for a *bagre* or a *mojarra*, which in any case they couldn't have cooked, because the fire or the smoke would have drawn the soldiers' attention. Raúl felt weakness overtaking his legs and damp smells burning his nostrils, and then he felt his head getting light. He remembered his false hunger strike at the Peace Hotel, reading Gorky, the dumplings that his self-sacrificing mother had made, and was secretly embarrassed to be thinking of novels at a moment like this.

"Let's stop," he said. "This isn't working."

Without having to say a word, there was a frightful understanding between the two of them that they would not get out of the jungle alive. Then Raúl took the documents out of the bag, the so-very-urgent documents that had got them into this mess, and said: "We better burn these. If we're going to die, they better not find them." But they couldn't light a fire (for the same reason they wouldn't have been able to cook a fish), so they decided to bury them. Ernesto suggested that they read them first, in spite of being forbidden from doing so: maybe there might be something in them, a clue, a hint, some bit of information that might help them find the camp. They were probably illusions of a dying man: improbable, desperate, toothpaste to deceive their rational minds. They didn't even have the energy to debate the advisability of violating the secret communications, or to speculate about the punishments they might be subjected to, they just divided up the documents without a word and began to read. Ernesto was the first to say what Raúl was already thinking:

"And for this they ordered us to cross the jungle?"

There was nothing in the documents: they were internal Party papers, all to do with the plenary they were going to be holding on the Tigre plains. There were lists of names, long bureaucracies, references to statutes of the Marxist–Leninist–Maoist Communist Party. A good part of the pages were taken up with a confrontation: Comandante Armando and Comandante Fernando were profoundly preoccupied, for they had detected in one dominant line in the Party a serious militaristic deviation that acted to the detriment of what truly mattered: the Bolshevization of the masses and the creation of a proletarian base. On other pages Raúl found a long discussion of a book he hadn't heard of, the title of which declared Colombia the first Vietnam of the Americas and the sentences that were quoted painted a chimerical picture that seemed taken more from the fantasies of distant leaders in the city than from the reality lived every day by the guerrillas. Raúl read that the guerrillas were liberating the north of the country from the yoke of the United States, that it had managed to create bases of support of more than ten thousand square kilometres and that sixteen municipalities in that region no longer sought the validity of the civil power of the Colombian government, lackey of Yankee imperialism. Sitting on the jungle floor, Raúl found only five plain words to fight against those revelations: *But this is not true.*

But he didn't say anything when he finished going through the pages. He shook his head to indicate there was nothing useful, though he didn't know what his companion hoped to find: a map, magical instructions on how to return to the Tigre plains? Ernesto didn't seem to have had any luck either, because as soon as he finished he stood up and began to soften the earth with the blade of his machete. With the last energy they had left, the two of them dug a hole with their hands, put the bag of documents in it as if they were burying a dead cat, covered it with reddish earth and covered the earth with leaves that were not dry, but still shiny and supple even though they were dead. Then they hung up their hammocks, so they wouldn't have to do it in the dark, and let night fall right there, since it made no sense to advance any further. Before falling asleep like that, with an empty stomach for the fourth or fifth night in a row, so weak and tired that he had a fleeting fear of dying in his sleep, Raúl dared to ask one last question that his comrade might be asking at the very same time: "Do you think we'll get out of this?" He was just expecting a simple answer to raise their spirits, but it provoked a genuine conversation, the most open he'd ever had with Ernesto, or with any other guerrilla fighter, in those long months of militancy.

They talked about their families, their training in faraway

countries, their nostalgias and their fear. Ernesto talked about his brothers – one of whom was in the Party, like him, while the other didn't want anything to do with politics – and his sister, who was not yet twenty but was already every inch a fully fledged revolutionary and destined for great things. Raúl talked about his father, who at that moment would be lying in his hammock in some part of Tierralta or Paramillo; and Sol, who had decided to carry on her militancy in the Cauca Valley, and about Valentina, in prison in Bogotá. He talked about old man Wang, the comrade at the alarm clock factory in Peking, who tackled problems with cryptic phrases. *When the light is gone and all is dark*, he used to say, *the only way not to go off course is to look back. Thus, seeing the light we've left behind, we can be sure of another that awaits us.* Ernesto said: "The Chinese are very odd."

The next day they woke up without urgency. They knew they should start walking, but, since they had no idea how to get anywhere, they didn't think there was any reason to rush. They bundled up their hammocks and began to walk north, or towards the point where north would be if the canopy was not deceiving them. They dragged their boots, making more noise than was prudent, but their muscles were not strong enough to lift the rubber soles off the carpet of leaves under which a venomous *mapaná* could be lurking. Raúl had a brutal intuition: this was his last day. In the depths of his consciousness he said goodbye to his mother, but nobody else, and he asked her forgiveness for letting himself die in this idiotic way. He was pondering these thoughts when he felt that the light was changing. Was it another optical illusion, like they'd had before? Maybe not, because Ernesto seemed to have picked up the pace: perhaps seeing what Raúl saw: a reflection had begun to appear on the tree trunks, a green that wasn't the same green as before, a green with a new and different light shining over it. Among the dense foliage, like a decoy that someone had placed at the end of a corridor, they saw a glare, and in seconds found themselves in front of a clearing the size of a stadium that they recognized, because months earlier they had been the ones who cleared it with their machetes. The *campesinos* had turned that new piece of scrub into a rice field, but Raúl stared mainly at the open sky, where clouds floated with an insolent freedom. He looked at Ernesto. They both knew that across the rice field they would find a sugar cane field, and, if they entered the woods by the side of the crops, two hours' walk would take them into guerrilla territory.

They hugged each other firmly, because they had come back to life.

XIX

At first there were vague jumbled explosions: repeated twinges of gloomy pain, the impression of being carried in her own hammock through the Cauca jungle, voices expressing pessimistic prognoses without Sol feeling the terror she should have felt. "She's going to die on us," a voice said, and another: "Leave it. There's nothing we can do about it." Among the mists of unconsciousness she recognized Guillermo's voice, then it wasn't Guillermo but her father, and then her father seemed to be the foreman from the clock factory, and even Carl Crook came to talk to her: "Don't worry, Lilí, everything's going to be fine." She remembered moments of being rocked in the bed of a pickup truck, suffering the potholes of the unpaved road as if they were needles stuck in her body, and in some moments she was back on the jungle trails hearing the rubber boots against the leaves on the ground and also the urgent voices: "Have they already given her blood? Was there coagulant there?" Sol stretched a hand to touch someone, to feel the contact of another hand, but found only the empty air. Sometimes she heard her own imploring voice: "Let my family know." But she didn't know if she said the words out loud, because nobody answered her. She wasn't even sure if these people whose presence she sensed were real. Maybe none of this was real.

Later she would find out what happened before she was shot in the back. There would be gaps, of course, missing pieces in a confusing tale. Sol knew that the detachment, gathered in assembly and led by Comandante Manuel, had found her guilty of all sixteen charges and condemned her to death, but she never knew why, after she tried to leave, after the commander shot her with the intention of killing her right there, they had taken her to a nearby camp where they'd given her first aid. "First they shoot me in the back and then they help me," she would say later. "Who can understand those bastards?" The fact remained that, to stay alive, she had needed all the luck in the world, as well as the compassion of a handful of people. It was not clear how that had happened. On the one hand was the good luck of having a hard rubber rucksack on her back at the moment she was shot, since the bullet had to go through all its contents before burying itself in her back. On the other hand, the guerrillas' internal bureaucracy had somehow allowed the news to reach Guillermo's ears; and Guillermo took the matter in hand, got her out of El Tambo and waited until she had recovered enough to make a longer journey, and a few weeks later he was taking her to Medellín. They were going to the house of her grandparents, Comrade Valentina's bourgeois parents, who represented everything Sol and her family had fought against for years.

"But why there?" Guillermo asked.

"Because I don't have anyone else," Sol said.

In other words, because her father was still in the hills, on the other side of Paramillo, and her brother was still on the

Tigre plains, and her mother was in jail in Bogotá. Her family was shattered and she was alone in the world.

"Well, not alone," Guillermo said. "I'm going with you."

"I can get there on my own."

"You couldn't get to the corner on your own," Guillermo said. "Let people help you, there's nothing wrong with that."

And so they had appeared early one morning, before first light, at the door of the house in Laureles. Grandfather Emilio opened the door with his face distorted by sleep, and looked at Guillermo with amazement and at Sol without visible surprise. "Grandpa, I've just arrived from Albania and I can't find my parents," she said. She didn't know what made her choose that lie over any other, but she didn't even have time to wonder about it. Don Emilio burst out laughing.

"Don't talk nonsense, dear," he said. "Your parents are guerrillas and you haven't come from Albania." And then: "But the important thing is you're here now. Welcome home. Here we'll share whatever luck you have."

It was like returning to life. Her grandparents took her to Talara, the farm they had in the mountains of Rionegro, an idyllic place reached by a road that ran through flower farms. There, breathing fresh mountain air, sleeping on a mattress under a freshly ironed sheet and a wool blanket that sometimes made her sneeze, Marianella began a slow recovery, not just of her wounded body. The doctors had not been able to remove the bullet, not having the instruments or facilities for a complex surgical operation, but her body had worked its magic and in a matter of months she was healthy again with the bullet inside. On the mornings of her convalescence, while those miracles were occurring in her flesh, Marianella woke up early and went out to see the skies of springtime, and sometimes, with a cup of coffee in her hand, she managed to forget that she was in hiding and that out there, in real life, right now there were two armies pursuing her and, if they found her, they would not hesitate to do her harm. She thought of her family, she wondered where they were, she worried about them. At those moments she also thought of Guillermo, and was surprised to find her gratitude mixed up with other feelings.

Guillermo came to visit her every now and then. It was not possible to know where he had travelled from each time, but he must have come from far away, because he arrived smelling of the road. He never stayed overnight, because her grandparents would not have approved, but during those long visits Marianella began to get an idea of his life. First she found out that Guillermo had three small children from his first marriage; then, that the mother of those children, his first wife, had died very young (but Guillermo never spoke of her cause of death); finally, that Guillermo had been thinking for several months of leaving the guerrilla army. Who could have imagined that a woman like Marianella, an uprooted bourgeois, would come along to show him the way out?

The six days spent with Ernesto in the jungle, four of them lost, changed Raúl in ways that were not immediately evident, but gradually began to show up over the following months. For example, he was not overly affected by the news about Orlando, who had been shot in the ambush and apparently survived for forty-eight hours with a shattered hip, bleeding out and keeping a brave silence and refusing to give the enemy any help, and died without too much pain – according to the official

406

version of events – in a village jail cell. It was as though his soul had hardened.

"Well," he said to Ernesto. "Better him than us."

At the end of the year another piece of news arrived that shook the camp: the death in combat of Comandante Fernando. They never knew the precise circumstances, but it was said that his detachment had been ambushed by the army in north-west Antioquia, very near the River Cauca, when they were on their way to the Tigre plains for the Party plenary. After he was sanctioned, a fall from grace that anyone else would never have recovered from, Fernando had embarked on a real political campaign from below, conquering the bases and maintaining the loyalty of those who were now his fervent followers, and he had won back so much esteem in the Party that in the last days of his life he was able to dream of becoming political secretary. He did not succeed in his first attempt, but it was clear that was why he was coming to the plenary on the Tigre plains: to overthrow the current secretary, Pedro León Arboleda. The last days of 1971 and the first of the new year – hot days of clear skies and friendly breezes rustling the tarpaulins and a light so white it hurt their eyes – were marked by the news, and for a long time it seemed as though Comandante Fernando's death was the only thing that had happened in the world. In secret, Raúl thought he'd been freed of something, and he had the confusing hope that a new future was opening for him in the guerrilla force.

The opportunity to confirm it presented itself sooner rather than later, when the commanders announced an important operation. Armando did not explain what the mission was, or where it was headed, but the mere announcement galvanized the troops. In those days they had moved a lot without Raúl knowing why, sailing south down the Sinú River, climbing up from the plains of San Jorge to the Nudo de Paramillo and sleeping on the highest part of the mountain, up where it was so cold the water would freeze overnight. High up there on the plateau, the air had thinned out so much that Raúl had trouble breathing, and envied the local *campesinos*, who climbed with the agility of Sherpas. From there they descended towards the west, and by the end of the day they'd reached the place where the detachment that had been entrusted with the intelligence was waiting for them. Now they found out about the mission, and were given maps with lines drawn in red ink and a sketch of the village they were going to take: San José de Urama. It was a village of cheap brick houses with zinc roofs, and it was surrounded by dense trees that made it blind to anyone coming from anywhere other than the two roads. The capture didn't have to be difficult, but Raúl would be in the vanguard: his training in China had turned him into the explosives man.

They left for the objective at three in the morning, after a brief pep talk in which Armando talked about the reasons for the revolution and the future of Colombia and reminded his men that they were all heroes, because they were fighting for the liberty of an oppressed people. An hour later they saw the lights of San José. At that point they were almost two hundred men, some who had come from very far away, surrounding the whole village. Advancing with them, in the darkness of the leafy vegetation, Raúl had the strange epiphany that all of them, himself included, were wanting to go into battle. In his rucksack he was carrying thirty sticks of dynamite and he had accepted that his mission was to blow up the door of the barracks where twelve men were sleeping, according to the intelligence reports. They took up a position opposite the police barracks. Armando, who was commanding the attack, made a gesture with his hand and Raúl understood: it was the moment to set the charge.

Raúl gave the wire to the comrade beside him and, while he unrolled it, he skirted along the wall to the door. At the end of the wire was the percussion cap, a device that Raúl had to place firmly in the dynamite to make sure it would work when the comrade pulled it, and he was just about to set it when a firefight erupted on the other side of town. They would later discover what had happened: a group of comrades had improvised a roadblock to protect the operation, even though nobody had ordered them to do so, with such bad luck that the first local who wanted to cross it was paralytically drunk, and such bad judgement that they didn't think it a mistake to shoot twice in the air when the drunk didn't want to stop. When he heard the shots, the comrade who had the wire in his hands pulled it hard, out of surprise or fright, and set off the detonator before Raúl had time to move away. The explosion of the percussion cap shattered his arm. The splinters ripped through his skin and pierced his flesh, and his arm and hand were covered in blood. Raúl felt an intense pain in his face and knew blood was streaming down one eye, but understood that his duty at that moment was to recover the dynamite, and he had barely managed to do that and return to the position when the police, alerted by the shots and the explosion, appeared at the windows and started firing at them. Dawn had begun to break when Armando told him he also had an injured ear; he reached up to feel it and found it incomplete, because the explosion had blown a chunk of it off. By now the heat of his skin and the sun's rays had dried the blood over the top of the gunpowder sprayed by the explosion, forming a paste so thick from his eyebrow to his jaw that there was no way to tell if his eye was still in its socket. The sounds of the world were confused, because the explosion had damaged his hearing, but he continued fighting, not knowing very well where he was firing, losing his perception of space, until he no longer knew what was going on.

The others told him everything during the retreat. The capture had been a resounding success: while some guerrillas were sacking the pharmacy and collecting the cash from the Caja Agraria, others entered a rich farmer's granary and distributed the grain to the people, and kept a couple of loads to take back to camp. They left with a generous plunder – tins of sardines and condensed milk, Saltine biscuits and *dulce de leche* – and it filled the comrades' backpacks. They started back up the Paramillo hill by the same trail they'd used to come down. Raúl listened to the stories with one side of his face, but without paying too much attention, because he still hadn't been able to confirm whether the explosion had cost him an eye. His rifle, a Korean M1 that was designed for wars fought from positions and not for crossing steep landscapes, weighed heavily on his shoulder. Armando had gone far ahead or was bringing up the rear; Raúl wasn't sure, and he looked around for him with his good eye without managing to find him. He was surrounded by his comrades from the camp and others he didn't know, but who were from the area. Three hours had passed since they left San José when they saw, a hundred metres off the trail, a house with a zinc roof, like the ones in the village but poorer, and they immediately went into combat mode.

Raúl received the order to place the dynamite they hadn't used in San José. He asked who was in the house and they answered with two words: "The enemy." He didn't know how they'd reached that conclusion, but it was obvious that they all knew something he didn't, and he could only obey. So he approached the house as he had the barracks, and set the charge as he had at the barracks, but this time he did connect the percussion cap and did have time to get back before the comrade at the other end of the wire pulled it and the percussion cap exploded and the dynamite exploded, making the zinc roof fly off in pieces, and leaving only the walls of the house standing. He had put the dynamite out in the open, and the uproar was so fierce that Raúl seemed to feel it in his guts.

"Come out and surrender," one of his comrades shouted, "and we'll spare your lives."

Only a couple of seconds passed before someone shouted from inside that yes, they'd come out, and the first silhouettes appeared on the doorless threshold. They were not soldiers: they weren't wearing uniforms and the weapons they held above their heads were not standard issue. There were four men and a woman. Raúl understood who they were, as he had heard people talk about those men – lumpen-*campesinos*, Commander Fernando called them – who were offering to defend whoever would pay them, like small, private, counter-guerrilla forces. None of the five offered the slightest resistance; they surrendered without anyone having to ask twice. That's why what happened was so unexpected: the comrades mowed them down then and there, without another word, and with enough precision to leave the woman unscathed. First with incredulity, then with horror, Raúl watched one of his comrades walk up to a fallen body that was still moving and finish him off with two machete blows. Then he turned to the woman, who had curled up in the middle of the execution and was screaming hysterically, and said:

"Go and tell them, so they learn their lesson."

The incident left him feeling sick. None of what he saw that afternoon bore any relation to what he'd learned in China, where the order was very clear: if the enemy was promised his life would be spared in exchange for surrender, that promise had to be respected, because that was the only way others would want to surrender later. But he didn't say anything: he didn't say the manoeuvre had been a mistake, or that those dead men were *campesinos* too, or much less that cruelty was not part of the revolution. The group advanced for the rest of the night and the whole of the next day. When they stopped to rest someone gave him some medicine for the pain in his face, and Raúl was so numb that he ceased thinking about the awful things he'd seen. He could only be grateful. He felt that his body was going to betray him at any moment, and thus, half-drugged, he even managed to forget that he was seeing the world out of a single eye. Twice, at rest stops that lasted a few minutes, he fell asleep on his feet, leaning on the long barrel of his M1, and he wouldn't remember when they arrived at a place where he could finally lie down. The next day, when he woke up, he found himself surrounded by a group of comrades. Among them was Carlos, the doctor who had chosen his name, who was sitting beside him with a bowl of hot water and rags made of old shirts.

"I don't know if I've lost my eye, comrade," Raúl said.

"Don't worry," the doctor said. "Let's take a look, keep still."

He began to cover his face with the wet cloths. The dry paste gradually melted away until his eye saw the light, or Raúl realized that clear daylight was coming in through that dazzled eye. He cried, but he didn't worry too much about hiding it: with a bit of luck, his tears of relief could blend with the water from the cloths.

His recovery was a small miracle. More than the pain from his burnt skin, more than the anguished fear of losing an eye, the strongest impression from those morose days was the novelty of guilt. Was it guilt? He had never felt anything like it, so it wasn't easy to recognize the feeling, but when he put that name to it nothing seemed out of place. He felt an urgent need to talk to his mother and a vague unfounded fear that something bad had happened to her in prison. In the humid nights he rolled up in his hammock like a chrysalis and glued his ear to the radio, not to look for stations with opera music, but to see if by some stroke of luck he could hear some news about his family. His body was still doing what it did: his skin was regenerating; his eye began to weep on its own without warning, as if it had its own woes, but every day he could see better and the skin of his eyelid no longer felt like it was about to break like the skin inside an eggshell. Sometimes he was awakened by phantom pain from his leishmaniasis, which had left a scar on his Achilles tendon. Although this was the least of his worries.

On one of those sweltering days, his detachment went to do some base work in a *campesino* hamlet very close to Tierralta. Raúl insisted on going with them, believing he would speed up his recovery that way. Actually, something had happened to him, and he didn't want to be alone. It was like a sort of melancholy, and he wouldn't have been able to explain it, so he fled from himself by accompanying the detachment, spending the morning with the *campesinos*, talking about the people's rights and the handover of our resources to international capital and the obligation to struggle against the oligarchs. At the end of the day, in those cooler hours, he was waiting for his comrades at the edge of a patch of bare land the locals used to play football when he heard a name that felt like a clap on the back of his neck:

"Sergio!"

He turned around in fright, and so abruptly that a comrade, thinking something else had happened, even aimed his rifle. His eyes scanned the lines of houses and saw what he was looking for: a young woman with some clothes in her hand – a shirt, some underpants – was walking quickly behind a naked child. "Sergio!" she shouted. "Come here!" That was it: a mother trying to dress her restive child. But the mention of that forgotten name shook Raúl to his core, and he could not get over the shock for the rest of the day. His comrades noticed his distraction and asked him several times if he was alright, because his face had a blank expression, like someone coming down with a fever, but Raúl couldn't explain what had happened to him because he couldn't understand it himself.

The last day of April, shortly after he turned twenty-two without anyone knowing, he was advised of his next mission: they sent him to visit some indigenous people. Raúl received the news with satisfaction, because he saw in the dispatch a show of confidence recovered after taking San José, but the task arrived at a bad moment: he'd spent several days tormented by toothache that wouldn't let him sleep. He decided not to mention it and not even let the pain show on his face, but he entered the commanders' tent feeling like his face might break at any moment. "We're going to explain how this will play out, comrade," Comandante Tomás said. "Are you ready?" And Raúl said yes, he was ready.

It was a reserve of Embera people on the banks of the River Verde, where the Paramillo mountains start to descend to the plains. Months before, on the way back from a long march, Raúl's detachment had spent the night beside the village, which consisted of half a dozen huts built around a longhouse. Shortly before they arrived, Comandante Tomás had regaled them with warnings about courtesy towards the indigenous people and respect for their customs. "You drink the chicha they offer whether you like it or not," he told them. They had not reached the huts yet when some of the Emberas came out of the darkness, armed with machetes and shouting in their language, and only calmed down when they recognized Tomás, who had been trying in vain to recruit them to the Party's cause. But they didn't look at him: the Emberas had fixated on Raúl from the beginning, and they did not stop looking at him while they walked to the longhouse, and did not stop looking at him while they introduced him to their chief, who they called the *jaibaná*. They all took their places around the centre. Tomás tried to sit next to the *jaibaná*, as he had on previous visits, and silence fell over the longhouse when he moved him aside with a gentle push and indicated that Raúl should sit there. It took this misunderstanding for Raúl to comprehend the nature of the insolent and inquisitive looks that still would not leave him in peace: no, it was not insolence or any sort of inquisitiveness, it was that his white skin and green eyes had something supernatural or magical to these men. The *jaibaná* was very clear when he said:

"We've been expecting you."

His name was Genaro. He spoke good but accented Spanish and sometimes slipped in words from his own language. That night, to everyone's amazement, Genaro drank his chicha while paying constant subtle attention to Raúl, and ended by asking Comandante Tomás to allow him to sleep inside the longhouse: it was a rare privilege that not even Tomás had received in all the time he'd been building relations with the Emberas, and he couldn't keep a flash of childish envy from flitting across his face. He had no choice but to agree, of course, and Raúl spent the night inside the sacred house, sleeping a few steps away from the *jaibaná*, while the rest of his comrades hung their hammocks outside, in the open air.

He didn't know that night what Genaro and his tribe had been expecting him for, but it didn't matter: the Party leaders had been looking for a way into the Embera community for a long time, and now it turned out that this blond city boy, who Genaro called "good *kahuma*", held the key in his hands. They explained to Raúl that the Party had a very valuable piece of information: in the zone where the longhouse was located, near the mouth of the River Verde, construction would begin within a few years on a hydroelectric dam that would ostensibly supply the whole zone, but would wipe out the Emberas. The documents Raúl read spoke of irreparable damage, and did so in solemn and alarming phrases: ruptures of an ancestral value system, uprooting of age-old customs, death of sacred rivers. They explained that the *bocachico* fish, an essential source of protein for the indigenous people and a vital part of their economy would completely disappear; the inevitable deforestation, they said, would lead to a spiritual imbalance among the Emberas. The Party had reached an agreement: their revolutionary duty was to take advantage of the situation to organize the indigenous people, teach them the value of protest and get them to rise up against the abuses of the oligarchs. The mission, as Raúl understood it, was to create a first cell among the indigenous people. "A single spark," Chairman Mao said, "can start a prairie fire." Raúl, it seemed, was the emissary of the fire.

So now, on the last day of April, Raúl went to bed with a new assignment in his head, but also with an intense toothache that was no longer just in his jaw, but sent electric shocks through all the bones of his skull. By morning the pain had become so unbearable that he could no longer keep it secret. "You can't go drink *chicha* like that," Comandante Tomás said. He summoned Comandante Carlos, who had only to peer inside Raúl's mouth to find an abscess and marvel that he'd been able to hide it for so long: the pain, he said, must have been severe enough to make most people faint. He operated immediately, which meant sitting the patient in a chair made of tree trunks, anaesthetizing him with a needle appropriate for a horse and removing the molar with a pair of surgical forceps of doubtful cleanliness. It was the spectacle of the day: the detachment, gathered round the tree trunk chair, assisted the struggle by shouting amid laughter: "United in combat, we shall overcome!" The molar put up no resistance, but Comrade Carlos prescribed two days of absolute stillness for the patient. Only after the rest, when there was no danger of haemorrhage or infection, did he give him permission to leave for the Embera village.

It was May by the time they set off. In the midst of a downpour that shook the branches and slapped the large leaves, Raúl, Comandante Tomás and a group of comrades approached the longhouse where the *jaibaná*, Genaro, awaited them. The strategy was very simple: they would be welcomed by the Emberas, Raúl would pretend to fall ill and Tomás would ask Genaro to look after him for a few days, the time it would take to complete the (fictitious) mission that had brought them to the zone. Genaro, of course, would welcome Raúl with open arms, and that would be the perfect opportunity for Raúl to tell him about the dam, about the damage it would do to the Emberas, about popular resistance and how the guerrillas could help them to demand their civil rights as well as ancestral ones. But those clear plans became cloudy sooner than expected, when Tomás told Raúl something he perhaps should not have told him at that moment.

It was a succession of misunderstandings. Maybe Raúl was making a face. His mouth was still hurting from the violence of the tooth extraction, and feeling the void with his tongue where his molar had been shocked him as much as feeling a stump where an amputated hand used to be; or maybe, it was simply that he still had phantom pain in the bones of his head. In any case, he was making a face: quiet, his brow furrowed, a certain discouraged expression. And maybe Tomás read it wrong, believing that Raúl knew something that he didn't actually know or that someone had told him what was already public knowledge, and believing that this was also the cause of his discouragement, the unease etched on his brow, his hostile silence. Maybe he believed it was a good idea to deactivate that discontent, because the success of this visit depended on him: what harm could it do, Tomás must have thought, to raise his morale before such an important mission?

"Well, comrade, congratulations," Tomás said. "You see how the Party gives Valentina all the help she needs."

That was how Raúl found out his mother was out of prison. That had happened two weeks before, but nobody had told him: for two weeks the detachment, or at least the commanders, had known that Comrade Valentina had been released after almost three months in detention and various legal strategies. But nobody had told Raúl. That night when the plan was already in motion – and Raúl was feeling ill in some vague way and Genaro had opened his arms and the rest of the comrades had gone on their way – and when Genaro had invited him to sleep in the longhouse instead of hanging his hammock in the trees, Raúl began telling him what they were planning in the capital: the construction of the dam, which implied flooding the region and diverting the rivers and messing up everyone's life for ever: that of the Emberas, yes, but also that of the *campesinos*. But he could not stop thinking about his mother for a single instant. Genaro listened to Raúl's words with patience. In his halting Spanish, he said: "Karagabí said so."

Raúl understood that it would be pointless to ask who that person was. "What did he say?" he asked.

"He left us a testament that he had created the water for us, for us to use her," said the *jaibaná* Genaro. "He said we must not touch anything: leave things as he made them. If not, a curse will befall us. And we Emberas will be no more."

They spoke of the matter several times over the course of the night and the next day, but Raúl had lost all his zeal and his attention had flown to other places. Valentina was free: but who was she with, and where was she? Had his mother returned to her family home in Medellín? Did his father know about her liberation, or his sister? Had she resumed her clandestine work, or was her cover irremediably blown? He used the same fictitious illness that had enabled him to stay with Genaro now to avoid him. He wanted to be alone, just to ruminate on the sensation of having been betrayed, and along the way he had somehow lost the inclination to complete his assigned job. So, he spent the whole day lying beside his rifle on the dirt floor, with his head on his pack, looking up at the cone of palm leaves that formed the roof of the *maloca*.

That night, when Genaro came to see him, his face was painted with genipapo resin, and his hand closed over a balsa stick the hilt of which was in the shape of a monkey's head. Two women came with him, both adorned with necklaces looped thrice around their necks, and colourful chaquira seeds quivering over their bare breasts. They washed their feet with the water from a red pail before coming in; one of them handed Genaro a bottle of aguardiente, and Raúl understood that this was a ceremony and that Genaro was getting ready to cure him – neither Tomás nor the other commanders had foreseen that this might be the consequence of their vulgar strategy. Genaro drank a swig of aguardiente, took a bunch of leaves that seemed freshly harvested and began to sing, shaking the leaves in the air between his face and Raúl's, and his song came out drenched in anise and saliva. He sang for two hours, and when he wasn't singing he was speaking in his language (speaking in the tone of someone telling an old story), but there was not a single moment when Raúl felt that he wasn't talking about him. It must have been two in the morning when the *jaibaná* leaned over him without standing up, grabbed his head between his powerful hands and placed his mouth, smelling of aguardiente, basil and wood, on his forehead, as if he were going to give him a kiss. But instead of kissing him he began to suck, and he did so with such force that Raúl could feel his teeth and thought he would have a wound the next day. Genaro let him go then, pushing himself away, took two steps and vomited on the ground, and Raúl had the incomprehensible certainty that there, in that stinking puddle, were his demons as well.

One morning Marianella woke up at the sound of wheels on the gravel at the front of the house, and looking out she saw her grandparents. Grandpa Emilio opened the back door and offered his hand to help someone out of the car. It was Luz Elena. Marianella ran out to hug her without feeling the pebbles cutting into her bare feet. She found a pale imitation of what her mother had been – the same body, yes, but her energy decimated and the face of someone who had lost her illusions – and she knew that something deeper than a mere setback had contaminated her life. She spent the following days there, in that house that had become a refuge, the only place in the whole world where she was safe. It was then, as the days passed, that a conversation began which later turned into a plan and, finally, a mission. For that, however, Marianella had to find out what had happened to her mother.

From the time when Fausto joined the guerrilla army, in the last months of 1969, Luz Elena had closed down her previous life, the one she lived in the Cabrera Cárdenas family's apartment, and she had moved almost completely to a safe house. It was a place that looked inoffensive from the outside, but inside was a small base of the movement where they hid medical supplies, ammunition and money in black garbage bags. After several months of clandestine residence there, months distinguished by her missions to Quito and Guayaquil, the Party directorship decided to put another responsibility in her hands: the custody of three children. They were Lorenzo's two sons and Camilo's daughter, two commanders who had not left the jungle for years and whose wives, for reasons nobody knew, had walked out on them.

So Comrade Valentina took charge of them as if she were a nanny, putting food on the table for them, taking them to school and to the doctor when necessary, always protected by her elegant clothes and pearl necklaces and upper-class manners. Of course, someone, a professor or a nurse, might have asked why a woman like her would be taking care of those children; but nobody ever did, perhaps because Luz Elena's authority prevented it, and it was obvious the Party counted on those class-based safe conducts. The children grew fond of her. Lorenzo's two were timid little boys whose spirits already bore the scars of this strange life, who had a sort of natural distrust of the world of adults, and only seemed calm with Valentina. The little girl, however, lived without apparent preoccupations: by the age of five she had changed residence and companions so often that she didn't even wonder when her next meal was coming. All that worked well – life in the safe house, being an impostor mother to the guerrillas' children – until Valentina was arrested. Nobody could do anything to keep those children from ending up at the Family Welfare Institute, where they were treated as abandoned and given a cot to sleep in and a dose of pity at regular intervals. Meanwhile, in her cell in Bogotá, Valentina waited in vain for a visit from some comrade, or at least the lawyer they'd so often promised her.

But nobody came to see her. During the thirteen months she was in prison, she did not receive a single letter from the Party, not even a line to make her feel she was not alone in the world. Valentina resorted to the last hope she had left: to ask her father for help. That was how Don Emilio, who never would have imagined that life would bring him such surprises, hired a lawyer in Bogotá so his rebellious daughter would not have to serve every day of her sentence. But this was not easy either, for Valentina welcomed the lawyer by informing him there was another prisoner, Comrade Silvio, and he must be defended as well. Don Emilio flatly refused, of course, for he was not about to help a *guerrillero*: let the communists take care of him. But Valentina was adamant. She told Don Emilio over the phone: "Both of us or neither." And so the two of them got out, and in front of the jail where Don Emilio was waiting they said goodbye and never saw each other again. Luz Elena returned to Medellín by plane with her father, with tickets paid for by the Cárdenas family's longing to be reunited.

Luz Elena's disappointment was heartrending. She felt betrayed by the Party, to which she'd given years of her life, her marriage and both her children. She returned to her city like someone returning to a strange place, not recognizing it and struggling to find her way round it, divorced from what she had once called her own. She knew the Party cadres had heard of her arrival and that they were looking for her. An unknown intermediary visited to bring her a message from the leadership:

they asked her to get the commanders' children out of the hands of social services. "You're the only one who can do it, comrade," they told her, but Luz Elena slammed the door in the emissary's face with all the force of her resentment. The next day they stopped her in the street. "They'll only hand them over to you, comrade, because you have custody. If you don't collect them, the commanders' children will be stuck there."

"It's obvious you don't know me," she said. "Tell them this: that I'm in no mood to do favours for anyone right now, especially for them, since they haven't even chosen to tell me where my family is."

Luz Elena had spent several days looking for a way to communicate with her son. Apart from an incomplete letter that reached her on one of her first days, she'd heard nothing from him the whole time she was in prison, and then, after insisting, she had received a reply from an emissary of the Party: Raúl had been killed in combat.

"My brother is dead?" Marianella said.

"That was the last news I received before leaving prison," Luz Elena said. "But I don't believe it. If that were true, we would have known."

"They would have notified us," Marianella said without conviction.

"Exactly," Luz Elena said. "Your father would know, for example, and he would have notified us."

During the following days, Marianella tried to make enquiries of her own, but without success. Her brother, dead? No, something told her the news was false, and it was not just the formidable capacity we have to deceive ourselves when it suits us. One of those mornings, after watching her mother cry more during the course of one breakfast than in her whole life so far, Marianella sat on the edge of her bed and said:

"So why don't we go and look for them?"

It was a spur of the moment suggestion, but her mother latched onto the offer instantly. Minutes later they were leaving Talara, in silence, both aware they were setting off on a journey that could end with a piece of news neither of them would ever recover from. Nobody had given Marianella authorization to do what she was doing; it occurred to her that she was perhaps about to violate several rules and aggravate her situation with the guerrilla army, but she didn't care. And so, after five hours, they arrived at Dabeiba; they crossed the village, left the car on a street where a car had never stopped and walked into the mountains. They kept going as far as the spot where the jungle vegetation swallows the trail, and from there on they followed a mule track. Marianella could not deny that she was surprised to recognize the way. Her legs had not worked so hard in a long time and the cold air stung her nostrils, but on she went as if her body had a memory that was not hers, taking turn-offs she would not have chosen, recognizing a sugar mill she'd seen only once, in passing, the day she and her brother and two other novice *guerrilleros* had walked this same route. They found the hamlet just as night was about to fall, and Marianella approached to describe her problem, ready to confront anyone's scepticism: but luck was on her side again, for the first person she crossed paths with was the same *campesino* who had given her money to pay for her fare to Medellín.

"Shit," the man said. "If it isn't the daughter of Emecías."

Marianella explained that she needed to find her father and her brother, and she needed to do so urgently. She reminded

425

them that she was Comrade Sol, who had served at the President Mao School and her brother was Comrade Raúl. The *campesino* listened to her patiently and then said that Comrade Emecías had been in the zone six months ago. He moved his hand in the air, in the direction of Tierralta, and said:

"He must be up there somewhere, about three days' walk."

"And could you find him? And could you look for my brother?"

"Sure," the man said. "What I need is time."

So they made a deal: the man would go in search of Emecías, taking him a message that they were looking for him and would bring him down to the hamlet.

"And what should we do?" Luz Elena asked.

"Come back in two months," the man said. "We'll meet right here with your papá."

"And my brother," Marianella said.

"Well now. I can't make any promises there."

With that agreement they said goodbye. Marianella and her mother began the trip home feeling the exhaustion of the journey in their shoulders. Luz Elena was out of breath so they talked only in very short bursts.

"The important thing is we've got confirmation," Marianella said. "That Papá is there, I mean."

"There's still your brother," Luz Elena said.

"We're going to find him, Mamá. I swear we're going to find him. And then we'll just have to figure out the most difficult part."

"Getting them out."

"I don't know how we're going to manage that," Marianella said, "so they let them go."

"Without doing anything to them, you mean."

"Without reprisals," said Marianella.

Luz Elena remained silent.

"I think I know how," she said. She was thinking about the children. She had grown fonder of them than her obligations advised, and in other circumstances her reserves of tenderness would have prevented her from even thinking of the blackmail that was already taking shape in her head, but this time the well-being of her own family was at stake. She took a deep breath and said: "If they want me to go get their children, they better let me see my family."

Marianella and Guillermo were married in May, a couple of months after Luz Elena recovered her freedom, in a private ceremony with a priest in attendance, so the grandparents' morals would be safeguarded. Photos from the moment Guillermo put the ring on her finger would survive. He was wearing a yellow shirt and an open jacket with many buttons, and Marianella was in white, a sleeveless white dress with a round neckline, but she had covered her bare shoulders with a heavy shawl that itched. She looked happy. Luz Elena, however, was not convinced of the wisdom of the decision.

"I don't see what you're getting married for," she said. "Go and live with him, but don't get married."

"But I'm in love, Mamá. Why shouldn't I get married?"

"Because you're not seeing things right. You don't realize."

"What?"

"That this isn't love," Luz Elena said. "It's gratitude. And that's not enough to make a life together."

XX

The message was clear, but it came without explanation: on the orders of Comandante Armando, Raúl was to relocate to Central Command on the Tigre plains. He would leave with a detail of five, and he would do so before dawn, because the meeting place was a three-day march away. It was not the most convenient moment to travel. In recent days, the detachment had been carrying out intelligence work for an important military operation: taking a counter-insurgency barracks. It was a large manoeuvre in which some two hundred men would participate; for Raúl it was also an opportunity to regain his confidence in his own abilities, which was still battered after the accident with the explosives (the consequences of which he continued to feel in his arm and face) and which did not improve after his visit to the Emberas. And now they were asking him to go somewhere else?

"And this is to do what?" he asked.

Tomás shook his head. "I know as much as you."

The next day, when the sky began to lighten, they had already been walking for two hours along the San Jorge river valley, in silence throughout, keeping a distance that suited Raúl very well: he wanted to be alone, alone with his uncertainties. What had happened, he wondered, for them to summon him in such an urgent way? Was it a reward that awaited him on the plains, or a punishment? The hours went by in these futile speculations, while he stopped where the group told him to, ate his cooked banana with rice and cassava and filled his bottle with water from the mountain streams. He strung up his hammock to sleep briefly and badly, off the ground where the mapanás slithered. The scout was from Córdoba with a teenager's scant moustache, but the wrinkles around his eyes betrayed an age that was not the same as his easy smile. Several times he tried to start up a conversation, without getting anywhere, and after the second day he stopped trying. By the time they reached the Tigre plains, the man had fallen into the same melancholy silence as Raúl, who didn't even have the presence of mind to apologize for his rudeness. His attention was elsewhere.

Raúl spent the night on the plains. The instructions were clear: the detail that had accompanied him from Tucurá would wait for him right there; Raúl, with a different detail, would continue in the morning to the next destination. The first group didn't know where Raúl was going, and the second knew that and nothing more. The rules of compartmentalization, that elaborate system of secrets, were the keys to the survival of any guerrilla organization, and Raúl was well aware that in that moment he was an actor in a play in which nobody knew more than their own lines. In the morning, before leaving, Comandante Armando revealed the next stage of his mission. "You're going to Galilea," he said. That was an uninhabited village in the Paramillo foothills. Then Raúl understood everything: he was going to see his father, Comrade Emecías, whose detachment had set up camp there.

"We've made a great effort so you can see each other," Armando said.

"But what for?" Raúl asked. "Why am I going to meet him?"

Armando repeated: "We're making a great effort."

It was a two-and-a-half-day walk to Galilea, and when they arrived Raúl discovered he'd barely covered half the journey yet: Galilea was not his final destination. Nobody had warned him, of course, because nobody knew: that information was also compartmentalized. The second detail was made up of people who were quieter and more circumspect, as if being from Central Command had conferred a certain abstract gravity on them, but they didn't know (or pretended not to know) any more than Raúl. He scrutinized their impenetrable faces when they stopped to eat, wondering if they recognized him or if they knew Emecías, but he was unable to clarify anything. When they arrived, one of them said: "We have orders to wait for you, comrade. So do what you have to do and let us know when we should be back."

At that moment his father came out to welcome him. They greeted each other more cautiously than Raúl would have liked. Never, since their separation, had they had the slightest contact, and Raúl realized, with some pain, that neither entirely trusted the other. It was like being back in the plot of *The Spy*. Then he asked:

"Do you want to tell me what's going on?"

"They're waiting for us," Emecías said.

"Who are?"

"Your sister and your mother," Emecías said. "A day's walk away. If you're not too tired, we can leave right now."

That's what they did. Raúl had the impression that his

father had aged. Almost three years had passed since they'd last met, and in that time Fausto had become an old man: he hadn't lost his hair, but it was all white now, as white as a swan's feathers. The skin of his face was stuck to his bones, and that fleshless body was what Raúl had felt when he hugged him. Never before had he understood so clearly the advantages of being stationed in a tropical part of the country, where there was lots of game to hunt – not just cows and peccaries, but also birds of all sizes – and where to fish all you had to do was wade into the river up to your knees when a shoal was swimming upstream and whack your machete into the sandy bed. Up here, not far from the bleak plateau, food was scarce, bodies seemed to close in on themselves and brows were always furrowed, and the damp cold would drain faces of blood, so everyone had the pallor of Bogotanos. Raúl would later find out that the detachment had committed grave military errors and that was why they looked decimated and depressed, and the demoralized combatants walked with their heads bowed and shoulders hunched, as if protecting themselves from the icy winds.

They hadn't been walking for a day but for a day and a half when Raúl found himself at the forest's edge. Emecías handed his rifle to the comrades who had brought them; Raúl, out from the protection of the trees, realized that he had been going down a steep hillside towards a road. Halfway between the woods and a path, fifty paces from the two men, a farmhouse stood out against the dark grey of the cloudy sky. "That's where they should be," Fausto said, and before Raúl could be afraid of not finding them, of having put them in a dangerous situation with all this manoeuvring, the origin of which he knew nothing, the door opened and they both came out, his mother and his sister, smiling and crying at the same time, walking towards them. Luz Elena hugged Sergio.

"You're here," she said. "You're not dead."

"I'm not dead, Mamá."

"You're not dead," she said. "You're here."

It was a long night, but none of the four would have wanted it to end sooner. They slept little, not because they had so much to tell each other, but because they talked about what they would do with the future. Raúl never entirely relaxed, as denunciations were not uncommon in the area, and the worst scenario would be to have to use the revolver he had on his belt. The house was small – a kitchen and one bedroom – and what little light there was made it look even smaller: from the thatched roof hung a single and very weak light bulb. Their host cooked a meat stew, which the men devoured and the women left, because they thought it smelled a bit off. Luz Elena, who hadn't known what to expect, had brought tins of tuna and sardines, condensed milk, three boxes of Mejorales and even a bottle of Agarol in case anyone was constipated, but what captivated Raúl were the Alka-Seltzer tablets, which he began to take as if to alleviate the heaviness not just of that meal but all the meals of the last several years as well. "You're fat," Marianella said. "I don't know how you did it, but you put on weight as a guerrilla." It wasn't fat, but inflammation, as a result of malaria and anaemia. Luz Elena saw it up close when she gave him the new shirt she'd brought him and asked him to try it on. Raúl took off the one he was wearing, and in the weak light the stretch marks on his belly shone.

"Oh, my poor boy," Luz Elena said. "It's as if you'd been pregnant."

After eating, when they sat down to talk, Luz Elena was the most direct. "We're leaving. We're leaving right now," she said. "They're all crazy here. We can't go on being a part of this." Emecías signalled that five hundred metres from the house was the group that was escorting him, and in the other direction, a couple of kilometres away, was the road to the sea, constantly patrolled by the army: to leave now, just like that, was unworkable and even suicidal, and would also condemn them to a life of persecution. But he was carrying his own disappointment, for during the last few years he had been embroiled in a debate with the National Directorate, and at the last congress, when he presented his criticisms, the only response he'd received had been an insulting choice: either he submitted to things as they were, or he resigned from the Party. Raúl, who had spent several months vexed by his disillusionment, discovered there, with his family, that he no longer felt able to go on. At his lowest moments he'd thought about deserting, yes, deserting like a coward, and it wasn't the strength of his convictions that had prevented him, but the disappointment he might cause his imprisoned mother, and the father whose admiration he had always sought. And now they were all here, under the same roof for the first time in three years, each telling their own tale of disenchantment and rage, trying to put into words the sensation that a force they hadn't managed to name had robbed them of three years of their lives. In the semi-darkness, Luz Elena was the first to say it:

"Well, that's it then. We have to find a way out. Tell me how we should do it, but as soon as possible."

It was not so easy. Guerrilla fighters who confronted the Party leaders ran the risk of being declared revisionists or counter-revolutionaries, and their future could be forever stained; those who left the ranks under a cloud, moreover, could suffer unpredictable reprisals. Luz Elena told them that Silvio, the guerrilla she'd been captured with in Bogotá, had just been tried by his detachment for reasons that were unclear. "Shot the way they were going to execute Marianella," she said. Silvio had nothing to do with it, but Luz Elena was putting together a list of grievances against a vague monster, and she was using whatever was useful to build her case. She would have liked their exit to be immediate: that it should happen then and there, that they would be living through their last minutes in the guerrilla army in this *campesino*'s house, that the four of them would walk through that door to return to Medellín, to the Cabrera family's life, to the future that awaited them. But Raúl refused, because none of his many disappointments justified desertion, and because his comrades were still counting on him for an operation.

Luz Elena could not believe it.

"For that you want to go back? This is over now, we've decided that it's over, and you want to go back. To see if this time they do kill you? I don't understand. I really don't understand."

Raúl just said: "They're waiting for me, Mamá."

They talked about getting false papers: identity cards, passports, criminal record clearance certificates with fake names, everything a military blockade might ask to see. "Guillermo can do that," Marianella said, and that's how her brother and father found out that she'd had time in those months to get to know a Party member, a widower and father of three, to fall in love with him and get married. He was a man of convictions as deep as the disappointment he was now feeling: by the time of what happened to Luz Elena, he had already been nursing uncomfortable doubts for some time. They also had to think about money, and then Raúl found out what had happened as soon as he and his sister left home: Comandante Iván had come to see Emecías to talk about the Party and its precarious economic situation, and Emecías, after consulting Luz Elena, had sold the family's properties – one of their two cars, the apartment in Medellín and a valuable lot on the outskirts of Bogotá – and every cent of the sales had gone into the Party's coffers. "We still have some money in the bank," said Emecías, "but we'll have to use it carefully." Outside they could hear the murmur of a nearby stream and, every once in a while, the snoring of the pigs. And so, there amid the sounds of the nocturnal countryside, a plan was gradually hatched.

By the time they lay down, the women on the bed and the men in their hammocks carelessly slung from the porch posts, almost everything was decided. But Raúl, who never really believed he was safe from a denunciation, had trouble getting to sleep. Any sound was a threat; the dark night was full of eyes and armed silhouettes. He decided to take a Mandrax tablet he had in his first-aid kit, and it was a mistake: the early morning hours filled with nebulous hallucinations that were not made of monstrous figures or threatening visions, but rather the incessant feeling of falling into a void, not a long fall, but a feeling of his body slipping down over and over again, and believing, each time, that this time he would find something to grab on to.

Never had he been so grateful to see dawn breaking, even if

it was the frigid dawn of the high plateau, which left frost on the windows and numbed one's hands. He climbed out of his hammock and walked over to one of the frosted windows: on the other side of it, his sister was folding the wool blankets while his mother smoothed her hair.

In the distance a rooster began to crow.

When Raúl returned to the Tigre plains, covering the same distance he'd walked five days earlier, nobody asked him any questions. That silence was enough for Raúl to understand what was evident: the commanders, without knowing everything, knew much more than they let on. His father had warned him. They did not know, of course, that the family had decided to give up the armed struggle; but they knew of Raúl's meeting with his mother, and they also knew his mother was blackmailing the commanders. It had already occurred to him that someone might retaliate just for that. "Don't go to Tucurá, stay here," his father had said. "I don't know what they know, but they know a lot. They have tried to convince me. Comandante Adolfo came to see me, he said he was sent by Central Command. He asked me not to go. My life is here, he said, they need me. It's better if you stay here. We don't know what might happen." Raúl was emphatic. "That's desertion," he said again. "I can't do that to my comrades." "But it's dangerous," his father said. And Raúl: "It's more dangerous to desert. That's really running the risk they might do something to you." Now, back in Tucurá, he saw the comrades who came out to meet him and two ideas flashed through his head: any of them would risk their life for him; any of them, by the same token, would kill him if he deserted. Coming back had been the right decision.

The operation they'd been planning for months took place two days after Raúl got back. According to the intelligence, the counter-insurgency group was occupying a *campesino*'s house a couple of days' march away. The detachment left the zone and walked all night and stayed in hiding the next day, so nobody would notice their presence; and everything seemed to be going well, as it was a clear night with no threat of rain that would slow everything down. They knew they were crossing a ranching area, and they knew that a large group of men on the move would always startle cattle and startled cattle would always stampede away with thudding hoofs; in such cases, hoping to keep the animal quake from giving away the guerrillas, a scout would go on ahead with a small group to frighten the beasts in the direction that best suited them. That's what they did this time, but things didn't turn out the way they should have, for during the night march the large group had split into two. The bolting animals found the gap between the two groups, and Raúl, leading the second group, found himself suddenly facing a stampede heading straight for him, a threatening herd bearing down on him in the darkness, twenty huge, heavy beasts whose implausible speed seemed to come out of a nightmare.

The first charge knocked Raúl over. He barely had time to roll over face down and cover his head with his hands. He never knew how many cows ran over him, but it was not fewer than three, and it seemed to him that those rock-hard legs stomped on him for several minutes. He stood up with difficulty when the stampede had gone, feeling his back wrecked by the hoofs, convinced that any of those blows would have killed him if they'd stepped on his neck. The next morning there was blood in his urine. When they reached the objective, he asked permission to take up a position in the rearguard, and could not have predicted Comandante Armando's response:

"Just the opposite, comrade. You're going first. Pick five men and take the gate."

Raúl thought that rash order might be a disguised privilege, a demonstration of confidence, but it could also be a sort of posthumous punishment: as if the commander knew Raúl was no longer one of them. He wondered fleetingly if he could, at that moment, refuse to do what he'd been ordered to do. If he did, what could happen to him? But he did not rebel: he fulfilled his mission as a combatant, chose five comrades he trusted and even got one of them to trade a rifle for a San Cristobal, which could fire in bursts. Chest to the ground, he dragged himself towards the gate of the property where the counter-insurgency soldiers had taken refuge. The grass was tall in this area where during the day the cows would graze, and it was difficult to move without blades of grass getting in his mouth or eyes, but at that moment his senses were elsewhere: in the darkness of night an attack was always possible. And so Raúl was attentive to the night sounds, trying to separate the slight noise of his comrades from the background noises, when four enormous dogs, the size of panthers, came out of nowhere and leapt on them with growls that struck fear into their bodies.

"What should we do, comrade?" asked one of the others.

"Shoot them," Raúl said. "Otherwise, they'll eat us alive."

It was a few seconds of gunfire. The dogs yowled as the bullets hit them and then sank into the tall grass, dead and dark, while what had happened dawned on the men: it was impossible that the counter-insurgents had not heard the shots, and perhaps in those very seconds were advancing towards them. Raúl gave the order to stay still: it was their only chance of survival.

So, face down in the pasture, they saw dawn break. When the rest of the group caught up with them, they advanced on the enemy's house and found it abandoned: Comandante Armando concluded that the stampede had been louder than they thought, and the enemy had had time to flee. Later, on the way back, Armando confessed to Raúl that he'd heard the shots and was sure he and the others were dead. Raúl couldn't tell if it was relief he heard in his voice, and he found himself lagging behind, trying to confront that novelty: he had been afraid. He realized it had never happened before. It was like an upheaval in the pit of his stomach, and it was also like a strange distraction, as if the urgency was not there, in the risk of losing his life in what might be a painful way, but in his mother's face, his sister's face, his father's face, which appeared to him as a reminder of all that awaited him if he survived. He had spent more than three years constantly feeling the nearness of death and the hope that it was not yet his turn, but that was not the same; and yes, he did wake up every morning with the mute satisfaction of living another day. But these last nights he had been afraid, truly afraid. *He was already on the way out*: that's what he was thinking without ever putting it into words.

Later he would find out that at that very instant when he was going through those absurd nights of stampedes and murdered dogs, Luz Elena was meeting with two Party members in Medellín and telling them her conditions: she would only go to pick up the commanders' children once her own son and husband were back home, safe and sound, with sufficient guarantees that nobody would carry out reprisals against them.

Of course, she reminded them of all that the Cabrera family had done for the Party, all the money, all the sweat, all the loyalty they had given since their return to Colombia; she reminded them that Fausto was respected and admired by the Communist Party of China, and she dared to say that without his name the Colombians would be nothing but an orphaned sect. But maybe it wasn't necessary, because in the end there was one simple truth: if things did not go as she said they should, the commanders' children would remain prisoners of the Family Welfare Institute. And the comrades understood that.

The following three weeks were the most arduous of his life. For the first time in his memory, Raúl felt that his destiny was not in the revolution, even if he was still there, in an encampment of revolutionaries, training with them, eating with them and singing the Internationale in unison with them. The commanders summoned him on one of those days to tell him that Central Command had been deliberating and, after lengthy discussions, had reached the conclusion that Comrade Raúl's training and talents could be put to better uses. That's why they'd made the decision to send him back to China, to continue his ideological and military studies in the best possible conditions, so he could be, when the time was right, indispensable to the revolutionary process of his country. It was a pantomime, of course, for Raúl already knew that the decision about his exit had been made, and the commanders knew that Raúl knew, but everyone played their roles brilliantly. Nights of mistrust and uncertainty followed, as well as something that could only be called nostalgia: nostalgia for what he would leave in the jungle, all the dreams, all the emotions, all the great projects he had once had, all the hopes he had brought back from his years in Peking, those strange years which culminated here: on this damp November morning when Raúl packed up his things and solemnly handed his rifle over to Comandante Tomás, and then took to the trail again: the same several days' march he'd done a month earlier, which this time would take him to Central Command, to his father, to the meticulous plan the family had designed so that the two of them, Emecías and Raúl, Fausto and Sergio, could return to the world safely.

The plan was complicated, but it was a matter of not running risks. Sergio arrived at the same rustic house where he had previously met his family; there, waiting for him, was his father, who had arrived the night before in the company of six comrades from his detachment. A brief ceremony that nobody had planned suddenly began to happen as if it had a life of its own. The guerrillas sang their anthems, the usual ones, but Sergio had never heard them sung with less enthusiasm.

> *Fatigue, hunger, bullets,*
> *nothing can stop me,*
> *because my hope is up ahead*
> *and that's where my duty guides me.*

Sergio and his father spent the night on their own, in a dense silence, as breaking it might send them down rocky paths with unpredictable consequences. Sergio would have liked to tell him how much he loved him, but he couldn't figure out how: it was as if they could no longer say things like that to each other. The only possible topic of conversation in those hours was that of the instructions: the next day a comrade would take them to another house, and from there, on horseback, they'd ride for several hours to the place where Marianella would be waiting for them in her car, with a change of clothes for each of them and the documents they'd need to return to Medellín without fearing the checkpoints.

"It's a bridge," Fausto said. "Near the road to the sea. If everything goes right there, nobody'll be able to stop us."

The next morning, very early, a sentry came and told them an army patrol was approaching. For a few minutes, Sergio thought it had been a mistake to hand over their weapons: he felt naked and vulnerable and civilian. When the same man came back with good news – the patrol had taken a different trail – Sergio wondered if he'd ever get used to a life that was not clandestine. Time seemed to have taken on its own rhythm and the snags piled up: the guide who was to lead them to the second house never showed up, and Fausto and Sergio had to accept the services of a dark-haired and dim-witted young man, son of a neighbouring household, whose mother offered him in these terms: "Adalberto is a little backward, but we've never lost him." In spite of a few unnecessary detours and a circle traced with a cartographer's precision, which made them lose an entire hour's travel time, Adalberto did end up getting them to the house where the horses were. They were alarmed to find that the person who was supposed to take them hadn't arrived yet, as nobody knew what could have delayed him so much, but in any case they had no choice but to wait: the rest of the trip could not be done on foot without it costing them another whole day. They sat in a dark corridor and waited, and when two hours had gone by they started to suspect that something had gone wrong in the day's scheme.

But then they heard horses' hoofs. When they went out to greet the rider, they were met with a caricature: he was an old-fashioned Antioquian muleteer complete with a *carriel* shoulder bag, palm-leaf hat and poncho, and he was so drunk that it was a miracle of his education that he was able to stay in the saddle. He brought the other two horses tied to the tail of his. "A sonofabitch," he shouted from on high. "That's what I am, a sonofabitch. How late I am, man, it's unforgiveable." Fausto tried to reassure him. "Calm down, calm down," he said. "It doesn't matter, we can still make it on time." "No, not on time, not nothing. No, señor: what I am is a sonofabitch. Let me tell you a secret: I'm inebriated." His tongue got tangled up in the word, and there was something admirable in the obstinacy with which he finally got it out. "I'm in-ee-bri-ay-ted," he said. "What a sonofabitch to do this to you, right?" He insisted so much, and it was so obvious that they would never get out of there until the man had received his rhetorical punishment, that Fausto got close enough to smell the stench of fresh vomit on his breath, and addressed him in perfect Castilian Spanish.

"Well, yes, actually, you are a son of a bitch," he said. "But let's get going now, please."

They had arranged a meeting place with Marianella at the entrance to the bridge, on a part of the shoulder where a car could stop without arousing suspicions, and also a precise time, seven at night, as it was advisable for them to move under the cover of darkness. She would be waiting for them there in her car; but it was dangerous to be out in the open and in plain sight of everyone, including the patrols it was not impossible they would run into around there, so Sergio and his father would hide at the edge of the road, protected by the vegetation

443

like in a Rousseau painting, and would wait for the signal before coming out of their hiding place. The car lights: that's how she would signal to them. On, off. On, off. Nothing could be easier.

That morning, at an early hour, Marianella had sought the help of her cousins. They were the sons of one of Luz Elena's brothers, and would have done her this favour even if their grandparents hadn't told them to. They checked over their jeep, a big, beige Nissan they'd all be able to squeeze into. The plan was to take a guitar and a pot of food, so they'd look like a family on a weekend outing, but Guillermo had an idea: they should also bring a couple of their children, a three- and a five-year-old, so the situation would look even more plausible.

"When the police see children they screw you over less," he said.

So that's what they did. Punctual and enthusiastic, Marianella's cousins picked her up along with the children and they left Medellín with plenty of time to spare. Shortly before arriving at Mutatá, as they came around a difficult curve, a bus that had misjudged the width of the road invaded their lane. Later they would tell how the elder cousin, who was driving, calculated the distances in a fraction of a second and thought it would be easy to swerve and avoid it with a yank on the steering wheel. It wasn't. The collision was head-on and only the bus's lack of speed as it was driving uphill prevented a tragedy. The Nissan ricocheted off the bus and its right tyre was punctured by one of the boundary stones that line Colombian roads to mark distances or commemorate accident victims. The tyre was flat; and then, when he crouched down to examine the chassis, their cousin discovered an even more serious matter.

"Is everyone alright?" he asked. "Are the kids OK?"

The children were crying, although they had suffered no more than a fright. Marianella, however, was beside herself.

"Now we're really fucked," she said. "Now everything's really gone to shit."

Crouched among plants, in a ditch in the mountains, Fausto and Sergio tried not to let impatience get the better of them. They couldn't see anyone on the bridge. The guide, who by then had sobered up, though he still felt guilty, offered to look for a car blinking its headlights. He went away and came back twice before he said:

"I don't see any cars, but there are some lights. This is very strange."

"What kind of lights?" asked Fausto.

"I don't know," the guide said. "All I know is that they're not car lights."

Before his father could stop him, Sergio jumped out of the ditch. "I'm going to go see," he said. He approached slowly, walking along the edge of the road, barely able to distinguish the gradient of the asphalt, the imprecise line of tar devoured by vegetation. It was a clear night, luckily, and a waning moon revealed the outlines of things. Suddenly a faint sound reached him and grew sharper as he walked: the strumming of a guitar. Were his ears playing tricks on him? Who was going to start singing in the middle of the night in a place as remote as this? There were voices, too, voices of children who were singing or playing (it was hard to tell). "Hush, be quiet," said a male voice. It was all too strange not to keep going, but Sergio realized those were the longest five hundred metres he had ever walked.

Then, abruptly, the music stopped, and Sergio knew they'd seen him, and in the middle of the night's black canvas two lights blinked on and off. But instead of feeling relieved, Sergio thought his luck had run out, because those were not car lights, no car in the world had lights like those two small eyes, too close together, like the lanterns of a group of explorers. They turned on and off, as if trying clumsily to make the signal, but they did not blink in unison, and the whole thing seemed like a bad theatre production.

Shit, he thought. He also thought: It's a trap.

Then he heard, in the silence of the night, his sister's voice.

"It's us," she said. "Are you both there?"

While Sergio and their father changed their clothes, Marianella told them what had happened: the accident, the bus that had waited for more than an hour, the fear of missing the meeting or of one of the mechanisms of fate, which seemed to be conspiring against the family, thwarting all their plans. The guitar had been the idea of one of their cousins, who had brought it along to convince whoever needed convincing that they were out for a drive in the country. By some lucky coincidence, there had been a torch in the Nissan's glove compartment, and the other was Marianella's, who had packed it without a thought – a guerrilla habit – in the bag with the documents she was now showing them, one by one, while she explained what Guillermo had managed to obtain.

There were the transitory identities that would enable them to get somewhere safe; later they'd get passports, but that would take longer and required recent photographs. Sergio did not pay too much attention at that moment, because part of his mind was still vigilant, watching every movement of the leaves under the timid moon, alert to every sound in the night. Seven people were waiting at the edge of a mountain road, and they would have looked suspicious to anyone; but they had no choice except to wait for the first bus that went by, although security precautions would require them to separate afterwards. Fausto would stay at Talara, the Cárdenas family farm, but Sergio would go on to Medellín, to spend the night in his grandparents' house, and then to Popayán, where Guillermo had a network of contacts and could get him a fake passport. When the bus pulled up, after half an hour that their nervousness stretched out, they hadn't had time to say goodbye, and Sergio knew that from then on they had to pretend not to know each other. He suddenly remembered the meticulous plans they had concocted in the *campesino*'s house, and was struck by the realization that he would not see his father again until they all arrived at the final destination of their escape. So, these were the last words they would exchange for a long time. It seemed his father was thinking the same thing.

"This is it," Fausto said. "See you in China."

They boarded the bus like strangers. Fausto sat in one of the first rows and Sergio walked to the back, many seats away, and from there he stared at his father's white hair, shining up ahead. Through the window he looked at those who were staying. His sister, a little blond boy, a little boy with black hair: long training had accustomed him to pretence, and his sister now seemed such a stranger to him that he didn't even feel the impulse to raise a hand and wave goodbye. There weren't many passengers on the bus. Sergio counted seven tired women and men; he imagined they were coming home after a long

447

day's work on a local ranch, one of the sugar mills higher up or a farm like their grandparents' farm. The street lights passed beside him and Sergio could think only that he had spent all the years of his adolescence, all those of his incipient adulthood, preparing himself for something that had not taken place. How much physical effort, he thought, how much mental stubbornness, how much discipline and vocation and how many sacrifices to be part of that marvellous mission: to bring about the revolution, create the new man, change this world into one where people suffered less or where nobody suffered. And now he was here: running away from all that with the single anxiety of not getting caught. What was this, if not resounding failure? At twenty-two years of age, travelling in a bus with fake ID, leaving behind everything he'd invested his whole life in, what was Sergio Cabrera if not a failure? This was what he was thinking when the bus stopped at a roadside shop. His father got out without looking back; Sergio saw him walk up to the wooden counter and order something. Then the bus pulled away and the white-haired head was left behind just as a whole life was left behind, closing without opening a new one. The bus continued on into the dark night along mountain roads, and Sergio thought that if there was an accident and the bus went over the cliff and he died at the bottom of the gully, there would be nothing to regret, nothing would have been lost, all things considered.

Two unreal weeks followed, lived outside the world, or between two worlds that framed Sergio's disoriented life: that of the guerrillas abandoned for ever and that of the empty future, which was like a blurry film poorly projected onto a bad screen.

Sergio spent the first night of his new life in Medellín, in his grandparents' house, where he almost burst into tears when he caught sight of himself in the hall mirror, as it was the first time he'd seen his own body, his own face, since he'd joined the guerrillas before he'd even turned nineteen, and he didn't entirely recognize himself in the hardened man reflected back at him. His mother had packed a suitcase and got together some money for him. Everyone treated him as if he were back from the dead, or, Sergio would think later, as if he were heading towards death, for nobody was at all sure about what might happen over the coming days, much less the coming years. Only the general outline of the plan had been fixed. Sergio would leave Colombia, would arrive in Mexico City, would meet Luz Elena and somehow they would fly together to Peking, where Fausto, if everything went well, would be waiting for them. When Sergio asked about Marianella, his mother's eyes widened.

"Well, she's going to stay, what did you expect?" Luz Elena said. "She's a married woman now and she's staying with her husband. And she has to be a mother to three children as well, imagine that."

"You don't think it's a good idea?"

"She made up her mind, and that's what she decided," Luz Elena said.

Sergio travelled all night. When he arrived at Popayán bus station, a man who was going to give him shelter while his papers were being prepared was waiting for him. He was an agronomist who lived with his Brazilian wife on the outskirts of the city. He had been a Party activist years ago, but without ever taking up arms, and very soon he had withdrawn entirely;

now he helped Guillermo once in a while with his personal missions. That's how Sergio found out that this man, political secretary of the Valle sector, leader of the patriotic front where they raised Muscovy ducks, had spent several years living a sort of revolutionary schizophrenia, as he had enough conviction left to carry on as an activist, but he devoted much of his energy to getting people out and protecting those who left. For Sergio, one truth was obvious: Guillermo was the only reason Marianella was alive. And now, thanks to him, Sergio had this comfortable bed in a house not entirely lacking luxuries on the outskirts of Popayán, and thanks to him a network of complicities had been set in motion to get him false papers.

A man came to the house to take Sergio's passport photo. Sergio asked how long until he would receive the document. The man looked at him mockingly. "It'll take as long as it takes." While he was waiting, Sergio took the risk of going into Popayán a couple of times. He did so with the collusion of the agronomist, who even offered a couple of pieces of advice, since Sergio did not know the city, and three years in the jungle had given him a craving for concrete and lights and traffic. Walking aimlessly around the new part of the city, he came across a theatre advertising a film with an incomprehensible title, A Clockwork Orange, and when he came out he felt the risk of visiting the city had been worth it.

The man who had taken his photo showed up unannounced one Saturday morning. The passport worried Sergio and at the same time made him smile: the page numbers were not consecutive, his badly pasted photo looked like a school project, and the distinguishing features listed did not coincide with the persistent truth of his face. According to the document, Sergio was a man of 180 centimetres in height, swarthy complexion, honey-coloured eyes and aquiline nose. "Dragon nose," his Chinese classmates had called him: that taunt, which had hurt his feelings at the time, now came back to him as something resembling nostalgia. No, he no longer had a dragon nose, or the green eyes that intimidated his classmates at Chong Wen School, nor was he called Sergio Cabrera Cárdenas, much less was he Raúl, the EPL comrade: his name was Atilio San Juan, and his profession merchant seaman. The process was obvious: two passports had been turned into one. And if it was obvious to him, Sergio thought, it could also be obvious to the authorities.

Luckily, the group of people helping him was aware of this. The day of his trip, the agronomist drove him to Cali airport, 150 kilometres or so north, as if he were just a regular passenger. During the three long hours of the drive, the man wanted to hear what Sergio had made of Kubrick's film, and then he explained broadly speaking what would happen. A young couple would be waiting for him in the terminal, in front of the check-in counters, and the three of them would then leave and walk around the building and go in through the kitchen. There weren't a lot of people involved in this operation, but they were all loyal to Guillermo, so there was nothing to worry about. The agronomist said this to Sergio without knowing that these words – *there's nothing to worry about* – had traditionally proved to be the best reason to worry about everything. But later, after entering the airport through the back door, beside bins of stinking garbage, and after walking between women with stained aprons and aluminium surfaces, Sergio found himself sitting in a departure lounge waiting for his flight and he regretted his own mistrust. He did not have to go through the immigration procedures, and that was the important thing: to make sure that no Colombian authority set eyes on his home-made passport. Once he'd left the country, it would be another story, but here, in Colombia, this grotesque document would not stand up to the slightest official scrutiny. When he boarded without any trouble, he thought the obstacle had been over-come. He was already in his seat when a flight attendant's voice came over the loudspeaker; she mentioned a technical problem and asked all the passengers to leave the plane.

Sergio felt in an irreconcilable way that everything had reached its end. The police had discovered and pursued him, or someone had sold him out: maybe the passport maker was an agent who'd infiltrated the group; maybe the agronomist or his Brazilian wife were not who they said they were. He disembarked with the rest of the passengers and took a seat again in the departure lounge, spent long minutes thinking about his mother and his sister, and about Guillermo, whose efforts had gone astray somewhere along the line. To live in fear, hunted, always looking over his shoulder: no, there had to be another life. And that life was there, within reach, but something had derailed it at the last moment, and it was only a matter of seconds before three police agents would arrive to arrest him, handcuff him and take him out of the airport towards this country's dungeons. Sergio was thinking of that, giving up everything as lost, when the flight attendant appeared and said loudly that the technical trouble had been resolved – a tyre had needed changing – that they appreciated everyone's patience and apologized, and that they could board the plane again: the flight to Panama City was ready for take-off.

Sergio thought it would be much easier to believe in God, in some god responsible for inventing this incident so that there, queuing up for the second time, boarding again the plane that would take him out of the country, he realized the enormity of his desire to leave, the visceral urgency of breaking with everything and starting from scratch. Those ideas remained fixed in his head minutes later when the plane took off and headed north, flying over the River Cauca and then over the mountains of the eastern cordillera of the Andes. It was a day of clear skies and Sergio saw the land through the little window with an insolent clarity: the portions of every shade of green in the world, the water of the rivers glinting like machete blades, the whole country where so many had done so much harm, where he had harmed as much as others. When the plane flew higher and clouds covered everything and the land was no longer visible, Sergio could only think in words of farewell. Goodbye, friends. Goodbye, enemies. Goodbye, Colombia.

XXI

According to what he told me himself, Sergio Cabrera came out of the Filmoteca de Catalunya forty-four years later, took a left at plaza Salvador Seguí and walked towards the Rambla del Raval. It was almost eleven at night. Beside him, in a silence that was not uncomfortable, was his son Raúl, who had just seen *The Strategy of the Snail* for the first time on a cinema screen, and, in it, his grandfather converted into a leader of a neighbourhood rebellion. "That role suits Tato," he'd said, and Sergio answered the way he liked to: "That's because he was playing himself." Raúl was very far removed from the stories they'd been talking about since Thursday evening, which now felt like a long time ago, until this Saturday, the final hours of which were coming to an end. They had been three days of interrupted conversations, interrupted not just by the commitments to the Filmoteca, but by the many things people never say that need to be said; three days in which Sergio would have liked to tell his eighteen-year-old son about the life of his father, who had just died at the age of ninety-two, aware that he had barely scratched the surface of that stubborn past.

In any case, Sergio managed to be briefly happy with Raúl. In Barcelona, they were just two people strolling, part of the formless beast of tourism, a father and son who lived separate lives in distant cities and who had now met to tell each other how much they loved and missed each other in the oldest way of all: by telling stories. Sergio had spent many years telling his friends about his life, at dinners or on trips, but nothing similar had happened with Raúl, because things didn't work like that in Fausto and Luz Elena's house: the past was not spoken of there. Now he realized he'd never told his son so many things, perhaps until now seeing him as a child who would not have understood them; and if he had ever explained where his name came from, he was sure that after this weekend it would be as if his son understood it for the first time.

"Fuck," Raúl said. "What a load of things lie behind my name."

"We could just say you're named after me," Sergio said. "And leave it at that."

He didn't tell him about the furious reactions from some of his Spanish relatives when they found out the origin of his name. Sergio, of course, would have liked to explain his reasons, but he knew very well that they weren't clear even to him. His first daughter was called Lilí, the name the Chinese had given to Marianella in the long ago time they'd spent in Peking; his second daughter's name, Valentina, was that of his mother in her years as a militant. It was as though he refused to let go of the past, even if it was sometimes the painful past that everyone in the family had tried to leave behind. That's what Marianella had done: years after leaving the guerrilla forces, when she'd already built a life with Guillermo – was married and expecting her first child – she spent a whole day on paperwork with a notary to officially remove her first name from all records.

Sergio remembered the letter in which she told him. "I got rid of Sol," she wrote. "I never want to hear that name again."

Marianella often spoke of that: of how much her guerrilla past still hurt her, of the almost physical efforts she had made to forget all that had happened in those years, of the regrets, the guilt, the hatred. Yes, that too, and Sergio, whose emotions never reached the nuclear intensity of those of his sister, understood very well what she meant, and also understood that his sister always lacked words to embody the depths of her disappointment. Some years later, reading Vasily Grossman's novel *Life and Fate*, Sergio found a sentence that knocked the dust off some of his most uncomfortable memories: *Sometimes men going into battle together hate each other more than they do their common enemy.* He sent Marianella a photograph of the underlined sentence, without any comments or gloss, and she replied with five bitter words: *There's nothing more to say.* Of course, she carried the past in a way that Sergio could not have understood entirely no matter how hard he tried, and everyone in the family remembered that medical appointment (in the 1990s) when the X-rays were showing worrying shadows and a doctor even spoke of lung cancer, later realizing that it was not malignant tissue that was showing up in the images, but the fragments of a bullet when a comrade had shot in the back.

When they arrived at the hotel, after walking past Fernando Botero's bronze cat, Raúl said to his father: "Will you buy me a drink at the rooftop bar?" It was a clear night; a breeze made the candles tremble inside their glasses and made life difficult for those trying to light cigarettes, and in the sky stars would have been visible were it not for the glow of the city. They sat down facing the dark tiled roofs, five seats away from the bar where

Sergio, three nights earlier, had seen Montjuic with new eyes and had begun to think of his father, of his Civil War stories, of his life as an exiled adolescent. By the time he was Raúl's age, Fausto Cabrera had fled his country and gone hungry in the Dominican Republic. At Raúl's age, Sergio was living his paradoxical Peking life as a Red Guard and privileged foreigner, and preparing to undergo military training with the Communist Party. What had Raúl done? Gone to school like all children, lived a few years with his father in Colombia, spent a normal Spanish adolescence that had brought him here, to a peaceful rooftop bar in a peaceful city, to order a San Miguel beer at the dawn of adulthood. Maybe this, the gift of normality, was better than leaving him a fortune. That's what Sergio was thinking when Raúl asked him why he hadn't gone to the burial.

"He was cremated," Sergio said.

"All the same, why didn't you go?"

"I don't know. Because I wouldn't have known what to say." There was a long silence that Sergio knew well: it was the silence of unsatisfactory answers. "I always had that trouble with him," he continued. "Tato was an actor, a reciter of poetry, a man who lived by his voice. I was never like that. Not with him. I never knew how to say things, and he hated that. He used to say my silences were torture. No, it wasn't worth going, what for? To remain silent, to torture him once more, one last time, with the silence he detested? No, it wouldn't have been worth it."

"And why didn't you send something?"

"Nobody told me I could," Sergio said. "And my sister wasn't going to go to the cemetery. Who would have read it?"

"I don't know, Papá. Anyone. Someone would have read it out and you would feel better right now."

"Maybe," Sergio said.

"And wasn't it painful not to be there?"

"Maybe," Sergio said again. "But you ask me why I didn't go and all I can tell you is that I don't regret it. Tomorrow you're going back to Málaga and Monday I go back to Lisbon, but these days here have been important. For me they have, anyway."

Raúl said: "For me too."

Sergio stretched out his hand and touched his son's face: almost a caress. He felt a new roughness against his palm, skin that was no longer a child's. Raúl was asking more questions and Sergio answered as best he could, just as he'd done on the previous days, but now, on the rooftop, he had an idea that absurdly had not occurred to him earlier. On his computer he had some photos from those times, and he could also write to Marianella to ask her to send a few more. Over the years, he'd been scanning old photos, because they were starting to deteriorate and nobody wanted them to be entirely lost, so it would be very easy to spend a bit of time searching through the hard drive, if Raúl felt like staying up late. Raúl raised his hand.

"Let's get the bill," he said.

In November 1972, Sergio and Luz Elena arrived in Hong Kong with the feeling of coming back from the dead. It was the end of their escape, or that's how it felt, because they had completed this long journey looking over their shoulders, sure that a series of faceless dangers awaited them somewhere. It seemed inexplicable that it had all gone to plan. It was inexplicable that Sergio had been able to get out of Colombia without mishap; it was miraculous that the merchant seaman Atilio San Juan had successfully got through immigration at Mexico

458

City International Airport, and that the disenchanted revolutionary Sergio Cabrera could have taken a taxi without anyone following him. But that's what happened: Sergio stayed at a hotel called Sevilla, on calle Bucareli, spent the afternoon looking at second-hand books on calle Donceles and that evening went to a scruffy cinema where they were showing *The Conformist*. And the next day, very early, he showed up unannounced at the Embassy of the People's Republic of China.

"My name is Li Zhi Qiang," he said. "My code is 02911730. I need to get in touch with the Party's Military Commission."

"The son of Specialist Cabrera," a man said. "Yes, he's already been here."

So Sergio found out that his father had covered the same route that he was now hurrying to cover, and he imagined him now installed, despite his convictions, at the Friendship Hotel. As the man explained, the embassy would be very pleased to organize his return trip to China, a complete itinerary that would go via Hong Kong and include the flight to Peking. "We understand that your mother will travel with you," the official said. "We understand she will be landing in a few days." Sergio confirmed it, but was left with the feeling, as uncomfortable as a badly sewn seam in the collar of a shirt, that the embassy staff knew more about his own life than he did himself.

During the long trip to Hong Kong, Luz Elena told Sergio all that had happened since they'd last parted at his grandparents' house. So Sergio heard that his mother, true to her word, had collected the commanders' children from the Family Welfare Institute and had been moved to tears by the children's hugs. It was hard for her to leave them in a clandestine flat of an urban cell, in the hands of people they didn't know, with no guarantee that anyone there would take good care of them, but Marianella assured her that her anxieties would reach the appropriate ears. They did so through Guillermo, whose contacts were still good despite the fact that he too had begun to make a life outside the guerrilla forces. They were living in Popayán, Luz Elena told him. Marianella had the opportunity to earn some money drawing architectural plans. One of Guillermo's brothers, an engineer, had set her a test, with no great expectations, just to try to help the family. But Marianella had demonstrated talent as a draughtswoman, which surprised her as much as it did everyone else. Everything seemed to be on track.

At the Chinese border, the official who took their passports looked long and hard at Sergio's, or rather, at merchant seaman Atilio San Juan's, and said: "This stays here." Sergio tried to protest or defend himself, but his Chinese, learned in Peking, was useless in Canton. Suddenly the apprehension and anguish and paranoia returned, for, in spite of the intervention of an interpreter, the passport did not go beyond the border, but stayed there, confiscated, like a stupid metaphor of a snared life. It was incomprehensible: the Chinese authorities had to know the passport was false, because otherwise they would not have allowed the entrance of someone whose name did not match up with his military code. Sergio hated Atilio San Juan, or rather envied him with the kind of envy that's so intense we confuse it with hatred. He envied him because he would have liked to be him: a merchant sailor with no past, with no regrets, no problems, boss of his own future, who slept well at night. For Sergio, on the other hand, the nights had turned into torment, and he frequently woke up with a sensation of enclosure he'd never felt before, and the darkness speed up his heart rate until his hand found the switch and turned on his bedside lamp. Then he would think of that Poe story about a cataleptic who was buried alive, and feel ashamed of himself. He didn't talk about that with anybody, because he didn't want them to think he was afraid of the dark like a child, and he didn't know how to explain what happened to him in any other way. He told himself it was a matter of time; that now, arriving in Peking to put a broken life back together, everything would gradually recover its normality. As they crossed the Chinese border, Luz Elena had said: "Isn't it strange that a person can walk from one world to another?" And maybe that's what it was, a change of worlds, that Sergio needed to be well again.

Peking was familiar, strangely familiar, and Sergio was happy to be back, but the happiness was not flawless, because something had broken in his relationship with Fausto. Sometimes it seemed as though his father had arrived from Colombia with an unspoken resentment, as if he blamed someone for the failure of his guerrilla adventure; he began to lead an isolated life, getting up very early for his sessions of t'ai chi ch'uan, having lunch on his own schedule at the restaurant. It was during those days that he decided that what happened in Colombia would not be spoken of at his table. It was like a contrived prolongation of the prohibitions of clandestine life, but the only thing he achieved was to corrode the complicities that had built up slowly over time. The silences at the table became as painful as the leishmaniasis wound quietly rotting away, without warning, until the damage was already serious. Sergio, against all expectations, discovered that he needed to talk about the guerrillas, and found ways to do so. He got in touch with his old friends from Chong Wen School, who organized a get-together in his honour that resembled a banquet: it was a table for twenty that ended where a dais began, and on the dais five of his former comrades took turns leading cheers to the international proletariat, singing songs beneath a colourized portrait of Mao to honour their Colombian comrade who had taken up arms with the People's Liberation Army of his country. For all of them, Sergio was a hero. It was impossible to explain that he saw himself as a fraud.

The best thing about his return was the reunion with Carl Crook. He arrived unexpectedly at the Friendship Hotel, not long before the last day of the year, because he'd heard a rumour that the Cabreras were back. He seemed taller than the last time they'd seen each other, even after taking off his Chinese cap that added a few centimetres, and he had grown an unkempt beard. He did not hide his disappointment when he found out Marianella had stayed in Colombia, but a timid smile of sad satisfaction appeared on his face when he heard of her marriage. "I find it hard to imagine," he said. "But if you say she's happy . . ." They talked of all this in long conversations in the hotel, in the Friendship Shop, in the Summer Palace where Carl had been the young boyfriend of a rebellious teenager. It was as if they had just realized they were friends: as if they'd put a name, after so many years of absence, to an old complicity. Sergio told Carl all that had happened to him in his three and a half years of life in the jungle. He told him about Fernando, about Isabela, about Sol and Valentina and the vampire bats, and he showed him the scars on his skin and on one of those many days he allowed himself the sentimentality of talking about other scars. Carl, for his part, gave him the latest news on what his family had suffered since April 1968, when the guards took David Crook out of his small cell and took him to Qincheng high security prison.

As soon as she found out about the transfer, Isabel began proceedings to try to free her husband. She tried to explain to anyone who would listen that it was a mistake, that the accusations of espionage were baseless, that David had spent twenty years working for communism. Her sons watched her move with dedication and industry and it never occurred to them that she would not succeed: Isabel always achieved what she set out to achieve. But one day, months after David's arrest, Isabel was arrested as well. There was nothing her children – three adolescent boys – could do against the machinations of the Cultural Revolution. China, the country where they had been born, grown up and whose language they spoke, had declared the Crooks a family of enemies, and the three brothers began a life of solitude that Carl always compared to what he had seen in the Cabreras.

"This is how the Colombians lived," he'd say to his brothers. "And if they could do it, so can we."

Paul, his youngest brother, learned to cook wonderfully well; Michael, the most physical of the three, took out his frustrations on his bicycle, or swimming at the hotel when the pool was open; Carl spent his time studying English, which he'd always seen from afar, like a second-hand tool, and in a short time he was not only reading Shakespeare, but doing so with pleasure. When Isabel was freed, as unexpectedly as she'd been taken, she told them where she had spent all those months. She asked them to lean out of the window of their own apartment in the Foreign Languages Institute and pointed up, towards one of the top floors of the tower block next door. "That's where I was," Isabel said. "Every day I saw you from there. And if any of you had looked up, you would have seen me." As soon as she was set free, Isabel immediately resumed proceedings to free her husband, and she did so with her hope intact, in spite of more than four and a half years having passed since his arrest. At first, nothing seemed to happen, but one night in May Isabel arrived at the apartment with her face transformed, gathered her three sons in the room with the Russian chairs and said:

"Let's go see your dad."

The encounter was not in Qincheng, but in a prison in the city. The guards led them to a classically constructed courtyard, which looked more like a temple than a prison, and there they waited for hours. Carl didn't know what he was going to find, and neither did his brothers. His father appeared freshly shaved; he had lost so much weight that his trousers were too big for him and, since they'd taken away his belt out of fear he might harm himself, he had to hold them up with one hand so they wouldn't fall down. Carl hugged him, his brothers hugged him, their mother hugged him and kissed him, despite such displays of affection running counter to Chinese custom. "If I'd met you in the street, I wouldn't have recognized you," David told them. His voice was not the same as Carl remembered and their conversation was cold, since the guards never moved more than a few metres away from them, but that's how the visit went: the family sitting on one side of a table and David opposite them, as if subject to yet another interrogation. But the important thing was that they were together, that David was alive and had not gone mad in the solitude of the prison. It was also permissible to think that something was changing in the

464

Party authorities, in the conscience of that anonymous power that was responsible for his imprisonment. Perhaps this visit was the prelude to better things, and perhaps a herald of liberty.

From then on, the Party allowed them to see him once a month. In those conversations Carl talked to him about Shakespeare, because nothing gave his father more pleasure, and his father told them about his life in Qincheng. His cell was a rectangle, four metres long and two wide, in which there were only three objects: a rickety bed, a toilet and a ceramic sink. Food came in through a hatch that opened at floor level: the prisoner would have to get down on all fours like a dog to receive it. He'd had time to read three times the four volumes of the complete works of Mao, in an English translation that Isabel had sent him at just the right moment; but he also did exercises, to strengthen his back, and he always did them in a position that allowed him to see the sky – the moon, a bird – through the barred window of the cell. One morning every two months they took him to a spacious cell with an open ceiling where he could see the sky and the branches of a tree that poked in; on the untended floor of the cell, in the springtime, weeds grew, and among the weeds, dandelions. David managed to pick three, one for each of his sons, and he saved them, without the guards noticing, between the pages of the Little Red Book. One day when they finally set him free, he would bring them this book as a gift.

Paul wanted to know if he was well treated. David explained that he had never been tortured, not even beaten. Of course, he hated what the guards did to him, the small insults and small humiliations, but he managed not to hate them; when they called him Mister Fascist with those voices full of hatred,

David was happy inside because hating fascism was a virtue. For months they deprived him of access to newspapers and the radio, and David discovered he needed news of the world more than music; so later, when they offered him the *People's Daily*, he did not hesitate to accept even though his Chinese was still mediocre. He set himself the task of perfecting it to be able to know which country had invaded the Soviet Union or how the war in Vietnam was going, and if the guards refused him the day's paper, David thought it must be because there was some news about his case. They interrogated him at regular intervals. The sessions began with the reading of some of Mao's words, painted in red ink on a larger than usual *dazibao*:

Indulgence for those who confess,
severity for those who resist.

But David had nothing to confess. On one occasion, in a moment of weakness – thinking of his sons, he explained, thinking of seeing them again – he invented a charge of espionage in the liberated territories, back in the 1940s, to see if they'd let him out once and for all. But the next day, repentant, he withdrew the confession, and he had never seen his interrogators so angry. That's why what they announced to him a few months later was so surprising: "Mr Crook, you are going to recover your liberty. It won't be a matter of days, of course, but it will be soon." They didn't tell him anything more.

The lives of the Crook family began to revolve around those monthly visits, now with the prospect of freedom on the horizon. What the three brothers and even Isabel did or stopped doing depended on the next interview, on what David had asked for: getting hold of documents by Lenin, Stalin and Mao, for a book he was writing in his cell; doing some physical exercise, yes, but always continuing to study, because Marx and Engels said at that age the mind is most receptive; keeping abreast of the workers' movement in England, planning their future. One of those days, Paul exploded: "What future if you're stuck in here? And you're always talking about working for the cause, for China. But look what China's done to you. Look what communism has done to you." Carl agreed: "The Cultural Revolution is the worst thing that's ever happened to us." David answered with a ferocity he had not used since they were children. "It's not the revolution's fault or communism's," he barked at them. "China has given us everything."

The visit ended with a bitter tension in the air. Since then, Carl said, they hadn't spoken.

"And now what's going to happen?" Sergio asked.

"I wish I knew," Carl said. "Sometimes I think that somebody somewhere already knows. And that's the most frightening thing."

At the end of the month, Sergio met with Carl at the Friendship Shop, and he seemed so nervous that he thought something bad must have happened. It was the exact opposite: David was getting out of Quicheng. The news should have made Carl unconditionally happy, but he seemed more apprehensive than satisfied, and his voice was evasive, as if he wished this meeting wasn't happening. Many days had to go by before Sergio would understand the preoccupations that were overwhelming him. During that time he lost track of him, as if they were living on different continents again, but at the beginning of February they met again, and Carl told Sergio the most general details of what had happened. David was summoned to an interrogation room, but not to receive accusations or deny charges of espionage with the same story as ever, but to listen to the verdict. It was a contradictory and absurd document: the first paragraph declared that the masses had taken David Crook prisoner under the charge of doing intelligence work for the enemy, the second paragraph called him "Comrade Crook" and expressed the desire that his activities continued to contribute to the friendship between the peoples of China and Great Britain. David was tempted to send them to the devil: this was an insult and slander. But then he thought that it would be better to sign the dishonour now and seek complete vindication later, from the privileges of liberty.

"He's home now, Sergio," Carl said. "He's gone back to work. That's the most important thing."

It was true. That was the definitive proof when a prisoner of the Cultural Revolution was freed: if they took up the work they'd been doing before, everything was fine; if not, they would always be under suspicion. In March, Isabel and David arrived at the Friendship Hotel with their sons, just as they used to arrive to swim in the Olympic-sized pool, but this time Sergio saw them walk up the stairs without looking at anyone and walk straight into a room where a committee of uniformed people awaited them. They were representatives from the Ministry of Public Security; they had received the letters of protest David had sent and had come to present a new verdict, or rather, the same verdict in different words. It was still true that the masses had taken him prisoner, but now the results of investigations carried out in accordance with the law had determined that David Crook had not committed any offence, and the Chinese government was declaring him innocent. The verdict continued by expressing the hope that the work of the comrade would contribute to friendship between the peoples of China and Great Britain.

Once his father was rehabilitated and his mother's innocence confirmed, Carl began a slow distancing from Chinese life. "I cannot live here," he told Sergio in their long conversations. "My father would never leave China, in spite of what they've done to him. But I cannot stay here, where we have suffered so much. And do you know what my father says? That suffering is good for human beings, as long as they manage to survive. I tell him he's right: when they don't survive, it's not so good." Carl spoke to Sergio with the strange awareness that nobody could have understood him better. In May, when he announced he was leaving Peking, he told Sergio that he would miss nothing as much as he'd miss their conversations, and Sergio didn't think he was exaggerating. "What are you going to do?" he asked. "I'm going to London by bus," he said with a smile. It was true, over the following six months, with an enormous rucksack on his back as his only luggage, Carl took trains and buses and more trains and a couple of boats to cross all of Asia and reach his father's city. He found work in a factory, and Sergio received letters in which Carl boasted of all he had learned in Peking, for his talent with tools made him an exceptional worker.

They spent Sunday morning looking at old photos, as they had spent the last hours of the previous night, while Barcelona went out to party in Raval and then went to sleep and then gradually woke up. They were so absorbed in that voyage into the past that they forgot to go down in time for breakfast and a woman with a pristine apron and Ecuadoran accent had to knock on their door to ask if they wanted the room made up. During the night, while they slept, Marianella had sent some scanned photos by WhatsApp, or sometimes photos of photos, taken in a hurry so Sergio could talk about them on the other side of the Atlantic: they were faces in black and white or in sepia tones (faces from a disappeared world) or buildings that evoked an emotion or a memory, and Sergio and Raúl sat on one of the unmade beds, both in pyjamas, filling the air in the room with words that were not words, but spoken captions. They had time, as the taxi the Filmoteca had booked for Raúl would come at one in the afternoon – which, for a flight that left at 3.30, was ridiculously early – and the plans they'd made the previous day, including a visit to the Miró museum and a walk up Montjuic, were suddenly supplanted by the luminous screens where the ghosts of the past manifested themselves.

Two photos provoked more conversation than the rest. In the first one was the group of children of specialists, who were studying Chinese language and culture before starting school. "There's me, and there's your aunt, of course: thirteen and eleven years old, look at us. We were children, Raúl. But there are the other Cabreras from the Friendship Hotel as well. There are our friends, the two in glasses. With one of them I went to kill birds in winter, because they ate the seeds. Many years later I learned that they'd gone back to Uruguay and joined the Tupamaros, another Guevarista guerrilla group. Sometimes it seems like everyone would have done the same, but it's not true. They did though, anyway, they returned to their country from China to wage revolution. It didn't go well for them either. They were in prison for some time and then went into exile in Sweden."

A whole generation – Sergio thought, looking at the photo

of the Uruguayan Cabreras – a whole generation of Latin Americans whose lives were pawned for an enormous cause. Where were they now? They lived in Sweden, yes, but where, and with whom, and with what memories of their time in arms, and with how much of a feeling that someone had stolen years of their lives? They were the sons of a poet, Sarandy Cabrera, a contemporary of Onetti and Idea Vilariño who translated Ronsard and Petrarch and wrote a prologue to the Spanish edition of Mao Tse-Tung's *37 Poems*. How had his life been? How had it resembled Fausto Cabrera's life, and how much influence had he had on his sons' decisions? Sometimes Sergio devoted his free time to combing through the labyrinths of the internet for their destinies, all those protagonists of his previous lives, and he knew that Sarandy Cabrera had died in 2005, in Montevideo. Now, in Barcelona, he wondered if either of his sons would have travelled from Sweden for his funeral.

In the other photo were Marianella and Carl Crook, arms

round each other and smiling in spite of saying goodbye: it was departure day, when everyone thought their years in China were over for good, and seeing the photo nobody would have thought the girl in the fashionable dress had just arrived from military training with the People's Army in Nanjing, or that the lanky youth had spent the previous night crying over his girlfriend's departure. "Your aunt was sixteen years old in this photo," Sergio told Raúl. "Two years younger than you." Sergio had taken the photo, but now, sitting beside his son, he could not remember if he was aware at the airport of all that was happening at once. It wasn't just that Marianella was going to Colombia, or that she was going to a war and that she was doing so with all the will of her stubborn convictions: in the hours that followed the photo, after the plane took off for Moscow, Carl went back to his family's apartment at the Foreign Languages Institute, and the smile in the photo turned into something else, as his father was locked up in Qincheng maximum security prison.

Then Raúl looked at his phone and said he was going to take a shower, since it was past twelve and he hadn't even packed. He rubbed a finger on the screen and said it was a shame the photo was wrinkled and yellow: had nobody thought it might be a good idea to take care of it? With that regret he went into the bathroom. Sergio leaned back on the bed with the laptop on his legs and stayed there, listening to the sound of the water running and his son moving about, going distractedly through the photos of his own archive and musing on his curious epiphany: Raúl lived in a world where such an aberration, a damaged or vanished photo, was inconceivable. Suddenly he thought of another photo that also showed the ravages of time, and had no trouble finding it on his computer. He could no longer remember who had taken it, but the occasion was unforgettable: the day Carl left China with the intention of reaching London and beginning a new life far from Peking, far from Mao, far from the prison where his father had left so many years of his life. There they were, at the train station, with Sergio occupying the place that five years earlier Marianella had occupied. In one of the photos, Marianella was

leaving for ever; in the other, it was Carl who was saying good-bye. They were similar photos, yes, but with such different histories behind them: two contrasting farewells, one who was travelling towards the revolution and another who was escaping from it. Then he remembered: the photographer was Paul, Carl's younger brother, and the camera was the Nikon Luz Elena had given Sergio when they returned to Peking, as a sort of vote of confidence in his future. And yes, the photo had been damaged, but Sergio didn't remember how, or when he'd developed the roll, and now, through an association of ideas, an old film-makers' saying sprang to mind: *Faith is believing in what the labs haven't developed yet.* That's how it was, he thought. He had always thought that it was fine not to believe in any god, but you had to have faith in the light. For whoever controls the light controls everything.

Now, looking at old photos sitting on an unmade bed in a hotel in Barcelona, the day after *The Strategy of the Snail* had been shown for the first time in a world without Fausto, Sergio realized his memory was starting to do what it did again. The previous night, a woman had asked what had been the most difficult challenge in making the film; he gave an answer about technical difficulties, but what he would have liked to say was very different: the most difficult thing had been to build the film around his father. For that was most of all a story about an old Spanish anarchist who organizes a neighbourly rebellion: a homage to Fausto Cabrera, a filial love letter in stills. With each snippet of dialogue, the framing of each shot, Sergio had wanted to tell his father how much he loved him, how grateful he was for so many things, how he felt that in some mysterious way he owed him his whole life, from his beginnings as a child actor in the early days of television to his director's seat on feature films. In between other things had happened – painful, uncomfortable, incomprehensible things – but *The Strategy of the Snail* would be the balm to heal all the wounds, the peace pipe, and keeping that in mind while he chose where to place the camera or gave an instruction to the actors, or while he let smoke out of a machine to see better which way the light was shining in a scene, was the biggest challenge of his life.

Then he remembered what happened on one of the afternoons of the shoot. He was about to film a scene in the interior of a demolished house, the facade of which was still intact, but the interiors of which had begun to be taken down in the fictitious world by the rebellious tenants, and at some moment Sergio wanted to know precisely which way the light was flowing, in that space of difficult shadows. He asked for the smoke machine and sprayed the place and that everyday miracle occurred: the rays of light became visible, straight, solid, so well-defined that a person might feel they could adjust them by hand. Fausto Cabrera, sitting in a chair on the edge of the scene, was studying his lines, and Sergio, as he looked at him, thought that memories were as invisible as light, and just as the smoke allowed him to see light, there must be a way to make memories visible, a smoke you could use to make memories come out of hiding, and adjust them and fix them for ever. Maybe what had happened in Barcelona during those days was nothing less. Maybe, Sergio thought, that's what he'd been: a man blowing smoke over his memories.

The film schools of Peking had closed in the first days of the Cultural Revolution, and nobody saw any possibility of them opening again. Not only were they closed, but damned: their repudiation had been fatally linked to that of Jian Qing, Mao's wife, an ambitious woman, a mediocre actress in other times, who had accumulated enormous power during the revolution and had wielded it with the aim of crushing any cultural manifestation that was not a celebration of Maoist ideas. Jian Qing had supervised everything that had anything to do with the stage, but her public image, since Sergio had left Peking in 1968, had suffered a brutal erosion, almost visible in the lines on her face and the rigidity of her smile, and now she was starting to blame all those who had been her accomplices for the excesses. It was even said that she was separated from Mao, but they were both hiding the truth for fear of what the movement might do. Fausto watched the whole spectacle from his private disenchantment.

"She's going to be utterly ruined and cinema is going down with her," he told Sergio. "If I were you, I'd start thinking about other things."

"But this is what I want to do," Sergio said.

"A person doesn't do what he wants, but what allows him to survive," Fausto said. "Later you can devote yourself to whatever you like." And he added: "Go and talk to the people at the Bureau. They can set you in the right direction better than anyone."

The officials at the Bureau of Foreign Specialists had the admissions of every faculty in Peking under their control. Sergio and Fausto went to see them one morning, and after two hours of conversation, Fausto had decided: Sergio would study medicine. He had been seduced by the Barefoot Doctors programme, the students of which spent three years studying at university and then went out to work among the peasants or workers. At the end of that period they were subjected to a vote by their patients; if their patients thought they were good, they could continue the programme to the final diploma.

"You will be close to the people," his father said. "It will be the most useful occupation if we go back to the guerrillas."

"What? We're going back?"

"One never knows. And it's not a good idea to get too far away from the revolution."

Sergio did not manage to complete three months in the faculty. By coincidence Luz Elena needed to have a hernia operation just at that time. Sergio went to visit her in hospital; he arrived at the very instant the nurses were wheeling her out into the recovery room, and he saw a nurse lift up her robe and he saw the fresh scar, discoloured from the antiseptic and with traces of dried blood, and he had to grab hold of the trolley in order not lose his balance. The doctor, one of his professors at the faculty, noticed what had happened and approached him discreetly to ask if he was sure this profession was for him. Sergio suspected the answer was a negative.

He confirmed it a few days later, when he faced his first anatomy lesson. In the Barefoot Doctors programme everything happened earlier than normal, as if the students lived accelerated lives; a few weeks after opening his first textbook, Sergio was already in a dissecting room. From afar he had seen how the professors took a dirty sheet off a dead body and pointed to its parts and named them, chewing their words. That day he stood beside the sheet, across from a classmate who looked at him shyly, and when the sheet was removed he found a woman with grey hair but firm skin and a line painted down her abdomen. The scalpel sank into the dead body without any blood coming out, and the next thing he remembered were the slaps from the professor, who looked at him with ill-concealed disappointment while Sergio came to after fainting.

"What's the matter, Comrade Li?" he asked. "Have you never seen a cadaver?"

Sergio didn't know what to say. He had seen dead people who'd been shot, or died of tropical diseases or accidents. But that was different: that was war, which leaves the dead by the roadside so one sees them and never forgets them. Sergio remembered each and every one he'd seen as if they were right in front of him, as the grey-haired woman's body had been. Why, then, had he been so strongly affected? Did peacetime deaths have more of an impact than those of war? Or perhaps the problem was much simpler: now that his revolutionary mission, for which he'd lived since childhood, was irremediably spoiled, he no longer had a place in the world and he never would have. During those days he wrote in his notebook: *There is nothing for me in China. Nor in Colombia. I haven't even turned twenty-four and I'm already wondering what to keep living for.*

On the afternoon of May Day, the Cabreras walked the several hours it took to get from the Friendship Hotel to Tiananmen Square. Among red flags and loudspeakers deafening them with revolutionary songs, a man approached to say hello to Fausto in heavily accented French. He was European but was wearing a Chinese jacket, and had wavy grey hair and lashes so long they seemed to comb his eyelids, and he was accompanied by a woman with a timid smile. Fausto introduced Luz Elena and the four of them exchanged pleasantries, and then they arranged to meet the following Sunday at the Friendship Hotel.

Later, Fausto explained that the man was Joris Ivens, director of one of the best films ever made about the Civil War: *The Spanish Earth*. Sergio recognized the name, of course, and also remembered the several times he'd gone to watch *Far from Vietnam* when he was in Paris. Ivens's part was the section he'd liked the best, and now he would have the chance to tell him.

So he made sure he was present on the following Sunday, when Ivens and his wife came to spend the day at the hotel. She was called Marceline Loridan and was also a film-maker. On her arm they saw the tattooed numbers from a concentration camp. Everything she said was elegant, informed and intelligent, and it was not surprising that she got on so well with Luz Elena. Sergio spoke of *Far from Vietnam* with an enthusiasm nobody could remember hearing him express before, and even Fausto must have noticed, because he mentioned it to Ivens. "He wants to study cinema," he said. "And he's no novice: he's acted with me, knows a bit about photography and has learned something about directing as well. But he'll have to wait until they reopen the schools, and who knows when that'll be."

Ivens turned to Sergio. Looking at him, but speaking to Fausto, he said:

"Well, he should come and work with me."

It turned out that Ivens had made two films on China and was preparing a third, an ambitious documentary in several parts called *How Yukong Moved the Mountains*. He'd spent more than a year filming and was convinced it would be his masterpiece. "Our masterpiece, to be precise," he said, placing his hand on Marceline's tattooed arm. The work was full of complications, and a young enthusiast who understood the mechanics of cinema, who spoke good French so could communicate

479

with him, as well as good Chinese to compensate for his own faulty command of the language, could be a great help. But later, after a week of working on the shoot, Sergio had become something much more than an assistant. Ivens was a hero to the Chinese, for he had portrayed their revolution with genuine understanding, but that carried a high cost.

"I haven't figured out if they treat me as a king or a spy," he told Sergio. "And you know, young Cabrera, that kings and spies have something in common: nobody tells them the truth. I need to know what's really going on in China. I need someone who knows the Chinese and understands them, someone who loves China, but loves it enough to be able to see its problems."

Sergio strove to be that person. He turned into Ivens's interpreter, but also his informer; he accompanied him to the Peking circus to speak to the artists and to a generator factory to speak to the workers. They spent whole summer days together, long days working for twelve hours at a time all over the city, from artisan workshops to the Peking Opera and then to the offices of a university professor, and Sergio was the first to be surprised when he discovered that he could speak knowledgeably of all those places: he had studied Chinese opera with his father, he'd worked at a clock factory, he'd been a Red Guard in his student days. And not only did he understand all the corners of Chinese life, but he could speak with all the inhabitants, no matter who they were, no matter what they did, and he did so separating, with the precision of a goldsmith, the truth from pretence and confessions from propaganda.

"Where have you been all these months?" Ivens said to him. "You would have made my work much easier."

It was a rhetorical question, but led to answers that were

not. In spare moments, while they ate ravioli or rounded off a long day of work in the swimming pool at the Friendship Hotel, with Marceline or while she took charge of another part of the documentary in another part of the city, Sergio told Ivens about his years in the guerrilla force, of the circumstances that led him to join and the reasons he decided to leave. Ivens listened to him with true fascination. "You have lived through a lot for someone so young," he said once. "We should tell your life story in a film." Sergio could not help but think that this man had filmed the Spanish Civil War along with Hemingway and given advice to Orson Welles. Ivens, for his part, grew fond of him, and even though he was half a century older and they could have been grandfather and grandson, their conversations had the complicity of a shared passion. "You remind me of myself when I was your age, Sergio," Ivens said. "You feel as if the world will end if you don't direct your first film right now. Let me tell you a secret: there is time."

Sergio, however, felt that time was running out: summer was ending, his work on *How Yukong Moved the Mountains* was ending, Ivens and Marceline's stay in China was ending. On the day of his return to Paris, Ivens said goodbye to Sergio with a promise: he would get him accepted into the IDHEC. The Institut des Hautes Études Cinématographiques de Paris would be a dream come true, of course, but Sergio never really believed it. When he mentioned the matter to his parents, in one of the dining rooms at the Friendship Hotel, he did so with neither excitement nor high hopes, and Fausto's reaction did not bother him as much as it should have. "First you have to graduate from university," he said. "After that, we'll see." Then Luz Elena interrupted: "But that's what he wants to do," she said. "He doesn't want to be a doctor, Fausto, or anything else. He wants to work in cinema. And that's because of you, so I don't see what the problem is." "In any case, he can't leave China," Fausto said. "He hasn't got any papers. He has no passport. He must be on an Interpol blacklist! He'd be arrested as soon as he set foot in Paris. Let's not waste time talking about what cannot be done." "Cannot because you don't want it," Luz Elena said, demoralized by then, and Fausto brought down his unanswerable conclusion: "That's not true. It can't be done because it can't be done." They had several versions of this conversation in the days that followed; Sergio listened to them as if they concerned someone who wasn't there, for it seemed to him that the life of a young man studying cinema in Paris was out of his reach. A person could fantasize as much as he wanted, but deep down Fausto was right: without a legal passport in his name, any intimation of independence was illusory.

In September, when he'd forgotten all about it, a letter arrived from Paris. *I am very sorry,* Sergio read. *There are too many prerequisites, too many obstacles.* He thought what had happened was predictable, the failure of good intentions. But then Ivens asked forgiveness for having taken the liberty of knocking on other doors, said he'd talked to some contacts at the London Film School and received a positive response. *If you want it,* he said, *your acceptance is assured.* Sergio did not show the letter to his parents, but for the first time a space opened in his routine for that unreal future. He began to take English classes in secret with a resident of the Friendship Hotel, the only place that was possible outside the Foreign Languages Institute. He had only to go down two floors to reach the professor's suite, but he also visited the Crooks a couple of times to practise without them realizing. He got to know the music of the Beatles – a memory from his adolescence, inseparable from Smilka's smiling face – and spent hours trying to figure out what Lennon was singing in "A Hard Day's Night", as if it might contain a key to the whole culture. That's what he was doing one evening, meticulously copying out an incomprehensible verse, when his mother came in with a package that had just arrived, by airmail, at the hotel reception. It was a legal passport, with the legal photo and legal name of Sergio Fausto Cabrera Cárdenas. Only the signature and fingerprint were false, for the obvious reason that someone who wasn't Sergio had gone to collect it in Bogotá.

Luz Elena had been conspiring for months to acquire the document. She did so with the help of her father, whose influence was still valid despite part of his family having fallen into communism. Don Emilio Cárdenas had only to make a couple of telephone calls to get Sergio's criminal record turned into a blank slate, with no past, a sort of secret amnesia; and once that was achieved, getting a passport, even if it had someone else's signature, was easier than he would have believed. Now, with the passport in his hand, with his face and name looking at him from legal pages and not from a handmade document that didn't even have consecutive page numbers, Sergio felt that life, the way he'd imagined it, was finally within reach. So during the following weeks, always with Luz Elena's complicity, he devoted himself to polishing the edges of the project, writing to the London Film School and receiving an enthusiastic response, writing to Joris Ivens and receiving his best wishes, preparing for the moment to present his decision to his father.

He did not expect Fausto to accept straight away, but neither Sergio nor Luz Elena could have predicted the vehemence of his reaction. They were in the Western restaurant when Sergio began to tell him what had been going on in these months, from his correspondence with Joris Ivens to the English classes, ending with the news:

"I'm going to London, Papá."

Fausto didn't care about people staring, or else his rage was stronger than his prudence, and he stood up, shouting. He accused the two of them of plotting the whole thing behind his back.

"You deceived me," he said. "No, this is worse than deceit: this is treason."

"Don't make a scene, Fausto," Luz Elena said. Sergio detected a serene authority in her voice that reminded him of previous confrontations. "Let's talk things over calmly."

"Calmly," Fausto said. "They betray me and then ask for calm."

"Nobody has betrayed you," Sergio said. "I just asked for help and she helped me; you didn't. This is what I want to do. I made this decision. I would have liked to do it with your support, but I don't have it. And I don't know what you were expecting, to tell you the truth. I wasn't going to stay here with my arms folded."

"What are you saying?" Fausto said. "What the hell are you saying? I've done nothing but support you my entire life."

"Not in this, Papá," Sergio said.

"This is a mistake," Fausto said. "You can study better here. The faculties are going to open up again in a few months, everyone says so."

"But I don't want to study here. I want to leave. I have everything ready and I'm going." Then he felt he could be more daring: "You've always told us about the help Grandfather gave you when you left the Dominican Republic. You wanted to leave, because you were going to be an actor, because you couldn't be an actor there. And your father gave you the money you were short, wasn't that it? Why can't you do the same? Why can't you be for me how your father was with you?"

"This is very different," Fausto said.

"It's the same," Sergio said. "I am your son and I need your help. I'm not even asking you for money. I have the money."

"Oh yeah? Where from?"

"From my traveller's cheques," Luz Elena said. "So he can settle in until he finds work."

"Now I see," Fausto said. "You want to make him bourgeois."

"What I want to do is help him," Luz Elena said. "And I can do what I want with my money."

"Well, I'm going to talk to them," Fausto said.

"Who?"

"So they won't let him leave," Fausto said. "Sergio entered with a false passport, don't forget. To leave, he needs someone to look the other way."

"And you would be capable of doing that?" Luz Elena said. "You would make a phone call to thwart your son's plans?"

"His plans, his plans," Fausto said. "And what about ours?" There was silence. "All the plans we've made," Fausto went on. "What's left of them?"

Sergio felt many years' worth of frustrations pounding in his chest, the ones he remembered and others he knew nothing about. "What plans?" he said. He heard his own voice and he noticed it had changed, but it was too late to rein it in. "What plans did we make, Papá? I'm asking you sincerely. I'm asking

485

because I don't know. I didn't make plans, Mamá didn't make plans, my sister didn't make plans. You did." He experienced a new clarity as he said it, as if seeing things for the first time. "The plan to come to China was yours, not ours. The plan to join the EPL was yours, not ours. Our whole lives. Our whole lives you've been making us believe that we were deciding, but it's not true: you decided. All my life I've done what you wanted, all my life I've kept quiet, trying to please you. But now I've realized, Papá. I've realized that keeping quiet is not a matter of temperament: it's a sickness. I've kept too quiet, I have, I've kept quiet to adapt to what others expect of me. And I've taken many risks, now I realize, I have lived a life of risks, but I haven't taken risks for myself, but for what people expected me to be, what you expected of me. And I don't want to be that anymore: I don't want to be the brave and promising youth. No more. This, this is what I want to do now. This is what I've decided to do now, these are my plans, mine, nobody else's. This is what I want to do with my fucking life."

When the pilot announced, in three languages, that they were beginning their descent towards the city of Lisbon, Sergio made some calculations and realized that at that very instant, in Barcelona, they'd be showing *The Art of Losing*, his adaptation of Santiago Gamboa's novel. People would watch the film without him; Sergio would not get to tell them how much he had enjoyed watching Gamboa tweak the lines of dialogue, nor how his father had reacted when Sergio suggested he appear briefly in the role of a priest at the Central Cemetery. At that moment Fausto remembered his appearance in Sergio's first feature film, *A Matter of Honour*, and said: "A priest again. As if I didn't know how to play anything else." Yes, Sergio could have remembered those anecdotes that evening, after the screening. But he would not, because he wasn't there; the retrospective was over for him. *No more looking back*, he thought then, playing with words, even though that's exactly what he was doing right now: now, descending through the Portuguese skies to the airport where Silvia was waiting for him, he was thinking about Fausto, who was dead, and about Raúl, who would be home by now.

He had said goodbye to his son on the Rambla del Raval, with the taxi door open and the driver showing his impatience, and Sergio seemed to sense that the farewell was not the same for both of them, and did not contain the same emotions. That was fine: something went from the sixty-six years of one to the eighteen years of the other. When the taxi had disappeared, Sergio went back inside the hotel lobby, and felt so lonely without Raúl that he wrote a WhatsApp to Silvia like a swimmer clinging to the side. But soon other words occurred to him.

I know that you need time and I don't expect our problems to solve themselves by magic, he said. *But I feel like I'm trying to find my way in the dark and it would do me a lot of good to know we're on the right track. What do you think?*

He waited for a reply for a couple of minutes – stubborn, elastic, stingy minutes – and then decided it would be better to go out. He spent the afternoon wandering around Barcelona, down the Ramblas to the statue of Columbus, along the Moll de la Fusta towards the Barceloneta, and then retraced the same route in reverse. The role this city had played in his life was a strange one, from when his father had gone up on the terraced roof to see Montjuic to his brief visit when the ship that was taking him back to Colombia stopped there. That trip closed the difficult year that began in the Friendship Hotel, in March 1974, with Sergio taking leave of his parents to travel to London. Luz Elena had to beg Fausto to come out and say goodbye to his son after weeks of not speaking to him. Since the night when Sergio revealed his plans, Fausto had fallen into a wounded animal's silence that he broke only to reiterate his accusations: they had betrayed him, they had violated family commitments. In vain Sergio explained that his decision to make films demonstrated the best of loyalties, because it would not have happened if he hadn't admired his father to the point of wanting to follow in his footsteps. Fausto eventually gave in: on the front steps of the hotel he said goodbye to Sergio with the world's coldest handshake, and walked back inside before his son had climbed into the taxi. Sergio's rage lasted for the whole trip via Moscow, Rome and Paris, and then the ferry from Calais to Folkestone, and then the train that took him to London. Before getting off the train at Victoria Station he looked at his passport. The port official had stamped it, and on the stamp was the date: it was June 7.

Today, Sergio said to himself, *my new life begins.*

It was strange to feel the same thing now, in Lisbon, arriving with Silvia in Benfica. It was also strange to feel like he was coming home, because Lisbon was not his city and never had been, and because he hadn't spent more than a few days in this apartment the previous week: a week that already belonged to another life. Returning from the airport to rua Ferreira de Andrade brought back the memory of the afternoon he'd received the news of Fausto's death by telephone. Now, looking for a parking space, turning the corner and walking to number

19, holding Amalia's sleeping body against his body throughout, Sergio counted the days since the last time this had happened, and it seemed implausible that so few days had passed. He mentioned it later, at dinner, but Silvia had something else on her mind.

"I'd like you to come to Coimbra," she said. "They're expecting us tomorrow. My family would love to see you."

Sergio agreed. "I'd love it too," he said. They were like magic words, for at the moment of saying them he felt a sudden relief and, with the relief, the accumulated exhaustion of the last few days, which made him think of the sandbags they put on bulls' necks before a bullfight. As soon as his head hit the pillow he knew he was starting to fall asleep, but he used the last vestiges of lucidity to tell Silvia that he had thought about so many things that weekend and he had made a decision: the first thing he would do when he got back to Bogotá was call Jorge Llano, the therapist, and talk to him. And he'd see how Gestalt might be able to help him.

The next day he woke up early. With the apartment still dark, he put on yesterday's clothes and went outside. The Lisbon sky was clear and the streets looked wet, as though they'd been cleaned at dawn, and the city seemed to have just been invented. Sergio walked around the block, passing the small park Amalia liked, but it was too cold in the open spaces, so he decided to go back sooner than he'd planned. He stopped in at the Pastelaria Califa for a coffee and to buy a couple of croquetes, and the woman at the counter recognized him and greeted him in Spanish, and Sergio felt so grateful that he bought six croquetes: two for each of them before they set off for Coimbra in a couple of hours. Then he imagined them. He imagined them in the car, as they had been on the way back from the airport – Silvia driving, Amalia sleeping in her car seat in the back, him in the passenger seat – but this time in the bright light of a sunny day. At the beginning of their relationship they had done this same trip together, maybe so Sergio could meet the Jardim Soares family; so now, walking between the Pastelaria Califa and Silvia's building, Sergio could imagine the route: they would drive down through Benfica to Belém and along the river until they reached the Expo grounds, before getting onto the motorway, and there they would see the water sparkling as it always did when the sun shone, and they would also see the clear sky and the wheeling seagulls, and the people beginning their days with their families as now Sergio, arriving at the apartment, began the day with his. Silvia opens the door for him and, as he walks in, Sergio realizes they are already having breakfast, and then he sets the *croquetes* down on the table and Amalia lets out a squeal of delight, and Silvia, who has her phone in her hand, holds it up and tells Sergio something he doesn't quite catch. She finishes chewing a mouthful, takes a sip of orange juice and reads the message Sergio sent her the previous afternoon, reads: *I know you need time*, reads: *I feel like I'm trying to find my way in the dark*, reads the question: *What do you think?* And she looks at Sergio and says:

"I think so, yes. I think we're on the right track."

AUTHOR'S NOTE

Retrospective is a work of fiction, but there are no imaginary episodes in it. This is not a paradox, or at least it has not always been. Rufino José Cuervo's *Dictionary of Construction and Rules*, to give an example I'm fond of, gives this meaning in the entry for the verb *fingir*: "To model, design, give shape to something, a) said of physical objects such as sculpture and similar, to carve." What I have tried to do in these pages is no different: the act of fiction has been to extract the figure of this novel from the huge mountain of Sergio Cabrera's experience and that of his family, as he revealed them to me over seven years of encounters and more than thirty hours of recorded conversations. The first, according to the voice archive on my phone, took place on May 20, 2013, in my study in Bogotá; in it, Sergio begins by talking about the series he had just finished making at that time, filmed partly in a haunted house (none of whose ghosts, to his dismay, ended up making an appearance), and then we got down to business. The last of these conversations was not with him, but with Carl Crook, who, on August 10, 2020, sitting in his house in Vermont, showed me over Zoom the Red Guard armband that had belonged to Marianella in 1967, and over the following

days was kind enough to translate fragments of his diary from Chinese for me. Between those two dates I exchanged countless email and text messages – with Sergio and Silvia, with Marianella and with Carl – and received photographs from their personal archives and consulted documents, the implausible survival of which seemed to me yet more proof of the stubborn insistence of the past, and while I wrote other books I was looking in the shadows for the form that best suited this one. By the time the coronavirus pandemic erupted, this novel was finding its voice and discovering its architecture. Now I am convinced that the writing gave order and purpose to the chaotic days of quarantine, and in more than one sense allowed me to conserve some semblance of sanity in the midst of that centrifugal life. In other words, ordering someone else's past was the most efficient way of contending with the disorder of my present.

The epigraph can be read (I would like it to be read) in that sense. The words appear in the preface of *Joseph Conrad: A Personal Remembrance*, a book by Ford Madox Ford that has given me company and sustenance, although my strategy has not been the same as his. The author endeavours to tell us the life story of a friend, and his whole sentence goes like this: "For, according to our view of the thing, a novel should be the biography of a man or of an affair, and a biography whether of a man or an affair should be a novel, both being, if they are efficiently performed, renderings of such affairs as are our human lives." I like the idea of interpretation, for that is what I found myself doing more than once with the events of Sergio Cabrera's life. My work as a novelist, faced with the formidable magma of his experiences and those of his sister, consisted of giving those episodes an order that went beyond a biographical recounting: an order capable of suggesting or revealing meanings not visible in a simple inventory of events, because they belong to different forms of knowledge. Novels don't do anything else. This is what we refer to, I believe, when we talk about moral imagination: to that reading of another life that consists of observing in order to surmise or of penetrating what is manifest to discover the hidden or the secret. Interpretation is also part of the art of fiction: whether the person in question is real or invented is, in practice, an inconsequential and superfluous distinction.

As well as the people mentioned, who gave me their time and lent me their memories – and allowed me to mould and sculpt them and give them shape – *Retrospective* owes a special debt to the gallantry of Santiago Gamboa, the complicity of Pilar Reyes and María Lynch, the editorial scalpel of Carolina López and narrative judgement of Ricardo Silva. To write the passages about the young Fausto Cabrera I used his book of memoirs *Una vida, dos exilios* (One Life, Two Exiles), just as I used *The Autobiography of David Crook*, the memoirs of Carl Crook's father, to reconstruct certain episodes from his life. Other people helped me in less tangible ways, sometimes without knowing it, and I want to put on record my gratitude (and free them of any obligation). They are Héctor Abad Faciolince, Nohora Betancourt, Javier Cercas, Humberto de la Calle, Guillermo Díez, Jorge Drexler, Luz Helena Echeverry, Gabriel Iriarte, Carmenza Jaramillo, Mario Jursich, Li Chow, Alberto Manguel, Javier Marías, Patricia Martínez, Hisham and Diana Matar, Gautier Mignot and Tatiana Ogliastri, Carolina Reoyo, Mónica Reyes and Zadie Smith. In another league is Mariana, who was a constant presence during the writing of this book while contending with the rest of the universe in this year of plagues.

JGV
Bogotá, October 2020

A NOTE ON THE AUTHOR

JUAN GABRIEL VÁSQUEZ was born in Bogotá in 1973. He is the author of five previous novels, including *The Informers* and *Reputations*, and two collections of stories, *The All Saints' Day Lovers* and *Songs for the Flames*. He is the winner of many prizes including, for *The Sound of Things Falling*, the International IMPAC Dublin Literary Award, the Gregor von Rezzori Prize and the Alfaguara Prize. In 2019 *The Shape of the Ruins* was shortlisted for the Man Booker International Prize and in 2021 he received the biennial Mario Vargas Llosa Novel Prize for *Retrospective*. His books have been translated into more than thirty languages. He lives in Bogotá.

A NOTE ON THE TRANSLATOR

ANNE McLEAN has translated Latin American and Spanish novels, stories, memoirs and other writings by many authors including Héctor Abad, Javier Cercas, Julio Cortázar, Gabriel García Márquez, Evelio Rosero and Enrique Vila-Matas. She has twice won both the *Independent* Foreign Fiction Prize and the Premio Valle Inclán, as well as sharing the IMPAC Dublin Literary Award with Juan Gabriel Vásquez for *The Sound of Things Falling*. In 2012 she was awarded the Spanish Cross of the Order of Civil Merit. She lives in Toronto.